NETSCAPE NAVIGATOR GOLD

Bryan Pfaffenberger

University of Virginia
Charlottesville, Virginia

AP PROFESSIONAL

AP PROFESSIONAL is a division of Academic Press

Boston San Diego New York
London Sydney Tokyo Toronto

This book is printed on acid-free paper. 

AP PROFESSIONAL
1300 Boylston Street, Chestnut Hill, MA 02167
World Wide Web page at http://www.apnet.com

An imprint of ACADEMIC PRESS
A Division of HARCOURT BRACE & COMPANY

United Kingdom Edition published by
ACADEMIC PRESS LIMITED
24–28 Oval Road, London NW1 7DX

ISBN 0-12-553151-6

Printed in the United States of America
97 98 99 00 IP 9 8 7 6 5 4 3 2 1

For Suzanne, always

Contents

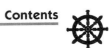

Introducing Netscape Gold

The World Wide Web may well be the most democratic mass medium ever created, in that Web users can *create* as well as consume content. That's right—you can create and publish your own Web pages, as well as surf the Web! Just think about the implications when compared with, say, TV. What makes the Web so vibrant, so exciting, and so cool is that you don't have to possess a large corporation's resources to make your message available.

Netscape Navigator Gold is the ultimate tool for both browsing the Web and publishing your own content. It includes two components:

- **Netscape Navigator** The most popular program by far for browsing the content of the World Wide Web.
- **Netscape Editor** A very impressive program that enables you to create your own content without having to do any programming in HTML.

This is the ultimate book on Netscape Navigator Gold, the only one you'll find that fully covers *both* aspects of the program—browsing Web content and creating Web content. With this book, you don't have to buy two books, one to teach you how to browse and the other to teach you how to create content. By the time you finish reading this book, you'll know how to extract the maximum from the Web, and what's more, you'll know how to create your own Web pages!

Introducing the Web

It's the fastest growing communication system in human history. It's loaded with useful information. And, it's fun. It's the World Wide Web. Academics, in their professorial way, call it a global hypermedia system. For you and me, it's an incredibly fun way that you can jump from one Internet computer to the next, just by clicking an underlined word or phrase called a *hyperlink*. After clicking the hyperlink, the Web goes to work, accessing the information you requested—which might be a document, a sound, an animation, or a movie clip. And who knows where you'll wind up? You might wind up browsing multimedia resources on a computer across the street—or halfway around the world.

The Web is entertaining, useful, fun, and—increasingly—just about indispensable. Many people, myself included, think that the World Wide Web is the opening salvo in the development of a global "information superhighway," knowledge of which will be required of any educated person.

The Web uses the Internet to transfer information. Global in scope, the Internet is a worldwide collection of computer networks that can exchange information using Internet standards. The data travels over just about every physical medium ever invented, including telephone lines, high-speed transcontinental trunk lines, microwaves, fiber optic cable, and even satellites.

Is the Web on its way to becoming a mass medium, akin to cable television in its penetration of U.S. households? Very likely. Here are some facts from Nielsen Media Research (http://www.nielsenmedia.com/commercenet/press.html):

- About 22 to 24 percent of people age 16 years or older currently have access to the Web in the United States and Canada.
- From August/September 1995 to March/April 1996, the number of Web users increased by 50 percent.

The Web is growing in other places too—like inside about 64 percent of Fortune 100 companies (according to *Forrester*), who are busily constructing *intranets*. An intranet is an organization-wide network that uses Internet technology to create a user-friendly information system. Within an intranet, you use the same tools you'd use to browse the Web and create Web content.

Whether you're planning to use Netscape on the Internet or a corporate intranet, you'll find that this book provides exactly what you need.

What Is Netscape Navigator?

To access the World Wide Web, you need an Internet connection and a program called a *browser.* A browser decodes the hidden symbols in Web documents, turning them into richly formatted documents replete with fonts and graphics. In addition, browsers also originate messages that locate and retrieve documents every time you click a hyperlink. Many people believe that Netscape Navigator is the best Web browser available—and I concur.

This book shows you how to master Netscape Gold, which includes Netscape Navigator version 3, the exciting new version of Netscape. You'll learn about all the new features of this major release, including all the exciting new plug-ins (accessory programs) that extend Netscape's capabilities. They enable you to view animations, 3-D virtual reality scenes, and live-action movies right on the Web pages you're accessing! This book fully covers all the new Netscape Navigator plug-ins (LiveVideo, LiveAudio, and Live3D), which enable you to view much of the Web's multimedia data without going through huge configuration hassles.

I've got version 1.1 or version 2, not 3! You can easily download the new version. Just choose Netscape's Home from the Directory menu, and look for links to download Version 3. Even if you've been using one of these previous versions without any problems, you should upgrade: Web authors are taking advantage of the new features that version 3 enables, so you'll miss out on some of the fun if you don't upgrade.

Netscape Navigator is much more than a Web browser, actually. Increasingly, Netscape is becoming the gateway to just about everything the Internet has to offer. Netscape Navigator could always access Internet resources

such as Gopher menus, FTP file archives, WAIS databases, and Archie file search services. Version 2.0 added electronic mail and Usenet newsgroups, and introduced Netscape Chat, which enables you to engage in real-time chatting with other Internet users.

Version 3 is even more impressive as a gateway to the Internet. New to this version is CoolTalk, which turns your computer into a long-distance telephone. To use CoolTalk, you'll need a sound card, a microphone, and somebody to call who also has CoolTalk (and the necessary computer equipment). Since your call traverses the Internet rather than telephone lines, there's no charge. Are long-distance phone companies happy about this? No. Will you be? Yes.

CoolTalk includes more than just long-distance telephone capabilities. It also includes a chat tool for text-based interaction, a shared whiteboard for textual and graphical data conferencing, and collaboration facilities that enable more than two people to participate. It's a little rough around the edges, you'll find, but you're looking at the leading edge of how people will communicate in the next century.

What Is Netscape Navigator Gold?

Netscape Navigator Gold includes all the features of Netscape Navigator, plus something very special: Netscape Editor, which enables you to create and publish your own Web pages. What's so super about Netscape Editor? Plenty. It makes Web content creation almost ridiculously easy!

Web Publishing without HTML

Do you remember when people using word processing programs had to insert funny codes in their documents in order to print with formatting? When I got my first PC in 1981, I had to type @CENTER(Hello, World) in order to center the text "Hello, World" in my document. Then Microsoft Word came along and made all that fussing with codes unnecessary. In brief, that's just what Gold is going to do for Web publishing.

In Web publishing, the codes in question are a lot like those old word processing codes—you have to mark up the text with special symbols. This is done using a markup language called the Hypertext Markup Language (HTML) to code content for display by Web browsers. A *markup language* identifies the components of a document, such as the title or heading, so that the browser can display it properly. HTML isn't very difficult, really—anyone can learn the basics of HTML—but it's extremely tedious to use on a day-to-day basis. And it's not worth expending the time to learn it if you just want to publish the occasional page.

With Gold, you can forget about HTML. You won't have to learn it! By the way, other books on Gold don't really seem to believe this, since they try to teach you a lot of HTML along with Gold. Why? It's unnecessary. To be sure, Gold can't do everything. For example, Gold 3.0 doesn't handle frames. You have to use HTML to create frames in your document. But Gold can create tables, and as you'll learn later in this book, you can use tables to lay out your page so that it looks like frames.

This book assumes that you don't want to learn HTML, and it doesn't throw HTML at you. The only exception is the inclusion of a few cool tricks that you can use to add neat stuff to your page!

Easy Publishing

Gold has something else going for it: one-button publishing. This is so cool that I can practically guarantee that you won't do it any other way!

In order to publish your Web page, you need to transfer your page (and its images) to a computer that's running a *Web server*, a program that makes your page available to the Internet. Most Internet service providers (ISPs) give their subscribers some disk space for this purpose. To transfer your page to your ISP's computer, you use FTP, the File Transfer Protocol. FTP can get pretty technical, though, and most people therefore think it's a hassle to publish their pages.

But it's not a hassle with Gold. After you configure Gold with the needed information, you just click the Publish button to transfer your page to your Internet service provider's computer. All the images are automatically transferred, too!

Is Netscape Gold Free?

Maybe. Netscape Communications grants a free license to use Netscape Navigator Gold if you are a student, faculty member, or staff member of an educational institution (K–12, junior college, college, or library), or an employee in a charitable nonprofit organization. For individuals, you also get a free license if you're using the program to evaluate whether you would

like to purchase an ongoing license. This period is limited to 90 days if you're using the program in a for-profit business setting.

If Netscape isn't free for you, you need to purchase a software license after the 90 days is up. To do so, just click the Software button; you'll see on-screen instructions for registration.

Why Do You Need This Book?

You've probably heard that Netscape is easy to use. It is, up to a point. But Netscape is a tool for accessing the World Wide Web (and indeed, the whole Internet). When you learn Netscape, you learn the Web *and* you learn the Internet. That's a lot to learn, and you'll need some help. You've come to the right place.

This isn't just a book about learning Netscape Gold, although we somewhat immodestly feel that it does a pretty good job in that department. It's about mastering Netscape *and* surfing the Web *and* exploring the Internet *and* creating your own Web content *and* publishing this content on the Web. It's five books in one—and you need all five. Anything short of that means that you wouldn't be getting the maximum out of this amazingly full-featured program.

So this book teaches five essential skills:

- Becoming an absolute, flat-out master of Netscape, using the tricks and techniques known only to those who grow pale from all-night Netscape Navigator sessions.
- Surfing the Web with an unerring aim, locating the cool, the informative, the useful, the wacky, and the irreverent.
- Using Netscape to harvest the incredible information and entertainment resources of the entire Internet, including Gopher, FTP, Usenet, Telnet, and Internet telephony.
- Using Netscape Editor to create great-looking Web pages, complete with all the bells and whistles, including sounds, animations, movies, and JavaScript programs.
- Using Netscape Editor's one-button publishing to publish your Web page quickly and easily.

No matter whether you're a beginner with Netscape or a seasoned vet of all-night surf sessions, you'll find that this book is packed with knowledge, strategies, techniques, and cunning tricks. It presents a comprehensive strategy for total mastery of the Internet and of Web content creation.

What's on the CD-ROM Disc?

Version 3 of Netscape Navigator offers three excellent plug-in programs (LiveAudio, LiveVideo, and Live3D) that greatly improve the program's ability to cope with multimedia files. This represents a major improvement over previous versions of the program, which required users to download and install as many as a dozen helper applications in order to view multimedia resources. It's an improvement, yes, but you'll still need helpers to cope with not-so-infrequently encountered data types such as MPEG videos, compressed file downloads, and more.

This book's CD-ROM disc comes to the rescue, offering all the helper applications you need to seal up the holes in Netscape's plug-in offerings. After installing the programs on this disc, you'll be able to browse the Web in confidence, knowing that your copy of Netscape can cope with just about anything the Web can throw at it.

For your Web publishing, you'll find lots of cool Web graphics, including icons, buttons, lines, and backgrounds.

To access all the goodies on the disc, just slip it into your CD-ROM drive. Use Netscape's File Open command to locate the file named WELCOME.HTM—after that, it's self-explanatory.

Please note that this book's CD-ROM disc doesn't include a copy of Netscape Gold. You can download Netscape Gold for free from Netscape's server, using the instructions in Appendix A. You'll find a cool FTP program (called WS-FTP) on this book's CD-ROM disc that you can use for this purpose. It's all set up and ready to go.

How This Book Is Organized

This book is designed for a fast start with Netscape. As the need arises, you can use the additional chapters to round out your knowledge of this

fantastic program, the Web, and the Internet. Before getting started, though,

- **Do you need an Internet connection and a copy of Netscape?** If you haven't got your Internet connection yet, be sure to read Appendix A.
- **Do you already have an Internet connection and Netscape Gold?** Flip to Appendix B, which tells you how to install all the cool plug-ins and helper applications on this book's CD-ROM disc. After you've read Appendix B, turn to Appendix C for information on configuring Netscape to use the programs you've installed.

Part I: Netscape Navigator Quick Start

Part I serves as an introduction to the Netscape Navigator part of this book—and if you're strapped for time, you can learn about 80% of what you'll need to know just by reading these three chapters.

In Chapter 1, "Getting Started with Netscape Navigator," you'll learn the parts of Netscape's screen, including what all those buttons do. It's worth a skim, even if you've already played with the program a bit. If you've used earlier versions of Netscape before, this chapter introduces the new features of the version 3 interface.

Chapter 2, "The Gentle Art of Web Surfing," provides an introduction for much of the rest of the book. You'll learn all the fundamentals of Web navigation the Netscape way. In addition, this chapter shows you some of the advanced functions of Netscape, which is a very powerful tool for accessing all kinds of Internet resources. If you've used previous versions of Netscape, you'll love how version 3 handles frames.

Chapter 3, "When the Surf Gets Rough," shows you how to deal with common error messages and other problems you'll encounter while you're surfing the Net.

Part II: Mastering Netscape Navigator

To get the most out of any fine computer program, you need guidance and tons of tips. You'll find what you're looking for in Part II, "Mastering Netscape Navigator." Even experienced Netscape mavens concede that they learn quite a bit from these chapters! When you finish reading them, you'll be an expert at using this outstanding program.

Chapter 4, "Change That Start Page," gets you started the right way, namely, with a default home page that's much more useful than the one

Netscape accesses automatically. You'll find this home page on this book's CD-ROM disc, and it's jammed with useful tools for navigating the Web.

Chapter 5, "Improving Netscape Navigator's Performance," shows you how to extract the maximum Web-surfing speed out of Netscape. You'll learn all of the tricks that experienced Netscape users discover the hard way, through experience. Even if you're using Netscape Navigator over a relatively slow modem (14.4 Kbps), you'll be able to browse the Web at a very good clip after reading this chapter.

Chapter 6, "Creating and Using Bookmarks," fully explores Netscape Navigator's improved Bookmarks menu, which enables you to save location information about Web sites you've visited. You'll learn how to organize your Bookmarks menu so that it becomes a treasure trove of Web information that you find useful.

Chapter 7, "Using Smart Bookmarks and SmartMarks," fully discusses the latest version of the Smart Bookmarks plug-in program, which adds advanced features to Netscape Navigator's already impressive bookmarks capability.

Chapter 8, "Managing Documents with Netscape Navigator," shows you how to save and print those fantastic documents you're downloading from the Net.

Chapter 9, "Customizing and Configuring Netscape Navigator," walks you through all those Preferences dialog boxes, highlighting the customization options that can really make a difference for you.

Part III: Grooving on Multimedia

Version 3 of Netscape Navigator comes with plug-in programs that greatly extend the program's multimedia capabilities. In addition, you can also use helper applications—programs that deal with the sounds, movies, and animations that plug-ins can't handle. Part III shows you how to explore the rich multimedia resources of the Web. After you read Part III, your copy of Netscape will come alive with awesome sounds, videos, animations, Java programs, and more!

If you haven't yet done so, flip to Appendix C to learn how to configure Netscape for the use of helper applications. Appendix B provides step-by-step instructions for installing the plug-ins and helper apps that you'll find on this book's CD-ROM disc.

Chapter 10, "Understanding Helper Apps and Plug-ins," thoroughly surveys the helper applications and plug-in programs that come with Netscape version 3. It also covers the helper apps that you'll find on this book's CD-ROM disc. In addition, you'll learn how to install and use plug-in programs that you can obtain by downloading them from the Internet.

Chapter 11, "Playing Sounds and Watching Movies," shows you how to harness the multimedia potential of the Web. You'll know how to deal with just about any sound or movie format that the Web can sling at you, including the new streaming sounds and live-action movies. Featured in this chapter are LiveAudio and LiveVideo, Netscape version 3's new plug-ins, which play most of the sounds and movies you'll find on the Web.

Chapter 12, "Viewing Adobe Acrobat Documents," shows you how to open and read richly formatted Adobe Acrobat documents. You'll also learn how to use the Acrobat 3.0 reader, which enables you to display Acrobat documents within Netscape's window.

Chapter 13, "Taking a Sip of Java," introduces the amazing new Web experiences made possible by Java, the new cross-platform programming language created by Sun Microsystems. Because Netscape can read and execute Java programs, you can access Web pages that contain Java code—and see amazing things happen on the Web pages you're viewing. Take the tour!

Chapter 14, "Exploring Virtual Worlds with Live3D," shows you how to navigate three-dimensional spaces with Live3D, a virtual reality plug-in that's included with version 3 of Netscape. The three dimensional worlds will appear within the Web pages you're viewing with Netscape. With Live3D installed, you can "walk" or "fly" through these spaces. Suddenly, the Web has three dimensions instead of two.

Part IV: It's Out There *Somewhere!*

Netscape Navigator isn't just a browser. Increasingly, it's an interface to everything the Internet has to offer. Part IV and Part V show you how to put all of the Internet's resources at your fingertips!

Chapter 15, "Exploring the Web with Netscape Navigator," shows you how to start exploring the World Wide Web. You'll get expert help from some of the Web's most ingenious and experienced travel guides!

Chapter 16, "Find It on the Web! (Search Engines and Subject Trees)," shows you how to find the information for which you're looking. The skills this chapter teaches are absolutely indispensable.

Part V: Exploring the Internet with Netscape Navigator

Chapter 17, "Sending and Receiving E-mail," shows you how to use Netscape's great built-in electronic mail capabilities. You'll learn how to make full use of cool new version 3 features.

Chapter 18, "Chat It Up," covers the brand-new version of Netscape Chat, an add-on program that lets you get involved in real-time conferencing via Internet Relay Chat. The new version is much improved over the previous one, and it's really fun to use.

Chapter 19, "You've Got a Call," covers the awesome new CoolTalk utility, which enables you to transform Netscape and your Internet connection into a freebie long-distance telephone system!

Chapter 20, "Digging Around in Gopher," shows you how to use Netscape Navigator to find and access the rich resources of Gopher, a menu-based Internet information system. You'll learn how to search with Veronica and how to find Gopher Jewels.

Chapter 21, "Ransacking FTP File Archives," shows you how to navigate the file systems of distant computers, finding and retrieving useful files and software. Special emphasis is placed on shareware.com, your key to more than 90,000 shareware programs.

Chapter 22, "Ranting and Raving in Usenet Newsgroups," fully covers the improved Netscape version 3 approach to Usenet. You'll learn how to post your own messages as well as read those placed by others.

Chapter 23, "Surviving Telnet and 3270 Sessions," shows you how to use Netscape to access the information stored in text-based computers, such as mainframe computers and bulletin board systems. With Telnet, another door opens to a huge variety of information, which you can access with Netscape.

Part VI: Creating High-Impact Web Documents

Here's your ticket to creating high-impact Web content without knowing any HTML!

Chapter 24, "Web Publishing Quick Start," gets you going with Web content creation the easy way, with Netscape's Web Page Wizard. In just a few minutes, you'll have created your first Web document.

Chapter 25, "Netscape Editor Fundamentals," introduces you to Netscape Editor, the Gold component that enables you to create Web pages without HTML.

Chapter 26, "Working with Text," fully covers all the ways you can enter and edit text with Netscape Editor.

Chapter 27, "Adding Headers, Lists, and Indents," shows you how to add formatting features that make your document easier to read.

Chapter 28, "Working with Characters and Fonts," helps you make your document come alive with character styles and fonts.

Chapter 29, "Choosing a Color Scheme," shows you how to make your document stand out with distinctively colored fonts, links, and even background graphics.

Chapter 30, "Adding Hyperlinks," makes you an expert in the hyperlinks that make the Web so cool. You'll learn how to link to your own documents as well as to any document on the Web!

Chapter 31, "Adding Images to Your Page," covers *in-line images*, the graphics that appear along with text in illustrated Web pages. You'll learn how to add images to your Web page and make them look great!

Chapter 32, "Creating Tables," shows you how easy it is to create tables with Netscape Gold. You'll also learn several neat layout tricks, the same ones professional Web designers use.

Chapter 33, "Bells and Whistles," doesn't teach you all the things that Web designers use, such as creating animated GIFS, producing sounds and movies, and writing JavaScript programs. These are advanced subjects. (For more information, see the forthcoming second edition of *Publish It On the Web* by Bryan Pfaffenberger, also published by AP PROFESSIONAL.) But it *does* show you how you can find and download public domain animations, sounds, movies, and JavaScript programs and include them in your Web pages. People browsing your page will think you've been doing this for years.

Chapter 34, "Publishing Your Page," shows you how to use Netscape Gold's cool one-button publishing.

Part VII: The Netscape Marketplace

Netscape isn't just a great Web browser and a tool for accessing Internet information. It's also the pathway to an amazing new world of Internet commerce, all based on secure, encrypted transmissions made possible by Netscape's Secure Sockets Layer (SSL) technology. In Chapter 35, you'll find a nontechnical, easy-to-understand introduction to this technology and why it's needed. In Chapter 36, you'll find an introduction to some of the first commercial sites on the Web—sites that enable you to use your credit card to order on-line. Let's go shopping!

Part VIII: The Appendices

This book includes six useful appendices, which will help you round out your knowledge and enjoyment of Netscape Gold:

- **Get connected** Appendix A helps you get connected to the Internet with the CD-ROM software packaged with this book.

- **How do I install the CD-ROM software?** Appendix B fully covers the installation of all those great helper programs and graphics on this book's CD-ROM disc.
- **Configure Netscape** Appendix C shows you how to configure Netscape to work with helper applications and plug-ins.
- **What does that command do?** Appendix D presents a quick reference guide to Netscape Navigator's menu commands, while Appendix E covers Netscape Editor.
- **Can't I use the keyboard?** Appendix F summarizes Netscape's keyboard commands in a handy table.

How to Read This Book

With Netscape Gold close by, naturally. Also, I recommend Mountain Dew for those all-night sessions (yawn). Check out the From Here section at the end of every chapter of this book for pathways to follow.

In addition, keep your eye out for icons. They provide cues and clues that help you find your way through this book. Here's a quick overview of this book's icons:

Here you'll find tips, shortcuts, suggestions, insights, and other helpful information about Netscape Gold.

We've tried to anticipate the problems you'll run into—and this icon shows where to look for solutions.

The Treasure Trove icon marks a cool Internet resource of some kind. Check it out!

Look here for inside information on the way the Web works and for fairly advanced information that might be of interest to you if you'd like to master Netscape Gold.

Acknowledgments

Writing a book such as this one isn't a solitary job for which an author should take sole credit—we get lots of help. I'd particularly like to thank Jeff Pepper (Sponsoring Editor), Katie Mulligan (Editorial Assistant), and Cindy Kogut (Production Editor). Many other people at AP PROFESSIONAL contributed as well; thanks to all. I would also like to thank my agent, Carole McClendon of Waterside Productions, for linking me up with AP PROFESSIONAL, and the great people at Netscape for making such a fantastic program!

Part I

Netscape Navigator Quick Start

Chapter 1

Getting Started with Netscape Navigator

On-screen, Netscape Navigator looks like most other Windows applications—with a few strange twists. What's the big "N," and why do comets shoot past it sometimes? And what's that funny broken key thing?

Whether or not you've already started surfing with Netscape (I'll bet you have), sooner or later you will want answers to such questions. You'll find them here, arranged for quick look-up. And if you're really busy, just scan "For the Time-Challenged," at the beginning of each chapter. This section hits the high points succinctly.

Are you a seasoned Windows user? You'll find lots of important stuff in this chapter about the features that differentiate Netscape from other Windows applications, such as the

For the Time-Challenged

- Netscape is preset to display the Netscape welcome page as its default home page. (You can change this if you want, as explained in Chapter 4.)
- Don't spend too much time trying to learn all the options on the menu bar. You won't use them frequently. With the exception of Bookmarks, the options you'll frequently use are available on the Toolbar.
- The Netsite box displays the URL (Uniform Resource Locator, the Web address) of the document you are currently viewing. (This box is called Location if you're accessing a server other than those made by Netscape Communications.)
- The doorkey icon tells you whether you're accessing a secure server (if it's broken, you're not).
- Hyperlinks, generally shown in color and underlining, enable you to access another Web document. Just move the pointer to the hyperlink, and click the left mouse button once.
- The big "N" (the status indicator) displays an animation while Netscape is downloading a document you've requested. At the bottom of the screen, the status bar tells you what you're downloading, and the progress bar tells you how much of the job is finished.

Toolbar's navigation buttons, the directory buttons, the broken key, and the hyperlinks. You can skim this chapter to get the information you need.

Are you a beginning Windows user? I'm going to assume that you know the fundamentals of using Windows 3.1 or Windows 95, such as how to start a program. But you'll find plenty of help for getting started with Netscape.

This chapter has the following sections:

- **What's on the Screen?** A visual guide to the features you see in Netscape's window. Get a quick overview!

- **Basic Window Calisthenics** Minimize, maximize, stretch, shrink—until you get it just right.
- **Quitting Netscape Navigator** Mommy, Daddy stayed up all night again!

Some of the pages I'm seeing look different than the ones in this book's screen shots! Good Web authors keep their pages fresh, and that's especially true of the Netscape pages you're about to see in this chapter: In fact, some of them change daily. Don't worry if what you're seeing on-screen doesn't exactly match the screen shot. In later chapters, you'll almost certainly find that a page or two mentioned by this book has disappeared from the Web. This can happen for many reasons. Again, it's nothing to worry about. It's nothing you're doing wrong. It's just the way the Web is.

Which Version of Windows Are You Using?

This book covers both Windows versions of Netscape, the 16-bit version for Windows 3.1 and the 32-bit version for Windows 95. The two versions of the program are almost identical, so all the instructions work for both versions of Netscape Navigator. If you're using Windows 3.1, don't be put off by the screen illustrations in this book—your version of Netscape will look almost exactly the same, except that you'll see the old, familiar Windows 3.1 interface.

Starting Netscape Navigator

Assuming you've already installed Netscape Navigator and are connected to the Internet (see Appendix A), you're ready to surf the Web.

To start Netscape Navigator:

1. Click the icon that connects you to your Internet service provider or the Microsoft Network.

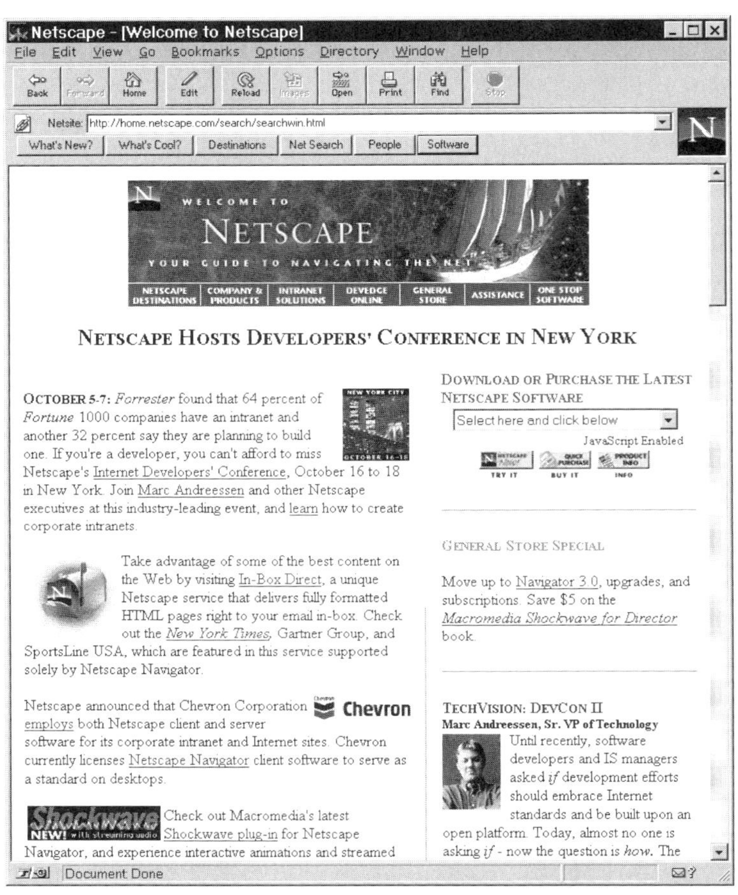

Figure 1.1 Netscape Navigator

2. Double-click the Netscape Navigator icon. If you're using Windows 95, you can choose Netscape from the Program menu, which you can access through the Start menu.

You'll see Netscape on-screen (Figure 1.1). To find out what you're looking at, read on.

What's on the Screen?

When Netscape Navigator starts, you'll see the program's window onscreen. The program icon (the big "N") displays an animation, informing you that Netscape is downloading information. In about a minute (or less, if you have a fast connection), you'll see the default *start page,* the page that appears when you start Netscape (or click the Home button).

Appearing within Netscape's application workspace, the default start page (see Figure 1.1) comes to you from Netscape Communications Corporation's headquarters in sunny California. In Netscape, as in any graphical Web browser, the default home page (also called the *start page*) is the Web document that the program is preset to display when started.

My start page isn't Netscape's home page! If you obtained Netscape from an Internet service provider (ISP) such as EarthLink TotalAccess, you may see a different start page. To see Netscape's home page, open the Directory menu and choose Netscape's Home.

My screen doesn't have some of the things shown in Figure 1.1! Somebody has messed with your Options menu, baby. On the menu bar, click Options. Below the first separator bar, look for options that don't have a check mark. These have been turned off. To turn them on, just click the option. Continue doing this until all the options have been turned on.

If you don't like the default Netscape start page, you can change it to something more to your liking. Find out how in Chapter 4.

The following sections detail the rest of the Netscape window, shown in Figure 1.2.

Title Bar

At the top of Netscape's window is the title bar, a standard Windows feature. Here, Netscape displays its own name. In addition, you see the title of the document you are currently viewing.

Where Does the Title Come From?

Web documents are written in the HyperText Markup Language (HTML), which enables Web authors to identify specific parts of the document, such as the title, headings, body text, and lists. The title bar displays the text that's marked with the <TITLE>...</TITLE> tags. If the document you're displaying contains the title "Sailing Page," you'll see "Netscape – [Sailing Page]" on the title bar.

Menu Bar

Below the title bar is the menu bar, which is just down the street from the neighborhood bar—but it's not five yet, is it? On the menu bar, you'll find the titles of Netscape's menus, from which you can choose additional options. Frankly, you won't use the menu bar very often—most of Netscape's most useful tools are available on the Toolbar (see the next section).

Here's a very quick overview of what's on these menus:

- **File** This menu enables access to a grab bag of display, storage, and printing options. You'll use it most frequently to open local files. A new feature with version 3: You can use this menu to open new Web or Mail windows.
- **Edit** This menu contains the standard Windows editing options, including Undo, Cut, Copy, Paste, and Find. The keyboard shortcuts are faster and easier. To use them, you hold down the Ctrl key and press the indicated key (for example, if you press Ctrl + F, you see the Find dialog box).
- **View** From this menu, you can choose options controlling the way Netscape obtains documents, but most of them can be chosen more quickly by using the Toolbar (discussed in the next section).
- **Go** Like the View menu, this menu contains several commands that are more easily accessed by clicking buttons on the Toolbar. But there's one gem: At the bottom of the menu, you see a list of the documents you've accessed recently. To go back to any of them, you just choose the document's name from the menu.

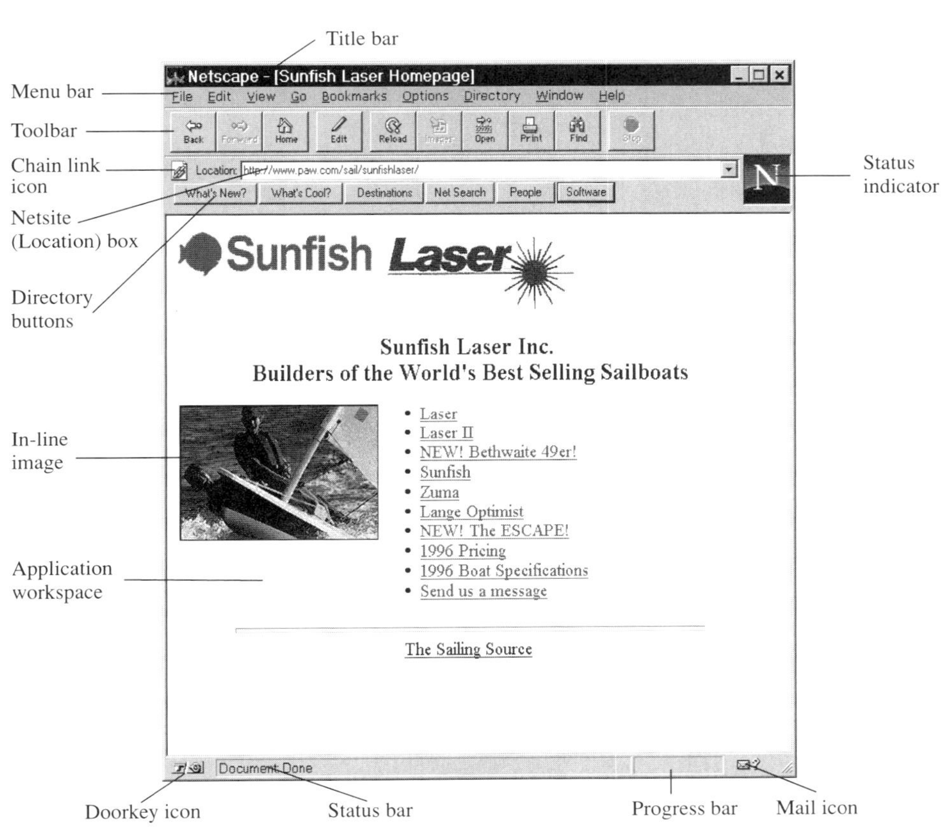

Figure 1.2 The parts of Netscape Navigator's program window

- **Bookmarks** This is probably the most useful menu of all. From it, you can choose options that enable you to create bookmarks. A bookmark is a saved document address that enables you to return to this document quickly, just by choosing it from the Bookmarks menu. You'll learn more about bookmarks in Chapter 6. *Note:* If you've installed the new Smart Bookmarks add-on, this menu has different commands. These commands give you direct access to Smart Bookmark's enormously cool features. You'll learn more about Smart Bookmarks in Chapter 7.

- **Options** This menu enables you to choose the way Netscape appears on-screen. Netscape is preset to display all of its optional screen features, such as the Toolbar, and that's the way I recommend that you use the program. In addition, you'll find lots of options for customizing Netscape, which are fully covered in Chapter 9.
- **Directory** This menu enables you to go directly to valuable Web resources, including search services. It duplicates the Directory buttons and gives a few additional options.
- **Window** This menu enables you to open new Mail and News windows, and also provides access to the Address Book, the bookmarks you've chosen, and the history list. You'll learn more about these features later in this book.
- **Help** This menu offers access to Netscape Navigator's on-line help directory—but hey, you've got this book. Much of the rest of this menu is a rather thinly disguised marketing tool.

I've got tennis elbow from using this darned mouse! I like to keep the use of my mouse to the minimum—and to do so, I make full use of keyboard commands. Look for the underlined letter in menu and option names. You can use these letters with the Alt key to select commands and options—without touching the mouse! To choose the View menu, hold down the Alt key and press V (uppercase or lowercase). To choose the Reload option in this menu, just press R. For a complete list of keyboard shortcuts, see Appendix F.

Toolbar

The Toolbar contains buttons, or tools, that enable easy access to frequently used Netscape commands. Here's a very quick once-over-lightly (you'll learn how to use these buttons in this chapter and the next):

Back — Go back to the document you just viewed.

Forward — Return to the document you went back from. This button isn't available unless you've displayed a document and then clicked the Back tool.

Home — Redisplay the default home page.

Edit	**Edit**	Open the current document in Netscape Editor.
Reload	**Reload**	Retrieve the currently displayed document again.
Images	**Images**	Turn off the automatic downloading of in-line images.
Open	**Open**	Type a URL (Web address) directly.
Print	**Print**	Print the document that Netscape is currently displaying.
Find	**Find**	Find text in the current document.
Stop	**Stop**	Stop downloading the current document.

Netsite (Location) Box

The Netsite box indicates the Web address (the URL) of the document you are currently viewing. When you access a non-Netscape Communications server, this box is called Location instead of Netsite. When you type a Web address into this box directly, it changes its name to Go To.

The chain link icon enables you to create a Windows 95 shortcut for the current page; just drag it to the desktop. If you drag the icon to the Bookmarks window, you create a new bookmark. This icon appears in the Windows 95 version only.

Directory Buttons

The Directory buttons enable you to access Web resources quickly. All of these options are also available on the Directory menu.

What's New!	**What's New**	Displays a list of new and interesting Web sites.
What's Cool!	**What's Cool**	Here are some Web sites that Mozilla likes. See you in a couple of hours.

Button	Name	Description
Destinations	Destinations	Starting points for Internet exploration.
Net Search	Net Search	Displays a great list of Web search engines (programs that search databases of Web documents). You'll learn more about searching the Web in Chapter 16.
People	People	Ways to find people on the Internet.
Software	Software	Click here to find out about Netscape's software upgrades.

Status Indicator

The big "N" lets you know when Netscape is downloading a document from the Web—it plays an animation (currently, comets shooting over the earth). When the document is finished downloading, you see "Document Done" on the status bar (at the bottom of the screen).

To return to Netscape's home page, just click the status indicator.

What's in a URL?

A URL has three parts. The first part (http://) indicates the type of resource you're viewing. If you're viewing an FTP file archive, the first part of the URL reads "ftp://," while a Gopher menu's URL reads "gopher://." The second part of the URL indicates the name of the computer you're accessing (such as home.netscape.com).

The third part of the directory indicates the path that Netscape must take to locate the document, and it also includes the document name (/home/welcome.html). Sometimes the third part of a URL is missing, which tells Netscape to look for and obtain the default document.

Do you really need to know all this? Not really, but sometimes you'll need to type URLs and it's important to do so correctly. For more information, check out Chapter 2.

Application Workspace

Here, Netscape displays the document you're currently viewing. You'll see text and hyperlinks, and you may also see in-line images (graphics that appear along with the text). If the document is bigger than the available window space, the scroll bars activate. You can click the scroll arrows, or drag the scroll bars, to bring hidden portions of the document into view.

Doorkey Icon

This icon indicates whether you're accessing a secure server. If you're not, the key is broken. Don't give your credit card number to any on-line vendor unless the connection is secure! If you're accessing a secure site, the key is unbroken.

Status Bar and Progress Bar

Next to the doorkey icon, there's a panel called the *status bar.* Netscape uses the status bar to display messages about what the program is doing. Most of the time, you can ignore these messages, unless you're curious to know what the program is doing.

Next to the status bar, you see a blank panel called the *progress bar.* When Netscape retrieves a document from the Internet, you'll see a graphical display indicating how much of the document has been obtained.

Mail Icon

If you've set up Netscape to read your Internet mail (see Chapter 17), you'll know when there's mail waiting for you: you'll see a little envelope followed by an exclamation point on the status bar. To open a mail window, just double-click this mail icon.

Hyperlinks: The Basics

Note that some of the words and phrases you see are highlighted with colors and underlining (if you're using a monochrome monitor, you'll see only underlining). These are *hyperlinks* (also called *anchors* or just *links*).

When you click on a hyperlink, Netscape locates the Web document that is linked to this hyperlink and initiates the transfer.

Try clicking one of the hyperlinks now:

1. Move the tip of the mouse pointer so that it's positioned over the hyperlink, and take a look at the status bar at the bottom of the screen. This displays the URL of the document to which this anchor is linked. Also, note that the pointer changes shape to a hand.
2. With the left mouse button, click the link. Forget all that double-clicking stuff; you just click once.

Several things happen now:

- The big "N" displays an animation (shooting comets). This tells you that Netscape is obtaining the document you requested, through a process called *downloading*. Incidentally, the official name for the big "N" is *status indicator.* (I like "Big 'N'" better.)
- The status bar indicates that Netscape is downloading a document.
- You see the new document within Netscape's application workspace.

What does "downloading" mean? When downloading occurs, Netscape transfers an entire document to your computer's memory, along with any associated graphics. This is called "downloading" because the information is coming from a distant computer to your computer. (As you might guess, the term *uploading* means sending information from your computer to a distant computer.) Once the document is in your computer's memory, you can scroll through it quickly. In addition, Netscape stores recently accessed documents in memory so that you can redisplay them quickly, should you wish to return to them.

Now try going back to the document you displayed previously. To do so, just click the Back button on the Toolbar. Take a look at the hyperlink you just clicked.

If you're viewing Netscape on a color monitor, note that the hyperlink you just clicked has changed color. This is a *visited* hyperlink, a hyperlink to a document that you've already seen. You can still click the hyperlink to redisplay the visited document, but Netscape wants you to know that you've been down that road before.

Basic Window Calisthenics

Like the window of any fine Windows application, Netscape's window can be adjusted until it suits your fancy. You can also minimize the program to an icon or maximize it to full size. The following instructions quickly detail these procedures; Figure 1.3 shows the on-screen window controls. P.S.—The Do-Nothing button really *doesn't* do anything. Access it at

http://www.wam.umd.edu/~twoflowr/button.htm

by typing this address exactly in the Location box (which changes its name to the Go To box) and pressing Enter.

Moving the Window

To move Netscape's window on the screen:

1. Move the mouse pointer to the title bar, hold down the left mouse button, and drag. You'll move the whole window.
2. When you've moved the window to where you want it to appear, release the mouse button.

Sizing the Window

To size Netscape's window:

1. Move the mouse pointer to one of the window's borders until the pointer changes shape, and drag the border.
2. When you've sized the window the way you want, release the mouse button.

Here's a neat trick: To size two borders at once, click on one of the corners and drag.

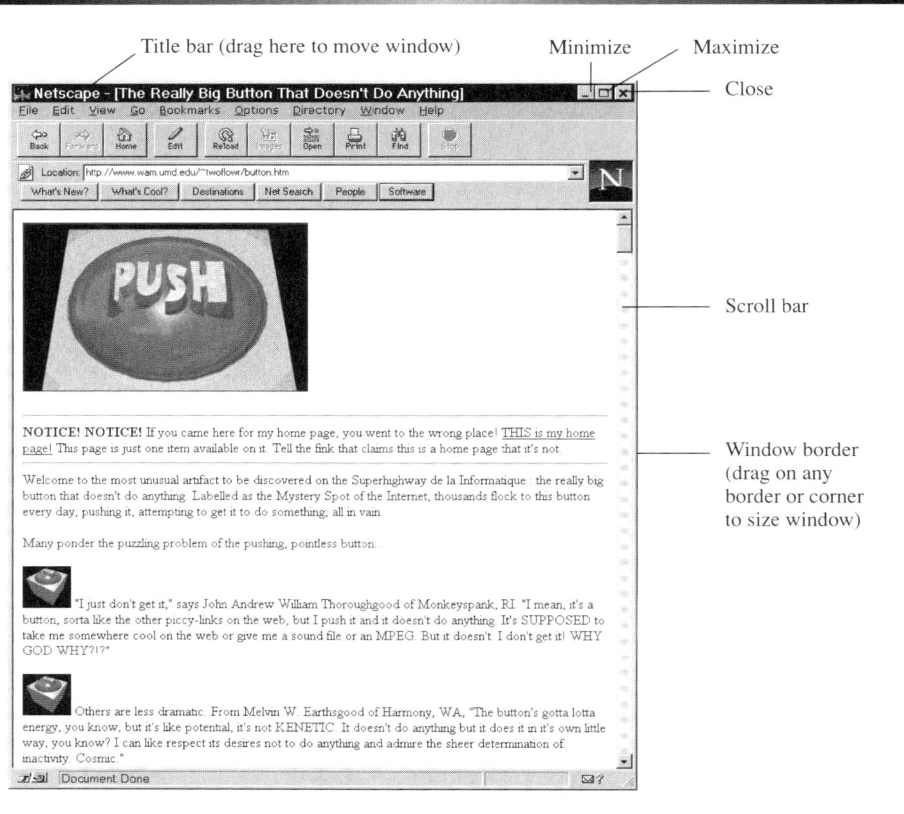

Figure 1.3 On-screen window controls

Minimizing the Window

To minimize Netscape's window:

1. Click the Minimize button. This shrinks Netscape down to an icon on the desktop (Windows 3.1) or a button on the taskbar (Windows 95).
2. To redisplay Netscape, double-click the minimized program icon (Windows 3.1) or the taskbar button (Windows 95).

Maximizing the Window

To maximize Netscape's window:

1. Click the Maximize button.
2. After you've maximized the window, you can restore the window to its previous size by clicking the same button.

Quitting Netscape Navigator

So, you're done. It's about 5 AM, isn't it? Hope you had fun.

To quit Netscape Navigator:

- From the File menu, choose Exit

  or

- Press Alt + F4

From Here

- Surf's up! Explore the Web, and access Internet resources, in Chapter 2.
- Running into problems—like that horrible "403—Access Forbidden" message? Check out Chapter 3, "When the Surf Gets Rough."
- Like to master Netscape Navigator, using the tricks known only to late-night confirmed hyperlink addicts? Check out Part II.

Chapter 2

The Gentle Art of Web Surfing

Wouldn't it be cool to learn how to surf the Web with the best of 'em, and in just an hour or two? If you agree, read this chapter. Sure, there's more to learn than this chapter covers, but you'll learn 90% of what you need to have some serious fun with Netscape. Plus, this chapter serves as a guide to much of the rest of this book. Later chapters explore its topics in more detail. By reading this chapter, you can learn which subjects you'd like to explore more deeply.

Just what does surfing the Web mean? It means exploring, discovering, navigating—and above all, being swept away by a series of awesome hyperlinks that you can ride all over cyberspace.

Netscape's your surfboard. You start by finding a cool Web document, one that's loaded with hyperlinks, and then begin exploring. As you navigate link after link, you'll connect with computers all over North America, Europe, Australia, and even more remote places. You can look forward to countless hours of discovery, fun, and even enchantment, with a bit of boredom thrown in (admittedly, not every Web site is worth accessing).

The surfing metaphor is darned appropriate: Sometimes you'll put your "board" on an amazing series of hyperlinks, and they'll carry you off to who-knows-where. And sometimes, admittedly, the hyperlinks you'll ride aren't very interesting, although (happily) some of them are so stupid that they are truly hilarious (see the following Treasure Trove). But there's gold in those links, as you'll surely agree. Have fun, and be sure to cancel tomorrow's appointments.

If you're curious to know what a really dumb Web site looks like, you'll find lots of links to dum-dum pages at the wonderful Useless Pages site,

http://www.primus.com/staff/paulp/useless.html

Webmaster Paul Phillips created this site after discovering that somebody named Kenny Z had typed his entire CD collection in an HTML document and made it available on the Web. Paul reflects that this was the first Web document that, as he puts it, "overtly crossed the line from tolerably frivolous to truly inane." Paul has since collected dozens of useless pages—you just have to check this out. For some reason, one of Paul's finds, the National Texture Administration's home page,

http://ftp.std.com/homepages/stevec/NTA/intro.html

just kills me. Maybe it's the link to "Man, the texturing animal." Read a treatise on fish and whale regurgitation, talk to Michael's cat, visit Edward's Scratch-n-Sniff Theater, read Dan's Dream Journal, and identify Ferret-Free Zones. To learn how to access a Web page by typing a URL directly, see the section titled "Typing a Web Address Directly," later in this chapter.

This chapter will benefit every reader of this book, and that's true even if you've already done some Web surfing with Netscape. In this chapter, you'll find a Web-savvy approach

to Netscape, the approach that experienced Netscape mavens use every day. Working through this chapter, even the stuff that seems obvious, will reveal the Netscape secrets and strategies that make this program the Web browser of choice.

For the Time-Challenged

- Remember to click just once when you click a hyperlink.
- A graphic with a blue border contains a hyperlink.
- Some graphics contain hyperlinks but don't have blue borders. To tell whether a graphic contains a hyperlink, move the mouse pointer over the graphic. If it changes to a hand shape, the graphic contains a hyperlink.
- To return to a document you've previously displayed, click Back or choose the document's name from the Go menu. To redisplay the document you were just viewing, click Forward.
- If you've accessed a multi-part Web page that has internal navigation buttons, learn how to use them. For finding your way around this web site, these buttons are much better than Netscape's Back and Forward buttons.
- When you access a document that contains frames, Netscape's window splits into two or more independently scrollable panels. To work with one of the panels, click within it.
- To access a Web page by typing its Web address directly, type it in the Location box and press Enter.
- If you get lost, click the Home button.
- To view movies, you need to install a helper application (see Chapter 11). Netscape is preset to play certain sounds.
- To locate documents on the Web, learn how to use search engines and subject trees.

A Word about Web Terminology

The Web's grown so fast that there hasn't been time to develop a consistent nomenclature—which doesn't help people who are trying to learn how to use it. Here are a few definitions to help you get started.

Page A Web document. Of course, many of these documents are longer than one page.

Home Page A Web document that's a "home" or a headquarters for a certain type of information. People like to set up home pages containing information about themselves, for example. Netscape has its own home page, the one you see every time you start the program.

Start Page The Web document that you see every time you start Netscape (or click the Home button). By default, this is Netscape's home page. You can change this, as explained in Chapter 4.

Web Browser A program that enables you to surf the Internet in search of Web pages.

Web Server A program that makes Web pages available to people who are browsing the Web.

Web Site A computer that's running a Web server. A Web site may contain lots of pages—maybe thousands of them. Unfortunately, many people use the term "site" as if it were synonymous with "page" ("That's a cool *site*" usually means "That's a cool *page*.")

URL The Web address of a Web page. I'll use the terms "Web address" and "URL" interchangeably.

There are more Web terms to learn, but these are more than sufficient to get you going.

Starting Netscape

Assuming you've already installed Netscape and configured your Internet connection (see Appendix A), you're ready to go. Unless you or somebody else (such as an Internet service provider who gave you a copy of Netscape) modified the default start page, you see Netscape's home.

By default, Netscape starts with a browser window. If you prefer, you can start with a mail or news window. To change the startup window, click General Preferences, click the Appearance tab, and choose an option in the On Startup Launch area. Chances are you'll want to start with the browser window.

Starting Netscape with Windows 3.1

In Program Manager, locate the Netscape program group, and double-click the Netscape Navigator program icon.

Starting Netscape with Windows 95

In the Start menu of Windows 95, click Programs, and then click Netscape to open the Netscape program group. Double-click the Netscape Navigator icon to start Netscape. You'll see Netscape on-screen, and the program displays the default start page (see Figure 2.1).

Using Windows 95? Eliminate all this Start-menu fussing by creating a shortcut for Netscape. The shortcut will appear on the desktop, where you can position it next to the Microsoft Network and Internet icons so thoughtfully provided by Microsoft (icons, I hasten to add, that you can't get rid of without knowing some system-level programming tricks.) To create a Netscape shortcut, click on the Netscape Navigator program icon and drag it to the desktop.

Netscape likes visitors—it helps them sell advertising space on their home page—but you should eventually change the default start page to something more tailored to your needs. It's really easy to do. For the lowdown, see Chapter 4.

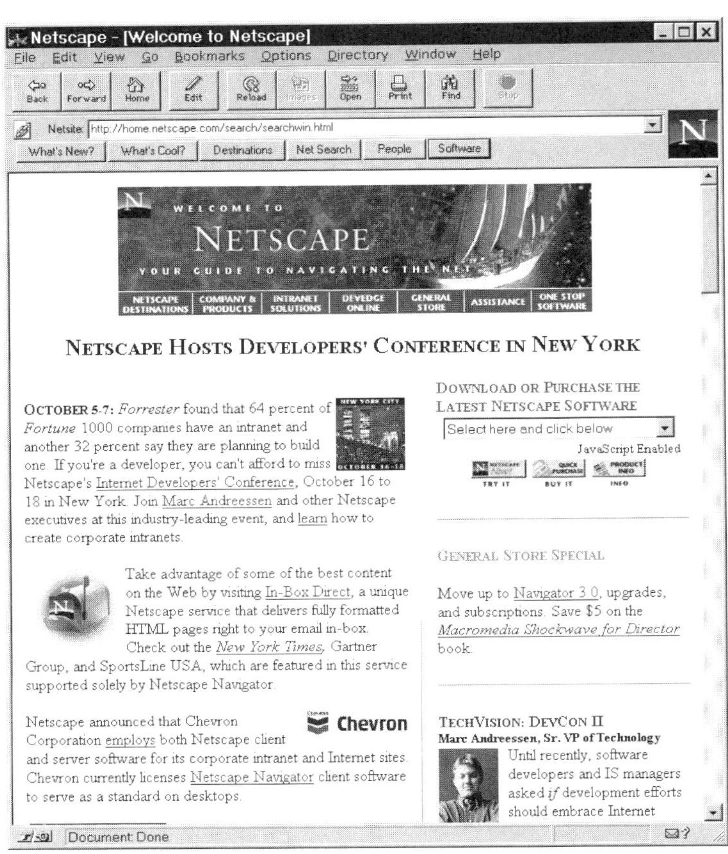

Figure 2.1 Default start page (Netscape Communications Corporation)

The Fundamental Maneuvers of Web Surfing

What makes the Web so much *fun* is its unpredictability—you start out clicking links from Netscape's home page (suggestion: click the What's Cool button to see a list of neat sites), and who knows where you'll wind up?

Experienced surfers know, though, that there are two kinds of surfing:

- **Grooving** This is good. Seriously good. When you're in a groove, you just can't seem to do anything wrong—you keep finding these *tremendous* sites, and the links from these sites take you to even more tremendous sites.
- **Thrashing** Everything you see is junk. On top of that, you're lost. You click and click, but there's nothing worth seeing.

Caught in a thrash? Get out of it by clicking the What's Cool button. You'll see Netscape's What's Cool page again. Try surfing from there—you can't go wrong. Check out a page, and click the Back button to go back to the What's Cool page again.

The Subtle Mysteries and Finer Points of Hyperlinks

You already know that hyperlinks appear in distinctive formatting (color and underlining, if you're using a color monitor). In addition, visited hyperlinks (ones you've clicked before) appear in a different, distinctive color. Here are a couple of additional points you need to know about hyperlinks:

- **Click *once*** To activate a hyperlink, you just move the pointer to it, and click. Yes, that's right—click once. Because many Macintosh and Windows functions are initiated by double-clicking something, you may have to unlearn the tendency to double-click. That second click may activate an unwanted hyperlink on the page that's about to be displayed, taking you to who-knows-where.
- **Some graphics contain hyperlinks** You can click these pictures to display a Web document. Here's how to tell whether an in-line graphic is a hyperlink: Look for a border around the graphic. With most browsers, the border appears in blue. Note, though, that Web authors are increasingly hiding the blue border (there's a way you can do this), since they believe that it's unaesthetic. When this is done, though, there's usually some indication on the graphic itself

that it's really a hyperlink. In Figure 2.1, for example, the Netscape Now graphic is a button—just the sort of thing you'd want to click.

- **Learn to use image maps** Some Web pages include graphics that have clickable regions, each associated with its own hyperlink. Such graphics are called *image maps*, although they don't necessarily look like a map. An example is the beautiful graphic at the top of Netscape's home page, which has a number of distinct areas. If you click one of these areas, Netscape displays the linked document. A great example of an image map is the White House Home Page (Figure 2.2). The whole screen is a clickable image map.

I can't tell whether this graphic contains a hyperlink or not! No blue border? It might still contain one or more hyperlinks. To find out, move the mouse pointer over the graphic. If it changes shape to a hand with one finger extended, then you know that the graphic contains a hyperlink.

I'm Lost! (Navigation Fundamentals)

Two exclamations are heard from beginning Web surfers: "Cool!" followed shortly by "Where am I!!?" Here's a very quick mini-course in Web navigation.

Going Back

At any time, you can go back to see a document you previously viewed. To go back, you click the Back button. If you just love toying with Windows' menus, you could choose Back from the Go menu, but mouse-haters are cheerfully invited to use the Alt + < keyboard shortcut. (< is the less-than symbol, which you'll find to the right of the letter M on your keyboard.)

Mouse lovers, here's a neat trick. To go back, just click the *right* mouse button anywhere within the document. From the pop-up menu, click Back.

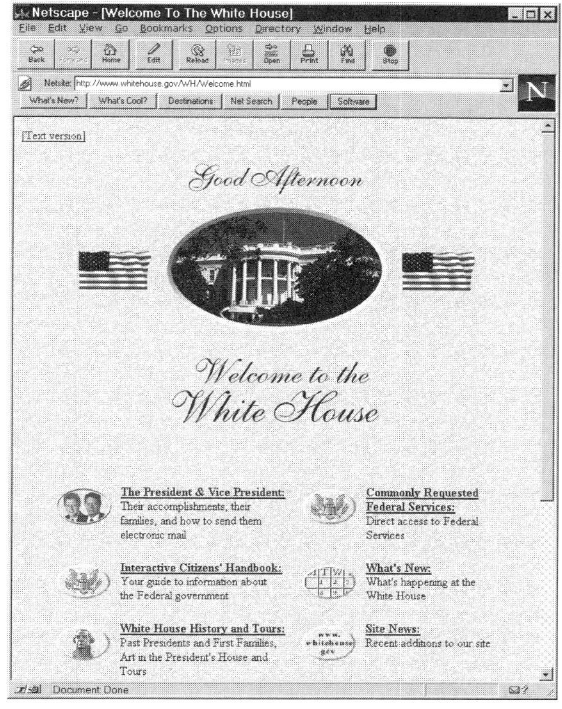

Figure 2.2 White House Home Page (http://www.whitehouse.gov/WH/Welcome.html)

If you're displaying a document in which the page has been broken up into two or more independent panels, called *frames*, clicking Back displays the next document in the selected frame.

Notice that going back is a lot faster than downloading the document in the first place? That's because Netscape stores a copy of recently accessed documents in a special memory area called a *cache*. The program can retrieve documents from the cache much faster than it can retrieve them from the network.

If you're trying to redisplay a document that you viewed several clicks ago, don't waste time by clicking the Back button repeatedly. Instead, open the Go menu and look for the document's name at the bottom of this menu. Note that sometimes Netscape doesn't save the names of all the documents you've visited. To find out why, see "There's a History to This," in Chapter 5.

Going Forward

Once you've gone back by clicking the Back button, the Forward button becomes available. Try it now (or press Alt + >).

If you like using the mouse, try this: Right-click anywhere within the document, and choose Forward.

If you're displaying a document with frames, clicking Forward displays the next document in the frame (but only if you've gone back in this frame).

So what does the Forward button do? It lets you return to the document you just went Back from. Oh, heck, it's easier to do than talk about.

The Forward button is dimmed! You're viewing the most recent document you downloaded, which means that you can't go forward. You can go back, or you can access a new Web document by clicking a hyperlink or typing a Web address.

Look for Internal Navigation Buttons!

Many Web sites offer more than just a page; they offer a *web*, and within this web each page has navigation buttons to help you find your way. A web (as opposed to *the* Web, the World Wide Web) is a collection of related Web documents, all stored on a single site; each document explores one facet of the topic at hand. Internal navigation aids help you find your way around in a web. Ideally, navigation buttons appear on every page of the web and look just the same, so you quickly learn how to navigate within the web.

If the web you're browsing has internal navigation buttons, by all means use them! Internal navigation buttons always give you the best way of navigating within a multidocument web. That's because the web's author knows just how the web is structured. The navigation buttons have been designed to help you navigate the web logically. You can use Netscape's Back and Forward buttons to redisplay pages you just accessed, if you wish, but the internal navigation buttons are your best bet.

You'll quickly learn to recognize navigation buttons, which are of two kinds:

- **Graphical Buttons** These are popular because they look neat, but they take forever to download on slow SLIP/PPP lines using modems. See Figure 2.3 for an example.
- **Text Buttons** These navigation aids download much more quickly because they're made from ordinary characters. See Figure 2.4 for an example.

I don't know what this darned navigation button does! Too many Web authors use button graphics that don't really suggest what's going to happen when you click on the navigation buttons—so don't feel bad, it's not you. Thoughtful Web authors include explanatory text along with the buttons, unless the buttons' meanings are so clear that it's obvious what they do.

It's a Frame-Up (Using Frames)

A very nice new feature of Netscape is support of *frames*, a set of HTML tags that enable Web authors to divide a page into several independently scrollable panels. When you access a document that contains frames, Netscape divides the application workspace into two or more panels. If there's more text in one of the panels than Netscape can display, the program automatically includes a scroll bar. You can use the scroll bar to bring the hidden parts of the panel into view.

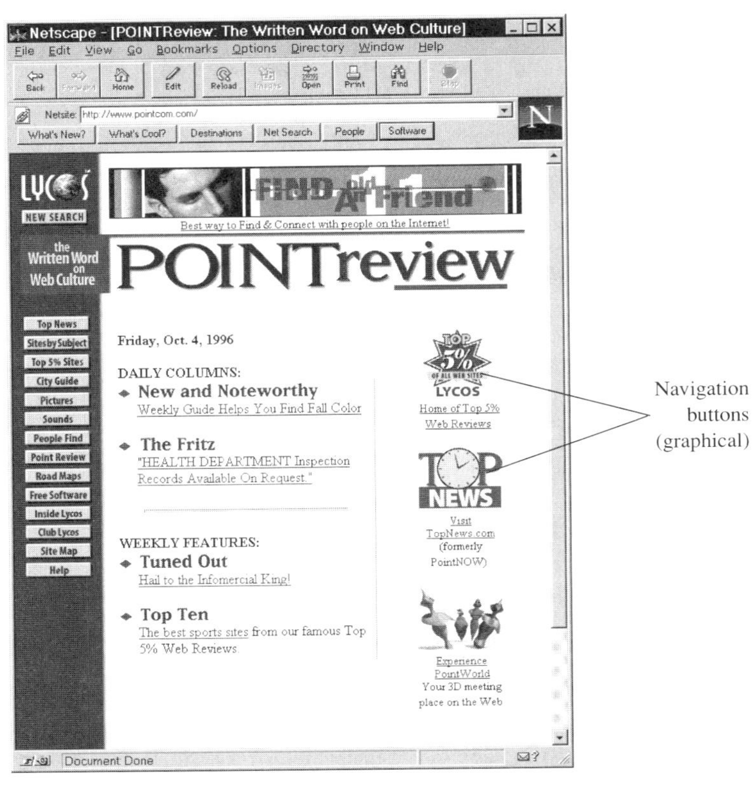

Figure 2.3 Graphical navigation buttons

Some Web authors may give you the option of repositioning the frame borders. If you'd like to do so, move the pointer to the border. If the pointer changes shape to a bidirectional arrow, you can adjust the border's position.

An obvious and appropriate use for frames is to keep navigation buttons on-screen at all times. With a one-page display, the buttons scroll out of sight as the user reads the document. With frames, a Web author can position the frame in a panel that stays put, even if the user scrolls the other

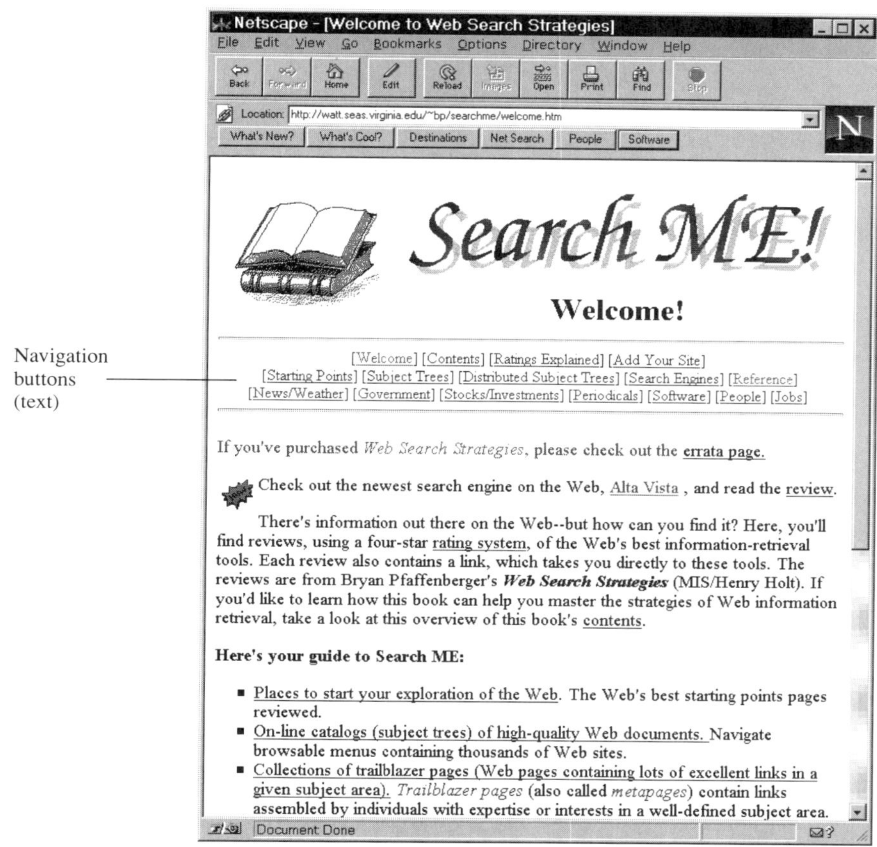

Figure 2.4 Text-based navigation buttons

panel (see Figure 2.5). Another obvious application of frames lies in computer-aided instruction. In Figure 2.6, you see an interesting explanation of the human eye; when you click on one of the features of the eye, you see an explanation in the right-hand panel.

Frankly, frames haven't been too popular among Web authors, and with good reason: In version 2.0, clicking Back propelled you backwards, completely out of the site. Version 3 fixes this problem by restricting the effect of the Back and Forward buttons to the selected frames. This works very

nicely, as you'll see. Display a frame document and then navigate around within one of the panels. Then click Back until you've gone back to the first document in that frame. If you click Back once more, you'll leave the site and see the previously displayed site.

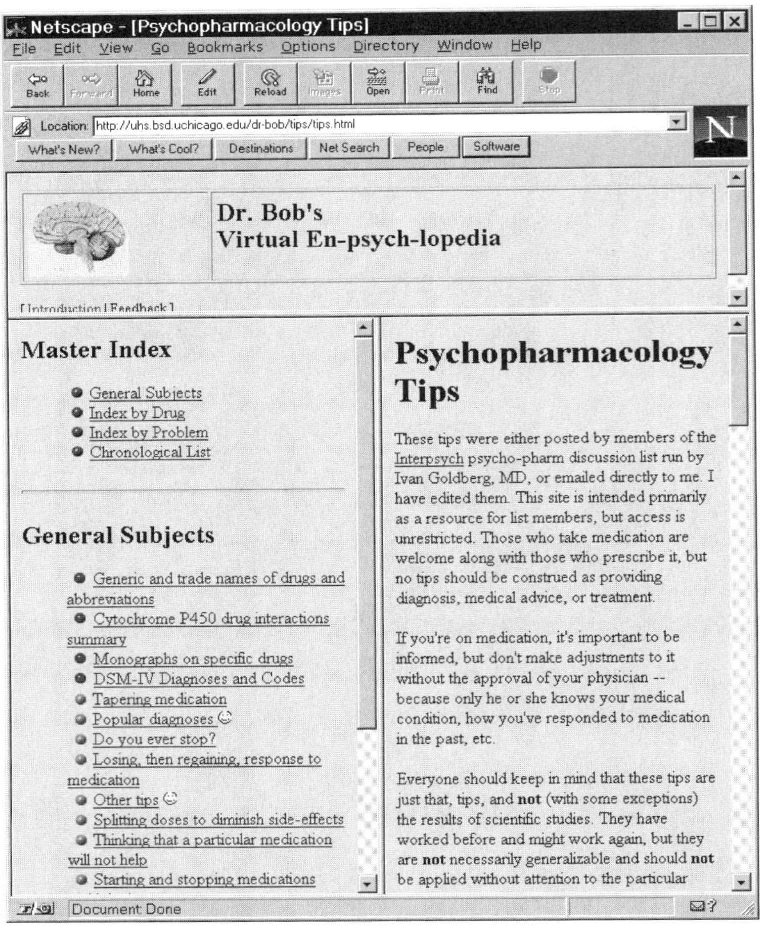

Figure 2.5 Navigation buttons positioned in left panel

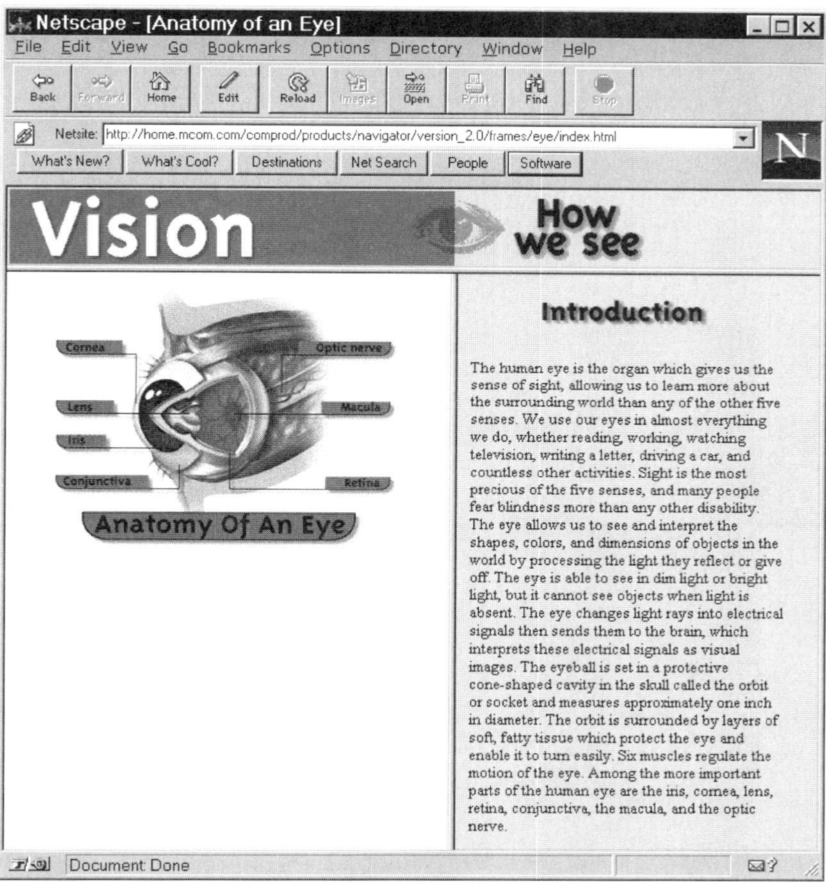

Figure 2.6 Frames used for computer-aided instruction

Java!

Here's the latest and probably the neatest thing on the Web. Java is a new programming language that is being developed by Sun Microsystems. Based on the popular C++ language, widely used by professional programmers, Java enables professional programmers to prepare mini-programs called

Java applets. New HTML tags enable Web developers to embed Java applets into Web pages—when you access such a page, things happen!

On pages containing Java applets, you'll see action where there was once nothing but static text and graphics—for example, words will whirl, blink, and fade. One of the coolest demonstration sites shows a simulated stock ticker tape, which scrolls past the screen at an impressive clip.While it does, three charts track your favorite stocks' price movements throughout the day. Most exciting, though, are a whole range of planned Web applications that will enable you to interact with a Web page and see the results immediately.

Netscape version 3 can run Java applets, and does so automatically. You don't need to do anything special, or learn any new commands. You'll just notice that the pages you download have added functionality.

This Java applet is taking forever to load! Some Java applets require downloading graphics and sounds in addition to the Java code, and this might require a minute or two. Be patient—chances are that the wait will be worth it!

Typing a Web Address Directly

You've picked up your copy of *Netguide*, and you've read about this seriously cool Web site. The only problem is, there's no hyperlink to this site on Netscape's default home page. How do you get there? You can type the Web address directly and go straight to the site, as this section explains.

Understanding Web Addresses

A Web address (URL) has three parts:

- **Protocol Name** This is the first part of the URL. It specifies the type of Internet communication standard (protocol) that's used to obtain this document. Web documents use the HTTP (World Wide Web) protocol, so you'll see *http://* at the beginning of Web addresses. You may also encounter *gopher://*, *ftp://*, and other protocol names.
- **Internet Address** In the second part of the URL, you see the Internet *domain name* of the computer that stores the resource you're

accessing. The parts of the domain name are separated by dots, as in *www.yahoo.com*.

- **File Location** The third part of a URL specifies the location of the resource within the file system of the computer you're accessing. You may see one or more subdirectory (folder) names in this section. The final component of the URL is the file name of the resource you're accessing. If it's a Web document, the file will end in *.htm or *.html.

A URL looks like this:

http://dmf.culture.fr/files/imaginary_exhibition.html

You don't have to type the "http://" part of a Web address. To locate the above URL, you could type dmf.culture.fr/files/imaginary_exhibition.htm.

Using the Open Location Dialog Box

To access a Web address by typing it directly, follow these steps:

1. From the File menu, choose Open Location, or use the Ctrl + L keyboard shortcut, or click the Open button.
2. In the Open Location dialog box, carefully type the URL. Be sure to copy the URL exactly, including the exact pattern of capitalization. Don't include any spaces.
3. Click Open.

I typed the URL, but it didn't work! Whoops. Well, there are several possible reasons. Here's a rundown:

- **You may have typed the URL wrong.** Even a little tiny mistake, like putting a period at the end of the URL or adding a space, can mess things up. Remember, too, that URLs are case-sensitive (uppercase and lowercase letters are different). If you find a mistake, just edit and correct it within the Location box, and press Enter to try again.

- **The author or site administrator may have pulled the plug on this site.** That wasn't very nice, was it? But it happens. Incidentally, some of the URLs in this book may have gone bye-bye in the interval between my writing and your reading—if you run into any of these, let me know (bp@virginia.edu).
- **Too many people are trying to access the site.** Netscape is trying, trying, trying to access the site; the comets keep shooting, but nothing appears . . . minutes go by, fruitlessly. Give up, and click Stop. Try again later—like 2 AM. So many people are surfing the Web that it's sometimes hard to get through to popular sites during prime daytime hours (10 AM to 4 PM).

Typing the URL in the Location Box

Here's a faster way to type the URL:

1. Click within the Location box. Netscape selects the current Web address.
2. Just start typing the new URL. The name of the Location box changes to Go to.
3. Press Enter when you're done typing the URL.

You can sometimes tell a lot about a Web resource by looking at its URL. For example, the URL on page 35 tells me that the document is located in a computer in France (the "fr" part of the domain name is a code name for France). I'll bet that the document is stored on a UNIX machine, too, since UNIX computers can handle long file names ("imaginary_exhibition.html"). A short file name with the *.htm extension is a dead giveaway that the computer is a Windows 3.1 system. Some more tips: In domain names, "edu" indicates a college or university, while "com" indicates a private company, "org" indicates a nonprofit organization, and "gov" indicates a government office of some kind.

Don't retype a URL if you want to revisit a site that you previously accessed by typing the URL directly—Netscape remembers the last ten URLs that you directly typed in the Location box. To choose one of them, click the down arrow at the right edge of the Location box.

How I Got Here, I Haven't a Clue (Go Home)

If you're really lost, you'll know it: hyperdisorientation sets in. (Hyperdisorientation is a well-documented malady of cyberspace, a recently discovered syndrome with distressing symptoms: Patients do not know how they got to where they are, haven't the foggiest idea how to retrace their steps, and babble incessantly about lost URLs.) Netscape provides a quick cure: Click the Home button. You'll see the Netscape welcome page again.

Help Me, Helper Applications!

Netscape can't do everything by itself, although it does a great job of displaying GIF and JPEG graphics. Sounds, movies, and animations are dinosaurs of a different color, though—the program needs helper applications, programs that start when they're needed in order to play a movie or sound.

Netscape version 3 comes with LiveAudio, a sound plug-in that's already installed automatically and ready to go, so let's give it a whirl. How about a selection from Neil Young's *Sleeps with Angels*? To access the *Sleeps with Angels* page, type the following URL directly:

http://www.iuma.com/Warner/html/Young,_Neil.html

By the way, note the comma and underline after "Young"—you need to type this URL exactly.

This is legit, incidentally; it's a 30-second excerpt from "Change Your Mind," one of the cuts from the album, and it's offered by Warner Brothers—for promotional purposes, obviously.

To hear the mono version of "Change Your Mind," click the Sun-AU (271K) option. (The other option, an 800K-plus stereo MPEG file, requires a custom sound player.) Netscape downloads the sound (this takes a while), and then displays the LiveAudio plug-in. You'll see VCR-like controls; just click the Play control to start the sound.

It won't play through my PC's little speaker! To hear the sound, your system must be equipped with a sound card and speakers.

When you're finished listening to the sound, you can "rewind" it and play it again, or just quit by clicking the LiveAudio close box.

I Want to See You Again, or, Setting Bookmarks

You've found a cool Web site, haven't you? And you want to know how to get back without having to click for six months, or type the URL, don't you? That's why Netscape lets you set bookmarks.

A bookmark is a URL that you've saved to a special list of ultra-cool Web sites, a list you have constructed yourself. Whenever you run across a Web site you like, just set a bookmark, as explained here.

To set a bookmark:

1. Display the Web page that you want to mark.
2. From the Bookmarks menu, choose Add Bookmark, or use the Ctrl + D keyboard shortcut.

Netscape adds the name of the document you're displaying to the Bookmarks menu. To visit this document again, just open the Bookmarks menu and choose the document's name.

I've added too many documents to my Bookmarks menu! This happens pretty fast, you'll find. Once you've added one or two dozen documents to your Bookmarks

menu, it isn't very much fun to use anymore. Time to get organized! Netscape provides a cool way to create submenus, so that you can pack dozens and dozens of bookmarks in this menu without creating something overwhelming to the eye. Flip to Chapter 6 for the lowdown on organizing your Bookmarks menu.

The Bookmarks menu is loaded with SmartMarks options—but no Bookmarks options! Great—you've installed SmartMarks. You'll be glad you did. To find out how to save bookmark items with SmartMarks, see Chapter 7.

Excuse Me, Where's the Subject Catalog? (Subject Trees and Search Engines)

Let's start with the bad news. It's really difficult to find information on the Web. Here's why. You've probably heard that the Internet is an experiment in controlled anarchy—there's no central headquarters of Internet, Inc. You don't have to get anyone's permission to hook up your computer or network to the Internet. So the Internet just grows and grows, hooking up an estimated 35 million people so far.

Because the Web uses the Internet for its communication base, the Web's just as gloriously disorganized—you don't have to ask anyone's permission to put documents on the Web. There's no single, central repository of records concerning Web documents.

With some 8 million Web documents now in existence (make that 12 million by the time you read this), we're talking about an information-retrieval nightmare. There's stuff on the Web concerning the chardonnays of Western Australia, the role of community networks in improving health care delivery, or the history of punk rock in the funkier districts of London—but good luck finding it, unless you're lucky enough to stumble on a trailblazer document that summarizes all the relevant links. (A trailblazer document, discussed in Chapter 15, stems from some charitable individual's attempts to sum up a number of interesting links, often on a single subject area such as gardening.)

Although there's no official, central database of Web documents, lots of clever computer people have been trying to solve the information-retrieval problem. They've taken two approaches, called *subject trees* and *search engines*.

- **Subject Trees** A subject tree is a subject-oriented catalog of URLs, organized by topic (such as "Astrology," "Astronomy," "Astrophysics," etc.). The "tree" part of the name comes from the catalog's hierarchical organization; under "music," for instance, you find branches of the tree, such as classical music, folk music, and techno-rave music. No subject tree is complete; it is a really big pain to keep one of these things updated. Most of the work is done by civic-minded volunteers, who have only so much time for such things. Out of some 2 million Web documents, for example, Yahoo—one of the best subject trees—indexes only about 32,000. On the bright side, though, Yahoo contains 32,000 *good* URLs. There's a lot of junk out there, but it doesn't pass the subject tree's screening mechanisms.
- **Search Engine** A search engine provides keyword searching of a database that has been compiled by a spider or worm (a program that automatically "crawls" the Web, finding Web documents and recording information about them). A search engine enables you to type in one or more search words (such as "Neil" and "Young"). The search engine then tries to match these search terms against a database of URL names and topics. Search engines and spiders are helpful tools, but bear in mind that they retrieve the chaff as well as the wheat: A search for CDs, for instance, will retrieve Kenny Z's useless list of his CD collection along with some on-line compact disc vendors and an unbelievable assortment of other stuff.

Let's take a look at subject trees in more detail; Chapter 16 delves into the mysteries of search engines.

Introducing Yahoo

No subject tree can hope to keep up with the thousands of new Web pages that appear every week. Every subject tree is therefore a selection from what's out there, and some are hipper than others. The hippest? Yahoo.

The name "Yahoo" stands for Yet Another Hierarchically Officious Oracle. On Yahoo's help page, you'll find a pull-down box that lets you choose words other than "Officious" if you like, including "Obstreperous" and "Odiferous." Self-effacing Yahoo may be, but you'll probably supply another "O" word: Outstanding. Actually, Yahoo means "a member of a race of brutes in Swift's *Gulliver's Travels* who have the form and all the vices of man"—but none of the virtues. Yahoo was created by David Filo and Jerry Yang, formerly computer science graduate students at Stanford University (until Yahoo swallowed them whole).

Accessing Yahoo

To access Yahoo, use this URL:

http://www.yahoo.com/

You'll see Yahoo's main subject tree (Figure 2.7).

Note the navigation buttons at the top of the page; you'll find them at the top of every Yahoo page. If you get lost, you can click "Yahoo!" to redisplay this page.

Exploring Yahoo

Now you'll see why Yahoo is called a subject tree. Click Government, and you'll see some of the main Government "branches" (subheadings), as shown in Figure 2.8. And if you click one of these subheadings, you'll see a page like the one shown in Figure 2.9; here you see document names.

Here's the cool part. These document names are living, breathing hyperlinks, which you can click just like any other hyperlink.

Have fun. There are over 50,000 hyperlinks in Yahoo!

Yahoo explorers, look for a pair of sunglasses next to a document's name. This indicates an especially good document of its type.

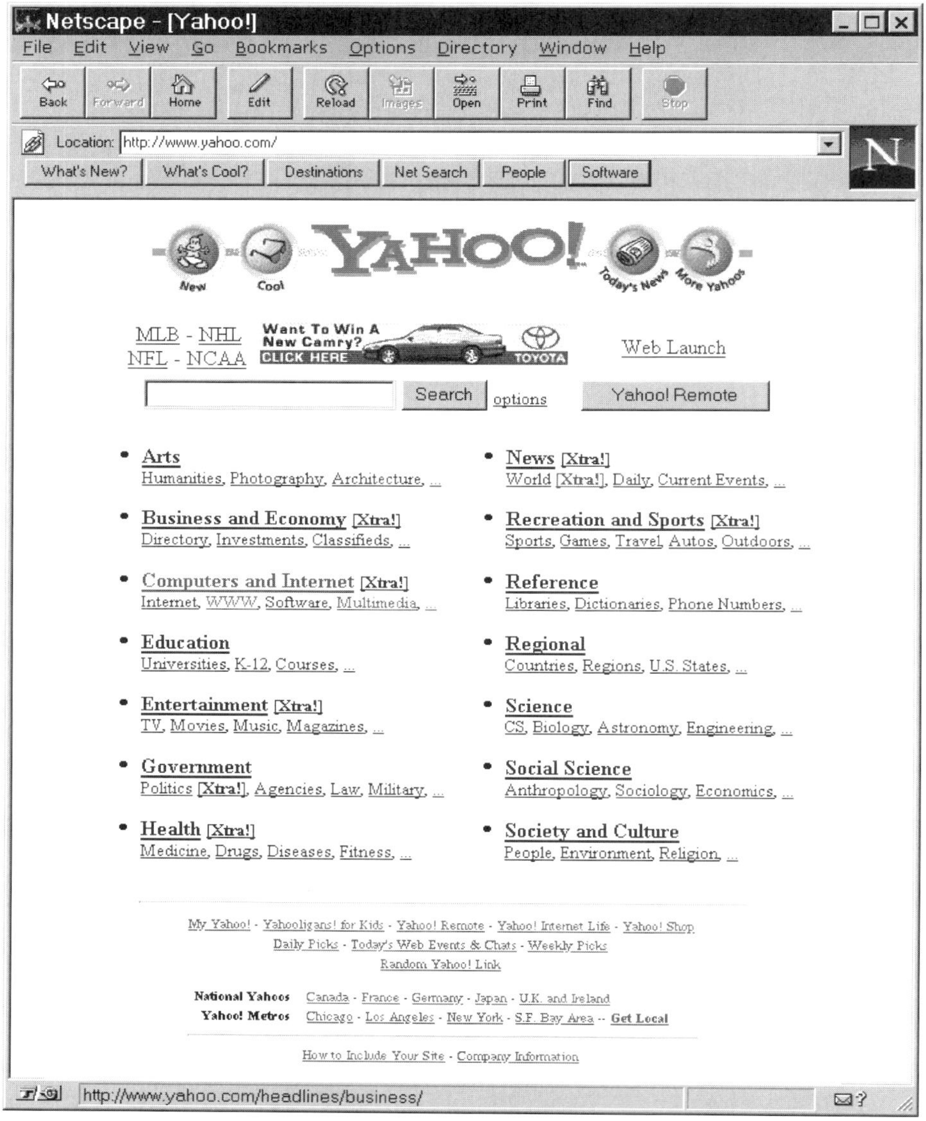

Netscape - [Yahoo!]

File Edit View Go Bookmarks Options Directory Window Help

Back Forward Home Edit Reload Images Open Print Find Stop

Location: http://www.yahoo.com/

What's New? What's Cool? Destinations Net Search People Software

New Cool YAHOO! Today's News More Yahoos

MLB - NHL
NFL - NCAA

Want To Win A New Camry? CLICK HERE TOYOTA

Web Launch

Search options Yahoo! Remote

- **Arts**
  Humanities, Photography, Architecture, ...
- **Business and Economy** [Xtra!]
  Directory, Investments, Classifieds, ...
- **Computers and Internet** [Xtra!]
  Internet, WWW, Software, Multimedia, ...
- **Education**
  Universities, K-12, Courses, ...
- **Entertainment** [Xtra!]
  TV, Movies, Music, Magazines, ...
- **Government**
  Politics [Xtra!], Agencies, Law, Military, ...
- **Health** [Xtra!]
  Medicine, Drugs, Diseases, Fitness, ...
- **News** [Xtra!]
  World [Xtra!], Daily, Current Events, ...
- **Recreation and Sports** [Xtra!]
  Sports, Games, Travel, Autos, Outdoors, ...
- **Reference**
  Libraries, Dictionaries, Phone Numbers, ...
- **Regional**
  Countries, Regions, U.S. States, ...
- **Science**
  CS, Biology, Astronomy, Engineering, ...
- **Social Science**
  Anthropology, Sociology, Economics, ...
- **Society and Culture**
  People, Environment, Religion, ...

My Yahoo! - Yahooligans! for Kids - Yahoo! Remote - Yahoo! Internet Life - Yahoo! Shop
Daily Picks - Today's Web Events & Chats - Weekly Picks
Random Yahoo! Link

National Yahoos Canada - France - Germany - Japan - U.K. and Ireland
Yahoo! Metros Chicago - Los Angeles - New York - S.F. Bay Area -- **Get Local**

How to Include Your Site - Company Information

http://www.yahoo.com/headlines/business/

Figure 2.7 Yahoo subject tree

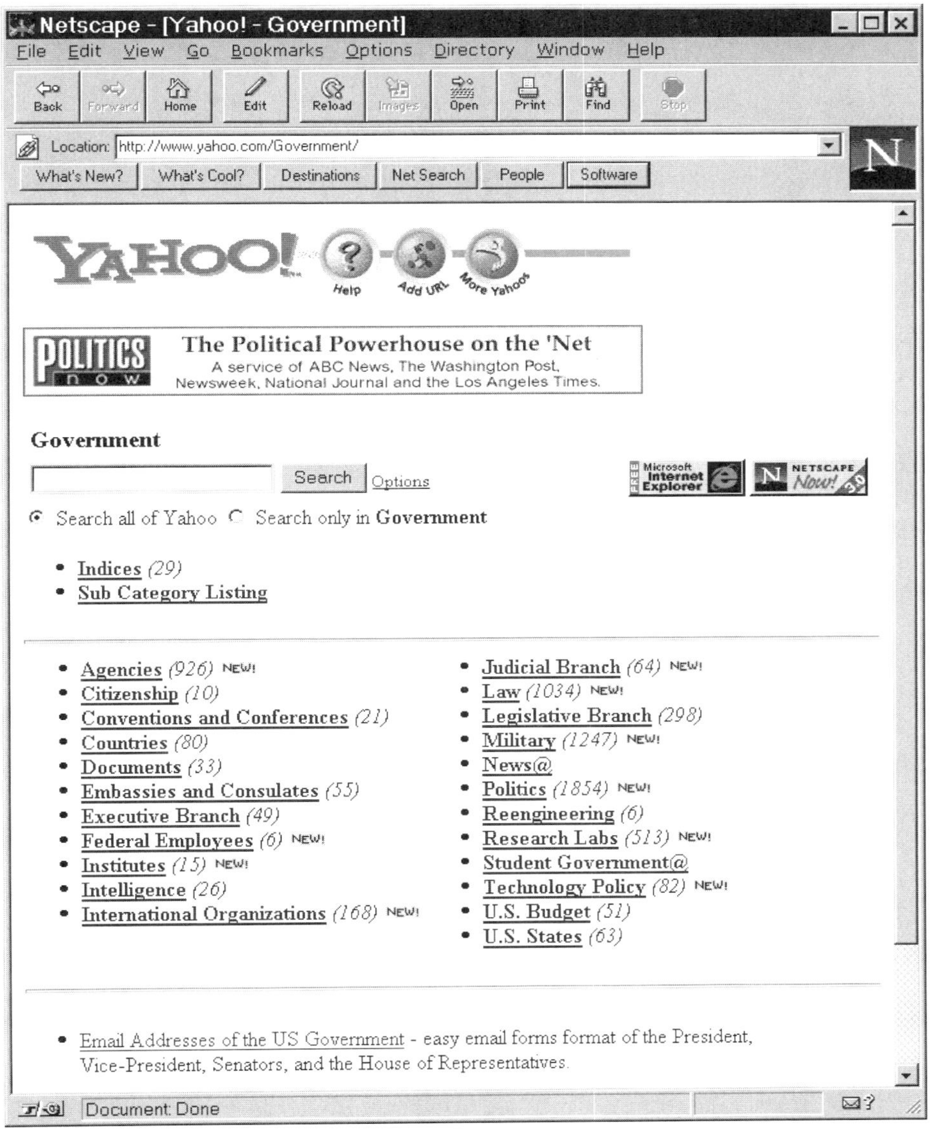

Netscape - [Yahoo! - Government]

File Edit View Go Bookmarks Options Directory Window Help

Back Forward Home Edit Reload Images Open Print Find Stop

Location: http://www.yahoo.com/Government/

What's New? What's Cool? Destinations Net Search People Software

YAHOO! Help Add URL More Yahoos

The Political Powerhouse on the 'Net
A service of ABC News, The Washington Post, Newsweek, National Journal and the Los Angeles Times.

Government

Search Options

Search all of Yahoo Search only in **Government**

- Indices *(29)*
- Sub Category Listing

- Agencies *(926)* NEW!
- Citizenship *(10)*
- Conventions and Conferences *(21)*
- Countries *(80)*
- Documents *(33)*
- Embassies and Consulates *(55)*
- Executive Branch *(49)*
- Federal Employees *(6)* NEW!
- Institutes *(15)* NEW!
- Intelligence *(26)*
- International Organizations *(168)* NEW!
- Judicial Branch *(64)* NEW!
- Law *(1034)* NEW!
- Legislative Branch *(298)*
- Military *(1247)* NEW!
- News@
- Politics *(1854)* NEW!
- Reengineering *(6)*
- Research Labs *(513)* NEW!
- Student Government@
- Technology Policy *(82)* NEW!
- U.S. Budget *(51)*
- U.S. States *(63)*

- Email Addresses of the US Government - easy email forms format of the President, Vice-President, Senators, and the House of Representatives.

Document: Done

Figure 2.8 Goverment "branch" of Yahoo subject tree

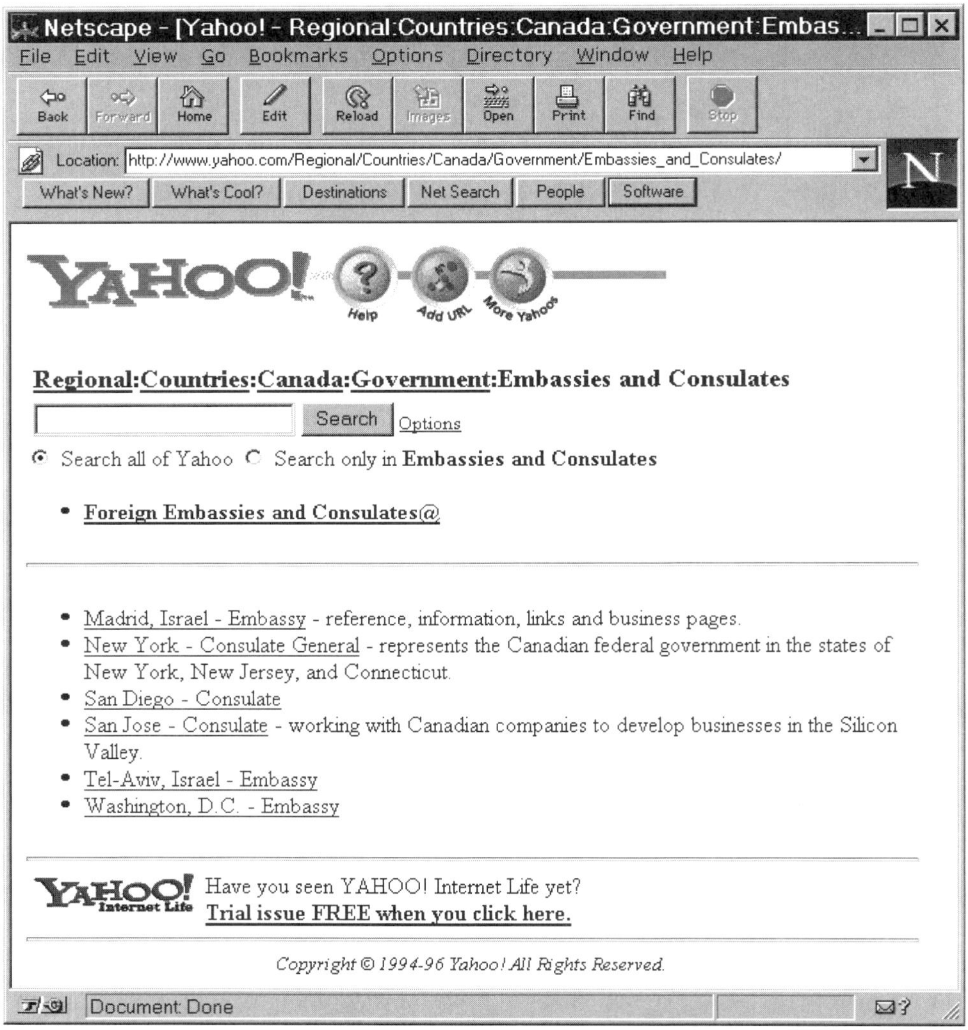

Netscape - [Yahoo! - Regional:Countries:Canada:Government:Embas...

File Edit View Go Bookmarks Options Directory Window Help

Back Forward Home Edit Reload Images Open Print Find Stop

Location: http://www.yahoo.com/Regional/Countries/Canada/Government/Embassies_and_Consulates/

What's New? What's Cool? Destinations Net Search People Software

YAHOO! Help Add URL More Yahoos

Regional:Countries:Canada:Government:Embassies and Consulates

Search Options

Search all of Yahoo Search only in **Embassies and Consulates**

- **Foreign Embassies and Consulates@**

- Madrid, Israel - Embassy - reference, information, links and business pages.
- New York - Consulate General - represents the Canadian federal government in the states of New York, New Jersey, and Connecticut.
- San Diego - Consulate
- San Jose - Consulate - working with Canadian companies to develop businesses in the Silicon Valley.
- Tel-Aviv, Israel - Embassy
- Washington, D.C. - Embassy

YAHOO! Internet Life Have you seen YAHOO! Internet Life yet?
Trial issue FREE when you click here.

Copyright © 1994-96 Yahoo! All Rights Reserved.

Document: Done

Figure 2.9 Documents listed in Yahoo

FROM HERE

- Change the default start page. To do so, flip to Chapter 4.
- Run into some trouble navigating the Web? Check out Chapter 3.
- Deal with an unwieldy Bookmarks menu in Chapter 6—or better yet, install SmartMarks or Smart Bookmarks and learn how to use these much-improved bookmark organizers (Chapter 7).
- Learn how to save and print the documents you display on the Web (Chapter 8).
- Learn more about starting points, subject trees, and search engines in Part IV.

Chapter 3

When the Surf Gets Rough

Netscape is loads of fun to use, but the Web isn't perfect. You will encounter many network-related problems while you're surfing. These aren't Netscape's fault, but part of Netscape mastery involves knowing what to do about them. This chapter discusses the things that can go wrong while you're surfing the Web—the black holes, the forbidden zones, the unplugged sockets, and more.

Even if you haven't run into the problems discussed in this chapter, it's still a good idea to skim it.

For the Time-Challenged

- If a site doesn't respond after a minute or two, give up and try again later.
- If you type a URL directly, make sure you type it correctly. A typing error could produce a DNS error message (the domain name is incorrect) or a 404 Not Found message (the document name is incorrect). Correct your typing and try again.
- Still getting a DNS or 404 error message? The site's down or the document's gone. Sorry.
- A 403 Forbidden message means that the document is not available to users from your Internet domain. This might mean the document is for local use only.
- Socket error messages generally indicate a temporary problem: Try clicking the hyperlink again.
- The other stuff discussed in this chapter falls into the minor nuisance category.

I Clicked the Hyperlink – and Nothing Happened!

The site you're trying to access is busy, busy, busy—so busy in fact, that it can't even transmit a message that it's too busy! Pathetic. Try again later—like at 2:30 AM.

If you're determined to get through to a site, open a new window in Netscape and let the original window keep on tryin'. Maybe the document you want will appear after a few minutes. Maybe not.

A site that just never responds is known to Web surfers as a Black Hole. If you've never had this experience, but would like to give it a try, there is a Black Hole simulation at the following URL:

http://ravenna.wwa.com/blackhole.html

Please do not click the Black Hole link (Figure 3.1). You will be caught in the Hole and unable to get out. Somehow, resist the temptation! (Actually, you can just click Stop and then Back to get out of the Hole.)

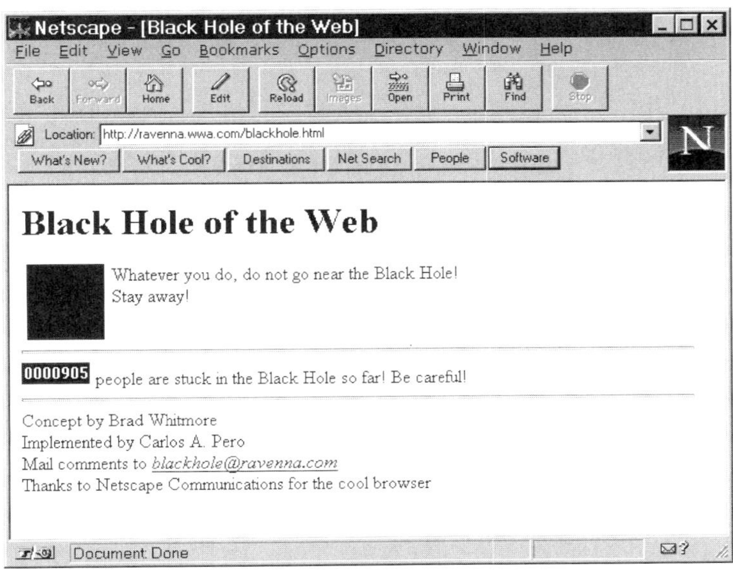

Figure 3.1 The Black Hole

It Says "Connection Refused By Server"!

The server's too busy. Try again later!

It Says "Document Contains No Data!"

Several things can cause this message. The author of the page might be in the midst of updating it. This message might also be caused by a network problem of some kind. Almost always, you can solve the problem by clicking the Reload button a few times.

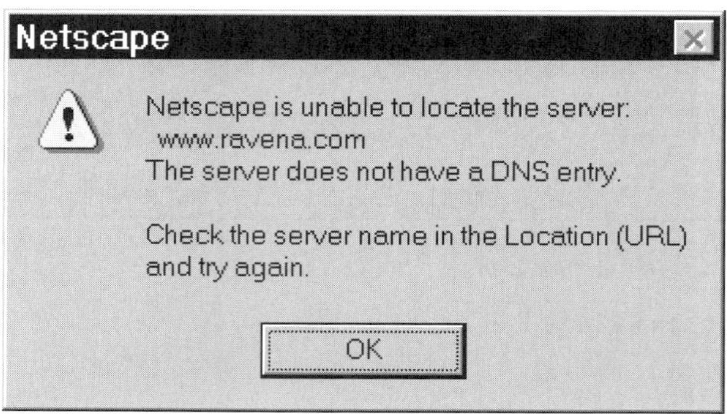
Netscape
Netscape is unable to locate the server:
www.ravena.com
The server does not have a DNS entry.

Check the server name in the Location (URL)
and try again.

OK

Figure 3.2 A DNS lookup gone astray

It Says the DNS Lookup Failed!

Netscape tried to access a Web site, but nothing happened, and then you see a dialog box with the message that the DNS lookup went awry (Figure 3.2). There are several possibilities here:

- Are you using a SLIP or PPP dialup connection? Check to make sure that you're still connected. Many dial-in systems are set up to hang up on you if there is no activity for a specified period of time, such as 10 minutes. (After all, other people are trying to access the system, and as far as anyone knows, you've probably gone fishing or something.) Use your SLIP/PPP dialer to re-establish the connection, and click the hyperlink again.
- Did you type the URL? You may have mistyped the domain name part of the URL (the part that contains the name of the computer you're trying to access).
- The computer you're trying to answer may have gone "Whoomp!" (That's the noise a computer makes when it's taken out of service and permanently disconnected from the Internet, in case you were wondering.)
- The DNS server might be overloaded. Try again later.

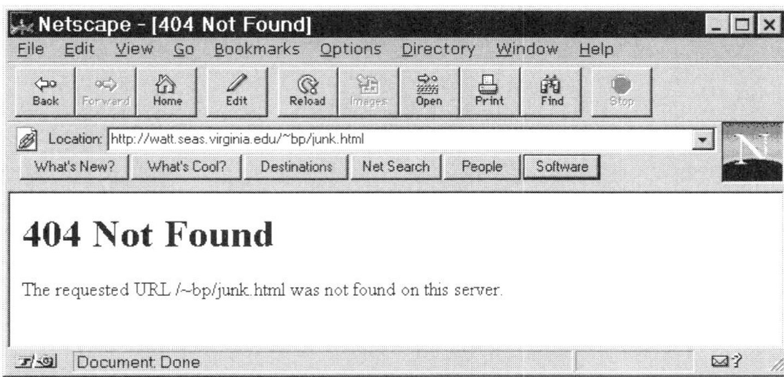

Figure 3.3 404 Not Found

It Says "Not Found"! (Error 404)

The domain name's all right—Netscape was able to contact the computer you're looking for—but, sorry to say, there's no document by that name located on the machine you've accessed (Figure 3.3). Did you type the URL yourself? If so, carefully check your typing and make any corrections, if necessary, right in the Location box. Press Enter to try again.

If you get the 404 Not Found message again, the document has probably been withdrawn from the server.

Wow! "Forbidden"! (Error 403)

Naughty, naughty! You weren't trying to access a sex site, were you? Sites with naughty pictures and stories tend to get restricted or shut down by system administrators, thanks to the fact that there are, apparently, about 20 million Web users with nothing better to do than hunt down erotic Web sites. With so many people trying to access the document, its host system can't function. Irate, the system administrator restricts access to the local domain only, and you see the "403 Forbidden" message. (Figure 3.4).

Figure 3.4 403 Forbidden

Sometimes you'll get this message when you're trying to access a non-naughty site. It probably means that the document you're looking for is of strictly local interest.

Horrors! A Network Error

Something went wrong with the network connection (Figure 3.5). Chances are good it's a temporary problem. Just click the hyperlink again.

If that doesn't work, check to see whether you're still on-line. High-speed modems are sensitive creatures—if there's a big-time error transmitting data, usually caused by a noisy line, they may down the connection without giving you any warning (thanks). Try reconnecting and accessing the site again.

It Says "This Site Has Moved"!

Well, make a note of the new hyperlink. Usually, pages such as this one include something you can click to get to the right place (see Figure 3.6).

Figure 3.5 Socket disconnected

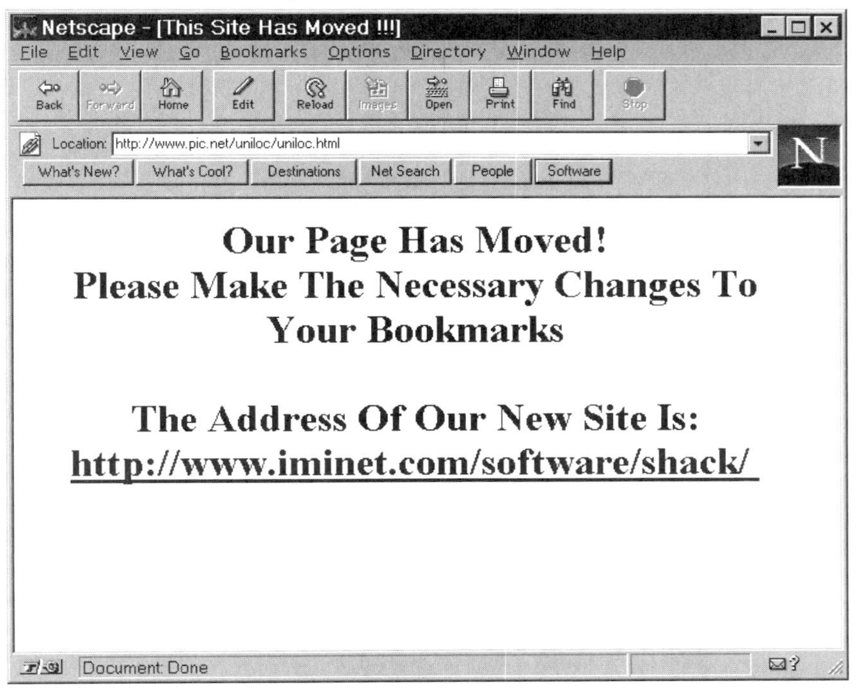

Figure 3.6 Forwarding address

They're Demanding a Password!

They can do that, if they like. And you can't access the page unless you type the correct login name and password (Figure 3.7). Probably, there's information on how to register—if you want to gain access to the site, do it.

It Says "The Information You Have Submitted Is Not Secure"!

And it isn't (Figure 3.8). Any message you send on the Web can be quite easily intercepted and read. That's why you should never, never, never send your credit card information, or any other personal information, via forms that you fill out in Web documents—unless, that is, you're accessing a secure document (see Chapter 35). This message is telling you that you're uploading (sending) information to a server that isn't secure. (Netscape knows.)

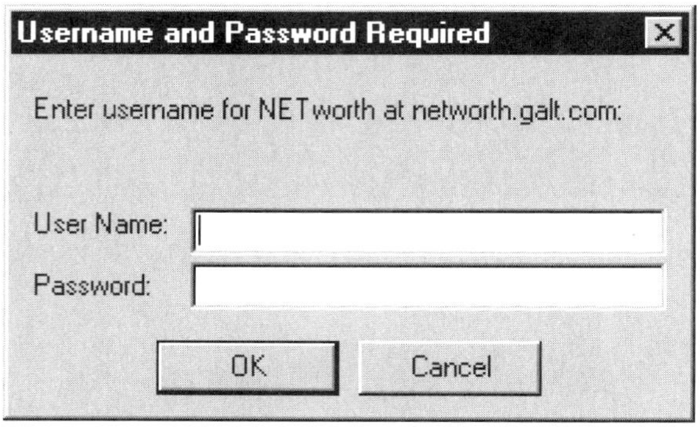

Username and Password Required

Enter username for NETworth at networth.galt.com:

User Name:

Password:

OK Cancel

Figure 3.7 Login name and password required for access

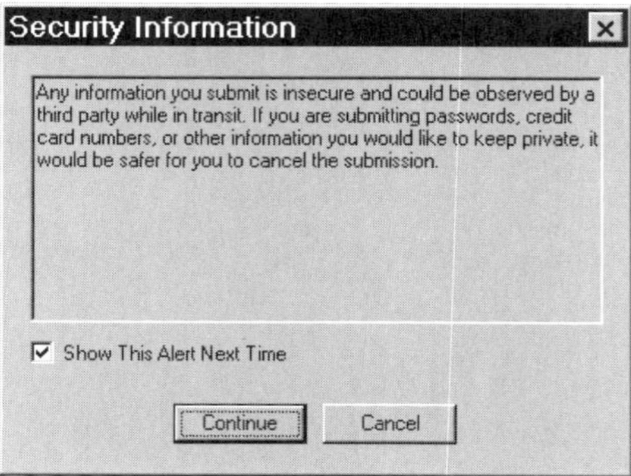

Figure 3.8 Warning about uploading information

This message gets a bit boring after a while. If you're tired of seeing it, and know better than to upload sensitive information to servers that aren't secure, you can stop Netscape from displaying it. From the Options menu, choose Security Preferences. In the General area, deselect Submitting a Form Insecurely. Click OK to confirm the change.

From Here

- Make the Web more accessible by changing your start page. Find out how in Chapter 4.
- Is Netscape running too sluggishly for your taste? Soup it up in Chapter 5, "Improving Netscape Navigator's Performance."
- Can't find your way back to a favorite site? Check out Chapter 6, "Creating and Using Bookmarks."

Part II

Mastering Netscape Navigator

Chapter 4

Change That Start Page!

You start Netscape, and every time you do, you see Netscape's default start page, at Netscape's headquarters in Menlo Park, California. Wouldn't you like to see something more useful, something more tailored to your Web-browsing needs? If so, you've come to the right place: This chapter shows you how to change the default start page, the page you'll see every time Netscape starts. (You also see this page when you click the Home button.)

What's the point of changing the start page? The improvement is more than cosmetic. A good start page gives you instant access to a huge variety of resources: starting points, subject trees, search engines, news, weather, sports, time-wasting diversions, humor, entertainment, and more.

You can choose any home page you like—this chapter shows you how to hunt down cool home pages and make them your own—or you can use the

For the Time-Challenged

- A start page is what you see when you start Netscape or click the Home button. You should change the default start page (Netscape's welcome page), substituting something of more personal value to you.
- This book comes with a home page called HOME.HTM, and it's a good choice. It's packed with useful hyperlinks that enable you to search for information, obtain news and weather reports, check out movie and video reviews, and much more.
- To install HOME.HTM as your home page, flip to the section "Changing Your Home Page," and follow the instructions carefully.
- Another good home page option is to use one of the many subject-oriented trailblazer pages of the Virtual Library, http://www.w3.org/hypertext/DataSources/bySubject/Overview.html. This is a good option for students, teachers, and professionals.
- You can save your bookmark list and make it your home page. For more information, see Chapter 6.

home page included on this book's disc, HOME.HTM. Either way, your enjoyment of Netscape and the Web will increase by leaps and bounds.

Every reader of this book should check out this chapter and change Netscape's default home page. It's easy, and you don't need to know any HTML. The home page that's included with this book will really increase your enjoyment of the Web.

Have We Got a Home Page For You!

On this book's CD-ROM disc is one heck of a nice home page called (you guessed it) HOME (actually, HOME.HTM). Part of it is shown in Figure 4.1.

At the top of this home page are two search engines: Infoseek and Yahoo. Below the search engines, you'll find links to the main subheadings. Here's an overview of the rest of HOME.HTM:

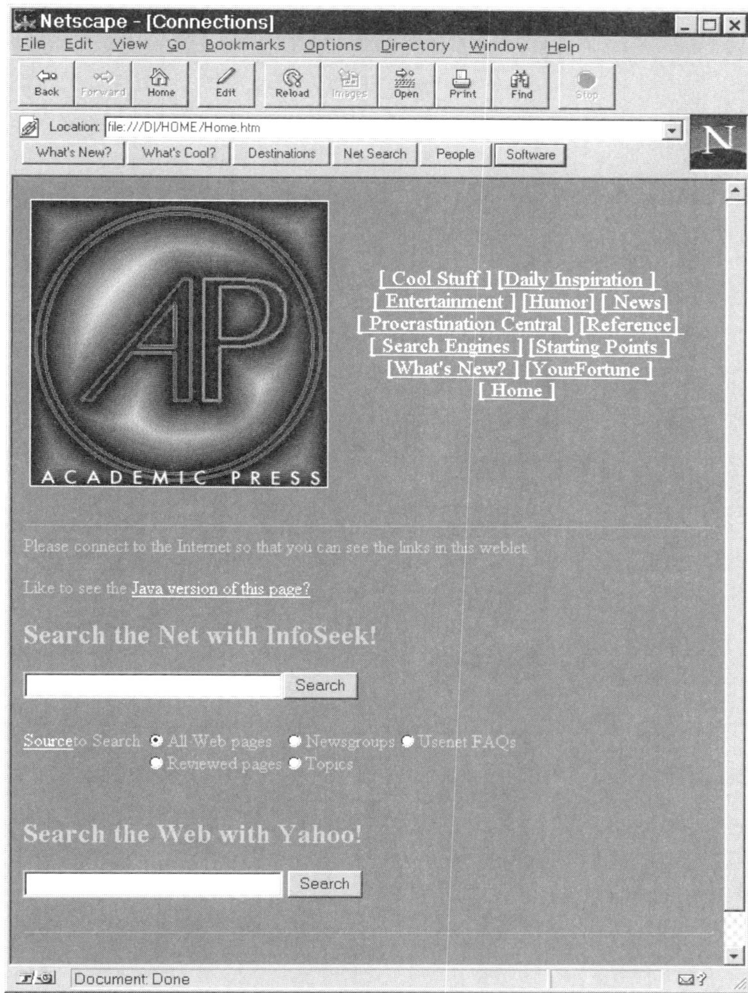

Figure 4.1 The home page that comes with this book (HOME.HTM)

Cool Stuff	Some of the most impressive and popular Web pages. If you're curious about what the Web *should* be like, take a look at these sites. You'll

	find a good selection of some of the Web's hottest sites, in a variety of subject areas.
Daily Inspiration	Check out the Deep Thought of the day, the quotations of the day, and more—including the Shakespearean insult of the day. Lots of fun stuff, and it changes every day.
Entertainment	The latest reviews of movies, videos, and music of all kinds.
Humor	Search for lightbulb jokes, play MadLib, and find out what happened to the guy who tried to use a $2 bill at Taco Bell.
News	Find out what's going on, from sources such as CBS News, the *San Francisco Chronicle*, and the *San Jose Mercury-News*.
Reference	Look it up on-line.
Procrastination Central	You didn't *really* want to get any work done, did you? Mr. Potato Head and Tic Tac Toe will make sure that you don't.
Search Engines	The best search engines, a click away.
Starting Points	Some great starting points pages.
What's New?	All kinds of new Web sites to explore.
Your Fortune	The Magic 8 Ball knows all, and if it doesn't, there's always the Fortune Cookie Server, an on-line Tarot reading, and the I Ching.

HOME.HTM doesn't contain thousands or even hundreds of hyperlinks; it contains just a few dozen. Apart from the hyperlinks in Cool Stuff, most of them share one element in common: They aren't boring, static pages that just show you the same text and graphics every time you access them. In Daily Inspiration, for example, you'll find lots of links that display something completely different at each access. Many other links connect you with fast-breaking news pages, which are updated frequently, and still others access databases that permit you to search for information.

HOME.HTM isn't perfect, since there's no way I could have anticipated all of your interests and hobbies. But it points the way. Use Netscape Editor and create your own start page!

CHANGING THE DEFAULT START PAGE

To change your default home page to HOME.HTM, follow these instructions:

1. Copy the Home folder (directory) from the CD-ROM disc to your hard drive.
2. From the File menu, choose Open File. Use the Open dialog box to open the file HOME.HTM, which is located in the Home folder you just copied to your hard drive. You'll see HOME.HTM on your screen.
3. In the Location box, select the URL of HOME.HTM, and press Ctrl + C to copy this URL to the Clipboard.
4. From the Options menu, choose General Preferences. You'll see the Preferences dialog box, which has seven tabbed pages.
5. Choose the Appearance page (Figure 4.2) by clicking the Appearance tab, if necessary (this page may already be on top of the "stack" of tabbed pages).

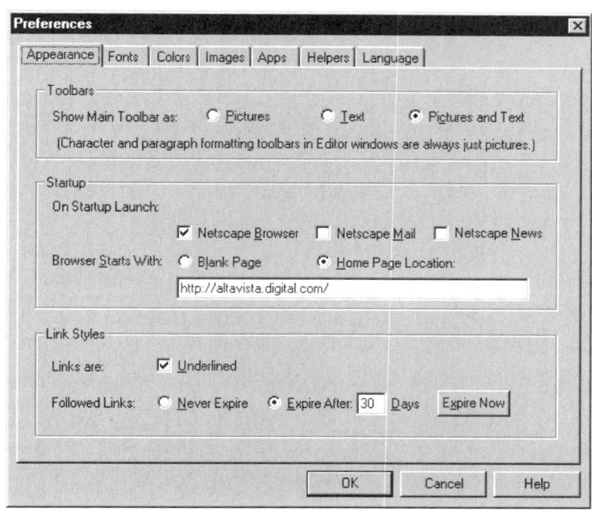

Figure 4.2 Appearance page (Preferences dialog box)

6. In the Home Page Location text box below Browser Starts With, select the existing URL. If you prefer to not use the mouse, just press Tab until the URL is highlighted.
7. Press Ctrl + V to paste the URL from the Clipboard.
8. Click OK.

More Great Start Pages

You'll find lots of great start pages on the Web. Here's a list of some of my favorites:

- Netscape's Destinations Just click the Destinations button in Netscape 3. You'll see a great selection of sites, organized by subject categories (Today's News, Business, Technology News, Finance, Sports and Fitness, Travel, Entertainment, and Shopping).
- **Nerd World Media** (http://www.nerdworld.com/) Here's a fun starting point that divides more than 8,000 sites into two major categories, Leisure and Knowledge; these categories are further broken down into a variety of subject headings. Hip and fun.
- **PC Computing's Web Map** (http://www.ziff.com/~pccomp/webmap/) Organized as a clickable image map, this starting points page provides a graphical entry point for popular sites in areas of interest to personal computer users, consumers, computer hobbyists, and parents.
- **Point** (http://www.pointcom.com/) Point is famous for its "top 5% of the Web" awards, which purport to identify the cream of the Web crop. A subject-oriented starting points page containing high-quality Web sites, Point indexes sites in the following subject areas: education, business/finance, entertainment, news/info, leisure activities, government and politics, science/technology, computers/Internet, shopping, arts/humanities, health/medicine, social and community affairs, kids, and "the road less traveled."
- **Search ME!** (http://watt.seas.virginia.edu/~bp/searchme/welcome.html) Here's the place to start your search of the Web. You'll find pages that list, review, and provide links to dozens of

information-seeking services, including search engines, subject trees, reference, news, periodicals, and more.

- **The Starting Point** (http://www.stpt.com/welcome.html) A very nice starting points page is called, appropriately enough, Starting Point, and it's made available by Superhighway Consulting, Inc. You'll find links to news, weather, sports, entertainment, business, investing, professional, reference, shopping, travel, magazine, and education sites.
- **The Whole Internet Catalog** (http://gnn.digital.com/gnn/wic/index.html) A part of the Global Network Navigator (GNN) service, the Whole Internet Catalog (WIC) lists 1200 of the best sites on the Web. Organized like a subject tree, but with far fewer entries, WIC groups sites according to the following subject categories: arts/literature, business, chat, computers, daily news, education, entertainment, government, health/medicine, Internet, kids & families, life/culture, personal finance, recreation, sports, science, reference desk, and travel.

To make any of these great pages your default start page, just type its URL in the Home Page Location box in the Appearance page in the Preferences dialog box, as described in the previous section.

Using a Trailblazer Page as a Home Page

A trailblazer page is a Web document that attempts to sum up the URLs pertaining to a particular subject, such as astronomy or wine (see Figure 4.3). If you're a student, teacher, or professional working in such an area, you may wish to find a trailblazer page and make it your home page, so that all these links are instantly available to you.

An excellent source of trailblazer pages is the Virtual Library, maintained at CERN (the Swiss birthplace of the World Wide Web). The Virtual Library is described as a distributed information system, and rightly so: The only page stored at CERN is the overview document (Figure 4.4), which lists the trailblazer page topics. Each trailblazer page is maintained by a volunteer and stored at the volunteer's

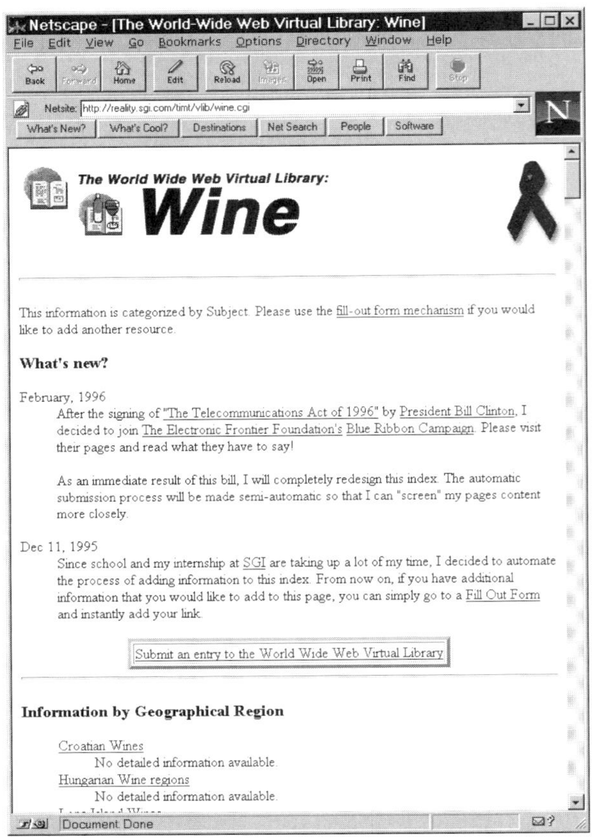

Figure 4.3 The Virtual Library's wine trailblazer page

Web site. Of course, this doesn't mean anything to you in practice; you just click away, and where you are—and where you wind up—doesn't really matter.

To access the Virtual Library's table of contents, use

http://www.w3.org/hypertext/DataSources/bySubject/Overview.html

Table 4.1 lists the subject headings current at this book's writing.

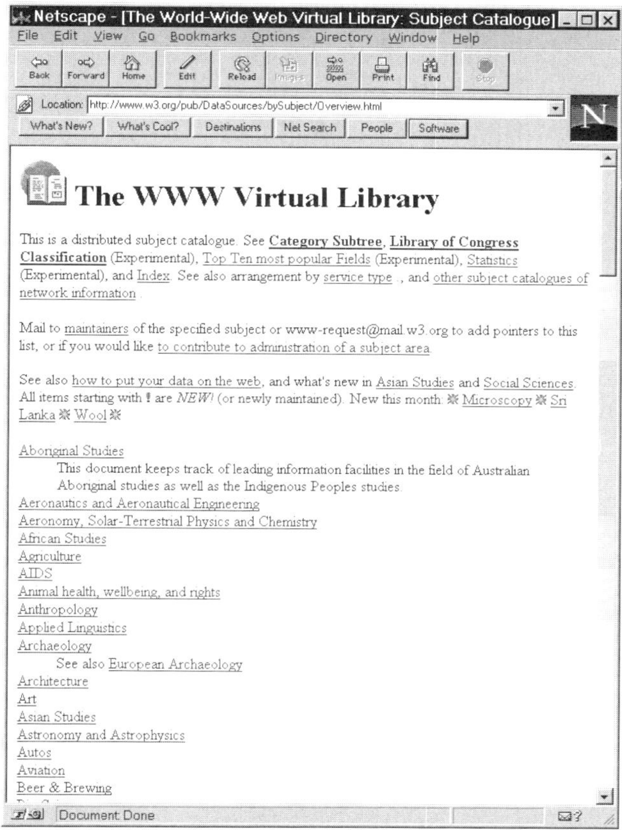

Figure 4.4 The Virtual Library's table of contents

If one of the Virtual Library pages (or some other page you see) looks like a good candidate for your home page, you can copy its URL and paste it into the Preferences dialog box. Here's how:

1. Display the page you want to use as your home page.
2. In the Location box, select the URL. To make sure you've selected all of it, click at the left edge of the box and drag all the way right.
3. Press Ctrl + C to copy the URL to the Clipboard.

4. From the Options menu, choose General Preferences.
5. Click the Appearance tab, if necessary.
6. Select the text that's currently in the Home Page Location box.
7. Press CTRL + V to paste the URL from the Clipboard. This action deletes the current URL and places the new one into the box.
8. Click OK to confirm.
9. Click the Home button to test your new start page.

You can search the Web for trailblazer pages. There are thousands of them, in every conceivable subject area. To learn how, see Chapter 16.

Table 4.1 Subject Headings in the Virtual Library

Aboriginal Studies	Ceramics	Epidemiology
Aeronautics and Aeronautical Engineering	Chemistry	Finance
Aeronomy, Solar-Terrestrial Physics and Chemistry	Coal	Fish
African Studies	Cognitive Science	Forestry
Agriculture	Collecting	Furniture and Interior Design
AIDS	Commercial Services	Games
Animal Health, Well-being, and Rights	Communications	Gardening
Anthropology	Community Networks	Geography
Applied Linguistics	Complex Systems	Geophysics
Archaeology	Computing	German Subject Catalogue
Architecture	Conferences	Gold
Art	Cryptography, PGP, and Your Privacy	Hazards and Risk
Asian Studies	Crystallography	History
Astronomy and Astrophysics	Culture	Human-Computer Interaction
Autos	Dance	Humanities
Aviation	Demography and Population Studies	India
Beer and Brewing	Design	Indigenous Studies
Bio Sciences	Developmental Biology	Information Quality
Biotechnology	Earth Science	Information Sciences
Broadcasters	Education	International Affairs
Cartography	Electronic Journals	International Development Co-operation
Central Asia	Energy	International Security
	Engineering	Ireland
	Environment	

Table 4.2 *Continued*

Italian General Subject Tree
Journalism
Landscape Architecture
Languages
Latin American Studies
Law
Libraries
Lighthouses, Lightships, and Lifesaving Stations
Linguistics
Literature
Logistics
Mathematics
Medicine
Medieval Studies
Meteorology
Middle East Studies
Migration and Ethnic Relations
Museums
Music
Mycology (Fungi)
Naval and Maritime
Neurobiology
Non-Profit Organizations
Nursing
Oceanography
Pacific Studies
Paranormal Phenomena—Archive X
Pharmacy (Medicine)
Philosophy
Physics
Physiology and Biophysics
Political Science
Politics and Economics
Publishers
Recipes
Recreation
Religion
Remote Sensing
Retailing
Roadkill
Russian and East European Studies
Science Fairs
Singapore
Social Sciences
Sociology
Spirituality
Sport
Standards and Standardization Bodies
Statistics
Sumeria
Sustainable Development
Technology Transfer
Telecommunications
Theatre and Drama
Tibetan Studies
Treasure
Transportation
U.S. Federal Government Agencies
U.S. Government Information Sources
Unidentified Flying Objects (UFOs)
United Nations and Other International Organizations
Vision Science
Whale Watching Web
Wine
Wool
World-Wide Web Development
Writers' Resources on the Web
Yeasts
Zoos

YOUR OWN YAHOO!

Here's a great trick for your home page: Access Yahoo (http://www.yahoo.com) and click the My Yahoo button. You can build your own custom home page, including news summaries in the areas you like, fifteen-minute-delayed quotes for up to 30 stocks and mutual funds, sports scores, weather, and links to reviewed Internet sites in your interest area (Figure 4.5). Cool!

You can make your My Yahoo page your default home page. Just type http://my.yahoo.com/ in the Browser Starts With area of the General Preferences dialog box (Appearance page).

Figure 4.5 My Yahoo provides a customized home page

From Here

- Is Netscape Navigator too slow for your tastes? Speed up the program's performance considerably by following the tips and strategies in the following chapter.
- Learn how to save bookmarks—or better yet, use the new Smart Bookmarks utility. See Chapters 6 and 7.

Chapter 5

Improving Netscape Navigator's Performance

By now, you've mastered the essentials of Netscape Navigator, and I'll bet you've had some fun exploring the Web. In this chapter, you go beyond the basics. You learn the time-saving tricks that Netscape mavens use to make Netscape run faster.

STOP! *PLEASE* STOP!

You just clicked a hyperlink. It looked interesting. But now you can see that it's going to be a pain. There are at least 50 pictures of the Brady Bunch. And it's taking forever to download. Stop the madness! Here's how:

- Click the Stop button

For the Time-Challenged

- ♦ If you've inadvertently clicked a hyperlink and Netscape begins downloading a huge, unwanted file, click the Stop button.
- ♦ To speed document downloading considerably (a plus if you're using a slow SLIP/PPP connection), turn off the automatic display of in-line images. You can selectively display an individual graphic by right-clicking it and choosing Load This Image.
- ♦ Don't go nuts trying to get back to a document by clicking the Back button—use the Go menu and the history list instead. While you browse, Netscape keeps a record of the documents you've visited in the current lineage (a series of documents that are all linked outward from a single, beginning document). While you're still within the lineage, you can go back to any of these documents by choosing a document name from the Go menu. If you begin a new lineage, however, Netscape erases the previous lineage's history list and begins a new one.
- ♦ Because Netscape erases a lineage's history list when you start a new lineage, you should begin the new lineage in a new window. (Each window's history list is separate.)
- ♦ If Windows messes up Netscape's screen display, choose Refresh from the View menu. If you've redisplayed a previously accessed document and suspect that the original may have changed, click the Reload button.

or

- Press Esc

or

- From the Go menu, choose Stop Loading

After you stop downloading, you may see part of the document onscreen, but it may show signs of its brutal treatment (for example, in-line images that didn't download will be shown with placeholders, like the ones in Figure 5.1). Just click the Back button to abandon this battle scene. If you feel sorry for the document and would like to give it an opportunity to live once again, click the Reload button.

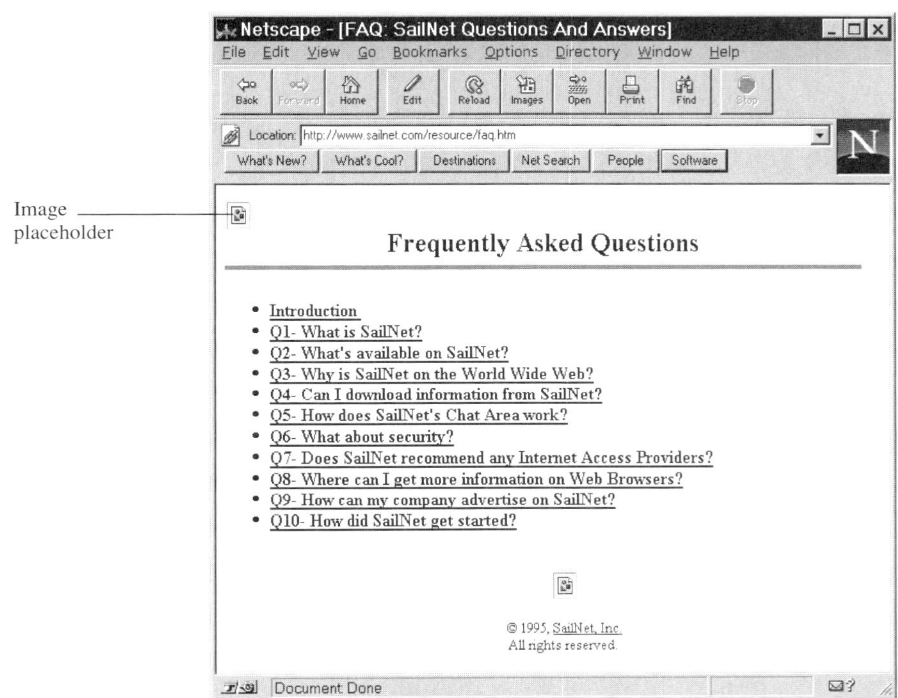

Figure 5.1 Document with image placeholders (produced by interrupted transfer)

This Document's Too Slow! (Too Many Images)

If you're accessing the Web over a SLIP or PPP connection, documents stuffed with in-line images can take forever to download. That's OK, if you're really interested in the pictures; after all, why else would you access the *Playboy* Home Page? (Of course, I only read the interviews.) Often, though, you're searching for some specific information, and the graphics—however pretty—serve only to delay your journey. For such Web ventures, you'd be wise to turn off the automatic downloading of in-line images. Here's how.

Using the Auto Load Images Toggle

In the Options menu, the Auto Load Images option is a *toggle command*. A toggle command has two states, on or off. When a toggle command is on, you see a check mark next to the command name. When a toggle command is off, there's no check mark. To change a toggle command, you choose the command. You can't really see what happens, because the menu disappears after you choose the command. If you open the menu again, though, you'll see that choosing the command did one of two things: It made the check mark appear (on), or it made the check mark disappear (off). It's simple, once you get the basic idea.

Let's assume that Netscape is automatically downloading in-line images, which is the default setting. That means there's a check mark next to Auto Load Images on the Options menu. You need to get rid of that check mark.

Turning Off Automatic Image Downloading

To turn off the automatic downloading of in-line images, do the following:

1. From the Options menu, choose Auto Load Images.
2. Just to make sure, click Options again, and look at the menu; there should be no check mark next to the Auto Load Images option. Press Esc to close the menu.

Hey, I turned off images! Why do I still see some of them? Netscape still displays in-line images if there's a copy in the cache. For more information on the cache, see "Increasing the Cache Size," in the next section.

You've turned off automatic image downloading. Great! Documents load quickly, but they aren't much visual fun anymore, are they? In place of the in-line images, you see *placeholders*, which to some people look like little crying robots. Well, read on.

Selectively Loading In-Line Images

After you've turned off automatic image downloading, you can view any single in-line graphic, just as you please. This is very cool. The technique uses that sophisticated right-clicking maneuver that gives a certain distinguished body language to your computer usage.

To view an individual in-line graphic (when automatic image downloading has been turned off):

1. Point to the image's placeholder, and click the right mouse button.
2. From the pop-up menu, choose Load This Image (to display the image within the current document) or View This Image (to view the graphic in a new, separate document). Netscape will download the image you've clicked (Figure 5.2).

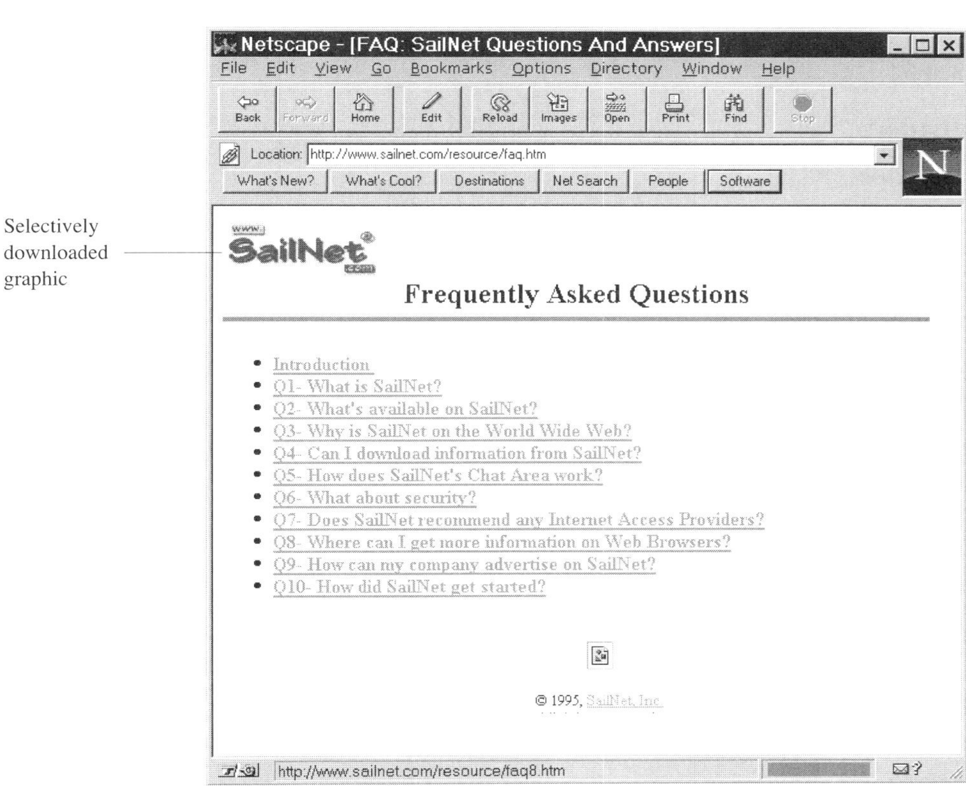

Figure 5.2 Image selectively downloaded

How do I know which image to download? The better Web authors provide text that explains what the image is for. Look for this text next to the placeholder.

Downloading All the Images in a Document

You can also download all the images in a given document:

- From the View menu, choose Load Images

  or

- Press Ctrl + I (the letter "I," as in "me")

  or

- Click the Images button

I don't care how long it takes to download the pictures! I want images on by default! No problem. From the Options menu, choose Auto Load Images again, so that the check mark reappears. By the way, you are a very patient person—or you have a very fast modem!

Increasing the Cache Size

A *cache* is a temporary storage location, like the ones thieves use to stash the loot until they get out of the pen. By the way, cache is pronounced "cash." Netscape uses cache memory to store recently accessed documents—and as you'll learn in this section, one of the best things you can do to increase Netscape's speed is to increase the size of the disk cache.

How the Cache Works

When you download a document, Netscape places the document in the cache. Should you wish to go back to a document you have viewed previously, Netscape locates and displays the document in the cache rather than retrieving it again from the network. Since cache retrievals are many times faster than network retrievals, this produces an impressive gain in Netscape's speed.

Where Does Netscape Store Cached Documents?

Netscape employs two caches, a memory cache and a disk cache.

- **The Memory Cache** This cache is a portion of your computer's random-access memory (RAM) that has been set aside for storing the most recently accessed documents. In comparison to network retrieval, retrieval from the memory cache is very fast; compare, for instance, how long it takes to download a new document and how long it takes to redisplay the same document by clicking the Back button. By default, Netscape sets aside 600 KB for the memory cache. Just how many documents the memory cache holds depends on the average size of the documents you've retrieved; a text-only document may require as little as 32 K, while a document loaded with in-line images may consume the entire cache. As you retrieve additional documents, older documents are flushed (removed) from the cache. At the end of your Netscape session, the memory cache is erased as you quit Netscape.
- **The Disk Cache** This cache is a portion of your computer's hard disk that, like the memory cache, has been set aside for storing the most recently accessed documents. By default, Netscape sets aside 5000 KB (roughly 5 megabytes) for this purpose. As you retrieve additional documents, older documents are flushed from the cache. Unlike the memory cache, the disk cache retains documents between Netscape sessions. Up to 5 megabytes of previously accessed Web documents are present on your disk, ready for fast retrieval should you access these documents again.

When Does Netscape Use the Caches?

The two caches come into play in the following situations:

- **When you access a visited hyperlink** As you know, Netscape keeps track of visited hyperlinks, hyperlinks to documents that you have previously accessed. These hyperlinks appear in a distinctive color. When you access a visited hyperlink by any means (choosing a bookmark, clicking a visited hyperlink, or typing the URL directly), Netscape contacts the server and attempts to verify whether the document has been altered since its last retrieval. If the document has been altered, Netscape retrieves a new copy. If

not, Netscape retrieves the document from the disk cache. By default, Netscape verifies visited hyperlinks every time you access one.

- **When you click the Back button** If you click Back, you're returning to a document that you have accessed in the current Netscape session. For this reason, it's probable that the document has not been altered since its last retrieval, so Netscape does not contact the server to see whether the document has changed. Instead, the program retrieves the document from the memory cache or, if it has been flushed from the memory cache, from the disk cache.

Here's a tip that may improve Netscape's performance and reduce unnecessary load on the Internet. From the Options menu, choose Preferences, and select the Cache and Network preferences. In the Verify Documents area, click Once per Session (the default is Every Time). With this setting, Netscape will attempt only once per session to verify whether the document has been updated. Should you once again click this document's hyperlink or bookmark in the same session, or type its URL, Netscape will retrieve the cache copy immediately, without accessing the server. This saves you time and reduces network load.

Should You Increase the Size of the Caches?

If you can, yes. Take the following quick quizzes to find out whether increasing the size of the caches is for you.

- **Increasing the size of the memory cache** Do you frequently find yourself clicking the Back button to go back to previously accessed documents? Do you run Netscape all by itself, with no other big programs running at the same time? Do you have 8 MB of RAM? If your answer to all these questions is "Yes," you can improve Netscape's performance dramatically by increasing the size of the memory cache. A cache that's 1000 KB will hold almost twice as many documents as the default 600 KB cache, but it will leave less memory for other applications. With a 1000 KB cache, there's a better chance that Netscape will be able to retrieve a redisplayed document from the memory cache, which is faster than the disk cache and much faster than network retrieval.

- **Increasing the size of the disk cache** Do you have at least 50 MB of free hard disk space? Do you frequently access documents that have lots of in-line images, and redisplay them in subsequent sessions? If your answer to both these questions is "Yes," you may wish to increase the size of Netscape's disk cache. You won't notice any difference until you try to redisplay a document you accessed several weeks ago; the larger the cache, the less chance there is that this document has been flushed from the cache. If it's still in the cache, retrieval will be much faster than network retrieval, which is Netscape's only option if the document isn't present in either cache.

For information on modifying the size of the caches, see the next section.

Changing Cache Size Defaults

If you've decided to change the default size of the caches, follow these instructions:

1. From the Options menu, choose Network Preferences.
2. In the Preferences dialog box, click the Cache tab. You'll see the Cache options, shown in Figure 5.3.
3. To change the size of the memory cache, type a new number in the Memory Cache box. The default size is 600 K. If you have lots of free memory, change this to 1000 K or 2000 K.
4. To change the size of the disk cache, type a new number in the Disk Cache box. Don't type a number that exceeds half of your available disk space.
5. Click OK to confirm your preferences and exit.

I'm out of hard disk space! After you increase the size of your disk cache and use your system for a while, you may run out of hard disk space—believe me, it happens. Just bear in mind that you can free up space—maybe a lot of space—by reducing the size of Netscape's cache.

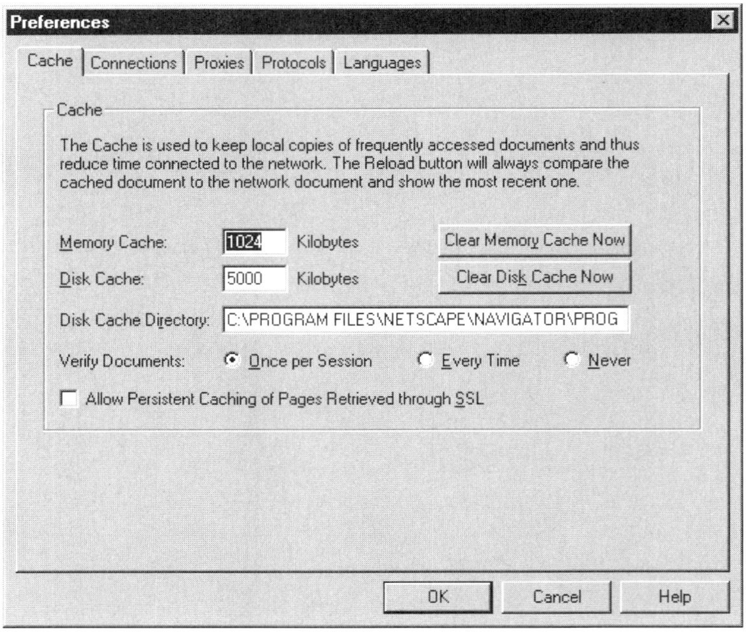

Figure 5.3 Cache options

Changing the Verification Frequency (A Super Speed Trick)

As you've just learned, Netscape stores a copy of visited documents in the disk cache. When you reaccess one of these documents, the program *verifies* the document. In brief, this means that the program contacts the original site to determine whether the document has changed since it was last downloaded. If the document has changed, Netscape downloads a new copy.

Verification is time-consuming—in fact, it cuts down the cache's performance considerably. Recognizing this fact, Netscape's designers set up the program so that it verifies documents only once per session. If you revisit the document later in the same session, the program loads it directly from the cache without verification—try it. As you can see, the second load is much faster. The speed is limited only by the data transfer rate of your hard disk drive.

So here's the super speed trick: You can change the verification setting so that Netscape *never* checks to see whether the document has changed. You can choose this setting in the Cache page of the Network Preferences dialog box—but before you do, consider whether you really want to do this.

What's the effect of changing the reload checking frequency to "Never"? A super speed improvement—you won't believe it. When you access a document that's in the cache, it loads very quickly because Netscape does not have to send a message out over the network.

But here's the danger. If the document you're accessing really *has* changed, you won't know it. Netscape will show you the copy that's in the cache. There might be some important new information in the new version of the document, the one that's available out on the Web—but you're in the dark. To be sure, you can manually initiate a check by clicking the Reload button (discussed later in this chapter), but you might forget to do so.

Because you might miss important new information by using the "Never" setting, you should think twice before changing the default setting (Once per Session). If you decide to go ahead and make the change, please put a big sign by your computer that says, "Remember to click Reload if you suspect the document has changed!"

To change the default verification setting:

1. From the Options menu, choose Network Preferences.
2. In the Preferences dialog box, click the Cache tab. You'll see the Cache options, shown in Figure 5.3
3. In the Verify Documents area, click Never.
4. Click OK to confirm your preferences and exit.

Should you use the "Every Time" verification option? Only if you're working with important, time-sensitive information, such as stock quotes. With this option, Netscape always verifies whether documents have changed before loading them from the cache. The result is sluggish operation, but you'll be certain that you'll never miss a change in an important document you're using.

When Should You Flush the Caches?

Netscape provides commands, found in the Preferences dialog box, that permit you to flush the memory cache and disk cache manually. The only reason

you'd want to do this is for security. Put bluntly, the cache provides an electronic trail, readable by a knowledgeable snooper, that tells where you've been browsing lately. If you're worried about this, flush the cache. Follow these instructions:

1. From the Options menu, choose Network Preferences.
2. Click the Cache tab.
3. To flush the memory cache, click Clear Memory Cache Now.
4. To flush the disk cache, click Clear Disk Cache Now. *Note:* This operation may take a few minutes.
5. Click OK.

Remember that deleting files doesn't destroy them beyond recovery—deleted files can be undeleted. To eradicate your traces totally, obtain a program that can "wipe" your hard disk so that all areas containing deleted files are overwritten with garbage data.

Finding a Document in the Cache

As you've just learned, Netscape downloads and saves a copy of the documents you've visited, up to the limits of the disk storage space that has been set aside for this purpose. Saved are every component of these documents, including the HTML text, GIF and JPEG graphics, and text files. And I do mean *every* component—every little button and rule, the cool icons and banners, the works.

Since these documents are stored in the cache, can't you go into the cache with File Manager (Windows 3.1) or Windows Explorer (Windows 95) and open them individually? Yes, but there's just one catch: Netscape renames all these files using a coding scheme that makes perfect sense to the browser but no

The Document Info dialog box contains lots of interesting information about a document. Listed are not only the document's URL, but also the URLs of all the Web resources included in the document (hyperlinks, graphics, the works). You can access any of these by clicking the URL, which is an active hyperlink.

sense at all to humans. The cache is full of files with names such as M0B8V1.gif and M0OB56LO.html. What's in 'em? Who knows? There are hundreds or even thousands of these files, and you'd go nuts going through all of them.

If you'd like to see one of these documents again, the easiest way is to use Netscape to locate the document on the Web, and let Netscape find and redisplay the cached version. Once you've done so, you can determine the cached file's name.

To determine the file name of a cached document:

1. Locate the document on the Web and display it using Netscape.
2. From the View menu, choose Document Info. You'll see the Document Info dialog box, shown in Figure 5.4

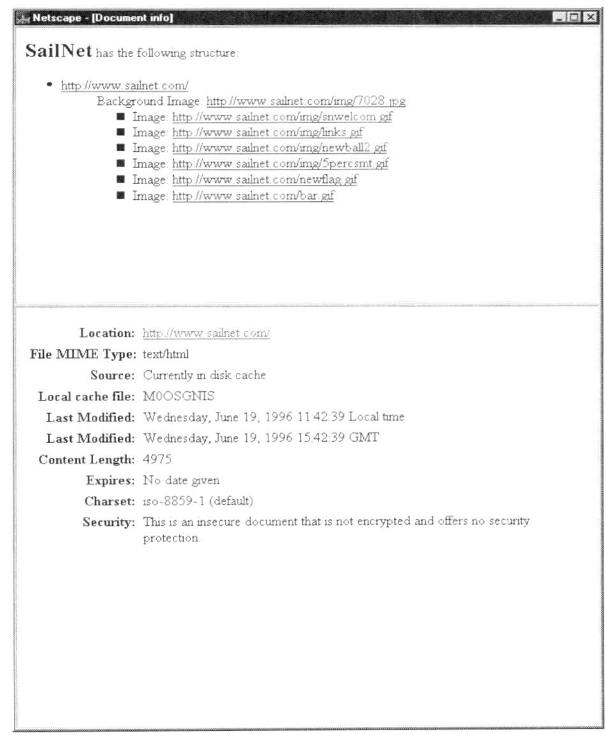

Figure 5.4 Document Info dialog box

3. In the lower panel, look at the Local Cache File area and note the name of the file. That's it!
4. Close the window.

There's a History to This (The History List)

After a good, long Web surf, you'll be wondering, "Where am I?" And after spending five hours in biancaTroll's house, you'll be thinking, "How do I get back to that *useful* page I saw half an hour ago?" You've surfed so many sites, you'd have to click the Back button six zillion times. But there's a better way, maybe. You may be able to use the history list to go back quickly to previously accessed sites.

Unbeknownst to you, Netscape has been keeping a record of your travels. The program knows where you've been. Fortunately, it doesn't know whether you've been naughty (you didn't fumble around in biancaTroll's bedside drawer, did you?). It just keeps a record of the URLs you've visited, with certain important limitations, which I'll explain in a minute.

Using the Go Menu

You'll find a list of recently visited sites on the bottom portion of the Go menu (Figure 5.5). To go back to a document you've visited previously in the current Netscape session, do the following:

- From the Go menu, choose the title of the document to which you want to return.

Using the History List

You can also go back to a document by using the History dialog box, as explained in the following:

1. From the Window menu, choose History, or use the Ctrl + H keyboard shortcut. You'll see the History dialog box, shown in Figure 5.6.

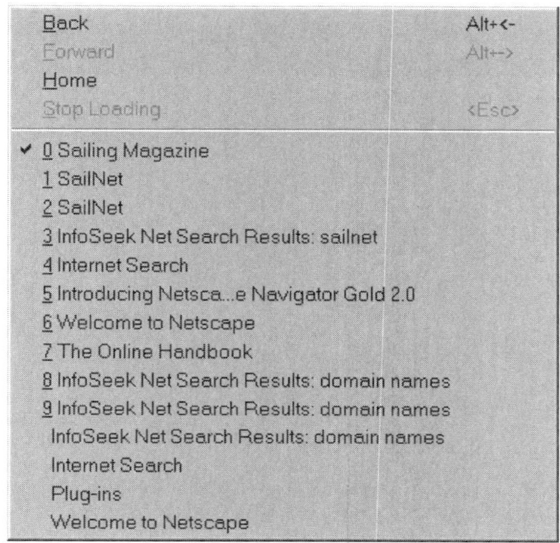

Figure 5.5 Recently visited sites on the Go menu

2. Highlight the document to which you want to return, and click Go To (or just press Enter).
3. Click Close.

Have you visited some interesting sites during this session? A quick way to add two or more bookmarks is to select the interesting sites in the history list, and click the Create Bookmark button (at the bottom of the History dialog box). To access the History dialog box, choose History from the Window menu or just press Ctrl + H.

Why the History List Erases Some of the Sites You've Visited

I just visited that site! I know I did! Why isn't the site listed in the darned history list? Sooner or later, you'll look at the history list, hoping to return to a site you visited a few clicks ago—and it's gone. This is very frustrating, and you'll

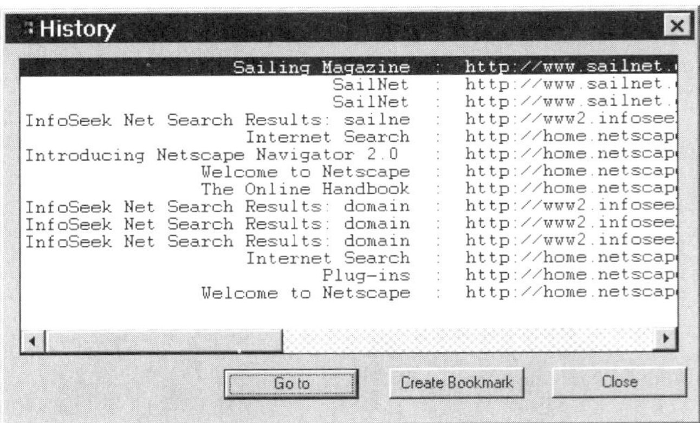

Figure 5.6 History dialog box

probably think it's a bug. It isn't a bug. There's a logic to it. That doesn't mean I like it, but at least there's an explanation—so here goes. Netscape's history list records only a single lineage of sites. A *lineage* is a series of hyperlinks that all extend outward from a single, source document.

Here's an example of a lineage. Let's say you start with HOME.HTM, and click the Virtual Library link. From the Virtual Library, you select the Wine page. From the Wine page, you select Napa Valley. From the Napa Valley page, you select Napa Valley Wineries, and so on. For this lineage, Netscape keeps all the links.

But then you get tired of browsing in this area, and go back to HOME.HTM. You select Stock Quotes to check out how your stocks are doing. They're doing fine, but check out the history list (in the Go menu, or look at the History dialog box). Hmmm! All the previous links have been erased. That's because you're in a new lineage.

Don't trust the history list to keep an exact record of every site you've visited. If you see a Web page that you definitely want to keep, choose Add Bookmark from the Bookmarks menu, and flip to Chapter 6 for more information.

When – and How – to Open a New Window

Now that you know how history lists work, there's another important thing to realize about Netscape: The program keeps a separate history list for each window.

Well, so what? Here's what: Whenever you start a new lineage, open a new window. If you do this, Netscape won't erase the history list in the last lineage's window, enabling you to go back to previously accessed documents (in case you get tired of the current lineage).

Just remember my motto: "New lineage, new window."

Working with a New Window

When you open a new window for Netscape, you see what appears to be a new, independent copy of the program—and as far as you are concerned, it is. In the new window, Netscape automatically displays the home page that you've chosen, just as if you were launching the program at the beginning of a new Netscape session.

The new window's history list is a copy of the previous window's list, but the window shows you the *oldest* document in this list—a veritable invitation to launch off in a new lineage, wouldn't you say?

Your subsequent actions in this window will not affect the history list in other Netscape windows.

To open a new window, do the following: From the File menu, choose New Web Browser.

Use this great trick to open a hyperlink in a new window. Point to the hyperlink, and click the right mouse button. From the pop-up menu, choose New Window with this Link. Netscape opens a new window. Instead of displaying the home page, the program displays the document you've chosen.

Here's another good reason to open a new window. If you suspect that you'll have trouble accessing a hyperlink, perhaps because it's lengthy or the site is situated on a 56 Kbps network in Tasmania, use the pop-up menu to open the link in a new window. While the new window is stalled pending retrieval of the document, you can switch back to the original window and continue enjoying the Web.

Increasing the Number of Windows You Can Open

How many Netscape windows can you open? By default, a maximum of four. If you wish, you can increase this setting.

Be aware that each new window you open consumes system resources; you'll rarely feel a need for more than four windows.

If you really want to increase this number, open the Options menu and choose Network Preferences. In the Preferences dialog box, click the Connections tab, and type a new number in the Number of Connections box. Click OK to confirm your choice.

Managing Multiple Windows

When more than one Netscape window is open, you can switch between them as you please. When you're done with a window, you can close it without quitting Netscape, as long as at least one other Netscape window is open. The following instructions detail these procedures.

To switch from one Netscape window to another:

- Click on the window you want to activate. This shouldn't be difficult, since Netscape cascades new windows (each new window is slightly offset from the others, enabling you to read the title bar of each open window).

To close a Netscape window:

- From the File menu, choose Close

  or

- Press Ctrl + W

When more than one Netscape window is open, the window-closing procedures just described close the window without quitting the program. When you're down to the last window, these procedures quit the program.

When to Reload, When to Refresh

On the View menu, you'll find options called Reload, Reload Frame, and Refresh. Here's what they do:

Reload	When you choose this command, Netscape goes back to the network and determines whether the document you're viewing has changed—and if so, a new copy is downloaded.
Reload Frame	This command works just like the Reload command, but it reloads only the frame that's currently selected.
Refresh	When you choose this command, Netscape retrieves a fresh copy of the current document from your computer's memory. The program doesn't check to see whether the document has changed.

When Should You Reload?

Only when you think there's a chance the document has changed since you last downloaded it. Here's why.

Netscape saves a copy of recently accessed documents in its *memory cache* (a special storage area designed for fast re-retrieval of documents). When you click a previously visited hyperlink, Netscape checks to see whether there's a copy of the document in the cache, and if there is, the program loads the cache's copy rather than retrieving the document from the network. In most cases, that's fine—the document appears much more quickly. But what happens if the original, network-based version of the document has changed? You wouldn't know this, because Netscape is showing you the old copy. If you suspect that the network version has changed, choose Reload from the View menu, or press Ctrl + R, or just click the Reload button.

If you decided to select the "Never" verification frequency (see "Changing the Verification Frequency," earlier in this chapter), bear in mind that the document you're viewing may not be the most recent version. To find out, click Reload.

When Should You Use Refresh?

Sometimes your Microsoft Windows system will fail to update the screen properly. This isn't really Netscape's fault. Windows is notoriously susceptible to screen update problems attributable to low memory or system resources. For example, the fonts might not look right, or the background color may have changed in a weird way. If this happens, choose Refresh from the View menu.

From Here

- The next set of skills you'll need to master involves Netscape's somewhat quirky bookmarks features. Check them out in Chapter 6.
- The best way to keep track of your Netscape bookmarks is to download and install the Smart Bookmarks plug-in. This utility is discussed in Chapter 7.
- Want to save or print a document or graphic? Find out how in Chapter 8.

Chapter 6

Creating and Using Bookmarks

You've just found the most awesome Web site. It holds the key to your dreams—nay, your job. And then, following links, you surf off in a zillion directions—only to find, to your dismay, that you've started a new lineage, somehow, and the darned history list has erased that awesome site's URL. (For the lowdown on lineages and history lists, see Chapter 5.) No matter what you do, you can't find it again. You give up in frustration, and late that night you sob softly into your pillow.

Don't let this happen to you: Set bookmarks.

In Netscape, a *bookmark* is a document title that you've added to the Bookmarks menu. In addition to the document title, Netscape saves the URL. To return to the document, you just choose the bookmark name from the Bookmarks menu. *Note:* In other browsers, a bookmark is called a hotlist item, and the bookmark list is called a hotlist. Hotlist item, bookmark—same thing. The next time you run into some Mosaic user who says, "You ought to

see my cool hotlist," you can sniff disdainfully and say, "We Netscape users call them bookmarks." Then run.

This chapter presents indispensable Netscape skills. In particular, you'll learn what to do when your Bookmarks menu gets overstuffed—a malady, you will find, that befalls every Netscape user, including you. A plus: This chapter's tutorials will prove invaluable in learning how to reorganize bookmarks, a crucial Netscape skill.

Isn't there a better way to do this? Netscape's bookmarks capabilities are much improved over the program's original version, but you'll still find that some operations are frustratingly difficult. You may wish to use a commercial add-on bookmark utility, such as Netscape's own Smart Marks program or Smart Bookmarks, discussed in Chapter 7.

Adding and Choosing Bookmarks

The simplest way to use bookmarks is to add them to the Bookmarks menu. To return to a bookmarked item, you simply choose it from the Bookmarks

For the Time-Challenged

- When you set a bookmark, the title of the Web page you've bookmarked appears on the Bookmarks menu.
- Very soon, your Bookmarks menu becomes too crowded. To alleviate this problem, you can create folders for your bookmarks. You do this within the Bookmarks window. After creating folders, you can organize your bookmarks by dragging them into the folders you've created.
- After you organize your bookmarks into folders, the folders appear on the menu and the bookmark items appear in pop-up submenus.
- By choosing What's New from the Bookmarks window's File menu, you can find out whether any of your bookmarked pages have changed since you last visisted them.
- To add new bookmarks to a specific folder, open the Bookmarks window, highlight the folder, open the Items menu, and choose Set to New Bookmarks Folder.

menu. The drawback of this technique, as you'll quickly discover, is an overly lengthy Bookmarks menu. When you get to that point, you'll want to organize your bookmarks, as discussed in the following section.

Adding a Bookmark to the Bookmarks Menu

You can add a Web document to your Bookmarks menu in two ways:

- **Right-clicking the URL** Point to the URL and click the *right* mouse button. From the pop-up menu, choose Add Bookmark for this Link.
- **Adding the bookmark after you download the document** From the Bookmarks menu, choose Add Bookmark, *or* press Ctrl + D.

Of the two methods for adding bookmarks, it's best to display the page and then use the Add Bookmark command (Bookmarks menu). This command places the page's title on the Bookmarks menu. If you right-click the page's hyperlink and use the pop-up menu, Netscape adds the URL to the Bookmarks menu. URLs are harder to read than document titles.

After you add a bookmark, the bookmark you've added appears on the lower portion of the Bookmarks menu (see Figure 6.1).

Choosing a Bookmark

After you've added a bookmark, you can choose it easily. Just click the Bookmarks menu, and click the bookmark you want. Netscape will download the document you've requested.

Introducing the Bookmarks Window

One of the most common complaints about Netscape, typically voiced by people who have been using the program for two weeks or so, is that the Bookmarks menu has become glutted with items. It's disorganized, out of order, too lengthy, and—for all these reasons—close to useless. The solution? Organize your bookmarks using the Bookmarks window.

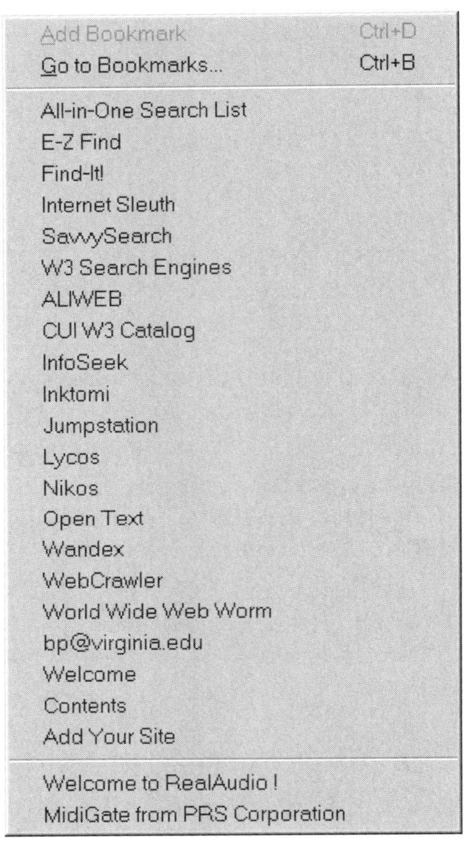

Figure 6.1 Bookmarks appearing on Bookmarks menu

Accessing the Bookmarks Window

To access this window, do one of the following

- From the Bookmarks menu, choose Go to Bookmarks

  or

- From the Window menu, choose Bookmarks

  or

- Press Ctrl + B

What You Can Do in the Bookmarks Window

The Bookmarks window provides tools for doing the following:

- **Organizing bookmarks** When you create a folder, a new submenu shows up on Netscape's Bookmarks menu. To place bookmarks into a folder, just drag the bookmark into the folder. This bookmark will then appear on a pop-up submenu in the Bookmarks menu. In this way, you can quickly customize the Bookmarks menu so that it contains dozens or even hundreds of your favorite documents. Within a folder, you can sort your bookmarks so that they appear in alphabetical order. Additionally, you can change the title of a page to something that's more descriptive.
- **Accessing bookmark pages** Just double-click any Web page's title. Netscape will display the page. If you can't find the bookmark in a lengthy list, there's a Find command that helps you look.
- **Finding out whether source documents have changed** The What's New command (File menu) enables you to determine whether any of the Web documents in your bookmarks list have been altered since you last accessed them.
- **Adding new bookmark items to a folder you've created** After you've organized your bookmarks list, you can choose which of the folders you've created that you want to display on the Bookmarks menu, and you can also choose the folder to which you'd like Netscape to add new bookmark items.
- **Importing and exporting bookmarks** You can easily exchange bookmark lists with other Netscape users by exporting your list and importing lists that people give you.

Here's a terrific bookmark trick that you can use if the Bookmarks window is open. To create a bookmark, just drag the chain link icon to the Bookmarks window, and release the mouse button.

The contents of the Bookmarks window are stored in a file called BOOKMARK.HTM, which you'll find in Netscape's directory. This file is actually a valid HTML document, which Netscape automatically creates. As you'll learn later in this chapter, you can open any valid HTML file using the File Open command in the Bookmarks window, and all the hyperlinks that this document contains will appear as bookmarks in this window. You can also give your bookmark file to anyone who uses Netscape or any other browser, so that others can open it and make use of the links you've found.

Organizing Your Bookmarks

Chances are that you have a lengthy, disorganized list of bookmarks, which you've saved directly to the Bookmarks menu. In the Bookmarks window, these appear in a list like the one shown in Figure 6.2. To organize your bookmarks, you'll want to create and name folders, and then drag the bookmarks into the appropriate folder. You may also wish to create *separators*, lines that appear on the Bookmarks menu, so that the menu looks neater. The following sections detail these procedures.

Creating Folders

To get your bookmarks organized, the first thing you need to do is to create and name folders. A folder is a storage place for your bookmarks.

Give some thought to how you want to organize your folders. Bear in mind that you can put folders within folders. Here's a plan that reflects my current interests and needs:

- Backpacking Stuff
- HTML Stuff
  - HTML Documentation
  - HTML Standards Docs
  - HTML Tips and Tricks
- Sailing Stuff
- Search Tools
  - Search Engines
  - Subject Trees

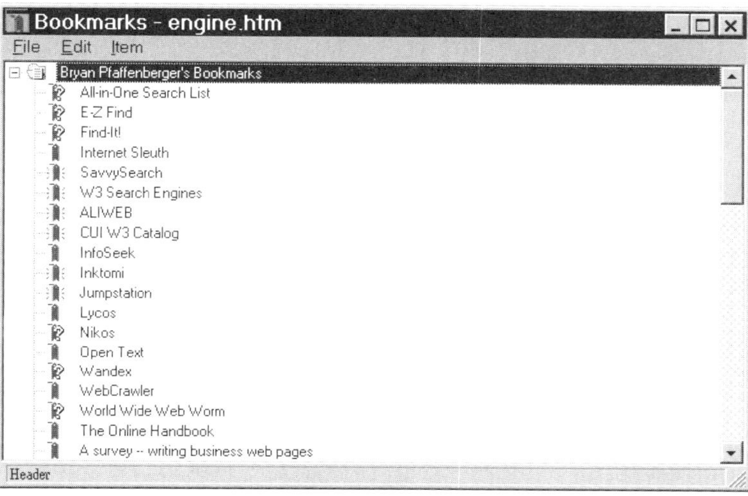

Figure 6.2 Bookmarks window with unorganized bookmarks

Don't worry about getting your folder organization exactly right the first time around. It's easy to reorganize your list.

To create a folder, do the following:

1. In the Bookmarks window, select the top item ("[Your Name]'s Bookmarks").
2. From the Item menu, choose Insert Folder. You'll see the Bookmark Properties dialog box, shown in Figure 6.3.
3. In the Name area, type the name for your new folder.
4. Click OK. You'll see the folder positioned beneath the selected item.

Adding Bookmarks to a Folder

It's easy to add bookmarks to a folder. Just select the bookmarks and drag them to the folder until the folder changes color, then release the mouse button.

Bookmark Properties
General
Name: New Header
Description:
Last Visited:
Added on:
OK Cancel Help

Figure 6.3 Bookmark Properties dialog box

Use these Windows shortcuts to select more than one bookmark item at a time. To select bookmarks individually, hold down the Ctrl key and click each of the items you want to select. To select a group of items, click the first one. Then hold down the Shift key and click the last one; Windows will select them all.

After you add bookmarks to a folder, you'll see that the Bookmarks window uses a tree-like diagram to show the list's logical organization (see Figure 6.4).

Adding Folders within Folders

Add additional folders and subfolders to flesh out the list's organization, as shown in Figure 6.5. To add a folder within a folder, just select the folder into which you would like to insert a folder. Then choose Insert Folder from the Item menu, and name the folder as described in the previous section.

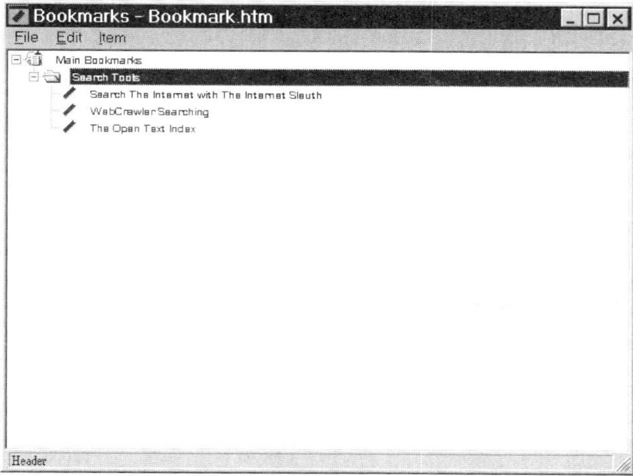

Figure 6.4 Tree structure of bookmarks list

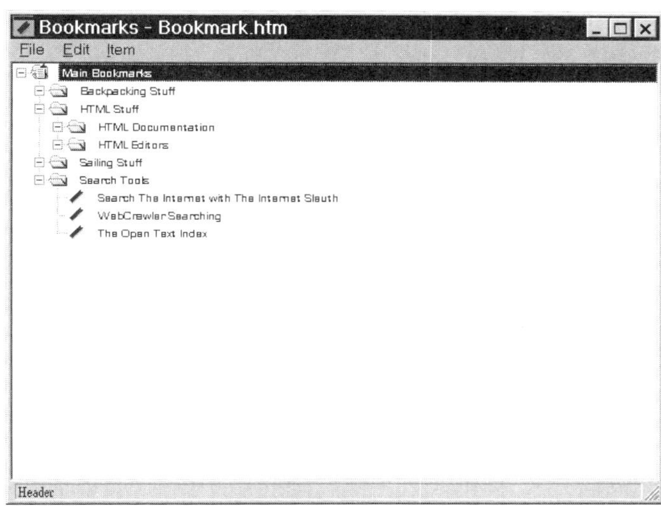

Figure 6.5 Bookmarks list after adding additional folders

Alphabetizing Bookmark Items

By default, Netscape alphabetizes the folders at a given level, but bookmark items appear in the order you added them.

To sort the items in a folder, follow these steps:

1. Select the folder.
2. From the Item menu, choose Sort Bookmarks. The items will appear in alphabetical order.

Making an Alias

If you'd like a bookmark to appear in more than one folder, you can do so quickly by making an alias. To do so, follow these steps:

1. Select the bookmark item.
2. From the Item menu, choose Make Alias. You'll see a copy of the item in the same folder.
3. Drag the copy to its new location in another folder.

Deleting an Item

To delete a bookmark item, simply select it and press the Delete key. (This just deletes the bookmark, by the way—it doesn't delete the original document out there on the Web.)

Looking at the Bookmarks Menu

The changes you're making in the Bookmarks window will be reflected in the Bookmarks menu. Top-level folders appear as items on the menu; when you click one of them, you see a pop-up menu containing the items you've added (see Figure 6.6). If you've added folders within folders, you get pop-up menus within pop-up menus.

Adding Separators

To clarify the logical organization of your Bookmarks menu, you may wish to add separators (lines that appear on the menu).

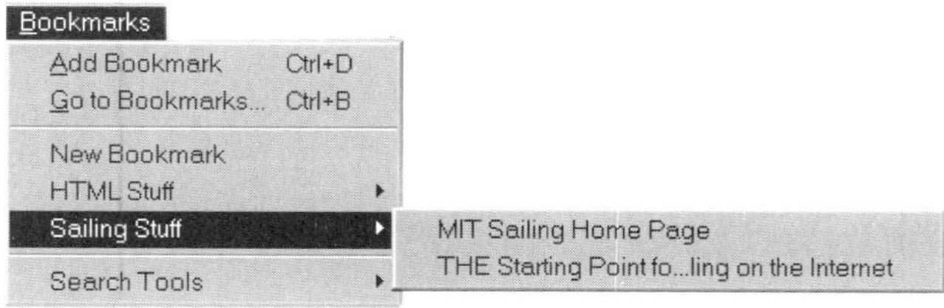

Figure 6.6 Pop-up menu containing added items

To add a separator, do the following:

1. Select the item above the place you want the separator to appear.
2. From the Item menu, choose Insert Separator.

If you don't like the placement of the separator, you can drag it to a new position within the Bookmarks window. To get rid of the separator entirely, select it and press Delete.

Reorganizing Folders

Once you've created your folders, you may wish to reorganize them. It's easy to do so. For example, suppose I've decided to create a new folder called Recreation, and I want to put Backpacking and Sailing Stuff into this new folder. To do so, I create the folder. Then I select the Backpacking and Sailing Stuff folders, and drag them into the new folder. Netscape includes the bookmark items, and any folders within folders, in the move.

Controlling the Bookmark List Display

Within the Bookmarks window, you can use the following techniques to control the way the list appears:

- To close a folder, so that only the folder name appears, double-click the folder icon. Alternatively, you can click the minus sign next to the

folder. After the folder closes, you'll see a plus sign indicating that the folder contains items.

- To open a closed folder, double-click the folder icon. Alternatively, you can click the plus sign next to the folder.

Adding a Description

If you would like to make some notes about a bookmark item, you can do so in the Bookmark Properties dialog box (see Figure 6.3).

To add a description, do the following:

1. In the Bookmarks window, select the item to which you would like to add a description.
2. From the Item menu, choose Properties.
3. In the Description box, type a description.
4. Click OK to confirm your comments.

Accessing Bookmarked Pages

You can use the Bookmarks window as well as the Bookmarks menu to access the bookmarks you've created.

To go to any bookmark listed in the Bookmarks window, just double-click it. The document appears in Netscape's window, not in the Bookmarks window. To see the document, switch back to Netscape's window.

Finding a Bookmark

In a lengthy bookmark list, you may have trouble finding a bookmark—especially if you've closed the folder in which it's stored. Let Netscape do the hunting for you.

To search for a bookmark item:

1. Select the folder where you want the search to begin (it proceeds downward from there). To search the entire bookmark file, select the top item.

2. From the Edit menu, choose Find. You'll see the Find Bookmark dialog box.
3. In the Find What area, type the text you want to find. Capitalization doesn't matter, unless you click Match Case. If a match is found, the program selects the item (if necessary, it opens the folder that contains the item).
4. To find the next matching item, click the Find Again button.

After you've exited the Find dialog box, you can still repeat the search with the same settings—just choose Find Again from the Edit menu.

Finding Out Whether Source Documents Have Changed

Chances are that the documents you've marked as bookmarks are pretty important to you—so naturally you'll want to know whether they've changed. Netscape can check the documents to find out whether they've changed. If any of them have, the Bookmarks menu will contain marks that indicate which of your bookmark items contain new material.

To determine whether source documents have changed:

1. Select one or more items.
2. From the File menu, choose What's New. You'll see the What's New dialog box, which enables you to look for changes in all the bookmark items or just the ones you selected.
3. Choose All Bookmarks to check out all the items, or Selected Bookmarks to check out just the ones you selected.
4. Click Start Checking. You'll see a dialog box that informs you how much time this operation will take. When it's finished, you'll see another dialog box informing how many documents, if any, contain changes.
5. Click OK to confirm, and look at the Bookmarks window. Documents that have changed are shown with a bright yellow flag.

Adding New Bookmarks to a Specified Folder

Once you've created folders for your bookmarks, you can select a new default folder to serve as the destination for new bookmark items. To do so, follow these steps:

1. In the Bookmarks window, select the folder you want to use as the destination for new bookmark items.
2. From the Item menu, choose Set to New Bookmarks Folder. In the bookmark item list, you'll see a check mark on this folder's icon.

Controlling the Menu Display

After you've added lots of folders and subfolders, your Bookmarks menu can seem cluttered again. If there's just one folder that you tend to use frequently, you can restrict the Bookmarks menu so that just this folder appears. To do so, follow these steps:

1. In the Bookmarks window, select the folder that you would like to appear on the Bookmarks menu, to the exclusion of all others.
2. From the Item menu, choose Set to Bookmark Menu Folder. In the bookmarks item list, you'll see a little menu icon on top of this item's folder icon. Only the items in this folder will appear on your Bookmarks menu. You can access the other items by opening the Bookmarks window, however.

Note that your choice of a folder as the Bookmark menu folder does not affect into which folder Netscape inserts new bookmark items. That's controlled by the Set to New Bookmarks Folder command, discussed in the previous section.

Exporting Bookmarks

One of the nicer points of Netscape is the program's ability to export bookmarks to a bookmark file, which you can then give to friends and colleagues (or whomever). These fortunate persons can then import the bookmark file, and your bookmarks will magically appear on their Bookmarks menu. This has created a certain amount of Internet traffic in bookmark files.

Another reason to export your bookmark file is that this enables you to create and store more than one bookmark file on your system. For example, you could create one bookmark file for your research on Civil War memorabilia, and another for your collection of hot Web sites. To learn how to open one of the bookmark files you've created, see the next section.

To export your bookmarks to a bookmark file:

1. From the File menu in the Bookmarks window, choose Save As. You'll see the standard Windows Save As dialog box.
2. Type a name for the file (be sure to use the extension .htm), and click Save.

Don't try to edit a bookmark file directly. It contains lots of secret, weird codes and other information that enables Netscape to import the file properly.

Opening a Local Bookmark File

If you've saved a bookmark file as just described, or if someone has given you one, you can open it. The new bookmark file replaces the previous one, so you'll see different options on the Bookmarks menu.

To open a bookmark file, do the following:

1. From the File menu in the Bookmarks window, choose Open. You'll see a standard Open dialog box.
2. In the Files of Type box, choose Source.
3. Locate and select the file you want to open, and click Open. Netscape replaces the current bookmark file with the one you just opened.

I want my old bookmark list back! No problem. Just open it using the instructions just given.

Importing Links from an HTML File

Here's a cool trick: With the Import command on the Bookmarks window's File menu, you can import all the links from any HTML document that you've saved on your local disk. They'll appear as bookmark items. The document headings will appear as folder names. This is pretty cool—try it out.

To import the links in an HTML file, do the following:

1. From the File menu in the Bookmarks window, choose Import. You'll see the Import Bookmarks dialog box.
2. In the Files of Type box, choose Source.
3. Locate and select the file you want to open, and click Open.

Netscape imports all the headings as folders and all the links as bookmark items. Note that the organization may not be ideal; you may have to rearrange the folders to make the list useful.

Creating Internet Shortcuts

If you're using the Windows 95 version of Netscape, you can easily create shortcuts to your favorite Web documents. The shortcuts will appear on your Windows desktop, where you can access them quickly.

To create an Internet shortcut:

1. In the Bookmarks window, select the item that you want to become an Internet shortcut.
2. Drag the item to the desktop, and release the mouse button.

You'll see the shortcut icon on the desktop. To access this document quickly, just double-click the icon.

From Here

- The Bookmarks window is pretty neat, but wait 'til you see Smart Bookmarks, the subject of the next chapter.
- Want to print or save the documents you're downloading—and how about those neat graphics, too? Find out how in Chapter 8.

Chapter 7

Using Smart Bookmarks and SmartMarks

Netscape's SmartMarks add-on program greatly improves the bookmark-organizing capabilities of Netscape Navigator. Available for both the Windows 3.1 and Windows 95 versions of Netscape Navigator, SmartMarks starts automatically every time you launch Netscape. Identical to SmartMarks is Smart Bookmarks, available from First Floor Software (800-639-6387). This chapter covers Smart Bookmarks version 2.0, which offers several excellent improvements over the impressive version 1.0 covered in previous editions of this book.

SmartMarks is available from Netscape in various commercial packagings of Netscape Navigator, (such as PowerPack), but you can obtain the program easily by getting yourself a

copy of Smart Bookmarks—and you can also download a free 30-day evaulation version (not currently available at Netscape's site). For more information, see First Floor's home page at http://www.firstfloor.com/eval.html. If you want to keep using the program at the end of 30 days, you pay a $25 registration fee.

For the Time-Challenged

- Smart Bookmarks is an add-on program that modifies Netscape's menus. To obtain the program, download it from First Floor Software's Web site or from the CD-ROM packaged with this book.
- Smart Bookmarks comes with more than a dozen predefined Smart Folders, containing the top 300 Web sites from Yahoo. To display these bookmark items, select a folder in the folder tree. The bookmark panel shows the bookmark items stored in the selected folder.
- The best way to add a bookmark item to a Smart Folder is to choose the File Smart Bookmarks option on the Bookmarks menu. This option enables you to choose the folder into which you would like to place the bookmark item. In addition, you can type a description and choose notification options.
- To update and download Web pages automatically, you create agents. An agent is a set of specifications for update scheduling, type of update, and copying to a local disk. After creating the agent, you can attach it to any bookmark you've saved.
- To see which sites have changed, select Agent Results in the folder panel. Double-click an item to see the changed page in Netscape.
- You can create a Web or Usenet search and save the search as a bookmark. If you then attach an agent to this bookmark, you can see at a glance whether a repeated search has retrieved any new links. This is a great way to stay in touch with rapidly changing areas of knowledge.

What's So Great about Smart Bookmarks?

Once you install Smart Bookmarks, the program automatically modifies Netscape's Bookmarks menu, presenting you with several new options and capabilities, including the following:

- Enhanced bookmarking capabilities. Although you can still use the Bookmarks window, if you wish, Smart Bookmarks provides an easier-to-use interface for creating, storing, and organizing bookmarks. In addition, Smart Bookmarks comes with 300 predefined bookmarks, arranged into more than a dozen preconfigured folders (see Figure 7.1), which echo the subject organization of Yahoo. You can add additional folders and bookmarks as you please.
- Full caching of document images as well as document text. You can reload these documents and view them even when you're not connected to the Internet.
- Add extensive comments to your bookmarks. Unlike the descriptions you type in the Bookmarks window, these comments are fully searchable.
- Set up automatic notification of changes to existing bookmarks, including changed or added links on a monitored page. You can link any bookmark with one or more *agents*, which you can customize to determine the frequency of notification and other options.
- Automatically receive bulletins regarding changes to a monitored site. (The site must support this feature in order for these bulletins to be received.)
- Search the Internet using the most popular search engines, with a single, simple user interface.
- Save successful searches, and have them monitored so that you're automatically notified when new or changed links appear in the retrieval list.

These features add up to a significant improvement in Netscape's overall functionality. Unless you're not really interested in storing and organizing bookmarks, Smart Bookmarks is a very wise choice. In this chapter, you'll

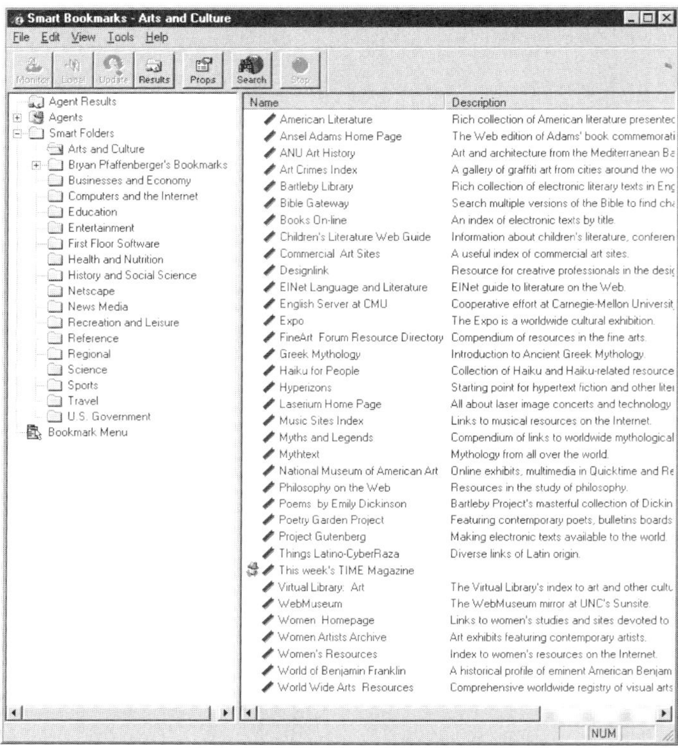

Figure 7.1 Preconfigured folders in Smart Bookmarks

learn how to get Smart Bookmarks humming—and after you do, you'll have vastly increased your ability to keep track of fast-breaking information developments on the Web.

This chapter focuses on Smart Bookmarks, but Netscape's version—SmartMarks—is virtually identical. However, you'll notice a few minor differences. For example, the menu items that appear within Netscape say Add SmartMark instead of Add Smart Bookmark. If you're using Smart-Marks, you can use this chapter as long as you keep these minor differences in mind.

Installing Smart Bookmarks

If you've downloaded Smart Bookmarks from the CD or First Floor's Web site, installation is simple.

To install Smart Bookmarks, do the following:

1. Using Windows Explorer (Windows 95) or File Manager (Windows 3.1), open the folder or directory that contains the Smart Bookmarks file that you downloaded.
2. Double-click the file name. The Smart Bookmarks installation utility starts.
3. Follow the on-screen instructions.

After you finish the installation, you'll need to restart your system.

Using the Enhanced Bookmarks Menu

After you install Smart Bookmarks, the program replaces Netscape's Bookmarks menu with two Smart Bookmarks options on the Bookmarks menu (Figure 7.2):

- **Add Smart Bookmark** Choose this command (or use the Ctrl + D shortcut) to create new bookmarks, just as you did prior to installing

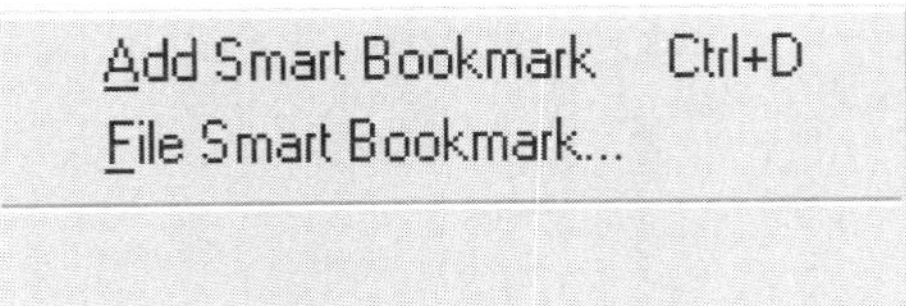

Figure 7.2 Bookmarks menu after installing Smart Bookmarks

Smart Bookmarks. You'll see your additions in the Bookmarks menu. Later, you can store these bookmarks in folders.

- **File Smart Bookmark** Use this command to store bookmarks with optional information, such as comments. You can modify the bookmark name, enter a description, and add keywords, which make it easier to find the bookmark. You can also choose the folder to which you would like to add the bookmark.

You also see a new option on the Window menu:

- **View Smart Bookmarks** This command opens the Smart Bookmarks window. You can also use the Ctrl + B keyboard shortcut.

Always use the File Smart Bookmark command to save your bookmarks from within Netscape. Doing so gives you the ability to determine which folder is used to store the bookmark. This eliminates having to clean up your Bookmarks menu later.

Understanding the Smart Bookmarks Window

The Smart Bookmarks window (see Figure 7.1) consists of two panels, with the folder tree on the left. In the right panel, you see the bookmark panel. It contains bookmarks that have been added to the open folder. To view the original document, just double-click the bookmark.

Below the menu bar you will find the following buttons:

Monitor Click here to link the selected bookmark to one or more agents, which can notify you if the page changes.

Local Click here to download a complete copy of the currently selected bookmark, including all the linked graphics, to a local disk. This will enable you to read the document even if you're not connected to the Internet.

Update	Click here to run an update on items you've selected for monitoring.
Results	If you see a change flag next to the selected item, click here to see a dialog box detailing the changes.
Props	Click here to view the properties of the selected item.
Search	Click here to start a Web search.
Stop	Stop downloading or checking for updates.

You'll find that these buttons provide access to the Smart Bookmarks tasks you'll undertake most frequently.

Using Smart Bookmarks: An Overview

I recommend that you tackle Smart Bookmarks in the following steps:

1. Begin by learning how Smart Bookmarks' folder tree works. Since this tree already contains many preconfigured folders and the top 300 Web sites from Yahoo, this should be a lot of fun!
2. Create and organize your own bookmark folders. You'll use these to store your favorite Web sites.
3. Add new bookmarks to your Smart Bookmarks folders. Add comments and keywords, if you wish. Assign an agent to each bookmark.
4. Create your own agents.
5. Look for icons informing you of changes in monitored sites. Use the Web Monitor, if you wish.
6. Search your folders matching keywords that you specify.

The following sections discuss these steps in detail.

Navigating the Folder Tree

Smart Bookmark's folders are arranged in a tree structure (see Figure 7.1). You can do the following with the folder tree and bookmarks panel:

- To view the bookmarks stored in a folder, just click the folder. You'll see the bookmarks in the bookmark panel.
- To view more details about each item (including the first few characters of the description and the date of last modification), open the View menu and choose Details.
- A plus mark indicates that a folder has hidden subfolders, which you can view if you wish. To view the subfolder names, click the plus sign.
- A minus sign indicates that the folder can be collapsed, hiding subfolders from view.
- The open folder's contents are on display in the bookmarks panel.
- To view the Web document linked with a bookmark, just double-click the bookmark. The document will appear in Netscape's window.

Creating New Bookmark Folders

To create a new folder, do the following:

1. Select the folder in which you want to place the new folder. To put the folder at the top-most level, select Smart Folders.
2. Choose New Folder from the File menu. You'll see the New Folder dialog box, shown in Figure 7.3.
3. In the Name area, type the name of your new folder.
4. In the Description area, type a brief description. You can also type keywords, if you wish, in the Keywords area. This will assist Smart Bookmarks in searching your folders.
5. Click OK. Smart Bookmarks creates the folder and automatically places it in alphabetical order among the other folders at the same level.

Organizing Folders and Bookmarks

You can reorganize the folder tree by placing folders within folders, and you can also delete unwanted folders. Within the bookmark panel, you can sort bookmarks by name or by date, and you can move bookmarks from folder to folder.

Placing Folders within Folders

Smart Bookmarks is a great utility, but here's one procedure that's not particularly obvious or easy: placing folders within folders. There's nary a word concerning this maneuver in the program's Help files, but your intrepid author has discovered the way.

To place a folder within another folder:

1. Make sure the destination folder is visible within the folder tree. If it isn't, click the plus sign so that it's visible.
2. Select the folder that's one level *above* the folder you want to move. For most of the existing folders, the folder that's one level above is

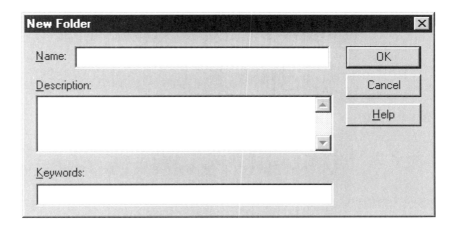

Figure 7.3 New Folder dialog box

the Smart Folders folder. After you select this folder, the folder you want to move will appear in the bookmarks panel.

3. Select the folder you want to move, and drag it from the Bookmarks folder to the destination folder. When the destination folder changes color, release the mouse button.

Deleting an Unwanted Folder

To delete an unwanted folder and all of its contents, just select the folder and press Delete. You'll see an alert box asking you to confirm the deletion of the folder and its contents. Click Yes to confirm the deletion.

Sorting Bookmark Items

Within the bookmarks panel, you can sort bookmark items by name or by date. To sort bookmark items, follow these instructions:

1. Select the items you want to sort. To select all the items, open the Edit menu and choose Select All, or just press Ctrl + A.
2. From the View menu, choose Arrange Icons. You'll see a pop-up menu with two options, Name (the default sort option) and Date.
3. Choose Name or Date to initiate the sort.

Moving Bookmark Items

To move a bookmark item to a different folder, display the item in the bookmarks panel and select it. Then drag the bookmark tile to the destination folder and release the mouse button.

Adding Bookmarks to Smart Bookmarks Folders

When you've found a site that you want to add to Smart Bookmarks, you have two options:

- You can add the item to the Bookmarks menu. Smart Bookmarks places the bookmark item into the Bookmark Menu folder.

(*Note:* This is not the same thing as the Bookmarks window, discussed in the previous chapter.) Later, you can drag the bookmark to a Smart Folder.

- You can choose the folder to which you would like to add the bookmark. This option is best because you don't have to worry about adding the new bookmark to a Smart Folder later.

Adding a Bookmark to the Bookmarks Menu

To add a bookmark item to the Bookmarks menu, open the Bookmarks menu in Netscape and choose Add Smart Bookmark (or just press Ctrl + D). Netscape adds the bookmark to the Bookmarks menu, and it also places a bookmark tile in a folder named after you (such as "Susan Smith's Bookmarks"). You'll find this in the folder tree in the Smart Bookmarks window. Later, you can move this item to a Smart Folder by selecting it and dragging it to a destination folder.

Adding a Bookmark to a Smart Folder

The best way to add new bookmarks to your Smart Bookmarks menus is to use the File Smart Bookmarks command, one of the new commands you'll find on the Smart Bookmarks (Bookmarks) menu. This command enables you to choose the folder in which you would like the bookmark to be stored. You can also type a description and choose notification options.

To store a bookmark in a Smart Folder:

1. In the Bookmarks menu, choose File Smart Bookmark. You'll see the Add Bookmark dialog box, shown in Figure 7.4.
2. In the Document Title area, you see that Smart Bookmarks has echoed the document's title. Change the document title to something more descriptive, if you wish.
3. In the Description area, type a short, informative description.
4. In the File Into Folder area, select the folder in which you want the bookmark item to be stored.
5. If you would like to have this site monitored, click the Monitor with an Agent checkbox.

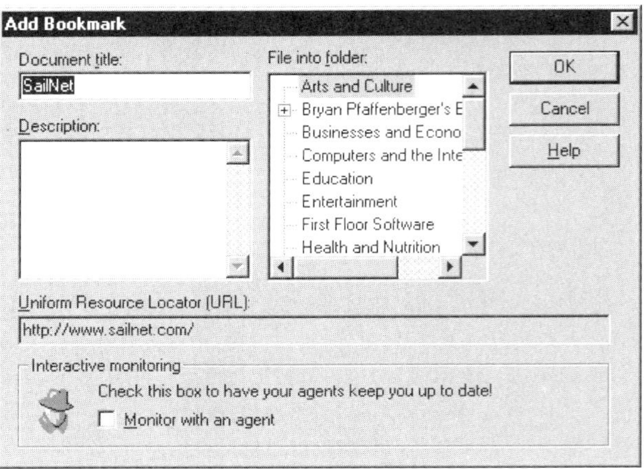

Figure 7.4 Add Bookmark dialog box

6. Click OK. If you chose Monitor with an Agent, you'll see the Select an Agent dialog box, which enables you to choose from a list of prepared agents. These include the following:

List/Searches	Monitors the links on bookmarks that list references to other pages, and informs you when new ones are added. By default, changes are monitored at 8 AM daily. No local copies are saved. This option is excellent if you're bookmarking a page that contains useful lists of links.
Local Copy	Makes a local copy of the document so that you can read it off-line. Changes aren't monitored.
What's New?	Monitors bookmarks at startup for changes.

You can also create a custom agent, if you wish. The process of creating a custom agent is described in the following section.

7. Click OK to create the new bookmark.

Using Agents

One of the most innovative characteristics of Smart Bookmarks is the programs' agents, which can check a bookmark for changes, make a local copy of the source document (including graphics), and even notify you when a linked page changes. Smart Bookmarks comes with three agents that you can use (List/Searches, Local Copy, and What's New?).

The existing agents give you a pretty good idea of what can be accomplished with agents. You may want to create your own, though, if you'd like to combine some of these functions in one agent (for example, you can combine updating with downloading local copies). Another reason to create your own agent is to modify the update frequency.

Creating a New Agent

To create a new agent, you use the Agent Wizard, as explained in the following steps:

1. From the File menu, choose New Agent. You'll see the Agent Wizard's first page (Figure 7.5).

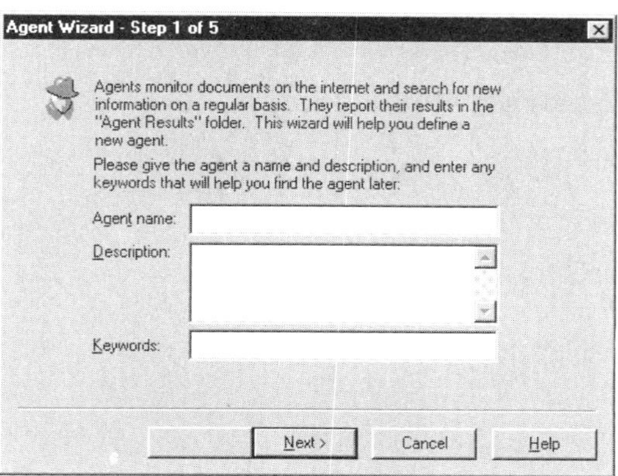

Figure 7.5 Creating an agent (first page of Agent Wizard)

2. In the Agent Name box, type a name for the agent.
3. In the Description box, type a brief description of what the agent does.
4. In the Keywords box, type one or more keywords to assist Smart Bookmarks in searching for this agent.
5. Click Next. You'll see the second page of the wizard, which enables you to select what the agent should do (Figure 7.6). Select one of the following:

    - **Monitor page changes** Changes will be reported in Agent Results.
    - **Monitor lists or search results** Reports new links to Agent Results. This is a good choice for trailblazer pages and searches.
    - **Monitor page changes and new links** This option combines the first two.

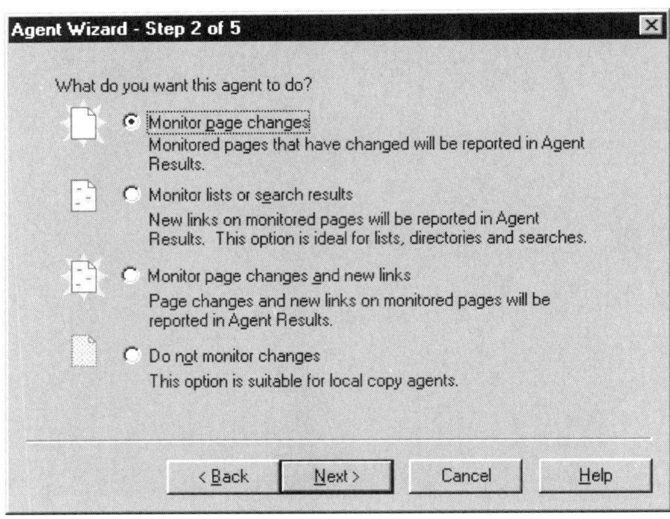

Figure 7.6 Creating an agent (second page of Agent Wizard)

- **Do not monitor changes** Choose this option if you want to create an agent that does nothing but download pages for offline viewing.

6. After choosing an agent type, click Next. You'll see the third page of the wizard (Figure 7.7), which enables you to select the update frequency. You can choose from the following options:

   - **Manually** Changes are checked only if you click the Update button.
   - **At program startup** Changes are checked when Smart Bookmarks starts.
   - **Every [user specified] minutes** Changes are checked at intervals you specify.
   - **Daily at [user specified time]** Changes are checked at the specified time of day.You can use this option to check for changes when you're out to lunch, or in the middle of the night when you're not using your computer. (Note, though, that your computer must be connected to the Internet in

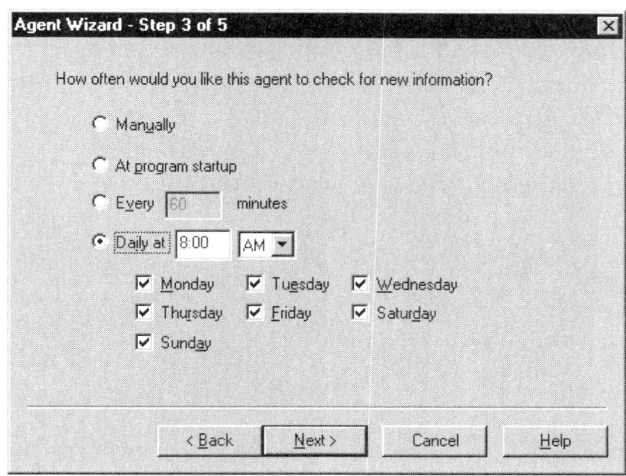

Figure 7.7 Creating an agent (third page of Agent Wizard)

order for the changes to be checked.) You can individually specify the days on which the checks should be performed.

7. Choose an update frequency, and click Next. You'll see the fourth page of the wizard, which enables you to choose local downloading. If the document is downloaded, you can view it off-line.
8. Choose whether you want local copies, and click Next. You'll see the fifth page of the wizard, which tells you you're done.

Note that the agent you've just created isn't assigned to any bookmarks yet. To assign the agent to a bookmark, just drag the bookmark to the agent's name in the Agents folder (in the folder panel). For more information, see "Assigning an Agent to a Bookmark," later in this chapter.

Changing an Agent's Properties

After you create an agent, you can change its properties (such as the update frequency). You may wish to do this, for example, if you've chosen to have your updates performed at program startup, but later find that this ties up your computer for too long. You can change the update schedule so that updates are performed when you're away from your computer.

Note that this procedure gives you more options and control than the Agent Wizard for the local copies option. For example, you can control whether local copies are saved with in-line images (by default, they are, but you can turn this off), and you can save copies of the pages to which a monitored item is linked.

To change an agent's properties, do the following:

1. Select the agent.
2. Click the Props button. You'll see the first page of the Properties dialog box, shown in Figure 7.8
3. Click the tab of the properties you want to alter:

   General This page enables you to alter the agent's name, description, and keywords.

   Schedule This page enables you to alter the schedule for updates.

Sensitivity	This page enables you to choose what the agent does (monitor page changes, monitor links or seach results, monitor page changes and new links, or turn off monitoring).
Local Copies	This page enables you to control whether Smart Bookmarks saves local copies (Figure 7.8). Offering more options than the Agent Wizard, this page enables you to specify whether you want graphics (in-line images) included in the local copies, as well as links to remote sites. You can also ask Smart Bookmarks to download copies of the pages to which that item is linked (one or two levels of links).

4. When you've finished making changes, click OK.

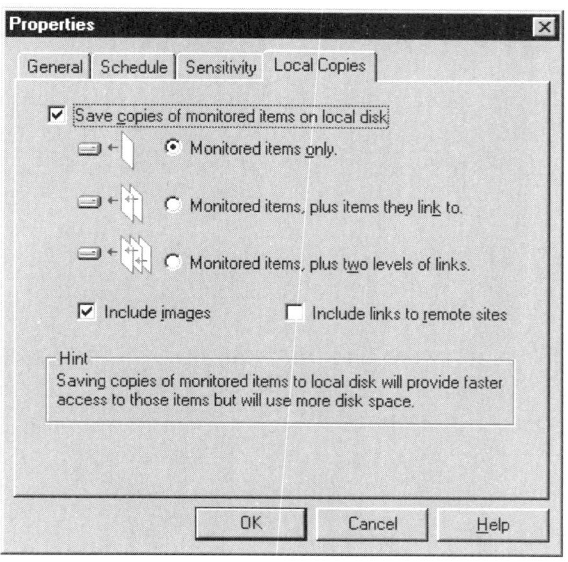

Figure 7.8 Local Copies properties

This agent is filling up my whole hard disk with Web pages! Be conservative in choosing the option that enables you to save local copies of monitored items plus the pages to which they're linked. These pages will load into Netscape much faster (since they're stored on disk). If you assign local copy agents to too many bookmarks, though, the result could be that Smart Bookmarks will be downloading literally hundreds of Web pages with all their graphics! Goodbye free disk space!

To save a local copy of a bookmarked page without having to alter the agent, just select the bookmark and click Local. But note that this button automatically assigns the Local Copy agent to the item, so be careful about using this too often (unless you have a gargantuan hard disk).

Assigning an Agent to a Bookmark

It's easy to assign an agent to a bookmark. In the folder tree, click open the Agents folder. Then simply drag a bookmark to the agent, and release the mouse button.

Another way to assign an agent to a bookmark is to select the bookmark and click the Monitor button. In the dialog box, choose the agent you want, and click OK.

You can also assign agents to bookmarks by using the Properties dialog box. To do so, select the bookmark and click the Props button. Click the agent tab, and click Add. Select the agent you want, and click OK twice.

Removing an Agent from a Bookmark

If you no longer want an agent to update one of your bookmarks, select the bookmark and click the Props button. Click the Agent tab, and select the agent in the Agents list. Click Remove to break the link between the agent and the bookmark. (Note that this does not delete the agent itself.)

Performing a Manual Update

If you chose the Manual option in the Schedule page when you created your agent, Smart Bookmarks doesn't check for changes automatically. To perform the update, click the Update button.

Viewing Changed Bookmarks

After you link a bookmark to an agent, the bookmark appears in the bookmarks panel with an agent icon next to it (a '40s-style detective). You can tell from the flags (symbols) next to the bookmark's name whether the source document has changed:

- **No change found** You see a blue slash mark (and nothing else).
- **Source page has changed, and you haven't seen the changes** You see a yellow star over the blue slash.
- **Source page has a new bulletin** You see an exclamation point over the blue slash.
- **A local copy has been saved** You see a very tiny disk graphic over the blue slash.

The flags can be hard to see on some monitors. If you're having trouble seeing them, open the View menu and choose Large icons.

In Figure 7.9, for example, you see a changed site with a bulletin, and another with a change flag.

To get a quick review of updates, just click the Agent Results folder. You'll see an item for each change that Smart Bookmarks has detected, as shown in Figure 7.9. To view the item in Netscape, just double-click it. After you read the item, the yellow star is removed from the item.

Creating and Saving a Search

One of the most advanced and useful features of Smart Bookmarks is the ability to create and save a search. You can save the search as a bookmark. If you then attach an agent to it, you'll see when the search shows new links. This is a great way to keep up to date on any subject. You can search Yahoo, Lycos, InfoSeek Guide, Web Crawler, Excite, Deja News, or Alta Vista. Alta Vista and Deja News enable you to search Usenet as well as the Web.

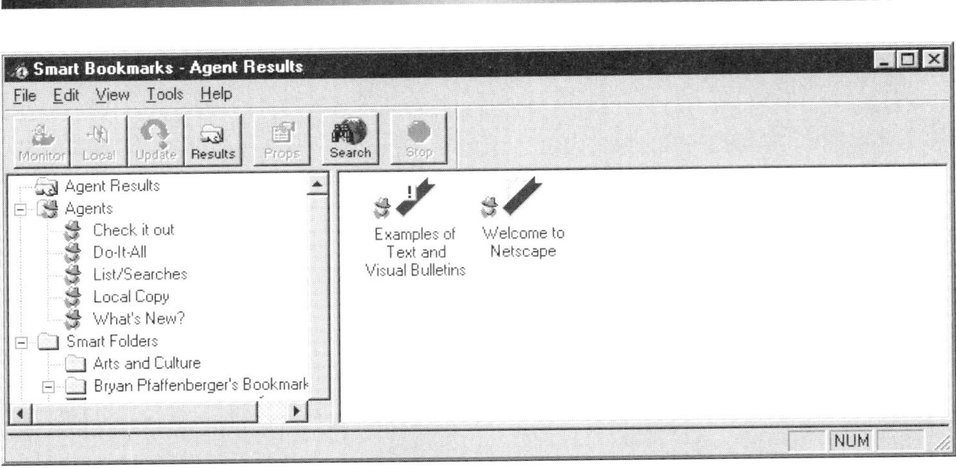

Figure 7.9 Agent Results list with two altered sites

The following instructions show you how to create a search, save it as a bookmark, and then attach an agent to the bookmark:

1. Click the Search button. You'll see the Web Search dialog box, shown in Figure 7.10.
2. In the Search the Web for New Pages list box, choose the search service you want to use. Because Alta Vista offers the largest database, I recommend this service for Usenet and Web searches.
3. In the first list box beneath the search service selection box (the one that says "contents"), choose the portion of the document you want to search. With all the services save Yahoo, your only choice is "Contents." With Yahoo, you can also choose Title, URL, or Comments.
4. In the second list box, the one that says "contains" by default, choose the match condition you want. "Contains" performs a substring search (that is, your search word is matched even if it occurs within a longer word). With some services, you can choose "Match," which forces the search engine to retrieve only those documents that contain the exact word you've typed.

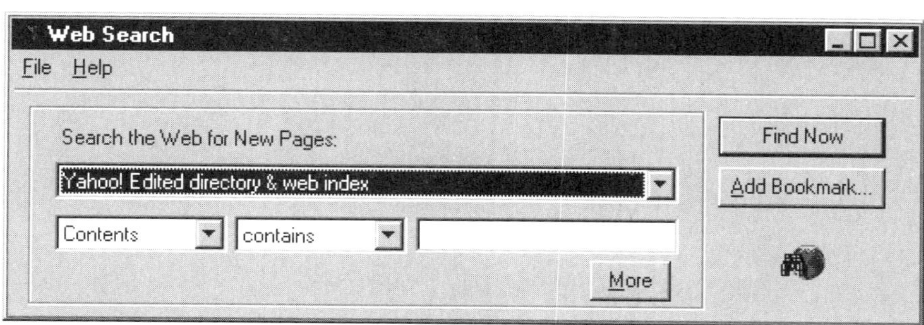

Figure 7.10 Web Search dialog box

5. In the third condition box, type the first search word you want to match.
6. If you want to add more search words, click More. You'll see an additional condition row. In the first box, choose "and" if you want to see only those documents that contain both of your search words; choose "or" if you're willing to see a larger retrieval list, in which items are retrieved if they contain one of the search words. Type the second search word. You can click More to add up to five search words, if you wish.
7. To create this search as a bookmark, click Add Bookmark. You'll see the Add Bookmark dialog box.
8. Change the name of the bookmark to something more descriptive.
9. Type a brief description.
10. Choose a folder in which to store the bookmark.
11. To attach an agent to this bookmark, click Monitor with Agent.
12. Click OK. You'll see the Select an Agent dialog box.
13. Select List/Searches.
14. Click OK. You'll see the Web Search dialog box again.
15. To perform the search, click Find Now. You'll see the search results in Netscape's window.

Now that you've created the search and saved it as a bookmark, remember to check the Agents Results folder to see if there's anything new!

If the search fails, you may have typed too many keywords. To broaden the search, try clicking the Fewer button and removing some of the keywords.

Searching Your Bookmarks

Once you've created hundreds or even thousands of bookmarks, you may have trouble finding a bookmark by manual means (going through all those folders and subfolders). Let Smart Bookmarks do the searching for you.

To search your bookmarks, open the Tool menu and choose Find Bookmarks. You'll see a search dialog box that's identical to the one shown in Figure 7.10, except that it's called Bookmark Search and it's set to search All Folders by default. To search a specific folder, click the folder icon and click the folder you want to search.

The Search Bookmark dialog box works the same way the Web Search dialog box does: You select the part of the record you want to search (you can choose from Name, Description, Comments and Bulletins, or Keywords) as well as the matching condition (contains, is, starts with, or ends with). You then type the keyword you want to match. If you wish, you can add additional search conditions by clicking More. To initiate the search, click Find Now.

Importing and Exporting Catalogs

In Smart Bookmarks, a *catalog* is a list of hyperlinks that is formatted and stored in a way that optimizes Smart Bookmark's functions. But these catalogs are not insulated from the Web. You can import any HTML file into Smart Bookmarks so that it becomes a new Smart Folder, and you can also export one or more Smart Bookmarks catalogs to an HTML file.

Importing an HTML File into Smart Bookmarks

You can import any HTML file containing hyperlinks into Smart Bookmarks so that it becomes a new Smart Folder in your folder tree. Smart Bookmarks ignores the text; it only stores the hyperlinks.

To import an HTML file into Smart Bookmarks so that its hyperlinks appear in a new folder:

1. Display the HTML file with Netscape.
2. From Netscape's File menu, choose Save, and save the file as a Source (*.htm) file.
3. In Smart Bookmarks, open the Tools menu and choose Import.
4. Use the Import dialog box to open the HTML file you just saved. You'll see a new Smart Bookmarks folder containing the hyperlinks in the file you imported.

Exporting Folders to an HTML File

Would you like to share your Web discoveries with others? You can do so by exporting one or more Smart Folders to HTML files. You can then mail the file to others, or give it to them on a disk.

To export one or more Smart Folders to an HTML file:

1. Unless you want to export everything in your Smart Bookmarks catalog, select the bookmark items or the folders you want to export.
2. From the Tools menu, choose Export. You'll see the Export dialog box, shown in Figure 7.11.
3. In the What Data to Export area, you have the option of choosing Sub-folders—to include all the subfolders in the selected folder(s)—keywords, or comments.
4. In the File Name area, choose a file name for the exported file.
5. In the Data format area, choose Bookmark HTML file.
6. Click OK to export the file.

To learn about new catalogs as they become available, open the Help menu and choose New Catalogs. You'll be connected to First Floor Software's Web site, where you'll find lots of interesting catalogs to download.

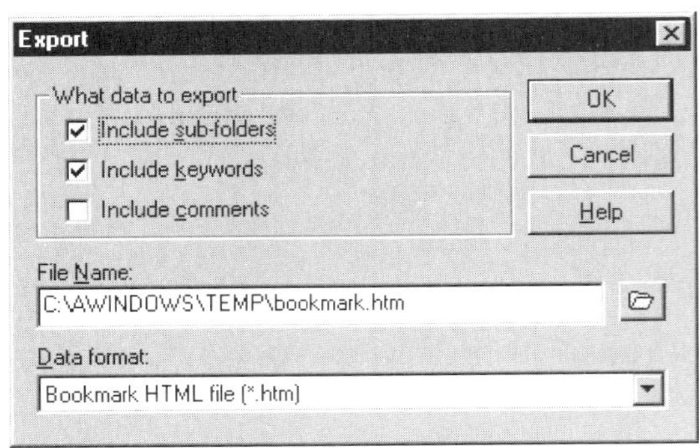

Figure 7.11 Export dialog box

Quitting Smart Bookmarks

This is going to be a very short section, because its main message is Don't, at least while Netscape is running. If you quit Smart Bookmarks while Netscape is on-screen, you'll lose the menu options that enable you to access Smart Bookmarks. You won't get them back until you start Smart Bookmarks again, which is a somewhat tedious process—especially considering that most of the default bookmarks are set to be checked when the program is launched!

Always quit Netscape and only *then* quit Smart Bookmarks.

From Here

- Learn how to save and print the documents you're viewing with Netscape Navigator. You'll find the lowdown in Chapter 8.
- Chapter 9 shows you how to use Netscape Navigator's customization options, so that the program looks and works the way you want.

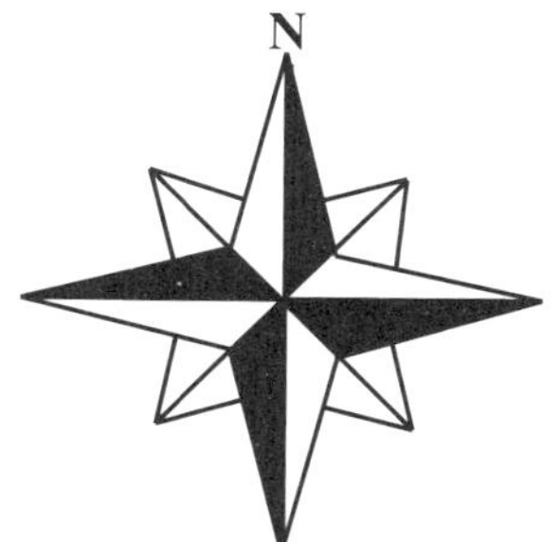

Chapter 8

Managing Documents with Netscape Navigator

While you're viewing Web documents with Netscape, you can select and copy text from the screen to the Clipboard, search for text, save the document to your hard drive (in HTML or plain text), save in-line images to your hard drive, print documents, and view the source HTML. This chapter fully discusses these document-handling aspects of Netscape Navigator.

Copying Text or Graphics to the Clipboard

You can easily select and copy any text or in-line graphic image that you see on-screen in Netscape Navigator. The copied text goes to the Clipboard, where you can paste it using other applications.

For the Time-Challenged

- You can copy text and graphics from any document that Netscape displays. The copied text or graphic goes to the Clipboard, where you can paste it using other applications.
- If you need to find text within a document you're displaying, click the Find button, type some search text, and click OK.
- To open a local document, use the Open File command.
- To save an in-line image to your hard drive, right-click it and choose Save This Image As.
- To print the document you're currently displaying, click the Print button.
- To view information about a document, choose Document Info from the View menu.
- To view the source HTML, choose Document Source from the View menu.

To copy text to the Clipboard, follow these steps:

1. Using the mouse, select the text on-screen.
2. From the Edit menu, choose Copy, or just use the Ctrl + C keyboard shortcut.
3. To paste the text using another application, use that program's Edit Paste command, or press Ctrl + V.

I tried to copy the darned text but I clicked a hyperlink instead! If the text you're copying contains a hyperlink, the copy operation can sometimes inadvertently turn into a hyperlink click. If this happens, click the Back button to return to the document. Try selecting the text again, but start by clicking *just outside* the text you want to copy, and carefully drag all the way over the text and release the mouse button just beyond the edge of the text.

To copy graphics to the Clipboard:

1. Point to the graphic with the mouse, and click the right mouse button. You'll see the pop-up menu shown in Figure 8.1.
2. Click Copy this Image Location.
3. To paste the text using another application, use that program's Edit Paste command, or press Ctrl + V.

I can copy, but I can't cut or clear this text! That's right. The Cut and Clear commands are enabled only when you've positioned the cursor within an editable text area.

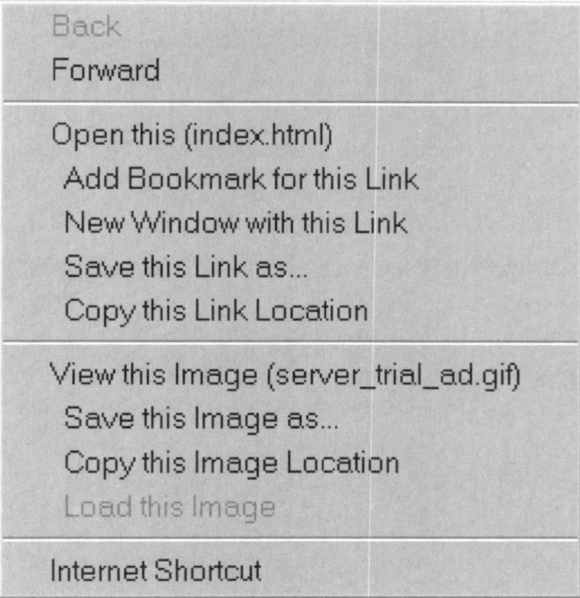

Figure 8.1 Pop-up menu (right-click)

Finding Text in a Document

You've just downloaded a humongous document, and you know it contains something of interest to you . . . somewhere. Don't wear out your eyes searching the text manually; use the Find button.

To search for text in the document that's currently displayed:

1. Click the Find button. Alternatively, open the Edit menu and choose Find, or press Ctrl + F. You'll see the Find dialog box, shown in Figure 8.2.
2. By default, Netscape searches down in the document and ignores capitalization. To search up, click the Up button. To match a capitalization pattern (for example, to find "Robert Frost" but not "morning frost"), click Match Case.
3. In the Find What box, type the text that you want to match.
4. Click Find Next. Netscape tries to find the text you've matched. If the program finds a match, it scrolls to the text's location and highlights it. The Find dialog box remains on-screen.
5. To find another match, click Find Next. To close the Find dialog box, click Cancel.

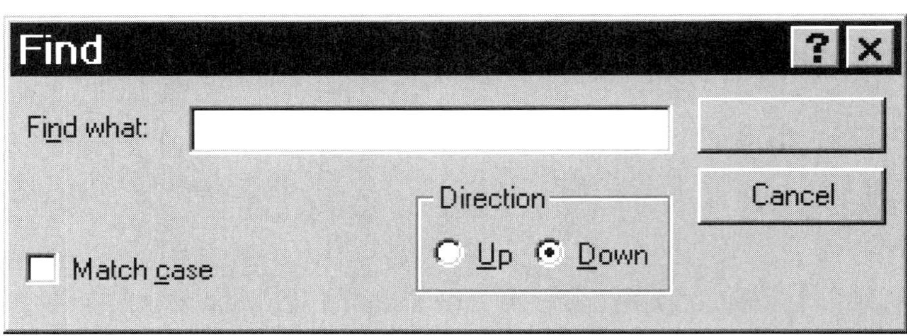

Figure 8.2 Find dialog box

After you close the Find dialog box, you can still repeat the search with the same settings—just press the F3 key, or open the Edit menu and choose Find Again.

Saving Documents

You can save any document that Netscape can display. It's easy to save documents in native HTML or plain text. But be aware that Netscape doesn't automatically save in-line images. To save a document with in-line images, you're in for some work, as the following sections explain.

If you're viewing a document with frames, you can only save the current frame, not the whole page. Reflecting this, the Save As command changes to Save Frame As when you're viewing a document that has frames.

Saving Documents in Plain Text

If you've downloaded a document that contains lots of interesting text that you'd like to save for future reference or use, you can save the document as plain text. With this option, Netscape removes all the HTML codes and hyperlinks.

If you just want a clean printout of the document, print it instead of saving it as plain text. Netscape's Print command produces an attractive-looking printout of the document, just as you see it on-screen—no ugly HTML codes.

To save a document as plain text:

1. From the File menu, choose Save As, or press Ctrl + S. You'll see the Save As dialog box (Figure 8.3).
2. In the Save as Type box, choose Plain Text (*.txt).
3. In the Directories list, choose the directory to which you would like to save the document.
4. In the File Name box, type a name for the document. Netscape suggests a name using the document's current title. Be sure to use the extension .txt.
5. Click Save.

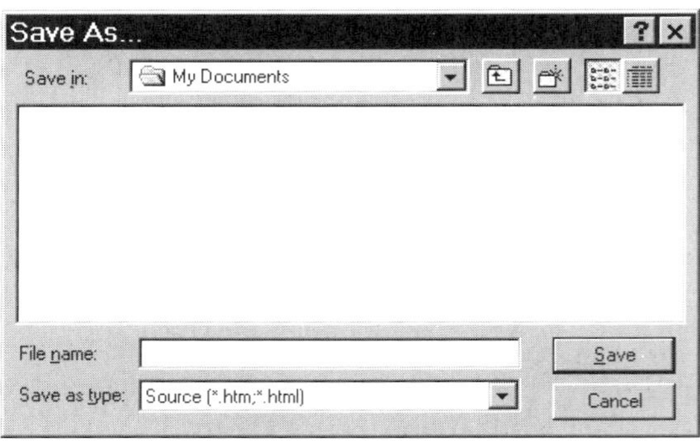

Figure 8.3 Save As dialog box

Saving Documents in HTML

The Web documents that Netscape displays are written in HTML, as you know. If you save a document in HTML format, you can reopen the document using Netscape's Open File command (File menu), and you'll see all the text formatting and hyperlinks that the document contains. But you may not see the in-line graphics, as explained below.

When should you save HTML documents? There's really only one good reason: You're learning HTML and you want to study the HTML coding. Don't make disk copies of documents in an attempt to cut down on network retrieval delays; Netscape already does this job for you automatically (see Chapter 5).

To save the document in HTML format:

1. From the File menu, choose Save As, or press Ctrl + S. You'll see the Save As dialog box, shown in Figure 8.3.
2. In the Save as Type box, choose Source (*.htm).
3. In the Directories list, choose the directory to which you would like to save the document.
4. In the File Name box, type a name for the document. Netscape suggests a name using the document's current title.
5. Click Save.

Why don't you see in-line images when you open an HTML file you've saved? To understand, you need to know the difference between a relative link and an absolute link.

- A *relative link* displays a graphic or document that's stored in the same directory as the document; it doesn't contain any path information other than, in effect, "Look in the same directory for this."
- An *absolute link* displays a graphic or document that's stored on some other computer, and contains complete instructions on where it should be obtained.

Now let's say you download an HTML file to your \docs directory, and open the file. Almost certainly, all of the in-line images were created with relative links. Netscape goes hunting for the graphics in the \docs directory, but they're not there, so you see lots of placeholders. Web authors are loathe to use absolute links for in-line images and for good reason: If you link to an image on somebody else's computer, what happens if that someone else decides to erase the image? Since you can't control this, it's easier and safer to use relative links for in-line images.

The moral of the story here is that Netscape doesn't do a very good job of letting you save documents to your disk for local, off-line browsing.

To save a Web page for off-line browsing, including all the page's graphics and even the documents linked to the page (up to two levels deep), use SmartMarks or Smart Bookmarks (as described in the previous chapter), and create a local copy agent. For frequently accessed pages, this is a great way to create a browsable local file system that doesn't require you to be connected to the Internet (except when you want to update the pages).

Viewing and Saving In-Line Graphics

Netscape's pop-up menu enables you to save graphics to your hard disk.

To save an in-line graphic:

1. Point to the graphic.
2. Click the right mouse button. You'll see the pop-up menu shown in Figure 8.1, earlier in this chapter.

3. Choose Save this Image as. You'll see the Save As dialog box. Netscape has automatically placed the graphic's name in the File Name box.
4. In the directories list, select the directory where you want to save the graphic.
5. Click Save.

I can't save the background graphic! That's right. Click as hard as you might, you can't download the background graphic. However, where there's a will, there's a way. From the View menu, choose Document Info. You'll see the information page for this document. The Background image is located right at the top. To save it, right-click it and choose Save Link As. Cool, huh?

Opening Local Documents

With Netscape, you can open any HTML or text file that's present on a disk in your computer. To do so, follow these instructions:

1. From the File menu, choose Open File, or just press Ctrl + O (the letter). You'll see the standard Open dialog box.
2. Use the folder tree commands to locate the disk and directory containing the file that you want to open.
3. In the Files of Type box, choose the type of file you want to open.

Printing Documents

By far the best way to produce a permanent record of a Netscape-accessed document is to print it. Netscape prints all the fonts and graphics just as you see them on-screen.

If you're printing a document that has frames, you can only print the current frame. Reflecting this, the Print command changes to Print Frame when you're viewing a document that has frames.

Choosing Page Setup Options

The Page Setup command on the File menu enables you to choose a number of print output options, including margins. To use the Page Setup dialog box, open the File menu and choose Page Setup. You'll see the Page Setup dialog box, shown in Figure 8.4.

In the Page Options area, you can make the following choices:

Beveled Lines Click here to print the beveled rules you see on-screen.

Black Text If you have a color printer, click here to suppress color printing of hyperlinks.

Black Lines Click here to print rules as a solid black line.

Last Page First Click here if you need this option to avoid having to hand-collate the printed output.

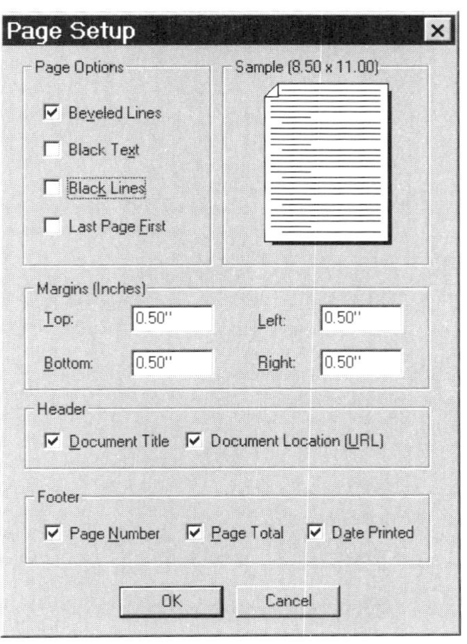

Figure 8.4 Page Setup dialog box

In the Margins area, you can change the margins by typing new measurements in inches.

In the Header area, you can choose to print the document title and the URL. It's a great idea to leave both of these selected—they're on by default—so that you can return to the Web location of a page you've printed.

In the Footer area, you can control page numbers, the printing of a total number of pages with the page numbers, and the date printed.

Previewing Print Output

To see what your document's printed output will look like, you can use the Print Preview command (File menu):

1. From the File menu, choose Print Preview. You see the Print Preview window, shown in Figure 8.5.
2. To see the next page, click Next Page. To return to the previous page, click Previous Page.
3. To view two pages in the same window, click Two Page.
4. To zoom in for a closer look, click Zoom In once or twice. Click Zoom Out once or twice to return to full-page view.
5. To exit Print Preview, click Close. If you would like to print, click Print, and see the next section for printing instructions.

Choosing Print Options and Printing Your Document

Depending on your printer's capabilities, you can choose from a variety of printing options before printing. Options found in most printers include selecting the page range and the number of copies to print. After you choose your options, Netscape prints your document.

To choose print options and print your document:

1. Do one of the following:

   In the Print Preview window, click the Print button
   or
   Click the Print button on the toolbar
   or
   From the File menu, choose Print
   or
   Press Ctrl + P

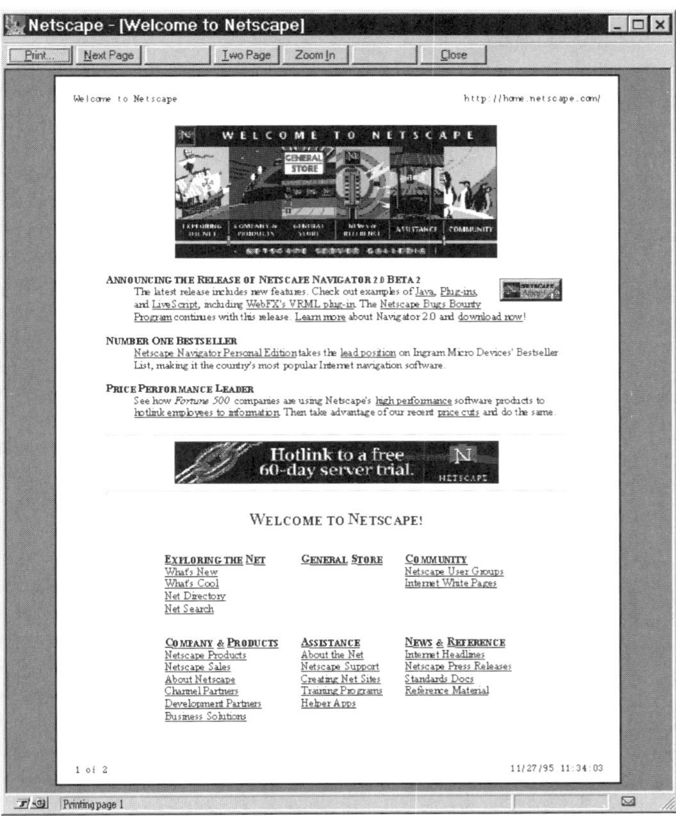

Figure 8.5 Print Preview window

2. You'll see the Print dialog box, shown in Figure 8.6.
3. If you would like to print just some of the pages in the document, select Pages in the Print Range area, and type the beginning page number in the From box and the ending page number in the To box.
4. To make more than one copy, type the number of copies you want to make in the Copies box.
5. Choose OK to initiate printing.

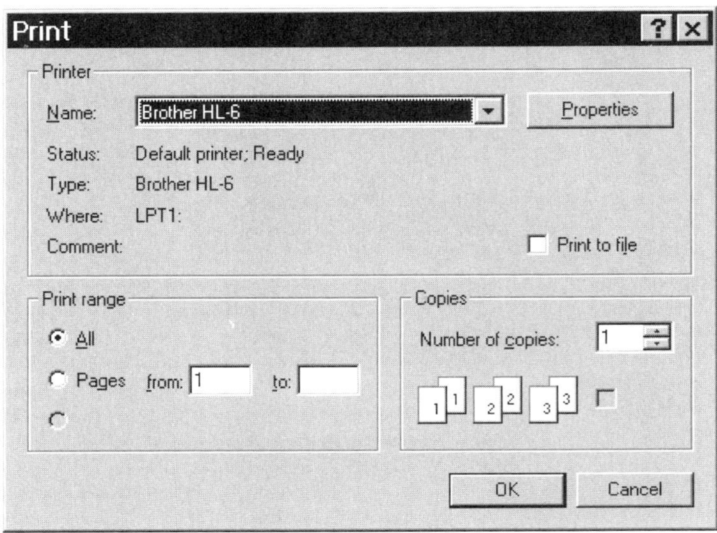

Figure 8.6 Print dialog box

Viewing Document Information

If you'd like to know more about the document you're viewing, open the View menu and choose Document Info. You'll see the Document Info about the document you're currently viewing, as shown in Figure 8.7. You'll find information that may prove helpful in certain situations; for example, you can find out from this window which file name Netscape has used to store the document in the disk cache.

Note that the Document Info page contains a list of all the hyperlinks in a document, including links to graphics. You can click any of these links to access the links and graphics referenced in the document. If you'd like to access and save all the graphics referenced in a document, this is the most convenient way to do so.

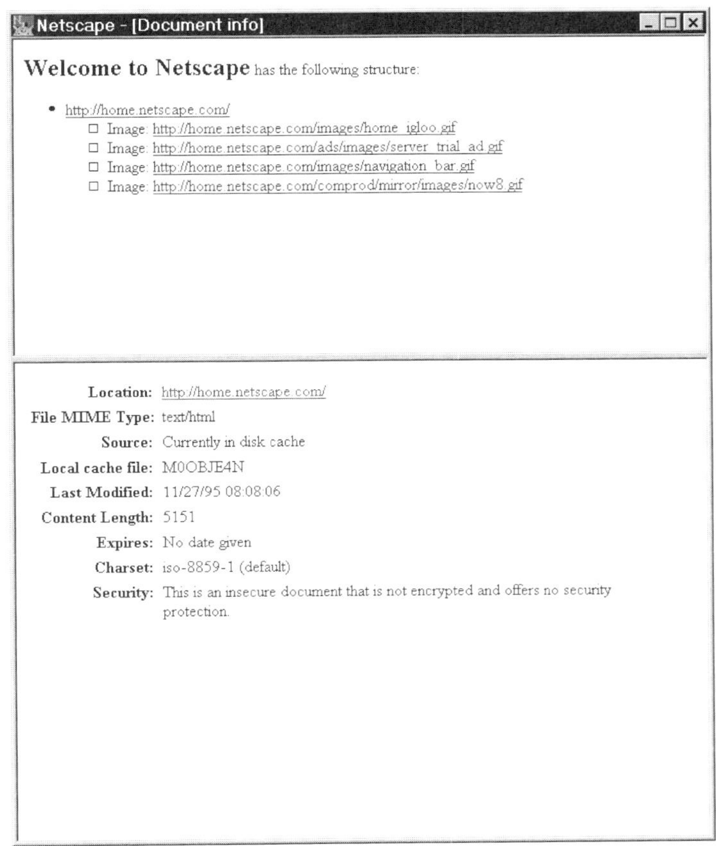

Figure 8.7 Document Info

Viewing the Source HTML

If you're learning HTML, the language used to code Web documents, you'll sooner or later access a particularly cool site and exclaim, "How did they *do* that!" Here's how you can find out. From the View menu, choose Document Source, and you'll see a colorful view of the underlying

HTML code (Figure 8.8). The colors help the eye to separate the code from the text.

From this screen you can select and copy snippets of HTML code verbatim, and paste them into HTML documents with which you're experimenting. Try varying some of the attributes to see what effect the variations have on the result.

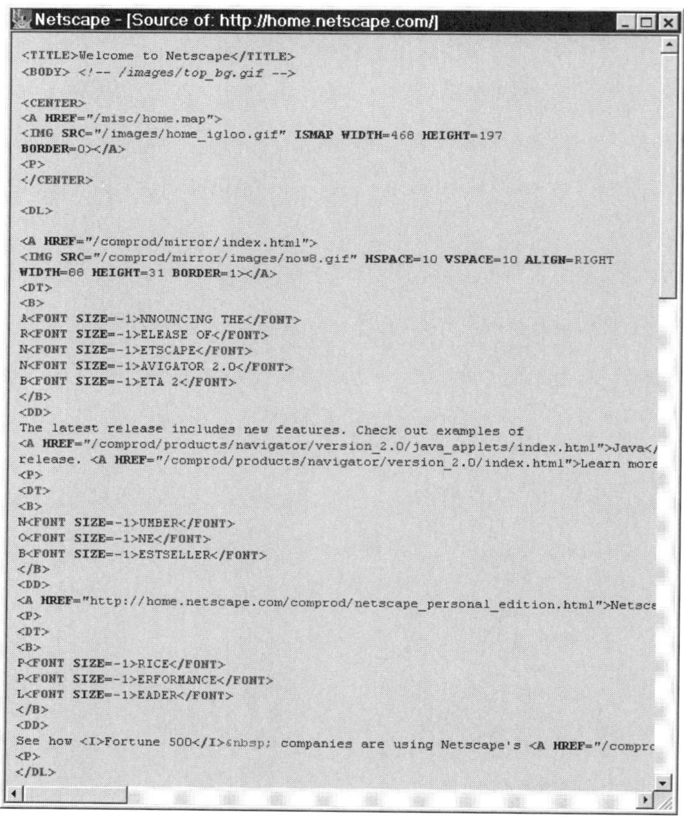


```
<TITLE>Welcome to Netscape</TITLE>
<BODY> <!-- /images/top_bg.gif -->

<CENTER>
<A HREF="/misc/home.map">
<IMG SRC="/images/home_igloo.gif" ISMAP WIDTH=468 HEIGHT=197
BORDER=0></A>
<P>
</CENTER>

<DL>

<A HREF="/comprod/mirror/index.html">
<IMG SRC="/comprod/mirror/images/now8.gif" HSPACE=10 VSPACE=10 ALIGN=RIGHT
WIDTH=88 HEIGHT=31 BORDER=1></A>
<DT>
<B>
A<FONT SIZE=-1>NNOUNCING THE</FONT>
R<FONT SIZE=-1>ELEASE OF</FONT>
N<FONT SIZE=-1>ETSCAPE</FONT>
N<FONT SIZE=-1>AVIGATOR 2.0</FONT>
B<FONT SIZE=-1>ETA 2</FONT>
</B>
<DD>
The latest release includes new features. Check out examples of
<A HREF="/comprod/products/navigator/version_2.0/java_applets/index.html">Java</
release. <A HREF="/comprod/products/navigator/version_2.0/index.html">Learn more
<P>
<DT>
<B>
N<FONT SIZE=-1>UMBER</FONT>
O<FONT SIZE=-1>NE</FONT>
B<FONT SIZE=-1>ESTSELLER</FONT>
</B>
<DD>
<A HREF="http://home.netscape.com/comprod/netscape_personal_edition.html">Netsc
<P>
<DT>
<B>
P<FONT SIZE=-1>RICE</FONT>
P<FONT SIZE=-1>ERFORMANCE</FONT>
L<FONT SIZE=-1>EADER</FONT>
</B>
<DD>
See how <I>Fortune 500</I>  companies are using Netscape's <A HREF="/compro
<P>
</DL>
```

Figure 8.8 Web page displayed using Document Source

From Here

- Customize Netscape Navigator in Chapter 9.
- Master the helper applications and plug-ins in Chapters 10 through 14.

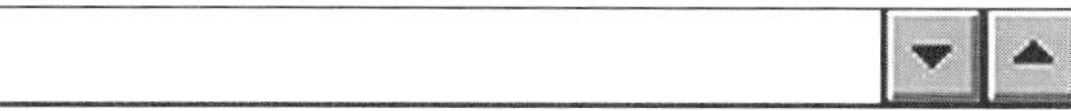

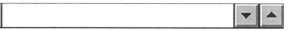

Chapter 9

Customizing and Configuring Netscape Navigator

Netscape Navigator is more fun when it works the way you want. You can choose the fonts you like, and you can also paint the screen with colors and even graphic backgrounds. On the Options menu and the Preferences dialog boxes, you'll find many more options that will make Netscape run your way. In addition, you'll find many essential configuration options.

New since Netscape release 2 is a much-improved method of organizing the Preferences options. There are now four Preferences commands (General Preferences, Mail and News Preferences, Network Preferences, and Security Preferences).

For the Time-Challenged

- Netscape doesn't give you much control over fonts; in the Fonts page of the General Preferences dialog box, you can select the base font and font size for the proportionally spaced font (which applies to most of the text on the screen) and fixed fonts (plain text documents and computer code). For the proportionally spaced font, choose one that you find highly readable.
- You can mess around with colors all you like, but I'll bet you get sick of seeing pink text on a chartreuse background and want the defaults back. Save yourself the trouble.
- In the Options menu, leave all the options on except Show Directory Buttons (which you can access in the Directory menu anyway).
- In the Images page of General Preferences, choose After Loading if you want the text to appear more quickly in downloaded documents.

This chapter discusses all the configuration options available in the Options menu, but you'll find more detailed discussions of some of them elsewhere in this book:

- For an in-depth discussion of cache configuration options, see Chapter 5, "Improving Netscape Navigator's Performance."
- For specific information on installing the helper applications that come with this book, see Appendices B and C.

Using the Options Menu

You'll find Netscape's most frequently chosen options on the Options menu. Some of these options are duplicated within the sea of Preferences dialog box options, but it's easier and quicker to choose them from the Options menu.

I can't figure out how these options work! To use the customization options on the Options menu, you need to understand that they're *toggles*. On a Windows menu, a toggle is an option that you can turn on or off using the same command. When the option is turned on (activated), you see a check mark next to the item's name. When the option is turned off, the check mark disappears. To turn off the Toolbar, for example, open the Options menu and look at the Show Toolbar option—since the Toolbar is visible, this option has a check mark. To turn off the Toolbar, choose this option. Open the menu again—you'll see that the check mark has disappeared. Believe me, this is a *lot* simpler than it sounds and you'll get used to it quickly enough.

Options Accessible on the Options Menu

Here's a quick overview of the customization options you can choose on the Options menu:

- **Show Toolbar** (default: on) Choose this command to hide or display the Toolbar.
- **Show Location** (default: on) Choose this command to hide or display the Location box.
- **Show Directory Buttons** (default: on) Choose this command to hide or display those nice big Directory buttons.
- **Show Java Console** (default: off) Choose this command to display or hide the Java console, which displays the Java code that Netscape is currently executing (if any).
- **Auto Load Images** (default: on) Choose this command to hide the automatic downloading of in-line images (you'll see placeholders instead); choose it again to redisplay the images.
- **Document Encoding** (default: Latin1) Choose this command to select the character set that Netscape uses to display the text onscreen. This option is useful if you're trying to read Web pages written in foreign languages, such as Japanese.

Which options are right for you? I'd recommend that you work with the Toolbar and Location boxes displayed, but you can skip the Directory buttons—they're accessible from the Directory menu.

Saving Your Options Choices

When you quit Netscape, the program automatically saves the choices you've made on the Options menu, and the program uses these options the next time you start it.

Choosing Options in the Preferences Dialog Box

As just mentioned, the most frequently chosen options are available on the Options menu—but there are loads more on the several pages of the General Preferences dialog box. This dialog box has the following tabbed pages:

Appearance In this page, you can choose options for the Toolbar, startup, and link styles.

Fonts In this page, you can choose a character set encoding (for displaying foreign languages), and you can choose fonts for each of these character sets.

Colors In this page, you can choose distinctive colors for links, followed links, text, and backgrounds.

Images In this page, you can choose the method Netscape uses to display the colors in downloaded in-line images, and you can also select options for the timing of image display.

Apps In this page, you can identify the helper applications Netscape uses to deal with Telnet and 3270 sessions. These options are discussed in Appendix C, "Configuring Plug-ins, Support, and Helper Applications."

Helpers	In this page, you choose the helper applications Netscape uses to display multimedia files, such as MPEG movies and RealAudio sounds. These options are discussed in Appendix C, "Configuring Plug-ins, Support, and Helper Applications."
Language	In this page, you choose the languages that Netscape tells a server it can accept. Very few servers are set up to work with this message presently.

The following sections detail the choices you can make in the Appearance, Fonts, Colors, and Images pages. You'll find detailed discussion of the Apps and Helpers pages in Appendix C.

Controlling Netscape's Appearance

You can change Netscape's on-screen appearance by choosing Toolbar options, startup options, and link styles.

To choose appearance options, open the Options menu and choose General Preferences. In the Preferences dialog box, click the Appearance tab. You'll see the Appearance options, shown in Figure 9.1.

Choosing Toolbar Options

Netscape's Toolbar is preset to display *pictures* (the cute little drawing of the house, for example, on the Home button) and *text* (the button's name). If you prefer, you can display only the pictures, or only the text. To choose one of these options, click the appropriate option button in the Toolbars area.

Keep the Toolbar in view—you'll use it frequently. To conserve space on-screen, try the Text option; this hides the pictures, making the Toolbar buttons as compact as the Directory ones. To hide the Toolbar entirely, open the Options menu and deselect Show Toolbar so that this item's check mark disappears.

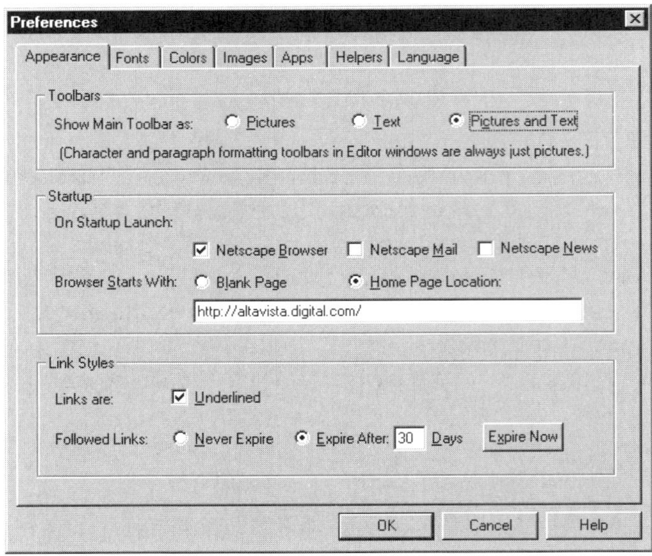

Figure 9.1 Appearance page (General Preferences)

Choosing Startup Options

By default, Netscape starts with a browser page that shows Netscape's home page. You can change the page that Netscape displays when the program starts. If you prefer, the program will start with a mail or news window instead of the browser window.

To change the default start page, type the URL you want to use in the Home Page Location box.

Want a faster startup? Choose Blank Page in the Browser Starts With area. Netscape will start much faster, but you'll see a plain gray screen until you access a Web site somewhere.

To start the program with a mail or news window, choose Netscape Mail or Netscape News in the On Startup Launch area. The default option is Netscape Browser.

You can start more than one window automatically. If you want Netscape to start with three windows—one each for mail, news, and browsing—just click all three options.

Choosing Link Styles

By default, Netscape displays links with a distinctive color and underlining. If you'd like to get rid of the underlining, deselect the Underlined option in the Link Styles area. I don't recommend this, though, because Web authors have gotten very creative in assigning colors to links; you can no longer count on links shown in bright blue. Without the underlining, you might not know what to click.

In this area, you can also control how long Netscape keeps track of the links you've visited. The hyperlinks you've visited appear in a distinctive color on-screen. By default, the program keeps track of these links for 30 days. You have the following options for visited links:

- If you would like Netscape to keep track of visited links forever, click Never Expire.
- To change the number of days that Netscape keeps track of links, type the number of days next to Expire After.
- To cause all your links to expire immediately, click the Expire Now button.

If you're security-conscious, bear in mind that visited links provide another way that a snooper can tell where you've browsed. Clicking Expire Now erases your trail of visited links.

Choosing Fonts

Netscape is designed to work with a number of standardized character set encodings. These encodings enable Netscape to display foreign languages. For each chararacter set, you can choose the following fonts:

- **Proportionally Spaced Base Font** This is the font used for almost all of the text you'll see on-screen. In a proportionally spaced font, each character is given a width proportional to its size ("m" gets

more space than "l"). The default proportionally spaced font is Times Roman.

- **Fixed (Monospace) Base Font** This is the font used for plain-text documents (such as README files in FTP file archives) and text marked with the <CODE> tag in HTML. (The <CODE> tag is used to give examples of computer programming code.) In a monospace font, each character gets the same amount of space, producing the effect of a typewriter. The default monospace font is Courier.

Because version 3 of Netscape can read the new <FONT FACE> tag, choosing base fonts is unnecessary—let Web authors do this for you. If the Web document you're downloading includes font choices, these will override your base font choice. However, the Web author's font choice won't appear unless the font is installed in your computer.

To change the base fonts if you wish:

1. From the Options menu, choose General Preferences. You'll see the Preferences dialog box, with the Appearance page displayed.
2. Click the Fonts tab. You'll see the Fonts page, shown in Figure 9.2.
3. In the For the Encoding box, the current setting is Latin1, which is the correct choice for English or European languages. If you would like to choose fonts for another character set, choose the character set from the list box.
4. Next to the proportional font setting, click the Choose Font button. You'll see the Choose Base Font dialog box, shown in Figure 9.3
5. Beneath the Font box, scroll until you see the font you want, and then click it. The highlighted font appears in the Sample box.
6. In the Size box, use the scroll bar to choose the size you want, or type a font size (in points) in the box.
7. Click OK to choose your proportionally spaced font.
8. Click OK to close the Preferences dialog box.

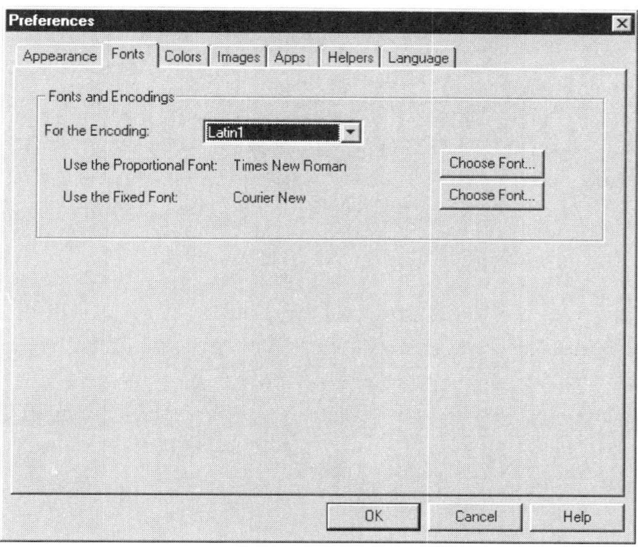

Figure 9.2 Fonts page (General Preferences)

Choosing Colors

Netscape provides several options for choosing colors:

Links	Hyperlinks you haven't visited appear in this color. By default, they're blue.
Followed (Visited) Links	Hyperlinks you've already visited. By default, they appear in lavender.
Text	All other document text. By default, it's in black.
Background	The default background is battleship gray. You can choose colors or, to make things even more visually confusing, a background graphic.

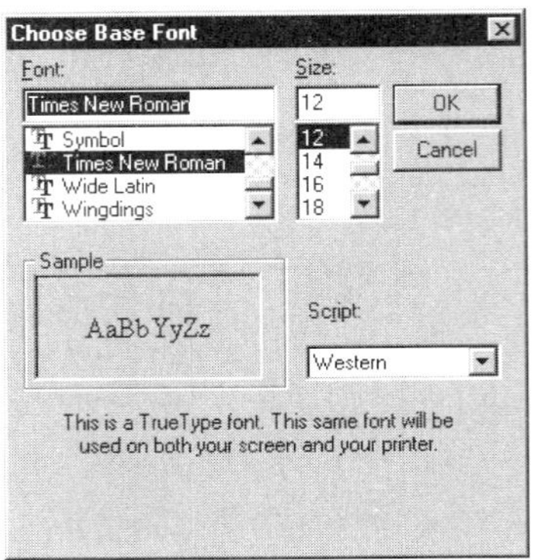

Figure 9.3 Choose Base Font dialog box

New to this version of Netscape is the ability to override Web authors' background and color choices—choices that were made possible by Netscape's own innovations (the Netscape extensions to HTML). Unfortunately, some Web authors choose colors and backgrounds that make their pages nearly illegible. By default, Netscape shows you the color and background choices made by the author of the page you're viewing. If you're trying to read a page with overly wild colors, you can hide them by clicking the Always Use My Colors box.

To change the default colors:

1. From the Options menu, choose General Preferences.
2. Click the Colors tab in the Preferences dialog box. You'll see the Colors preferences, shown in Figure 9.4
3. To choose a color for Links, click the top Choose Color button. You'll see the Choose Color dialog box (Figure 9.5).
4. Click the color you want, or click Define Custom Colors to see the color model (right side of Figure 9.5). Move the pointer until you've defined the color you want, and click Add to Custom Colors. Then click the color you just created.
5. Click OK to confirm your color choice.

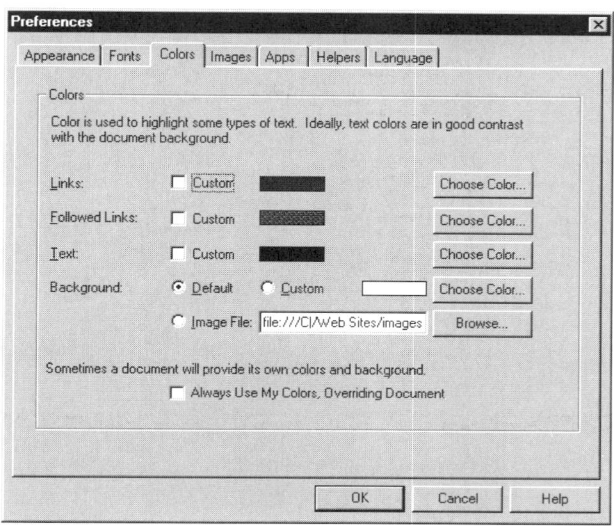

Figure 9.4 Colors page (General Preferences)

6. Repeat steps 3 through 5 for Followed Links and Text, clicking the appropriate Choose Color box.
7. To set the background, click Custom and choose a color, or click Image File and use the Browse button to select a JPEG or GIF graphic.
8. Click Always Use My Colors if you really want Netscape to override incoming documents' color choices. I'd suggest leaving this option off.
9. Click OK to confirm your choices.

For a super collection of background patterns, check out

http://home.netscape.com/home/bg/index.html

You can download any of the patterns by right-clicking the pattern you want and then choosing Save this Image As.

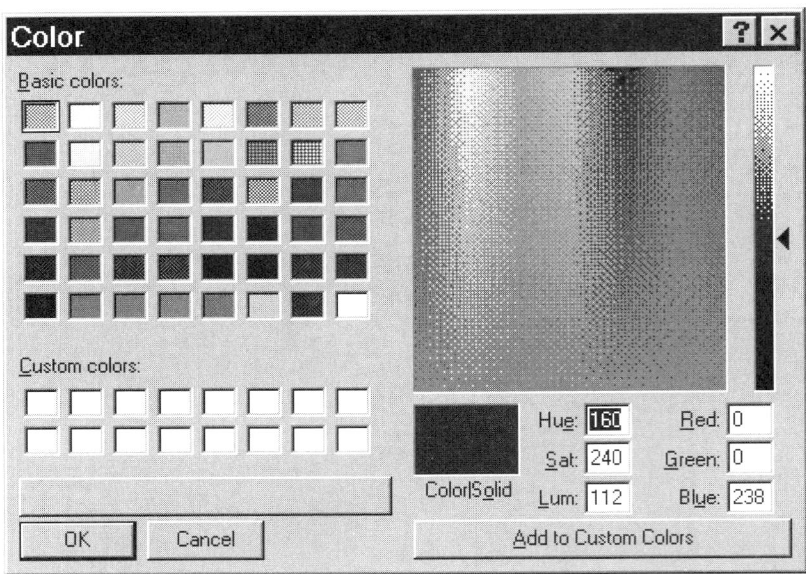

Figure 9.5 Choose Color dialog box

I'm sick of this! I want the defaults back! No problemo. Just open the Colors preferences again, deselect all the Custom check boxes, and click Default in the Background area. Click OK to confirm, and you're back to boring-old-gray background with boring-old-black text. Want your colors back again? Sheesh, make up your mind! Well, you can get them; the Preferences dialog box retains your color choices. Open the Colors preferences again, select the Custom boxes, and restore your background by clicking Image File.

Controlling Image Options

Netscape provides a variety of options for downloading images. You can use the Options menu to specify whether Netscape downloads images automatically. In the Preferences dialog box, you can choose how Netscape interprets image colors, and you can also select the timing of image display. To display the image options, open the Options menu, choose General Preferences, and click the Images tab. You'll see the Images page, shown in Figure 9.6.

Choosing Color Display Options

By default, Netscape automatically determines the most appropriate method of color display for your color monitor. If you would like to change the image display options, choose one of the following:

Dithered In a dithered image, Netscape simulates a color that your monitor can't actually display. It does this by grouping tiny dots of colors that are within your monitor's capabilities, so that this area

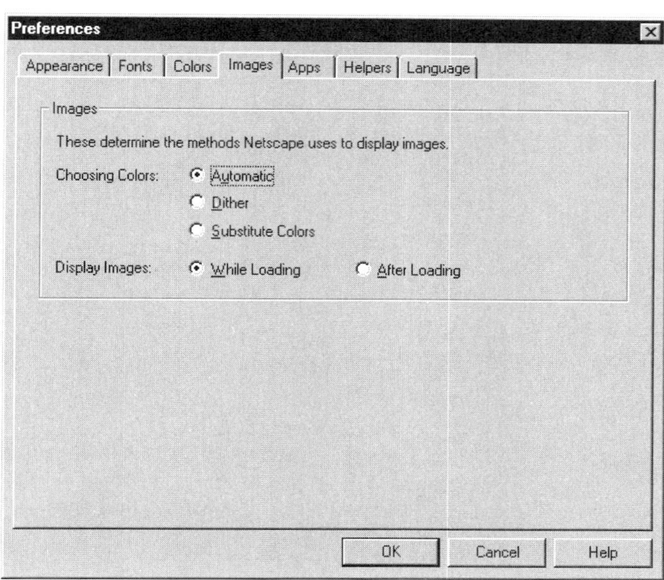

Figure 9.6 Images page (General Preferences)

	appears to have the correct color. Dithered images are closer to the original's true colors, but they take much longer to download.
Substitute Colors	Choose this option if you would like Netscape to use your monitor's closest color in place of the image's true color. If you choose this option, some colors may not look quite right but images will download faster.

Choosing Languages

Netscape Communications is one of America's new global-savvy companies, as you'll discover when you click the Language tab of the General Preferences dialog box (Figure 9.7). With this page, you can choose your *language*

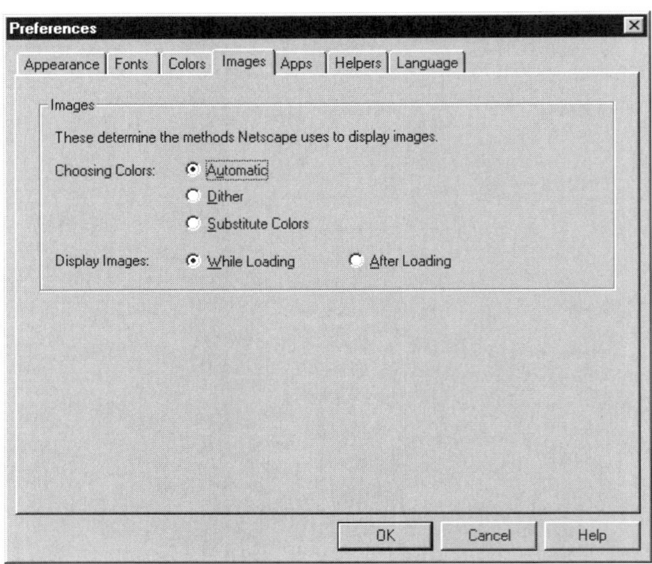

Figure 9.7 Language page (General Preferences)

priority. A language priority is a code that Netscape sends with your page request. This code tells the server which language you'd prefer, if alternative versions of a document are available.

Not very many servers take advantage of this capability (yet), but it's worth choosing your language preference in case you run into one that does. To specify your preference, select your top language priority in the Language/Region area, and click the right arrow to add your language to the Accept list. To change the prioritization of the languages in the Accept List, select a language and click the down arrow button to lower the language's priority.

From Here

- For an in-depth discussion of cache configuration options, see Chapter 5, "Improving Netscape Navigator's Performance."
- Choosing mail preferences? See Chapter 17.
- For information on choosing news (Usenet) preferences, see Chapter 22.
- For specific information on installing the helper applications that come with this book, see Appendices B and C.

Part III

Grooving on Multimedia

Chapter 10

Understanding Helper Apps and Plug-ins

Netscape can't handle all the types of data out there on the Web—at least, not without help. Sure, Netscape can read HTML, and the program can handle GIF and JPEG graphics natively. (By *natively*, I mean on its own, without any outside help.) It can also decode Java instructions (see Chapter 13 for more information about Java). But there's much more out there—so much, in fact, that Netscape couldn't possibly include enough program code to handle everything the Web is capable of slinging at a browser. Linked to Web pages are sounds, movies, animations, live radio broadcasts, live TV broadcasts, spreadsheets, virtual reality worlds, and even a model railroad (I am not making this up—check out http://rr-vs.informatik.uni-ulm.de/rr/).

For the Time-Challenged

- ♦ Netscape needs help to deal with the huge variety of data types available on the Web. This help is needed to play sounds, videos, animations, and other multimedia resources, as well as to cope with spreadsheets, virtual reality worlds, and other neat things that are popping up on Web pages.
- ♦ To deal with these data types, Netscape has always been able to work with helper applications. Netscape version 3 can work with plug-in programs.
- ♦ When Netscape is properly configured, a helper application starts after Netscape has downloaded some data that it can't deal with directly, such as a sound. The helper application runs in its own window.
- ♦ Plug-in programs work differently. They actually extend Netscape's capabilities so that the program can display multimedia data within Netscape's window.
- ♦ Streaming audio and video technologies enable you to start listening or watching without waiting for the whole file to download. There's some sacrifice of quality, though.

Here's something fun: A collection of links to pages that connect bizarre devices to the Web, including clocks, coffee machines, pets (!), robots, spy cameras, and more. Check out

http://www.yahoo.com/Computers_and_Internet/Internet/Interesting_Devices_Connected_to_the_Net/

In order to deal with all the data that's accessible on the Web, Netscape needs two kinds of help:

- **Helper Applications** These are programs that Netscape starts when it encounters a type of data that it can't handle directly. All versions of Netscape can work with helper applications. You'll find lots of them on the disc included with this book. Appendix C shows you how to configure these helper applications.
- **Plug-ins** These are programs that modify Netscape so that it can deal directly with data of a certain type. For example, the Live3D

plug-in enables Netscape to directly display virtual worlds—and you can navigate inside of them in three dimensions!

This chapter introduces helper applications and plug-ins. The rest of the chapters in Part III show you how to use these programs after they're installed.

Please remember that you must install helper apps before you can do some of the things described in this chapter and the remaining chapters of Part III. For more information on installing the helper apps and plug-ins included with this book, see Appendices B and C.

Absolutely the coolest thing about Netscape version 3 is the great suite of plug-ins that are included with the program. These include LiveAudio (sounds), LiveVideo (Windows movies), QuickTime (Apple movies), and Live3D (VRML virtual reality worlds). Distributed with Netscape, these plug-ins are installed and configured automatically—which means, happily, that you start using multimedia resources immediately without worrying about huge configuration hassles, which you had to do in previous versions. Thanks to these plug-ins, this chapter isn't as important as it used to be, but you'll still need to install and configure a few helper applications to deal with data types that the Netscape plug-ins don't recognize.

Help Me, Helper Apps

In brief, a helper app is a program that's designed to start automatically when data of a certain type is encountered.

For example, suppose you click on the name of a file that was compressed by PKZip, a popular compression utility. Your browser looks for PKZip—and if the program is present on your disk, the browser starts PKZip and the file downloads and decompresses automatically.

When you've configured your browser to work with helper applications and they work correctly, it's cool. Here's an example. Suppose you click on a hyperlink for an MPEG video. If everything's working smoothly on your system, your browser starts an MPEG helper application, downloads the video, and you see it on-screen (Figure 10.1).

What Types of Helper Apps Are Available?

To deal with all the types of data you'll encounter on the Web, you'll need to equip your system with the following helper apps:

- **Sound Players** Sounds are stored in a variety of file formats. When you click a hyperlink that accesses a sound, Netscape determines the format in which the sound file is stored and starts the appropriate sound player. The LiveAudio plug-in that comes with Netscape can play most of the sounds you'll encounter on the Web, but you'll still need a helper application for stereo MPEG sounds. **Please note**: In order to play sounds on your Windows system, you'll need a sound card and speakers.
- **Video Players** Videos, animations, and movies are stored in several formats. Netscape's LiveVideo plug-in can handle Windows (AVI) movies, but you'll still need a helper application for MPEG and QuickTime movies.
- **File Decompression Software** Many of the files you can obtain with Netscape have been compressed. This cuts down on disk space

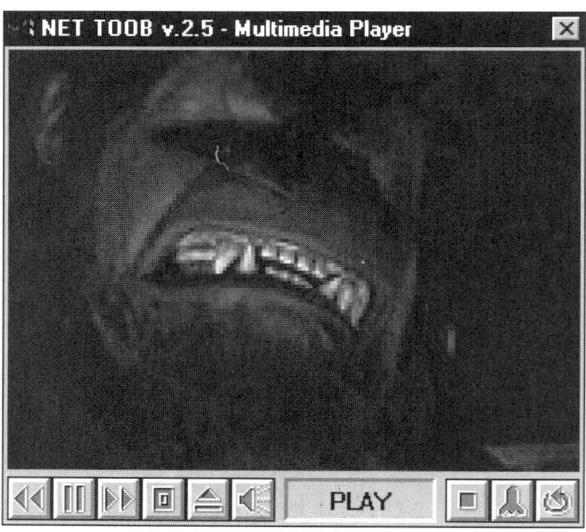

Figure 10.1 MPEG video played by helper application (NET TOOB)

usage as well as bandwidth usage when the files are transferred. After you configure Netscape to use WinZip, the file decompression software included with this book, Netscape will start WinZip automatically after you download a compressed file.

- **File Viewers** Netscape displays HTML documents beautifully, but many authors find that HTML does not meet their formatting needs. For this reason, they sometimes save their documents in formats that require special reading software. In increasing use among Web authors is Adobe Acrobat. To display Acrobat documents, you need the Adobe Acrobat helper application.
- **VRML Viewers** VRML is short for Virtual Reality Modeling Language. If you've got a VRML viewer, you can access and explore three-dimensional worlds on the Web. (If you've ever played the popular game Doom, you've explored a three-dimensional world.) You can view VRML worlds with the Live3D plug-in included with Netscape.
- **Telnet Viewer** To access Telnet sessions, you need special software that can communicate with large mainframe computers. Included with this book is the National Center for Supercomputing Application's (NCSA) Telnet for Windows.

Where do I get the helper applications I need? You've already got it. The CD-ROM disc packaged with this book contains all the helper software you need.

How Does a Helper Application Work?

Here's an illustration. Suppose you click a link to a sound. When Netscape accesses the sound, the program realizes that it doesn't have the capability of dealing with this data. But it downloads the data anyway. Then it looks for, and launches, the appropriate helper application. The helper application appears in a new, separate window and plays the sound.

Hey—How Did Netscape Know Which Program to Launch?

Netscape may be a great program, but it's not all-knowing. Like other browsers, Netscape relies on *MIME extensions* to determine which kind of data the program is accessing.

What's a MIME extension? MIME is short for Multipurpose Internet Mail Extension. Originally, MIME was a standard for enabling Internet e-mail users to exchange graphics, sound, and video files. Since its creation more than a dozen years ago, MIME has been adapted for use with the Web. The valuable thing about MIME is that it provides a standardized way of associating *file extensions* with certain types of data.

If you've used MS-DOS, you're familiar with file extensions, those three-letter additions to file names that come after the period. When Netscape encounters a sound (such as "beep.au"), the program looks at the extension. It then consults a table and finds out which program—if any—is associated with the ".au" MIME type.

What the heck does "*.mpg" mean? You're looking at a DOS or UNIX wild card. It means, basically, "any file with the extension .mpg." The computer nerd types on the Web love to write MIME types this way; don't let it put you off.

To get your helper applications to work, you must associate each of the MIME types with the specific helper app you've installed. Appendix B tells you how to do this. Your helper apps won't work until you've configured them by following these instructions!

What's on the CD-ROM Disc?

The CD-ROM disc packaged with this book contains helper applications that round out Netscape's capabilities, enabling you to deal with just about any type of data you'll encounter on the Web. For installation instructions, open the file Welcome.htm, which you'll find on the CD-ROM disc.

Here's a list of the programs for Windows 3.x systems (they'll also run on Windows 95 systems):

- **Adobe Acrobat Reader for Windows 3.x (Version 2.1)** Using this program, you can display and print documents with rich formatting and graphics. It's copyrighted but freely distributable.
- **Autodesk Animation Player for Windows 1.00** This program enables you to play movies recorded in the Autodesk (*.fli) format. There aren't too many of these, but if you run into one, you've got

the player you need. The program is freeware (copyrighted but freely distributed without charge).

- **MidiGate 5.C.2** This program enables Netscape to play MIDI files. In brief, MIDI files are text files containing coded instructions to a MIDI playback device. Most sound cards are able to play MIDI instructions, although the sound isn't very impressive unless you have a pricey wave-table synthesis sound card. (A wave-table synthesis sound card contains recordings of actual musical instruments, which are used to synthesize the musical sounds from MIDI files.) A shareware program, MidiGate costs only $10. The program may be used free of charge for an evaluation period of 30 days; subsequently, you'll need to send the registration fee to PRS Corporation, 502 Kinwick Centre, 32 Hollywood Road, Hong Kong. *Tip:* Check out the Classical MIDI Archive, which I'll discuss in the next chapter. *Note:* Because MidiGate is a Visual Basic application, you'll need the file VBRUN300.dll to be installed on your computer system.

- **NCSA Telnet for Windows** This program enables you to access the resources available at Telnet sites, which are widely accessible through the Web and through Gopher.

- **NET TOOB** Unlike MPEG Play and most other movie players, this player is capable of dealing with almost all the video formats you encounter on the Web: MPEG, QuickTime, and AVI (Windows). It's a shareware program that will run only for two weeks after you first install it. The registration fee is $14.95. For more information on NET TOOB, see http://www.duplex.com/. To pay the registration fee, call (508) 741-5500 between 9 and 5 Eastern Standard Time. Alternatively, you can send the registration fee by check or credit by writing to Duplexx Software, 35 Congress St., Salem, MA 01970.

- **QuickTime for Windows 2.03** This program, included courtesy of Apple Computer, plays videos and animations created in Apple's QuickTime format. It's freeware (copyrighted but distributed without charge).

- **RealAudio 1.0** This helper application plays RealAudio sounds. Although the quality is similar to a rather tinny AM radio, RealAudio sounds start playing very soon after you access them. For voice recordings, the convenience makes up for the poor sound. The RealAudio 1.0 player is designed for users of 14.4 Kbps dialup lines.

- **WHAM (Waveform Hold and Modify) Version 1.33** This versatile sound player can handle Soundblaster (*.voc), Silicon Graphics/Apple (*.aiff), and Sun/NeXT (*.au) sounds and provides many features for modifying the sounds you download. It's shareware. If you find WHAM useful, please send a check of $25–30 to Andrew Bulhak, 21 The Crescent, Ferntree Gully, VIC 3156, Australia.

- **XingSound Freely Redistributable Audio Player** This sound player enables you to listen to sounds recorded in the MPEG audio format. The version of XingSound included with this book (and widely available on the Web) is a monoaural program that employs the Windows audio driver, producing acceptable (but not spectacular) results. For high-quality stereo playback, you can purchase the retail version of XingSound from Xing Technology Corporation, 1540 West Branch Street, Arroyo Grande, CA 93420 (info@xingtech.com).

Please support the shareware concept by registering the shareware helper apps that you've found useful. Shareware authors are dependent on your willingness to pay registration fees. I think you'll agree it's a great concept: You get excellent software at a very reasonable price, since shareware authors don't have to pay marketing and advertising fees. But it all depends on you.

When Helper Applications Don't Help

Lots of people have trouble with helper applications. Here are two things that can go wrong:

- **Installation** Before you can run the helper program, you must obtain it and install it on your hard drive. This is often a major pain because these programs aren't included with most browsers. You have to find them and download them yourself.

- **Configuration** You have to configure your browser to work with helper applications. This is done by associating a *data type* (a specific kind of data, such as a Windows sound) with the program that's designed to deal with it. For example, you can associate .zip (compressed) files with WinZip, the Windows version of the popular PKZIP compression utility.

Installing and configuring helper applications takes time and a little bit of computer smarts. I'll bet that at least half of the people browsing the Web haven't configured their browsers to work with the most common data types, such as videos, animations, and sounds. And as a result, their Web isn't very lively. Don't let this happen to you.

Even if you can get helper applications running correctly, there are two additional reasons why they're not very satisfactory. First, helper applications run in their own window. Although this isn't a serious problem, it takes your attention away from the Web page you were viewing, which remains static. Wouldn't it be cool to see the action and hear the sounds without having to leave the page you're viewing? That's why Netscape features plug-ins, which are described in the next section.

It says "Unknown File Type!" As the alert box (Figure 10.2) explains, you've started downloading a file, but Netscape doesn't know how to deal with this type of data. Apparently, you haven't configured the program to work with the appropriate helper application. If you've already installed the helper apps as described in Appendix B, you still need to configure Netscape to use them, so click Pick App and use the Open dialog box to locate the plug-in. That takes care of the configuration (for this data type only).

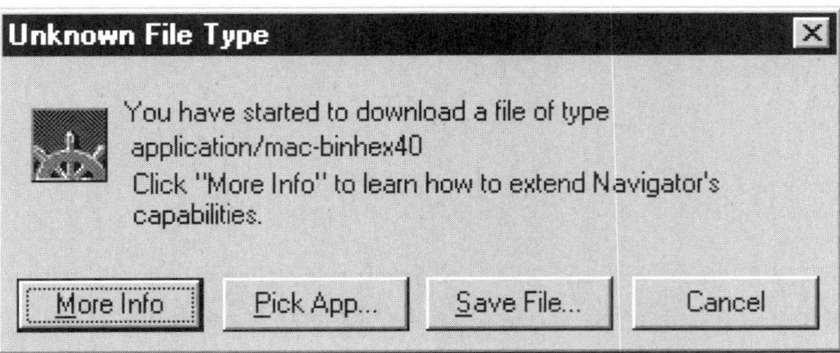

Figure 10.2 Unknown File Type alert box

An Overview of the Installation and Configuration Process

Appendices B and C cover installation and configuration in detail, but here's a quick overview.

1. Create a directory within Netscape's directory. Call this directory HELPERS.
2. If the file is a *self-extracting archive* (*.EXE) file, double-click the file. This may start an installation program; if so, tell the program to install the file in the HELPERS directory. It may also just decompress the files in an MS-DOS window and then stop. If so, use File Manager or Windows Explorer to look for a SETUP or INSTALL program, and run this.
3. After installing the helper application in the HELPERS directory, open Netscape and display the Helpers page of General Preferences.
4. Locate the data type that the helper application is supposed to deal with, and link this data type to the helper application you just installed. For specific instructions, see Appendix C.

This process may sound a bit complicated, but you can do it. Happily, you need to configure your helper apps only once, and it's done.

What happens to sounds, movies, and other downloaded data after you play them with helper applications? They stay in the temporary directory, the one that's listed in the Temporary Directory area of the General Preference dialog box's Apps page. If you would like to save the multimedia resource or hear it again, you can locate the file in this directory. That's nice if you really want to play it again, but in time this directory may become cluttered with unwanted sounds and movies, which can consume quite a bit of disk space. Housecleaning is in order: After using Netscape for a while, open this directory and get rid of the multimedia resources that you don't want to keep. As you'll see later in this chapter, plug-ins deal with multimedia files differently; they go to the cache, which has built-in upper limits on how much of your hard disk it can consume.

Plug in to This!

Netscape Navigator's program architecture enables you to install *plug-ins.* A plug-in is a program that, after installation, extends Netscape's capabilities. What's really cool about plug-ins is that, unlike helper apps, there's no separate program to fuss with—the plug-in becomes part of Netscape, seamlessly extending its capabilities.

Compared to a helper application, a plug-in program is a pleasure to use. To be sure, you still have to obtain and install the plug-in, but after that it's a piece of cake. There's no configuration hassle, and the plug-in operates automatically. Best of all, the action takes place right on the Web page you're viewing, not in a secondary window such as the ones that helper applications use. In Figure 10.3, you see the very impressive results you'll

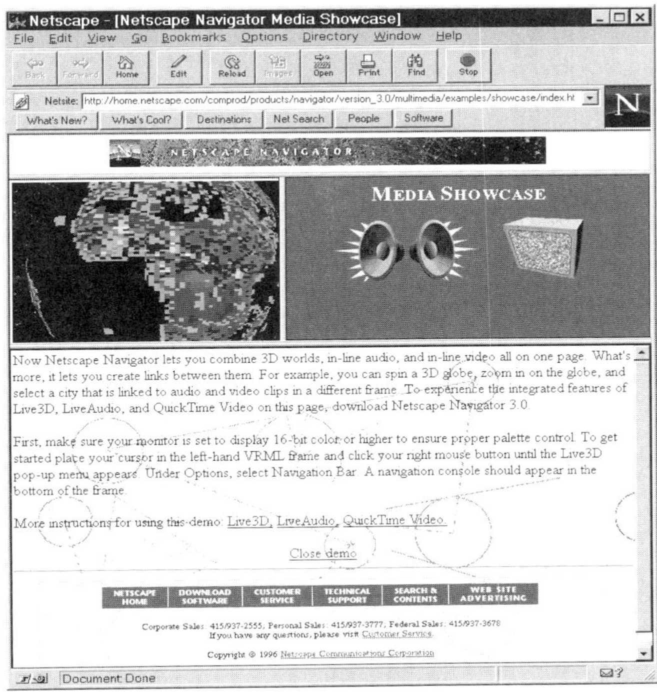

Figure 10.3 Data display within Netscape's window via plug-in (Live3D)

get after installing a virtual reality plug-in. Such a program enables Netscape to display three-dimensional spaces, which you can explore using the special controls that the program adds to Netscape.

Netscape 3 comes wth an impressive suite of plug-ins ready to go. Here's what's included in the standard distribution of the program:

- **LiveAudio** Plays *.au, *.aiff, and *.wav sounds.
- **LiveVideo** Plays Windows (*.avi) movies in-line.
- **QuickTime** Plays Apple QuickTime (*.mov) movies in-line.

An expanded version of the program includes the following, in addition to LiveAudio and LiveVideo:

- **Live3D** Netscape's VRML plug-in.
- **CoolTalk** The plug-in for Internet telephony.

Getting Huge Quantities of Additional Plug-ins

Dozens of plug-ins are available that do lots of additional things, and you can download many of them for use during a free evaluation period (or just for free).

The best place to look for plug-ins is Netscape's plug-ins page, currently accessed by clicking the Software button and following the links for downloadable components. Another excellent place to look is Stroud's Consummate Winsock Apps List, which has pages for Windows 95 and Windows 3.1 plug-ins. There are several places where you can find Stroud's nifty page; try http://www.hkstar.com/cwsapps/.

Here's a list of some of the more interesting plug-ins currently available for downloading (note that these versions were designed for Netscape 2.0, and may not yet be available for version 3.0):

- **FutureSplash** This plug-in enables Netscape to display vector-based animations, which require a lot less downloading time than graphics-based animations. Since this is technologically superior to the animations you're viewing right now, it may catch on!

- **Cool Fusion** With this plug-in, you can view streaming Windows (AVI) movies, even if they weren't prepared with this in mind, and the videos appear in-line within the document.
- **Crescendo** Although LiveAudio can play MIDI sounds, this plug-in enables streaming MIDI delivery, so that Web pages can have active background music.
- **PointCast Network** PointCast is a free broadcasting service that makes news, weather, and sports scores available on-screen. This plug-in enables Netscape users to receive PointCast broadcasts.
- **Microsoft PowerPoint Animation Player & Publisher** This plug-in enables PowerPoint users to publish PowerPoint presentations on the Web.
- **Quick View Plus** This versatile plug-in enables you to view just about any file, including spreadsheet, word processing, database, graphics, presentation, and compressed data, within Netscape's window. More than 200 file formats are supported.

Installing Plug-ins

Plug-ins are easy to install. Generally, you download them to a temporary directory on your hard disk. With File Manager (Windows 3.1) or Windows Explorer (Windows 95), display and double-click the downloaded file's icon. This will start an installation program that automatically installs the plug-in in the correct directory (the PLUGINS directory in Netscape's folder) and configures Netscape to use it. When you start Netscape, the program examines this directory and loads all the plug-ins it finds there. Compared to helper applications, what could be simpler?

I configured Netscape to use my helper app, but this plug-in takes over! Yes, it does, and it's supposed to. Where a plug-in and a helper application are both installed for the same data type, the plug-in takes precedence. Generally, you'll want to use the plug-in instead of a helper app, because plug-ins offer superior technology (for example, many plug-ins

show multimedia data in the same window as the Web document you're viewing).

Using Plug-ins

Plug-ins are also very easy to use. When you click a link to a multimedia resource that a plug-in recognizes, Netscape downloads the file and starts the plug-in.

This is taking too long! There are those who feel that Netscape's plug-in technology is pushing the technological envelope too far, especially for people who are using slow 14.4 Kbps modem lines. Downloading a huge VRML world that has lots of linked sounds and graphics can be an exercise in frustration, unless you really like sitting around for 10 minutes, anxiously watching the status line for the long-awaited "Document Done" message. If you find the wait too frustrating, think twice before accessing pages that are rich in multimedia resources (or if you do, click Stop).

What happens to the multimedia files that Netscape downloads for plug-ins to play? Unlike the files destined for use by helper applications, they go to the disk cache. (For more information on Netscape's caches, see Chapter 5.) The good thing about this is that you won't have to worry about deleting unwanted multimedia files from your temporary directory. On the other hand, it's harder to locate and save multimedia files that you'd like to keep on your local system.

If you've just run a plug-in and really want to keep the multimedia resource you've just seen, open the Cache directory and sort the files by date (in Windows 95, you do this by opening the View menu and choosing Arrange Icons by Date). The resource you've just downloaded should be at the top of the list. Copy this file to another directory and rename it so you can tell what's in it.

Getting into the Stream of Things

The latest wrinkle in Web multimedia is *streaming* data. With streaming audio and video, the sound or movie arrives as a data stream, which the plug-in starts playing immediately. For example, when you click a RealAudio sound, the player kicks in and starts playing the sound almost immediately. The wonderful thing about streaming data is simply this: You don't have to wait for the whole darned file to download before things start happening. (That's probably the biggest drawback of helper applications.)

What's sacrificed with streaming audio and video? Quality, mainly. With RealAudio version 2, the sound can approach the quality of an FM radio station, as long as the Internet isn't too busy. In other words, if you're accessing a RealAudio sound at about 3 AM, you'll probably get good results. At peak usage times, the signal may fade in and out, as if you were trying to listen to a car radio at the fringes of the reception area.

Despite the reduction in quality, you'll probably like streaming audio and video—it's neat to have the multimedia start right away. I'll admit that I like streaming audio (especially for voice) more than streaming video, which—at best—gives you herky-jerky motion in a postage-stamp-sized window. You'll need a very fast Internet connection to make streaming video look good.

From Here

- Have you installed and configured your helper apps yet? If not, please go directly to Appendix C. Do not collect $200, and most of all, don't go to the next chapter—the stuff that's described there won't work until you've installed the helper apps.
- You did install the helper apps? OK. Check out Chapter 11 for the lowdown on sounds, movies, and animations.
- In Chapter 12, you'll find a thorough discussion of Adobe Acrobat, including the use of the new Amber reader.
- Explore three-dimensional virtual worlds! Check out Chapter 14.

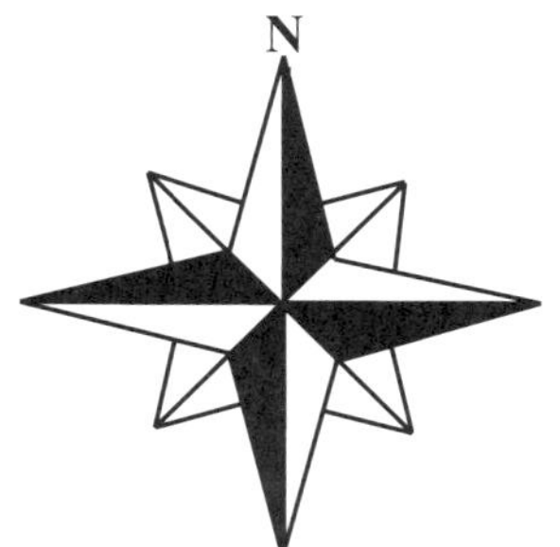

Chapter 11

Playing Sounds and Watching Movies

It's hypermedia time! Assuming you've installed and configured the helper applications and plug-ins you want to use (please see Appendix C), you can click links to sounds, movies, and animations—and things start to happen. In this chapter, you'll learn how to work with the many types of sounds, videos, and animations you'll encounter on the Web.

This chapter assumes that you've installed the helper applications included on this book's CD-ROM disc and configured Netscape to start them automatically. For information on installing these programs, see Appendix B.

For the Time-Challenged

- After Netscape downloads a sound, you'll see the sound player. Look for a VCR-type Play button to initiate the sound, unless it starts playing automatically. You can use the VCR-type controls to pause, stop, "rewind," or "fast-forward" the sound. When you're finished listening to the sound, exit the sound player.
- After Netscape downloads a movie, you'll see the movie player. Look for a VCR-type Play button to start viewing the movie. When you're finished watching the movie, exit the movie player.

Downloading Sounds

When you click a sound link, Netscape starts downloading the sound to the current temporary directory. This directory is the one listed in the Temporary Directory area of the Apps page (General Preferences). After downloading is complete, Netscape starts the appropriate plug-in or helper app (assuming these have been installed and configured).

Don't forget, if you see the Unknown File Type alert box after Netscape downloads a sound (see Figure 10.2, in the previous chapter), this means that you haven't yet configured Netscape to use the correct helper application. For information on configuring helper apps, see Appendix C.

Listening to Sounds

To listen to sounds on your Microsoft Windows system, you must equip your computer with a sound card and speakers. The applications discussed in this section won't play through your computer's tinny little standard speaker.

After you configure Netscape to work with helper apps as described in Appendix C, the program automatically detects the type of sound file you are downloading and starts the appropriate player.

Understanding Sound File Formats

Here's a list of the sound file formats that you're most likely to encounter on the Web; each is followed by the MIME type that's associated with the sound, the name of the program that Netscape launches when you access a file of this type, and a brief description of what to expect in terms of sound quality. Note that Netscape launches these programs only if you've configured Netscape according to the instructions in Appendix C.

- **Silicon Graphics/Apple sound (audio/x-aiff)** These sound files have the extension *.aif, *.aiff, or *aifc. When you access one of these sounds, Netscape starts LiveAudio. You don't often encounter these sounds.
- **Sun/NeXT sound (audio/basic)** This is a Sun/NeXT (*.au or *.snd) sound. When you access one of these sounds, Netscape starts the LiveAudio plug-in. *.au sounds are fairly compact and generally of low quality; they're often used, though, to provide a small-size "sampler" of a much bigger MPEG sound file.
- **WAV sound (audio/x-wav)** This is a standard Microsoft Windows sound. When you access a WAV sound, Netscape starts the LiveAudio plug-in. The sound quality depends on how the recording was done—there are a number of options, ranging from low-quality monoaural to high-quality stereo—but it's probably going to be very good.
- **MPEG sound (audio/x-mpeg)** This may prove to be of very high quality—at best, near-CD quality in stereo. When you click an MPEG sound, Netscape starts Xingplay (Windows 3.x systems) or the Media Player (Windows 95 systems).
- **MIDI sound (audio/midi)** MIDI sound files are compact—they consist only of ASCII text. When you click a MIDI sound, Netscape starts the remarkable MidiGate. What you hear depends on the quality of your sound card. If you've got a wave-table synthesis card, the sound might actually be pleasing to the ear. If your sound card uses FM synthesis, it will sound like some kid playing a $29 electronic organ.
- **RealAudio sound (audio/x-pn-realaudio)** When you access a RealAudio sound, Netscape starts the RealAudio player. RealAudio sounds begin playing almost immediately after you access them, but don't expect good sound quality—it's OK for voice but barely acceptable for music.

The following sections discuss the techniques you use to play each of these sounds.

When Netscape downloads a sound or any other multimedia resource, the program places a copy of the file in the current temporary directory. To find out where this directory is located, open the Options menu, choose General Preferences, and click the Apps tab. Look in the Temporary Directory box to see the current temporary directory setting. I recommend that you create a directory called Temp to store downloaded files; this ensures that the downloaded files don't clutter up Netscape's directory. After you create this directory, type C:\temp in the Temporary Directory box and click OK.

Using LiveAudio

When you access a Sun/NeXT (*.au), Silicon Graphics/Apple (*.aiff), or Windows (*.wav) sound, Netscape downloads the sound to the current temporary directory and launches LiveAudio (Figure 11.1).

To play the sound, just click the Play button. You can also pause the sound, adjust the volume (with the slider control), stop the sound, and play it again (by clicking Play once more).

Figure 11.1 LiveAudio

Here's a quick guide to the controls you'll find on Netscape Audio Player's control panel:

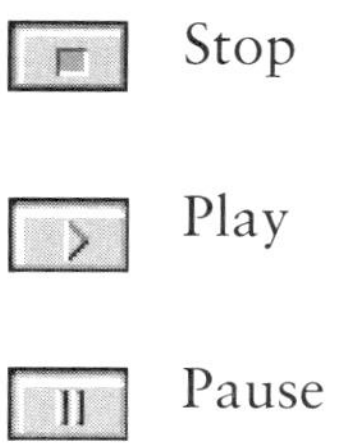

Stop

Play

Pause

In addition to these controls, you'll see a slider control (see Figure 11.1) that enables you to control the sound's volume.

Using the XingSound Player

When you access an MPEG (*.mp2) sound with the 16-bit (Windows 3.x) version of Netscape, Netscape downloads the sound to the temporary directory and launches the XingSound Player (Figure 11.2).

Here's a quick guide to the controls you'll see on XingSound's simple control panel:

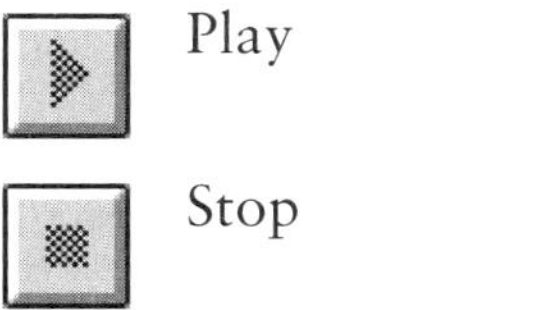

Play

Stop

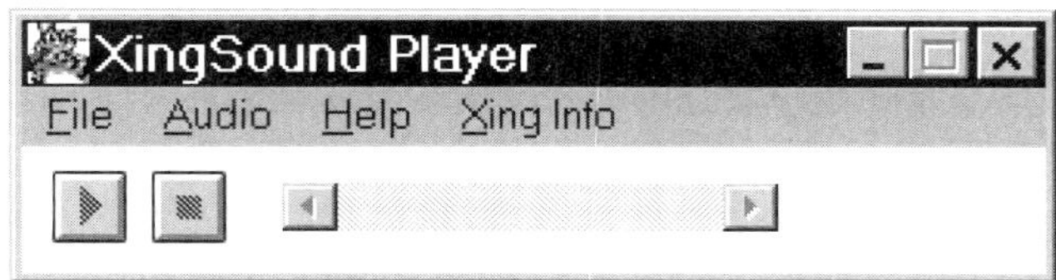

Figure 11.2 XingSound Player

In addition, you can drag the slider to the place where you want the sound to start playing.

Like to find some cool sounds on the Web? Check out the "Sites With Audio Clips" metapage at

http://www.eecs.nwu.edu/~jmyers/other-sounds.html

The creation of Jennifer Myers, it's an awesome collection of aural resources that's sure to keep you busy for hours.

Using MidiGate

Perhaps the coolest helper app that's included on this book's CD-ROM disc is MidiGate, which plays MIDI files. A MIDI file, in case you don't know, is an ASCII text file that contains a representation of musical tones and effects.

When compared to other sound file formats, MIDI has a huge advantage in that it's very compact—a 10-minute harpsichord sonata, for example, requires only about 10K of disk storage space and downloads very quickly.

The down side of MIDI is that your computer's sound card will probably play the MIDI file with quality reminiscent of a cheap electronic organ.

When you access a MIDI sound file, Netscape downloads the file to the temporary directory and launches MidiGate (Figure 11.3). The sound starts playing immediately.

There's quite a lot to MidiGate, especially if you're a MIDI hobbyist. Our concern here is just to play the sounds you'll encounter on the Web, so we'll keep it simple.

Figure 11.3 MidiGate

Here's a quick guide to the controls you'll find on the MidiGate control panel:

 Rewind to the beginning

 Fast forward

 Stop

Exit

Position of current selection in queue, if more than one sound has been loaded

Displays Queue dialog box, which enables you to open more than one sound for continous playing

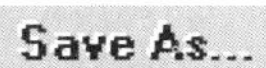

Open a MIDI sound file on disk

Save As... Saves the current sound with a different file name

There's no slider control on MidiGate's control panel, but you can still click the sound progress bar to indicate where you'd like the sound to start playing.

You'll find some stunning repositories of classical MIDI sound files on the Web. Check out the Classical MIDI Connection

http://206.96.214.4/~raborn/index.html

and the astonishing Classical MIDI Archives

http://www.prs.net/midi.html

which contains more than 1,500 MIDI files. Cool!

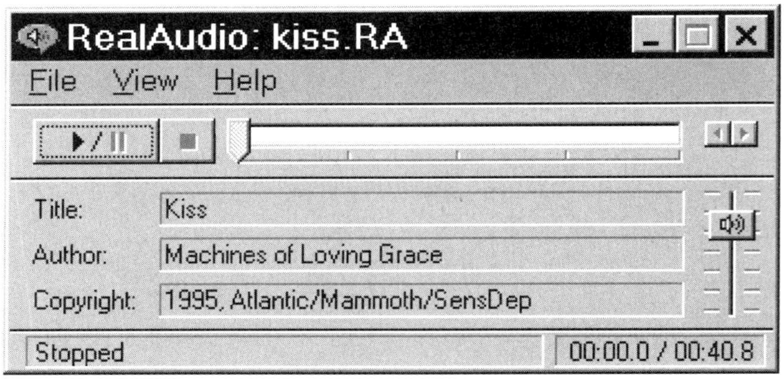

Figure 11.4 RealAudio player

Using the RealAudio Player

You'll find two kinds of RealAudio sound files on the Web:

- **RealAudio Version 1** You can download and listen to these files using a 14.4 Kbps modem.
- **RealAudio Version 2** To listen to these files, you'll need a Pentium computer and a 28.8 Kbps modem. These files are often flagged with a RealAudio 28.8 icon. To play them, you'll need to install the RealAudio plug-in, which is available from Netscape's plug-in download site.

When you access a RealAudio 1.0 sound file (*.ra), Netscape starts the RealAudio sound player, shown in Figure 11.4, and you hear the sound almost immediately. The RealAudio dialog box shows the title of the sound being played, the author, and the copyright holder, if any. You'll also find the following controls:

Play/Pause

Stop and return to beginning of sound

Rewind

Fast Forward

Adjust the volume using the slider control.

It sounds really garbled! If you've heard some good sound, but all of a sudden the quality goes way down, chances are the data stream has run into a roadblock on the Internet. (It happens.) Just be patient—the quality will probably come back up in a few moments. If not, you'll see a dialog box informing you that the quality is unacceptable. Try accessing the site later, when the Internet's not so busy.

One of the most valuable resources to be found anywhere on the Internet is accessible from the RealAudio home page (http://www.prognet.com/index.html): full-length audio files of National Public Radio (NPR) news programs, including All Things Considered and Morning Edition. If you heard a story on an NPR broadcast and you'd like to hear it again, you can do so by accessing RealAudio's home page and clicking the NPR button. At this writing, RealAudio required that you register and obtain a password—there's no fee or obligation for this, however. You'll also find links to RealAudio versions of ABC news broadcasts.

VIEWING MOVIES

You'll find thousands of movies on the Web, but don't expect too much in terms of quality. Every movie, digital or otherwise, is simply a succession of still images (called *frames*); in a high-quality movie, the frames go by quickly enough that the brain is tricked into seeing smooth motion. To keep file sizes down, the creators of most of the digital movies you'll find on the Web kept the number of frames per second to a minimum, which results in a very jerky presentation that won't trick your eye, your brain, or anything else.

It's taking a half hour to download this movie! Unfortunately, movie files tend to be big and bigger—the one I'm downloading right now is about 2.5 MB. On a 14.4 Kbps modem line, a file that large will take many minutes to download. If it's taking too long, remember that you can switch back to Netscape and browse elsewhere while the file's downloading—or you can cancel the download, skip the whole thing, and go down to your video store and rent a real movie.

The best movie formats offer sound as well as video. As with the digital sound just discussed, you'll need to equip your Windows system with a sound card and speakers if you wish to hear these sounds.

Understanding Movie File Formats

Like sounds, the digital movies you'll find on the Web are stored in a variety of file formats, so you'll need more than one movie viewer. Here's a quick overview of the movie file formats you're most likely to find on the Web. Also indicated here is the MIME type, the file extension that's used with the type, and the application that Netscape will launch when you've accessed one of these movies (assuming you've installed the software according to the instructions in Appendix C).

- **MPEG (video/mpeg)** MPEG is short for the Motion Picture Experts Group, an industry consortium that meets periodically to define digital video standards. At present the MPEG-1 standard defines a relatively low-quality video standard. MPEG movies, stored in *.mpg files, aren't much to write home about, you'll find, and they require huge files. When you access an MPEG file, Netscape will start NET TOOB. If you're using Windows 95, you can also play MPEG movies with the Windows Media Player.
- **QuickTime (video/quicktime)** Originally created by Apple Computer, the QuickTime format is now an international standard, and it's better than MPEG. In addition to offering good compression and performance, QuickTime offers near-CD-quality digital stereo sound. Stored in *.mov and *.qt files, QuickTime movies are played by the QuickTime plug-in that's distributed with Netscape. You can also use NET TOOB, if you prefer.
- **Video for Windows (video/x-msvideo)** The Windows movie format (*.avi) offers another high-quality movie standard with digital

stereo sound. Not as efficiently compressed as QuickTime movies, the files are very large but the quality is good. Windows movies are played by LiveVideo.

In addition to these movie formats, you can also display streaming video with the VDOLive plug-in, which you can download from Netscape's plug-in site.

I just downloaded an 8 megabyte movie, and it plays for only three minutes! And the picture's the size of a postage stamp! Don't say I didn't warn you. Is network video here yet? Use your own judgment, but I'd say no. Right now, it's an amusing diversion at best. Movies aren't going to become a significant attraction on the Web until better compression techniques are developed and people have much faster Net connections.

Using NET TOOB

The shareware program NET TOOB, included on this book's CD-ROM disc, is a versatile movie player that can handle MPEGs, QuickTime movies, and Video for Windows movies. (In order to view QuickTime movies with NET TOOB, you must first install QuickTime for Windows.) I recommend that you use NET TOOB for viewing MPEG movies (LiveAudio handles Windows and QuickTime movies).

When you've configured NET TOOB to play the movies you download, the program will start automatically after downloading is complete. You'll see the NET TOOB video player (Figure 11.5). Here's a quick rundown of the controls you'll find in this window:

 Rewind

 Pause

 Fast forward

 Stop

Close video player

Turn sound on/off

Choose video size

Choose resolution (in frames per second)

Choose continuous play or play once and quit

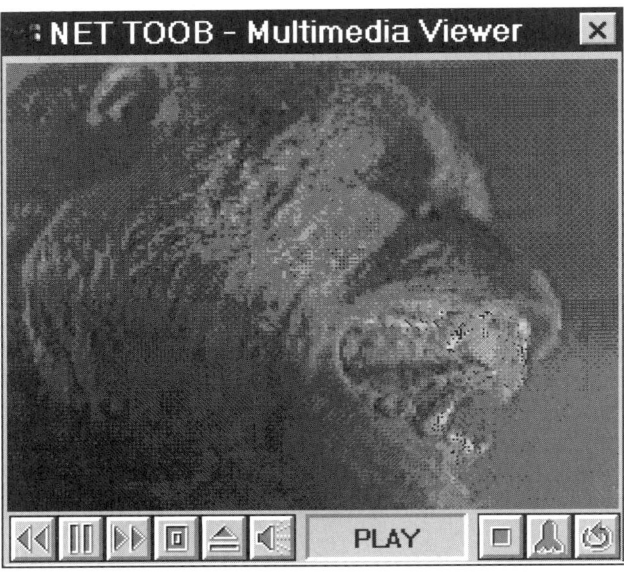

Figure 11.5 NET TOOB display window

NET TOOB plays the video with continuous looping. Try experimenting with the different sizes; at the smallest size, your computer can display the video with sufficient numbers of frames per second to trick your eye into seeing continuous motion. This effect collapses with larger sizes. When you're finished playing the video, click the Close Video Player button.

Can I see that video again? Sure. Netscape wrote the downloaded file to the temporary directory. From Program Manager (Windows 3.x) or the Start menu (Windows 95), choose NET TOOB. You'll see the NET TOOB control panel. To open a video file, click Select Video File and open the temporary directory. Use List Files of Type to select the type of video file you're opening—Video for Windows (choose AVI video), QuickTime (choose QTW video), or MPEG (choose All Files).

Using LiveVideo

When you access a link to a Windows (*.avi) movie, Netscape displays a new page and starts downloading everything on it, including the video file. Unfortunately, this could take quite a while. Check the status line; you'll see an estimate for how much longer it will take to finish downloading the file. Whatever you do, don't exit the page by clicking Back, because that will stop the download!

When the movie has finished downloading, you see the finished page (Figure 11.6). The movie looks like an in-line image, but when you click on it, the movie starts playing. It's cool to see the movie on the same page, without an intrusive, separate window starting. To see the movie again, just click it.

Using the QuickTime Plug-In

Like the LiveVideo plug-in, the QuickTime plug-in displays the movie in-line (along with the text and graphics of a Web page). When you access a link to a QuickTime (*.mov) movie, Netscape displays a new page and starts downloading the file. As with Windows movies, this could take a while; it's a good time to get a cup of coffee or chat with a co-worker! Where the movie will appear, you'll see a QuickTime logo while the movie is downloading. Finally, the movie appears in the window, framed within the

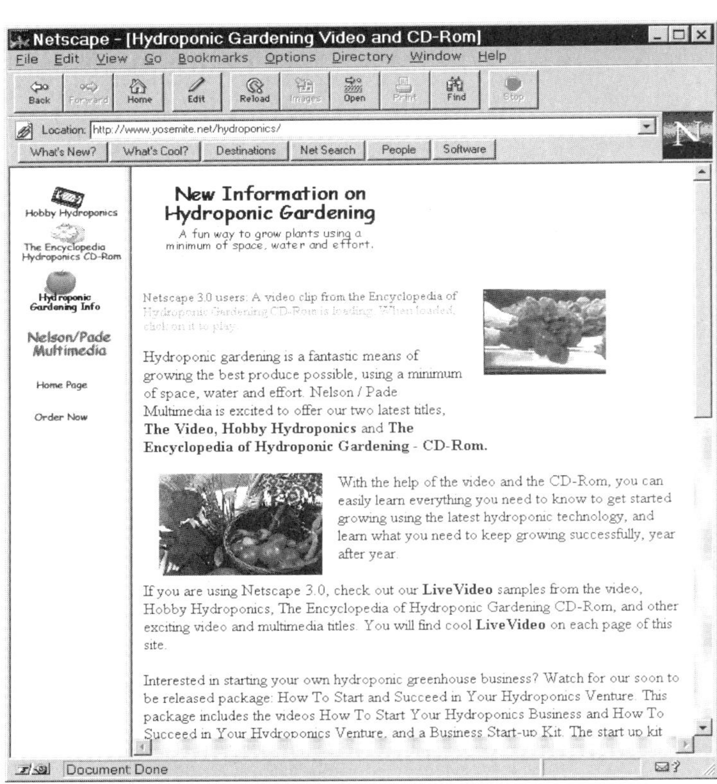

Figure 11.6 LiveVideo

QuickTime player; in Figure 11.7, you see the player in the lower right corner. Here's an overview of the VCR-type tools you'll find in the player:

Volume

Play/pause

Rewind

Fast Forward

In addition to these controls, you can use the slider to position the start of the film where you want.

Figure 11.7 QuickTime in action

Introducing Streaming Video

Thanks to Netscape's new plug-in capabilities and some key technical advances, streaming video is now possible. With streaming video, you get two impressive capabilities:

- **In-line video that starts playing almost immediately** A live-action video can appear within a Web page, just as in-line graphics now appear. But you don't have to wait five minutes for the whole file to download. When you click an in-line video, the video starts playing almost immediately—with stereo sound.
- **Dynamic adjustment** Some users are accessing the Internet by means of slow, 14.4 Kbps means, while others have faster modems, and still others have very fast network-based connections. A one-size-fits-all approach would saddle modem users with jerky, unconvincing videos, or unnecessarily punish users of fast connections by depriving them of the quality that their systems can support. With dynamic adjustment, the plug-in detects the speed of the connection and adjusts the quality automatically (lower for slow connections, higher for better connections).

Streaming video has come to the Web today thanks to VDOLive, a plug-in for Netscape version 2. Created by VDOnet, a small Israeli company, the plug-in enables Web authors to embed streaming video within their Web pages. At 14.4 Kbps, the quality isn't anything to write home about—the audio's fuzzy, the picture's the size of a postage stamp, and the action's herky-jerky—but quality improves markedly at 28.8 Kbps.

After you've installed the VDOLive plug-in, you don't need to do anything special to view a VDOLive movie—just access a site that's offering a VDOLive movie. At some sites, you'll see in-line video; at others, you'll see the video in a separate Web page. But all the action's within Netscape.

You can get a good idea of streaming video's potential by taking a look at KPIX's VDO Video Library. The San Francisco-based TV station offers videos on earthquake preparedness, hidden hikes in the Bay Area, Hawaii's innovative health plan, and much more. If you're viewing the videos with a 28.8 Kbps modem, it's a lot of fun. Check it out at http://www.kpix.com/video/.

From Here

- Learn how to view Adobe Acrobat documents in Chapter 12.
- Try out some Java sites in Chapter 13.
- Explore three-dimensional virtual worlds in Chapter 14.

Chapter 12

Viewing Adobe Acrobat Documents

When you view HTML documents with Netscape, you'll see Netscape's interpretation of the underlying HTML tags. The formatting is simple and effective. Unfortunately, HTML does not include tags needed for more complex document formats, such as multiple-column text or footnotes.

To provide richer document formatting, some document authors prefer to encode their documents using a proprietary document format. One such format is the PostScript page description language, familiar to users of laser printers. PostScript can also generate richly formatted screen displays, but this requires a reader capable of decoding the PostScript commands. Such readers exist—GhostScript is an example—but Adobe, the originators of PostScript, have developed a set of extensions to PostScript, called Adobe Acrobat, that produce superior results on-screen. You will encounter growing numbers of Acrobat documents on the Web (for an example, see Figure 12.1), and you

Acrobat Reader - [TIMES.PDF]

File Edit View Tools Window Help

Friday
January 12, 1996

Internet Edition

Eight pages
© 1996 The New York Times

TimesFax
FROM
The New York Times

FROM THE FRONT PAGE

Budget Battle Turns To Campaign Fodder

WASHINGTON — There was little mourning among political consultants when the budget talks were suspended this week. The strategists were already planning Congressional campaigns that revolved around the great, unresolved differences between the two parties on balancing and reconfiguring the Federal budget; the lack of a deal just makes those differences sharper.

"I haven't lost a lot of sleep over it," said Stan Greenberg, who polls for the Democratic National Committee. After weeks of surveys and voter research, Democrats are convinced that their party can prosper mightily if it presents itself as the last line of defense against Republican cuts in Medicare, education and environmental protection.

As Democratic consultants see it, Republican incumbents enter the 1996 campaign with a crippling record of votes on those issues, and the lack of a budget deal means they have no overarching accomplishment to outweigh those votes.

Republican strategists counter with a very simple theme that takes into account the lack of a budget deal, (or, perhaps someday, a less-than-perfect budget deal) as well as the stalling of other high-profile parts of their legislative agenda: Their party tried to bring about the fundamental change the voters demanded in 1994, but the Democrats blocked them.

By ROBIN TONER

Gingrich Hits Clinton on Budget Plan

WASHINGTON — Insisting that a balanced budget plan was "within our grasp," President Clinton called on Congressional Republican leaders to renew the drive for an agreement Thursday. But he was instantly rebuffed by Speaker Newt Gingrich, who accused him of misleading the public in "a political game."

The deep difference between the two sides in the drawn-out budget battle was made starkly clear when the President held a televised news conference to declare his own optimism that a deal can be reached "if we set aside partisanship and work to seize this moment."

"We shouldn't let our fundamental agreement on a balanced budget," Mr. Clinton declared, "be held hostage to a narrower agenda that seeks to prevent America from giving Medicare to senior citizens or quality nursing home care or educational opportunity for young people or environmental protection to all of us."

Mr. Clinton was soon castigated by Mr. Gingrich for accusing the Republicans of seeking excessive "cuts" in Medicare, Medicaid and other social welfare spending when the financing of these programs, Mr. Gingrich said, would actually be increasing.

"It was a very disappointing press conference," Mr. Gingrich commented in Seattle after watching the President on television during a West Coast fund-raising trip. "It does not give me much encouragement."

By FRANCIS X. CLINES

Peru Convicts American Woman of Treason

LIMA, Peru — Lori Helene Berenson of New York was convicted of treason Thursday by a secret Peruvian military court and sentenced to life in prison for aiding Marxist guerrillas who prosecutors said were planning to seize the Peruvian Congress and abduct lawmakers.

The widely expected verdict was announced six weeks after Ms. Berenson was arrested in an anti-terrorist police operation that also led to the capture of 22 other people after an all-night shootout in a Lima suburb. But the sentence came as a surprise, especially since prosecutors had requested a 30-year prison term, the minimum penalty for treason in Peru, and reflects the Government's tough policy toward insurgent groups.

Ms. Berenson is expected to be moved soon to Yanamaygo Prison in Puno, a special prison for terrorists situated in the Andes. Lawyers for Ms. Berenson, 26, said a treaty between the United States and Peru allows her to serve her sentence in the United States after all judicial appeals have been completed. But the lawyers said their client had indicated no desire to serve her time in the United States.

By CALVIN SIMS

Fear of Diseases Drives Britons From Beef

LONDON — For centuries, beef has held pride of place at the British table. All that may change. Despite pledges by Government ministers that British beef is safe, consumers by the droves are giving it up for fear that meat from diseased cattle could cause a degenerative brain disease.

The Government emphasizes that no link has been established between bovine spongiform encephalopathy, commonly known as mad-cow disease, and Creutzfeldt-Jakob Disease, a rare brain disease fatal to humans.

Since November, when the scare erupted, the Ministry of Agriculture, Fisheries and Food has trotted out scientists and reports suggesting that it is unlikely for a disease to cross the "species barrier" and that even if it did, regulations are in place to keep the diseased portions of cow carcasses out of the human food chain. But the scare refuses to go away. For every scientist who says beef is safe, there is one who says it may not be. The debate over a possible link rages in British medical journals.

The public is voting with its fork. According to a research organization, 1.4 million households have stopped buying beef.

The decline began in November and by mid-December, sales were down 25 percent.

By JOHN DARNTON

1 of 8 | 100% | 8.50 x 11.00 in

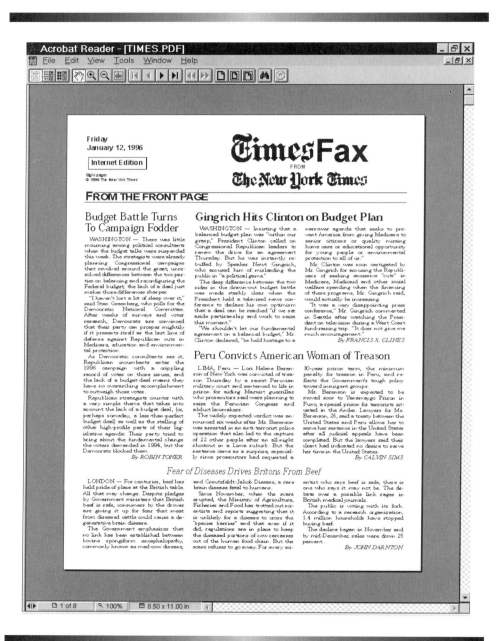

Figure 12.1 New York Times (TimesFax) displayed by Adobe Acrobat

For the Time-Challenged

- Acrobat enables you to download and view richly formatted documents, no matter on which brand of computer they were created.
- Once you've downloaded a document, you can easily navigate through it by using the Acrobat toolbar.
- The Amber plug-in enables you to view Acrobat presentations in-line (that is, within Netscape's window) and to download just one page at a time.

can read them with the Adobe Acrobat Reader software included with this book.

In Adobe's nomenclature, Acrobat documents are *portable documents*—and it's a great term. Unlike richly formatted documents created with word processing programs such as Microsoft Word, Acrobat documents can be viewed and read on any computer system for which an Acrobat reader has been provided (and there are Acrobat readers for almost all commonly used types of computers). Acrobat is a major plus for large organizations, in which people using many different types of computers must be able to exchange richly formatted documents and don't have time to translate them. And it's a natural for publishing on the Web.

Adobe has added lots of new features to the basic Acrobat design, by means of plug-ins. The coolest of the lot is Weblink (included in the version of Acrobat on this book's CD-ROM disc), which enables Acrobat authors to incorporate Web links into their Acrobat documents. And with Weblink installed in the Reader, you can access Web documents by clicking links, just as you would within Netscape.

If you're using the Windows 95 version of Netscape, you can take advantage of the amazing new Acrobat Amber plug-in, which enables you to view Acrobat presentations within Netscape's window. What's more, you can view one page at a time—there's no need to wait for the whole presentation to download before you can start viewing.

This chapter begins by discussing the Adobe Acrobat helper application, which runs in a separate window. If you're using Windows 95, you can take advantage of the Amber plug-in, which is discussed later in this chapter.

Downloading an Acrobat Document

Adobe Acrobat documents are stored in *.pdf files (the "pdf" is short for Portable Document Format).

When you click a link to an Adobe Acrobat document, Netscape downloads the document and starts the Acrobat Reader. When the downloading is complete, the Acrobat Reader starts and appears in its own window. You use the Acrobat Reader's controls to page through the document.

Understanding the Acrobat Reader Window

The Acrobat Reader window has its own toolbar, which offers the controls discussed in the following sections. You'll rarely use the menu commands.

Choosing a Display Mode

Acrobat enables you to view the document three different ways. The default mode is the Page Only display mode, and it's the one you'll probably want to use most often.

Page Only Display Mode In this mode, the default mode shown in Figure 12.1, the Adobe Acrobat document fills the window.

Bookmarks and Page Mode In this mode, you'll see a vertical list of bookmarks in the left panel of the page, with the document displayed in the right panel. These bookmarks are like hyperlinks. You can click them to display a page other than the one you are viewing. You may encounter some Acrobat documents that take advantage of this feature.

Thumbnails and Page In this mode, you see a vertical list of thumbnail (postage-stamp-sized) images of the document's pages in the left panel, while the document is displayed in the right panel (Figure 12.2). To go to one of the pages, click the thumbnail image.

Acrobat Reader - [BUILDTR.PDF]

File Edit View Tools Window Help

Trends Magazine, October 1994

Building the Information Superhighway

By Edward R. McCracken

Extraordinary advances in digital technology are the foundation on which the global information infrastructure is being built. Once in place, it will forever change the way we do business.

There is a growing consensus today, among a wide range of leaders, that the world stands at the brink of a communications revolution, and that the coming changes will have an unprecedented impact on commerce and society and on the flow of information among corporations, governments, communities, and individuals. At the center of these imminent changes is the development of a global information infrastructure that will provide a means of moving all types of digital data—text, graphics, video, audio, and photographs, alone or in combination—from one place to another, worldwide, at extremely high speeds. A crucial component of this network will be a global web of high-capacity fiber-optic cable that, instead of electrical signals, transmits pulses of light.

Popularly known as the information superhighway, this infrastructure—made practical by rapid advances in digital technology—will be in place in many areas of the world within just a few years. And parts of it, such as an interactive digital television network soon to be tested in 4,000 Orlando, Florida, homes, will be a reality before the end of 1994. The concept for a global information infrastructure was derived in part from the success of smaller systems already in operation, such as the Internet computer network, cable television, and telephone services. However, the information superhighway will be far more comprehensive and diverse.

The term "information superhighway" is appropriate because it provides an image analogous to the shape that this impending convergence of computers, television, and telephones will take. Much as a highway system expedites vehicular traffic for pleasure and commerce, the information superhighway will facilitate the movement and management of data, audio, and video. Taking the analogy a step further, each home, school, business, medical center, or other institution will have its own on- and off-ramps. However, unlike a highway system, the coming

"Building the Information Superhighway" 1

1 of 4 100% 8.50 x 11.00 in

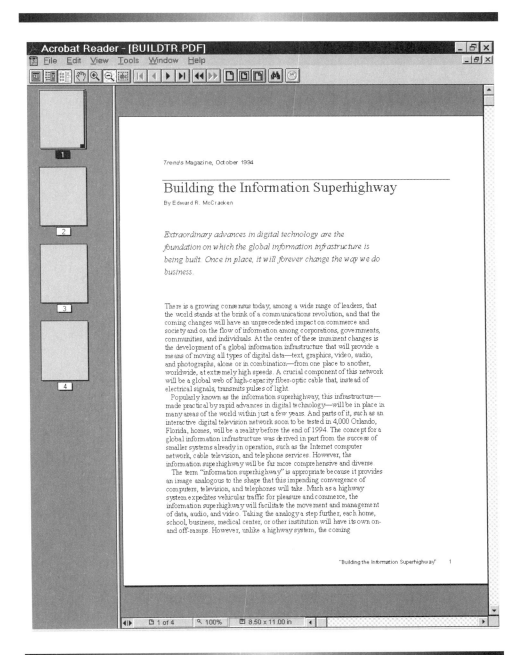

Figure 12.2 Thumbnails and Page mode

Navigating Through the Document

Use the following buttons to navigate through the Acrobat document:

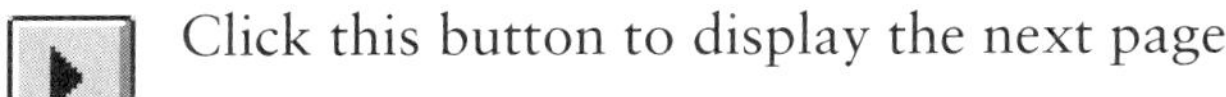

Click this button to display the next page.

Click this button to display the previous page.

Click this button to display the last page.

Click this button to display the first page.

Click this button to go back to the previously displayed page.

Click this button to redisplay the page you were just viewing.

Sizing the Document On-Screen

To get a closer look at a portion of the page, use one of the following tools:

Click this button to increase the magnification.

Click this button to decrease the magnification.

Click this button to turn on the hand tool, which lets you bring hidden portions of the document into view.

Note that some Acrobat documents contain author-defined articles, which are designed so that you can page through them almost automatically. To find out whether the document has articles, open the View menu and choose Articles. You'll see a list of the articles the document contains, if any. To read an article, select it and click OK. The Reader will display the beginning of the article. Just click the mouse button to page through the article automatically.

You can also size the document by clicking one of the three page size buttons, which are situated near the right end of the toolbar:

 Click this button to display the page at 100% magnification.

 Click this button to fit the page to the window.

 Click this button to fit the width of the page to the window.

Reading the Document in Full-Screen Mode

You can also read Acrobat documents in full-screen mode, in which the page takes up the whole screen. From the View menu, choose Full Screen. To view the next page, press Enter, the right arrow key, or the down arrow key. You can also click the left mouse button. To view the previous page, press the left arrow or up arrow key. When you are finished paging through the document, the program switches back to the normal display mode (you see the Adobe Acrobat Reader in a window).

Finding Text in an Acrobat Document

If you would like to search for text in an Acrobat document, click the Find tool (the button with binoculars). In the Find dialog box, type the text for which you want to search. Click the Whole Word option to avoid retrieving embedded strings, and click Match Case, if desired, to match the capitalization pattern you have typed. To search backwards, click the Find Backwards option. Click Find to initiate the search. If the program finds a match, it highlights the matched text on-screen. Press F3 to find the next occurrence of the same text.

If no match is found, you'll see a dialog box asking whether you want to continue searching from the beginning of the document. If you click OK, the program continues the search. Should this search fail to retrieve a match, you'll see an alert box informing you that the text could not be found.

Copying Text and Graphics to the Clipboard

If you find text in an Adobe Acrobat document that you would like to copy to another document, click the Select button (the one with "abc" on the button face), and select the text. Then open the Edit menu and choose Copy, or press Ctrl + C.

You can also select and copy graphics. To do so, open the Tools menu and choose Select Graphics. Then drag a selection box around the graphic you want to copy. From the Edit menu, choose Copy, or just press Ctrl + C.

Printing the Document

To print the Adobe Acrobat document you are viewing, follow these steps:

1. From the File menu, choose Print.
2. In the Print dialog box, choose printing options, if you wish. You can print all the pages (the default setting), the current page, or a range of pages. You can also choose to print more than one copy. Additional options may be available, depending on your printer's capabilities.
3. Click OK to start printing.

I can't save this document! You're right—there's no Save option on the Reader's File menu. What gives? Simple—there's no need. Netscape has already downloaded the Acrobat document to the directory listed in the Temporary Directory box (Apps page of the General Preferences menu item). Unless you deliberately erase it, there it will stay. Even after you quit Netscape, you can open the Adobe Acrobat Reader and load this document using the Open command in the File menu.

For an introduction to the extremely cool things that can be done with Adobe Acrobat and the Web, check out the following URL:

http://www.adobe.com:80/Acrobat/PDFsamples.html

You'll find Acrobat versions of Shakespeare's plays and sonnets, the Declaration of Independence and other historical documents, Aesop's fairy tales, and lots of other very interesting things. Don't miss Sun Tzu, *The Art of War.*

Using the Amber Acrobat Reader

If you're using Windows 95, you can take advantage of the Amber plug-in for Netscape.

This plug-in enables Netscape to view Acrobat files within Netscape's window, and what's more, only one page downloads at a time—you don't have to wait for the whole presentation to download before reading.

There's more! Like the progressively displayed JPEGs you're used to viewing with Netscape, Amber progressively displays a page, beginning with the text first. And to speed things even more, Amber uses *font blitting*—which means that fast substitution fonts are used first, followed by the true fonts only after everything's finished downloading.

Amber is a major step forward in making Acrobat documents more accessible on the Web.

From Here

- Take a look at the most exciting thing to hit the Internet since Netscape itself—Java. You'll find a complete introduction in Chapter 13.
- Explore three-dimensional worlds with Netscape's Live3D plug-in. Find out how to use it in Chapter 14.

Chapter 13

Taking a Sip of Java

Java is many things—a programming language, a key innovation in the history of computing, even a step into a new technological world. For Netscape users, though, it's fun, most of all. With Java, those static Web pages come alive with action, which can include sound, animation, and video. And these pages also provide *inter*action, enabling you to make choices or input data and see the results immediately, right on the page you're viewing.

In this chapter, you'll take a tour of some of today's best Java sites, and you'll learn more about what lies behind Java—and why some people think that Java will change the face of computing forever.

For the Time-Challenged

- Helper programs aren't a very good solution for Web multimedia. They run in a separate window. Worse, if you don't have the helper software, you're out of luck—you can't use the multimedia file. Java solves both problems by downloading the needed software (called an *applet*) along with the multimedia material. You then see the multimedia presentation within Netscape's window.
- Java is a new programming language that's beautifully suited to the Web environment. Unlike other programming languages, a Java program generates a *byte code*, which is expressed in plain ASCII characters that any computer can read. A Java interpreter, designed for a particular computer, transforms the byte code into instructions designed for a particular computer.
- Although Java contains many measures to safeguard computer security, users have been somewhat rattled by a continuing string of discoveries concerning security loopholes, and malicious Java applets are appearing on the Web. Until these problems are solved, you may wish to restrict your Java browsing to recommended sites or even turn off Java altogether.
- Netscape 3 contains a built-in Java interpreter, so you don't need to do anything special to run Java programs. When Netscape accesses a Web page containing a Java applet, Netscape downloads the code and runs it.
- JavaScript is a subset of Java that enables amateur programmers to bring rich, interactive features to their Web pages.

Java – What's the Big Deal?

You've done some serious surfing now, and I'll bet you've run into this problem: You've clicked on something, but Netscape tells you that it doesn't recognize the file you're trying to access. What's going on? The problem: You don't have the right helper program. So you've got two choices, neither of which is terribly satisfactory: You can skip the file, or you can download it and then try to find a helper program that will run it.

What's so cool about Java is that, when a Web page includes Java code, Netscape automatically downloads the program, called an *applet,* that is

needed to make things happen. Your computer than executes (runs) the applet, producing action—and interaction—right on the Web page you're viewing.

Helper programs aren't about to go away, though. Java's very useful, but it works best when the programs being downloaded are relatively small. As you'll see in the next section, where you'll take a look at some excellent Java sites, these programs do simple things, such as displaying an interactive crossword puzzle or a real-time clock. For now, you'll still need helper programs to play sounds, watch movies, and run animations.

What about Security?

Java's a great idea, but it has raised concerns about computer security. For example, what if someone wrote a destructive prank program that masqueraded as a legitimate Java applet? The original Java language specification sought to prevent this by ensuring that Java applets can't do destructive things, such as erase files.

Unfortunately, these measures weren't sufficient, and researchers have unearthed a series of holes in Java that could enable malicious programmers to do nasty things. As each of these problems has been discovered, Netscape and Sun have developed solutions and implemented them in the latest versions of Netscape.

It's something of a pain to upgrade to the latest version of Netscape—you have to download and install the program, which can take about a half hour—but it's wise to do so. The latest version incorporates the latest security fixes!

Hey, this applet is consuming all my computer's memory! Welcome to reality. Hostile Java pages are appearing on the Web. Some of them consume memory or system resources maliciously, forcing the user to quit and restart. A particularly evil one paints the screen black and prompts for your password to restore access (a blatant attempt to steal passwords). Efforts are underway to remove such sites from the Web, but the antisocial mentality of a small minority of computer programming enthusiasts virtually ensures that they'll pop up time and again. If you're curious to see what kind of

damage malicious Java applets can do, check out http://www.match.gatech.edu/~mladue/HostileApplets.html—but please, don't click any of the links!

Because of the potential for Java security leaks, you may wish to consider turning Java off entirely, at least until you're satisfied that the problems have been solved. To do so, open the Options menu and select Network Preferences. Click the Language tab, and deselect Enable Java and Enable JavaScript. If you subsequently find a site that you believe to be authentic and wish to view the Java applet in action, turn these options on again and reload the page.

For the latest on Java security problems (and their solutions), see Java Resources (http://www01.ix.de/ix/raven/Web/Java/Security.html). Also, take a look at the Java Frequently Asked Questions—Applet Security page (http://java.sun.com/java.sun.com/sfa/index.html).

It says "Type your user name and password to restore service"! Please, please, please, *don't fall for this trick!* Computer criminals want your user name and password so that they can carry out crimes such as unauthorized access, vandalism, and theft on-line. If you access a Web page that demands the user name and password you use to gain access to the Internet, quit Netscape immediately and do not return to the site. *Note:* This doesn't apply to bona fide Web pages that require you to type a special user name and password, different from those you type to access the Internet, in order to access services to which you have subscribed.

A Tour of Java Sites

You don't need to do anything special to run Java programs—with Netscape, it's all automatic. When you access a site that contains Java code, you'll know it—there are placeholders where the Java action will take place, and it takes a while for the code to download and execute. Once it does, things start happening!

Note that Java is so new (at this writing) that relatively few Web sites incorporate Java code. That's going to change quickly, especially since Netscape incorporates a Java interpreter! By the time this book reaches you, many Java sites will have appeared besides the ones listed here, which have a "demo" flavor to them. But it won't be long before some of the Web's top sites begin incorporating useful Java applets.

If you're nervous about Java security, browsing these sites is a great way to experience Java without fear. These are bona fide sites that don't contain any malicious applets.

EarthWeb

The name makes this site sound as if it's an environmental trailblazer page, but it's not—it's the headquarters for a Java development team. And what a team! EarthWeb is a New York-based company that specializes in Web site development using Java. When you access EarthWeb (http://www.earthweb.com/java/), you'll find a series of demonstration applications. They'll give you a pretty good idea of what Java can do.

Here's a sampler of what's on the site at this writing (on the Web, things change, so you can be sure this page will have been updated when you access it):

3-D-Netris The popular game takes on new meaning in a rotatable 3-D display.

Jigsaw Puzzle Drag the pieces to the square, and see if you can win.

Maze This will a-maze you! This fascinating program generates and solves its own maze. To start it, just click within the maze.

Throw the Ball Catch the ball by clicking and dragging. Release the button while moving the mouse to throw the ball! See Figure 13.1 for an illustration.

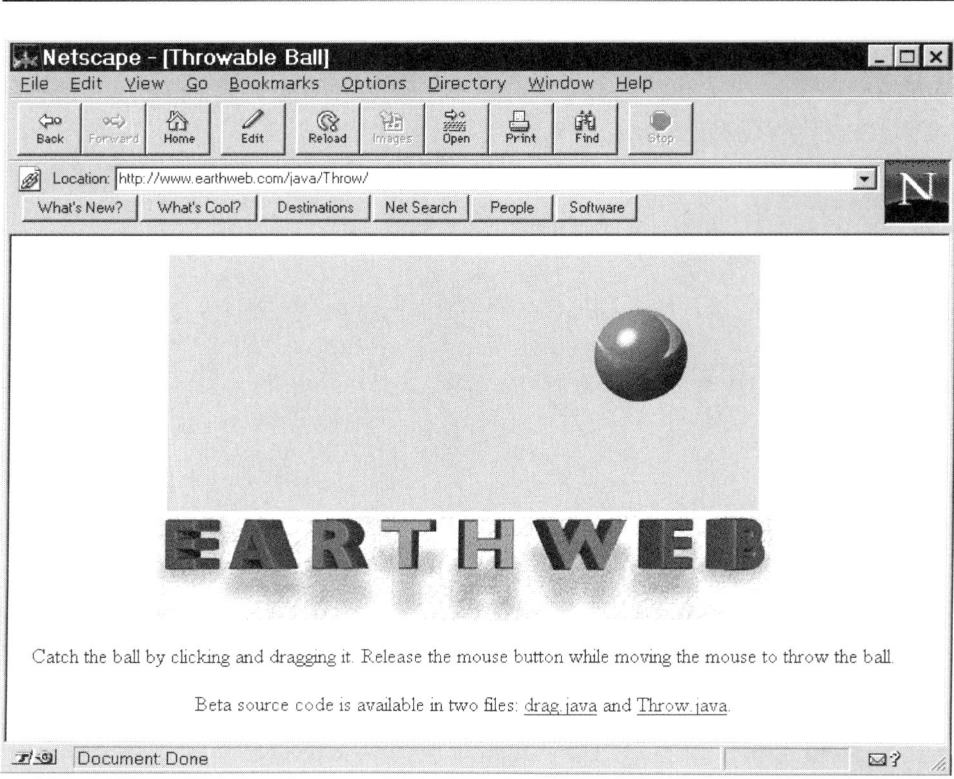

Figure 13.1 EarthWeb's bouncing ball

Don't miss Gamelan (http://www.gamelan.com/about.html), an EarthWeb project that summarizes tons of Web-based information about Java. Included are dozens of Java applets that you can try. Don't miss The Impressionist! Incidentally, in case you're curious, *gamelan* is the name of the traditional gong orchestral ensemble of the Indonesian archipelagos of Java and Bali.

Robert's Online Loan Pricer

Like to know how much that new sailboat is going to cost you every month? Here's a great demonstration of Java's ability to create interactive pages: It's a loan payment calculator, but with a twist—You type in any four of the five needed lines of information, and the Java applet does the rest (Figure 13.2). To access this site, use http://www.ripley.org/~robertl/option-pricer.html.

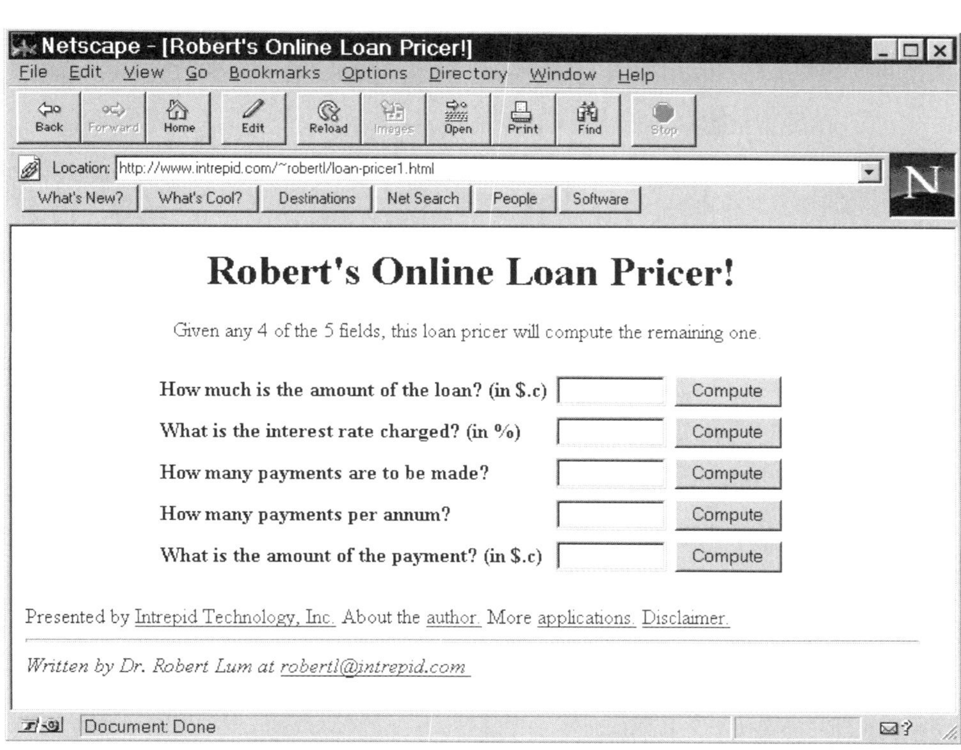

Figure 13.2 Robert's Online Loan Pricer

Solitaire

If you're wondering whether Java applets can have enough functionality to really *do* something, check out Solitaire (http://w3.gwis.com/~thorn/BetaSol.html). Shown in Figure 13.3, this site displays an impressive Solitaire game, which is bound to keep you busy for a while!

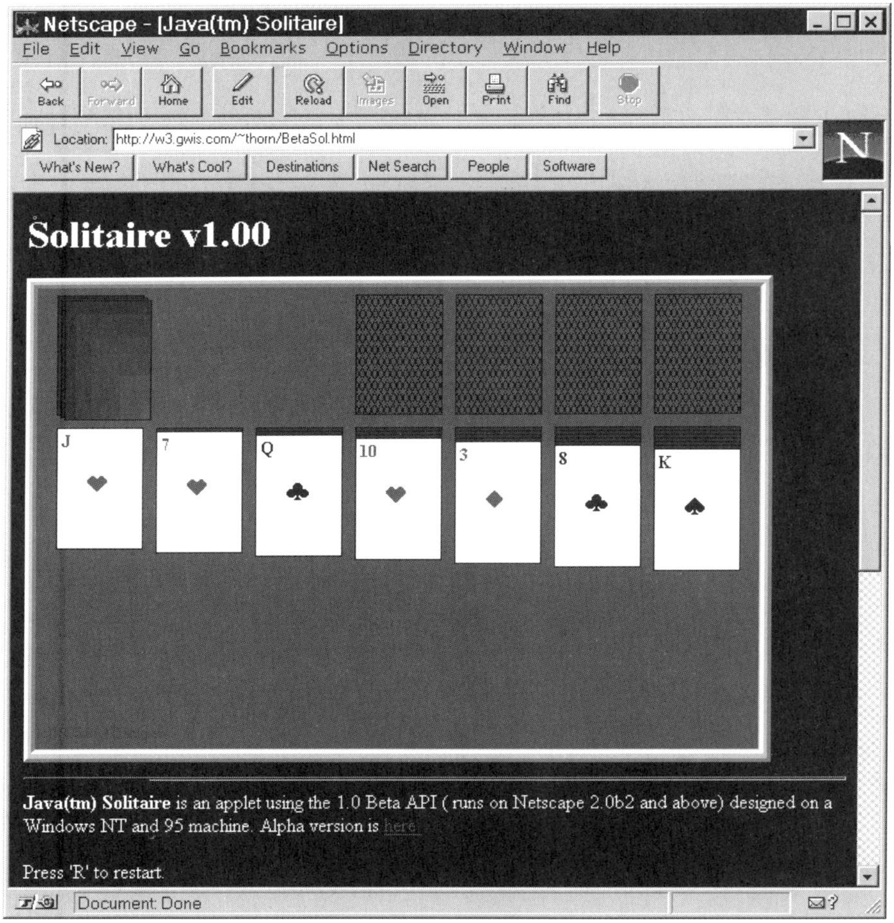

Figure 13.3 Solitaire

Where Did Java Come From?

You may be surprised to learn that Java got its start before the Web did. Java creator James Gosling, a programmer at Sun Microsystems, conceived of Java in early 1991—and at that time, Gosling thought that Java would be used to program consumer electronic devices. Specifically, Java would be used to create programs for TV set-top devices which, from the early 1990s and pre-Web perspective, were a sure bet to bring the Information Age into the home.

As Gosling initially conceived Java, the language would have to work with any kind of computer processing unit, since consumer electronic devices would surely have lots of different processors installed. Thus Java was intended to be *platform-independent* from the beginning, meaning that it would work with just about any processor made. As you'll see, that's one of the reasons it works so well with the Web—but we're getting ahead of the story.

The TV set box idea didn't work out—it seems that interactive television is always about to happen, but never quite makes it—but Java didn't die. Looking at the rapid growth of the World Wide Web, Gosling and his colleagues quickly realized that the Web, not interactive television, provided the perfect vehicle for disseminating Java applets. They created the first Java-enabled browser, called HotJava, to demonstrate what Java could do in tandem with the Web. Then Netscape Communications Corporation announced that the next version of their browser would include a Java interpreter—and the rest, as they say, is history!

Ironically, something like the TV set-top box is appearing in stores right now—but it's not designed for interactive television. On the contrary, it's a small computer (sans disk drives), priced at about $500, that enables you to access the Web!

What's JavaScript?

One of the most wonderful things about the World Wide Web is that just about anyone can learn HTML and put up a Web page. Java's great, but many Web enthusiasts fear that Java will raise the technology bar, preventing nonprogrammers from creating interactive Web sites. Thanks to JavaScript, a subset of Java designed for use by nonprogrammers, this pessimistic scenario may not occur.

Gosling and his team started with a programming language called C++, but quickly found that it was too quirky to serve their purposes. Taking the best ideas from C++ and other programming languages, they devised a new language from the ground up. Java would have the following characteristics:

- **Simplicity** Reacting against the oddly named key words and other deficiencies of previous programming languages, Java's developers wanted the language to be easy to learn and use.
- **Object-Oriented** In an *object-oriented* programming language, programmers create and polish small program modules, each of which accomplishes a certain task, such as displaying a dialog box on the screen. Once this module (called an *object*) is tested, it can be copied and used in any program. As an object-oriented language matures, programmers create hundreds and even thousands of objects, which can be put together to construct new applications in short order.
- **Robustness** Java eliminates some of the programming traps that bedevil users of C++ and other programming languages. By encouraging good programming habits, Java helps to ensure that the Java programs you run will be bug-free.
- **Architecture Neutral** This is probably the most amazing thing about Java—its ability to run on any kind of computer ever made. Unlike all previous programming languages, a compiled Java program doesn't generate binary code, which is tied to the instruction set of a particular processor. Instead, it generates a *byte code*, a list of intermediary instructions that can be expressed in ASCII characters that any computer can deal with.
- **Interpreted** To translate the byte code into instructions that a specific computer can read, you need a Java interpreter. Netscape has its own, built-in Java interpreter, so you're ready to go!
- **High Performance** All these innovations wouldn't add up to much if Java performed sluggishly. To ensure high performance, Java introduces a number of important innovations. Among them is the Java *garbage collector*, a program that runs in the background, cleaning up disused memory so that a program always has the maximum amount of memory to run.

- **Multithreading** A good program can do two or more tasks at once, so Java incorporates multithreading. In multithreading, two or more separate program processes, called *threads*, can execute at the same time.
- **Security** Programs bandied about over the network pose security problems, but Java incorporates a number of advanced protection measures to safeguard your system.

JavaScript enables anyone who's able to learn HTML to create rich, interactive sites. The cool thing about JavaScript is that it enables you to become the master of ceremonies for the events on a Web page. For example, when a user clicks a button, a portion of the script jumps into action and performs a function, such as searching a database for information or running a prepackaged Java applet.

From Here

- Your excursion into the incredible new capabilities of Netscape Navigator 3 isn't quite done yet! For the next step, take a look at Chapter 14, where you'll experience your first taste of virtual reality, thanks to the Live3D plug-in.

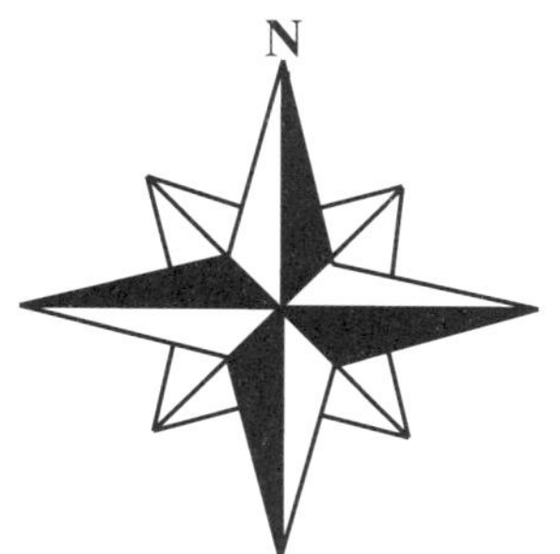

Chapter 14

Exploring Virtual Worlds with Live3D

By now, you're probably impressed with what the new Web can do, thanks to the impressive capabilities of plug-in programs and Netscape version 3. In this chapter, you'll learn how to view virtual reality presentations, which are the most amazing things to hit the Web yet—or the most useless, depending on your point of view.

What's virtual reality? Different people define it in different ways—cyberpunk author William Gibson calls it a "shared consensual hallucination," while others, perhaps more down to earth, prefer to term it an "experience in three-dimensional computer graphics." However you

define virtual reality, it's best experienced first-hand. Thanks to Live3D, a plug-in developed for Netscape Navigator version 3, you can.

This chapter provides an in-depth introduction to virtual reality and Live3D, beginning with the scripting language, VRML, that makes it all happen. You'll learn how to work with Live3D's navigation commands—yes, they differ from Netscape's—and you'll take a tour of some of the Web's hottest virtual reality sites. You can obtain Live3D by downloading the program from Netscape's home page.

Introducing VRML

Short for Virtual Reality Modeling Language, VRML got its start at Silicon Graphics, a California-based firm that had developed Open Inventor, a three-dimensional programming language. In 1994, computer programmers Mark Pesce and Tony Parisi started thinking about a "virtual reality markup language" for the Web, along the lines of HTML, the markup language that's used to create Web pages. Mark and Tony shared a belief that the Web is too "flat." To be as intoxicating and enchanting as possible, they argued, the Web should reveal three-dimensional spaces, which you could explore as if you were walking into a huge castle.

After a vigorous discussion on Usenet, Pesce and Parisi settled on a subset of the ASCII version of Open Inventor as the basis for VRML. Silicon Graphics graciously agreed to place this language in the public domain so that VRML could proceed. By early 1995, a draft specification of VRML 1.0 had been produced.

As currently specified, VRML provides the tools needed to describe a scene in three-dimensional detail. The scene consists of objects (such as cones, cubes, or rectangles), which can be nested within other objects. Like HTML, VRML includes the ability to embed hyperlinks within the objects that a programmer creates. In South of Market (SoMa), a VRML world created to navigate the streets south of San Francisco's main thoroughfare, you may find your way to the offices of *Wired* magazine—and when you click the front door, you'll wind up at HotWired's home page.

Virtual reality is best explored while wearing a stereovision headset, which tricks you into believing that you're physically inside the computer-created space. Viewed from Netscape's perspective, the three-dimensional worlds created by VRML are inviting, but don't produce the exclamations of wonder often heard from those donning headsets for the first time. Still,

For the Time-Challenged

- The Virtual Reality Modeling Language (VRML) was developed by Silicon Graphics, Inc., and released into the public domain. Currently standardized in version 1.0, VRML enables programmers to create three-dimensional virtual worlds. These worlds can contain hyperlinks.
- To explore virtual worlds, you can use Live3D, a plug-in program for Netscape version 3. When Netscape encounters a VRML world, the program automatically starts Live3D.
- Live3D has several navigation modes: walking, spinning, looking, flying, and pointing. The easiest is walking. If you get lost, just click the reset button on Live3D's toolbar to begin at the entry point.

VRML offers something that headset-based systems don't: the possibility of creating vast hyperlinked worlds that one could explore endlessly, just as one can now explore the Web via ordinary hyperlinks.

The newest wrinkle on the VRML scene is the Moving Worlds specification (VRML 2.0), which is backed by 56 leading Internet companies. Created by Mark Pesce, Moving Worlds enables VRML designers to integrate Java applets, leading to some interesting possibilities for interactive VRML worlds. And that's not all. Moving Worlds scenes can incorporate animations, sounds, videos, high-resolution graphics, text, and hyperlinks.

Using Live3D

A product of Netscape Communications Corporation, Live3D functions as a plug-in program for Netscape 3. It transforms Netscape into a program capable of exploring three dimensions, instead of the usual two.

When Netscape encounters a VRML world, the program automatically starts Live3D, and you'll see the Live3D command bar in the lower portion of the window (Figure 14.1). If you click the question mark (?), you'll see tips on mouse techniques on-screen.

Navigation Modes

There are six navigation modes in Live3D:

- **Walking** You explore the world at a slow speed, remaining on an unchanging, flat plane. This is the best way to explore most of the time.
- **Flying** Currently, this mode is accesible only from the pop-up menu. It's like walking, except that you're in the air. Dragging the mouse with the left button controls your pitch, roll, and yaw; the A key provides forward thrust; and the Z key provides backward thrust. This is a good mode when you've got a lot of ground to cover, or you want to pretend you're a superhero.
- **Spinning** In this mode, you can rotate the world right in front of your eyes. Often, this is rather disconcerting, and it's difficult to restore the plane and angle of attack that you had when you started.
- **Looking** This mode enables you to turn your "head" left or right, or up or down, without moving. Use this mode to inspect a room you've just entered. It's less confusing than walking around, because it's hard to turn a tight circle when you're walking.
- **Sliding** In this mode, you can "slide" left or right, or move up or down, without rotating the scene. This is a great mode for doing things like getting around obstacles or going through second-story windows.
- **Pointing** This mode enables you to point to an object on the screen. When you click the left mouse button, you go to it automatically. This is lots faster than navigating "on foot."
- **Accessing Views** Many VRML worlds have more than one saved *viewpoint*, a vantage point that's particularly attractive. To see a list of viewpoints, click the right mouse button and choose ViewPoints from the menu.

I'm lost! It's pretty easy to get confused. Just remember, you can go back to a stable, comprehensible scene just by clicking View on the toolbar. Sometimes this is the opening scene. In worlds that have more than one saved view, click-

ing View takes you back to the beginning of the current view. Either way, you'll be able to proceed without confusion.

Accessing a VRML World

Now try it yourself! To get started with Live3D, you'll need to access a VRML site. Here's a great place to start: Planet Italy (http://www.construct.net/projects/planetitaly/Spazio/VRML/sienawrl.gz). You're inside a cafe in Siena, Italy. This world is loaded with surprises, including neat links to travel information about Italy. Enjoy!

Ooooh, is this slow! In a virtual world that has lots of hyperlinks, don't count on rapid navigation—every new "world" requires downloading at least 50 KB of information, and maybe as much as 300 KB. All this is going to work much better when we all have 10 MB/sec connections, huh?

Have you ever played Doom? If so, you've got a real advantage, because most of Live3D's commands duplicate the popular (if violent) shoot-'em-upper. Don't count on seeing anything quite as responsive as Doom's three-dimensional world; the worlds you're about to enter have to be downloaded from the Net, which is considerably slower than your computer's hard disk.

Navigating in Three Dimensions

Getting around in a VRML world takes a bit of practice, you'll find. Also, Live3D offers many keyboard control options that aren't apparent from the screen. This section shows you how to master three-dimensional navigation, using all the tricks that Live3D has to offer.

Tricks to Use While Walking

When you walk with Live3D, you move within the virtual world at a manageable pace. Start with walking until you've mastered the basic maneuvers.

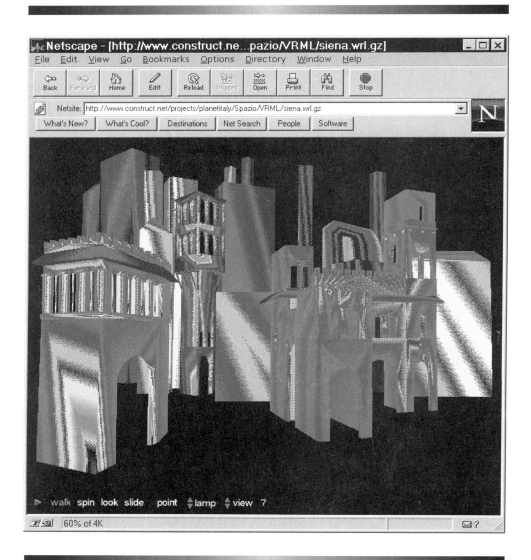

Figure 14.1 Live3D in action (Planet Italy)

Here's a rundown of the many tricks you can use while walking:

- To start walking, click "walk" on the Live3D control panel (at the bottom of Netscape's window).

- To move ahead, press the up arrow or hold down the left mouse button and drag up. To go back, press the down arrow, or hold down the left mouse button and drag down.
- To turn right, press the right arrow key, or hold down the left mouse button and drag right. To turn left, press the left arrow key, or hold down the left mouse button and drag left.
- To slide (move right or left without turning in either direction), hold down the Alt key and drag the mouse in the direction you want to slide.
- To look around, hold down the Ctrl key and drag in the direction you want to look.
- To move faster, hold down the Shift key.
- To get to something quickly by pointing, hold down the Ctrl key and left-click the object.
- As you move, you can tilt your head up by pressing the Z key, or down by pressing the A key.
- If you come to a doorway, it might be openable—to find out, get close to it and press the Spacebar.
- To orbit around the entire scene (you'll have to try this to see what this means), hold down the right mouse button and drag.
- Here's how to take a quick tour of the world. To cycle through the saved viewpoints, click View on the toolbar and click the up arrow until you're back at the beginning.

Spinning (Basically, Don't)

Spinning can be very disorienting and really isn't recommended for most worlds. It's cool sometimes, though, to see a geometrical object spinning before you. If you start spinning and can't restore a navigable plane, just click View to go back to the beginning of the selected view.

It's too dark in here! Well, turn on the light! Click Lamp, and click the up arrow until the scene's bright enough for you.

Accessing Viewpoints

If the world you're viewing has more than one saved view (click open the pop-up menu and choose ViewPoints to find out), by all means visit them. They've been chosen to give you the best possible angles on the world. Here are some view tips:

- To return to the begining of the current viewpoint, click View on the toolbar or press Ctrl + V.
- To see the next viewpoint, click the up arrow on the toolbar (next to View) or press Ctrl + right arrow.
- To see the previous viewpoint, click the down arrow on the toolbar (next to View) or press Ctrl + left arrow.
- To go to a specific viewpoint, right-click the scene and choose ViewPoints from the pop-up menu.

Using the Pop-up Menu

If you click the right mouse button anywhere within a virtual world, you'll see Live3D's pop-up menu (Figure 14.2). On this menu you can make additional choices about the way Live3D operates. Here's a quick rundown:

- **ViewPoints** This option enables you to choose from one or more predefined viewpoints.
- **Navigation** With this option, you can choose the same navigation modes that you'll find on the toolbar, with the addition of Fly. What's great about this option, though, is that it enables you to choose some great operating defaults, including Stay on Ground When Walking and Collision Detection. I recommend that you turn on Stay on Ground When Walking; leave Collision Detection off unless you really want to go around all those walls (instead of going through them, like Caspar the Ghost).
- **Lights** This option enables you to toggle the Headlight on or off (by default, it's on). You can also choose shading and intensity options.

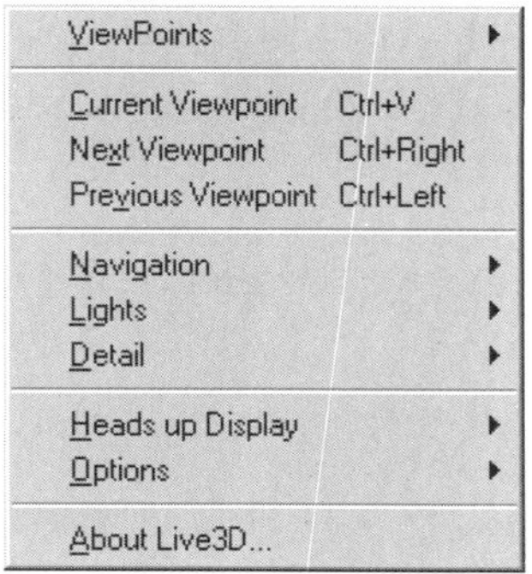

Figure 14.2 Live3D's pop-up menu

- **Detail** With this option, you can set the type of image detail Live3D uses. You can display the image as a solid (the slowest setting), a wireframe, or a point cloud (the fastest setting).
- **Heads up Display** This option enables you to select various navigation aids. You can turn on cross hairs that show where you've clicked and enable navigation help (this is the same as clicking the Help question mark on the command bar).
- **Options** Here, you can choose some additional options that control how Live3D displays the 3D scene, including Fast Rendering, Motion Blur, and Always Display Back Faces. Try some of these out!

The Best VRML Sites

To see what people are doing with VRML, check out Live3D's What's Cool site, located at http://www.paperinc.com/wrls.html. My favorites:

- **Intel Inside** (http://www.intel.com/procs/ppro/intro/vrml/nav.wrl) Fly into a Pentium Pro microprocessor (Figure 14.3). When you get right up to the processor's case, you'll see hyperlinks appearing on the wall. Click any of these to see more information on the Pentium Pro microprocessor.

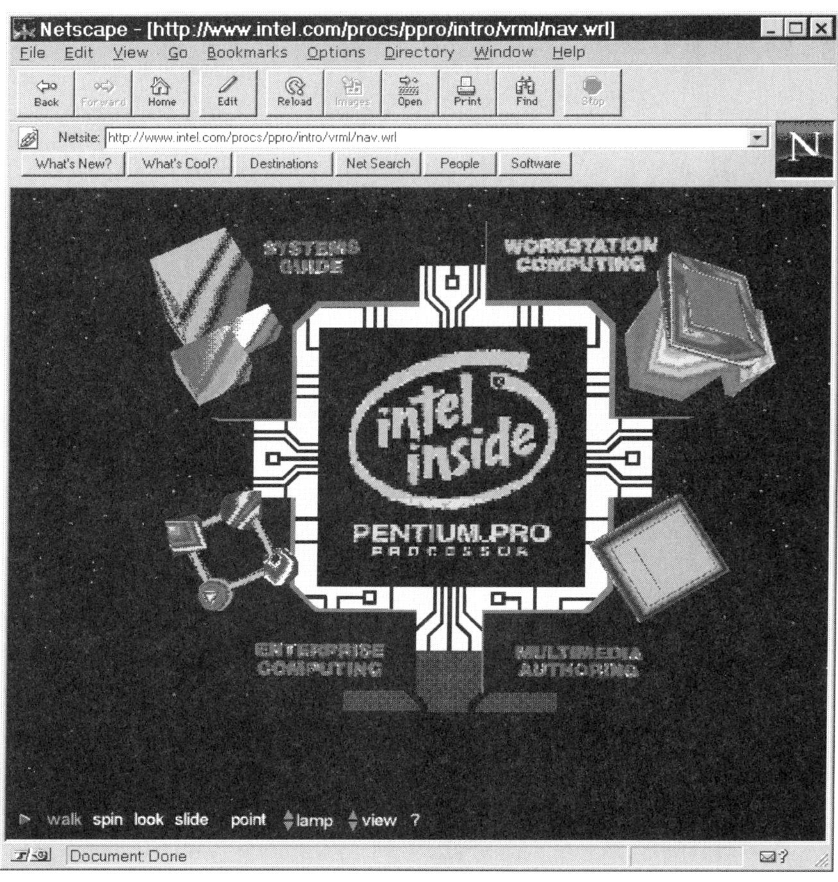

Figure 14.3 Intel Inside

- **ORC's Fractal Landscape** (http://www.ocnus.com/cgi-bin/fracland.wrl.gz) You'll want to fly over this one.
- **SoMa** (http://www.hyperion.com/planet9/worlds/vrsoma.wrl) Here's an incredible world that simulates Multimedia Gulch, an area dense with multimedia- and graphics-related firms situated along Howard Street, just south of Market Street (San Francisco's main drag).

Is Virtual Reality Good for Anything?

Good question, and one you well might ask after exploring some of the early virtual worlds on the Web. All in all, they're pretty crude, and downright slow over a SLIP/PPP line. But there are plenty of ways virtual reality in general, and VRML on the Web in particular, may prove of value. Consider these:

- An engineer could design a part and view it from all angles prior to making a physical prototype—and then share the design with engineers located elsewhere in the world.
- An architect could create an interior plan of a major construction project, and make it accessible on the Web so that clients from all over the country could see it.
- A physician could visualize a portion of a patient's body prior to surgery and go deeply within the simulated physique, exploring organs and other structures.

When placed on the Web, virtual worlds experience precisely the same multiplication effects that other Web resources do—that is, they become accessible to far more people, and benefit proportionally from the vastly increased feedback, than applications based on a single, non-networked computer system. If there's really a practical dimension to virtual reality, it will happen on the Web.

From Here

- This chapter concludes this book's survey of Web multimedia. In Part IV, you'll learn how to make full use of the Web's search tools.

Part IV

It's Out There *Somewhere!*

Finding It on the Web

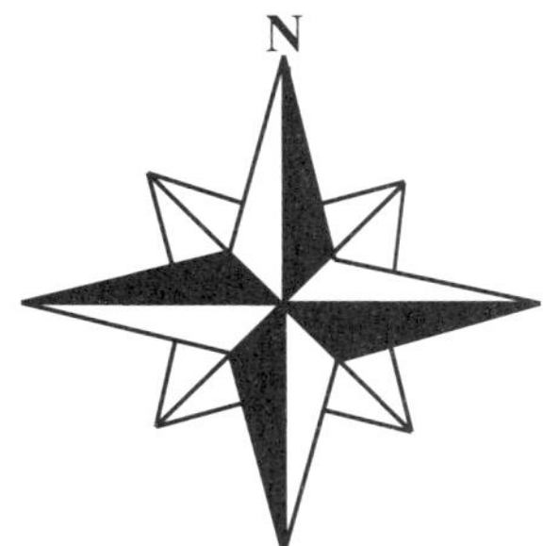

Chapter 15

Exploring the Web with Netscape Navigator

It's a big Web out there, with several hundred million documents. One thing's for certain: You're going to need help finding information. Surfing alone won't do it.

Fortunately, there are plenty of people who are trying to help. In this chapter and the next, you'll learn how to make full use of Web documents that people have created in an attempt to help you find your way. I call these *trailblazer pages*. They don't attempt to be complete, up to date, or even 100% accurate—those URLs come and go—but they can be invaluable. Chapter 16, on subject trees and search engines, covers Web information resources that *do* try to be comprehensive. But for now, you're looking for good places to launch your exploration of the Web, and this chapter points the way to some very useful resources.

For the Time-Challenged

- Trailblazer pages point the way toward Web information resources.
- Use starting points pages to begin your exploration of the Web.
- Locate metapages in your areas of interest.
- Check out "Best of the Web" pages to see what's cool.
- Use "What's New" pages to keep up with new Web developments.

Please note that some of the URLs mentioned in this chapter may have joined the dead byte heap of history by the time you read this. Still, I've chosen most of these documents because they appear to be more or less stable, so most of them should be up and running when you read this book.

Introducing Trailblazer Pages

Pioneers, explorers, adventurers, helpful souls—whatever you want to call them, they're the saints of the hour. Often on a purely voluntary basis, they've gathered the best of the Web (and sometimes the weirdest of the Web) into collections of hyperlinks. I divide this fast-evolving class of documents into the following categories:

Starting Points These are Web documents that are intended to help neophytes get started with the World Wide Web. Some are created and maintained by organizations, but the better ones are voluntary efforts by individuals.

Metapages These pages attempt to summarize all the links in a particular subject area. If you can find one in your area of interest, you will find it very helpful.

Most Popular Links What everyone is accessing, largely because people read pages like this to find out what everyone is accessing.

Best of the Web What some people (or more likely, one person) think the best sites are—a cyberspace Top Ten.

Cool Links I'm not sure what the difference between "Best" and "Cool" is, but see for yourself by checking out these pages. Be prepared to waste at least five hours.

Worst of the Web A relatively new and praiseworthy development, these pages list sites singled out for wasting Internet bandwidth with unnecessary junk (such as a list of some guy's T-shirts).

Weird Links Compilations of links to the Web underground. Forget sex, incidentally; there are too many dateless geeks out there looking for sex sites. When one appears, it gets inundated with several million accesses per day, which overloads the server and brings the computer to a halt. The service provider screams bloody murder, and the site gets shut down. A Sports Illustrated swimsuit site made a brief appearance, but after getting 7.2 million accesses in the space of 48 hours, it was withdrawn.

What's New These resources try to keep track of the deluge of new Web documents.

Starting Points Pages

Starting points pages stem from the ancient past (maybe two years ago) when the Web was completely unfamiliar to people. Created by organizations such as the European Center for Particle Physics (CERN), they provide a good point of entry for people accessing the Web for the first time. They include lots of links that introduce you to fundamental Web concepts, such as "What is a browser?" You'll also find links to subject trees, search engines, Usenet FAQs (Frequently Asked Questions), Internet documents of all kinds, and What's New documents.

The World Wide Web Home Page

Does the Web have a home? Yes, and it's called the World Wide Web Consortium (Figure 15.1), or W3C for short. W3C is a nonprofit industry consortium based at the Massachusetts Institute of Technology (MIT). The organization's mission is to promote technical standards that will ensure the Web's stable evolution and that Web products will all work with each other.

The W3C site (http://www.w3.org/pub/WWW) is a great place to keep up with fast-breaking developments on the Web. You'll learn about new developments in HTML, graphics and 3D on the Web, fonts, style sheets, and much more.

Figure 15.1 W3C home page

Netscape's Destinations Page

To access one of the best starting points on the Net, just click the Destinations directory button. You'll see the Destinations page, shown in Figure 15.2. There's lots of cool stuff, including today's news and links drawn from a variety of topical areas.

Figure 15.2 Netscape's Destinations page has links to high-quality sites that show off Netscape's technology

Excite Reviews

Excite not only offers one of the Web's better search engines, but also offers reviews of Web sites—more than 60,000 of them—in a variety of topical areas (http://www.excite.com/Reviews/; see Figure 15.3). On the title page, WebWatch offers pointers to some of the most interesting pages around.

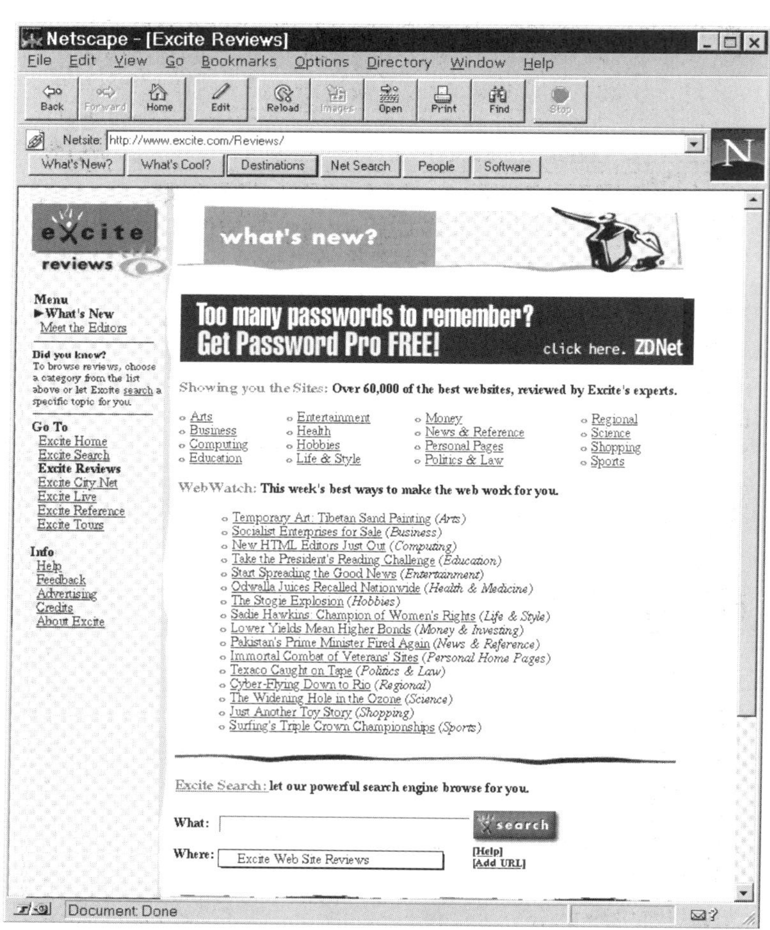

Figure 15.3 Excite offers rated reviews of 60,000 Web sites

Lycos Sites by Subject (a2z)

Another search engine, Lycos, offers a starting point (http://a2z.lycos.com) that you'll want to visit (Figure 15.4). Called a2z, this service offers a subject guide to hundreds of popular pages in a variety of subjects. The reviews aren't as critical or helpful as Excite's, however.

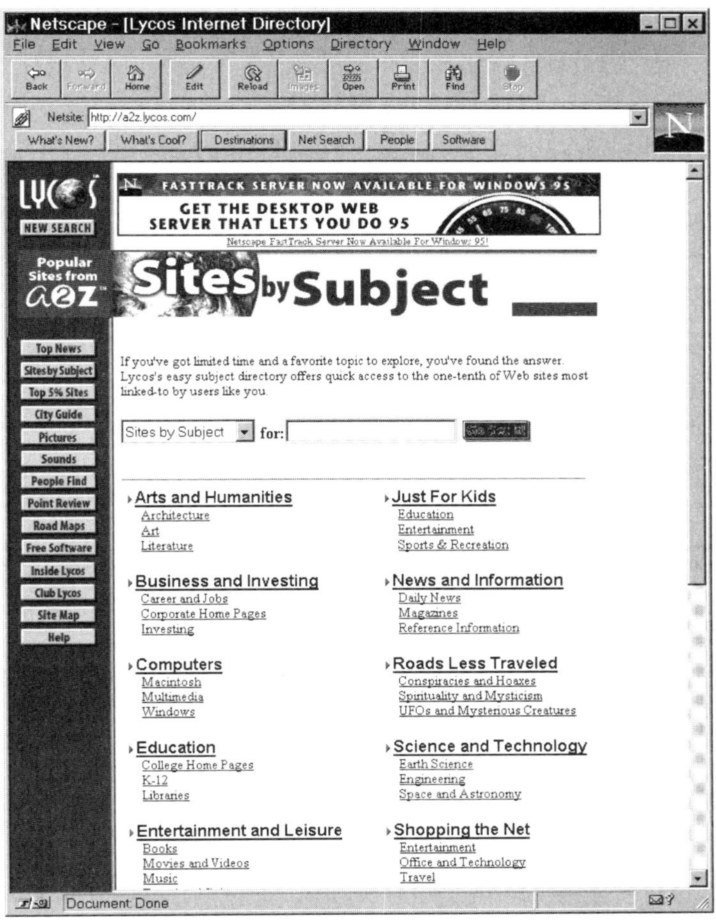

Figure 15.4 Lycos a2z home page offers reviews

DisInformation

You've probably heard that the Web is loaded with propaganda, paranoia, conspiracy theories, UFO sightings, catastrophe scenarios, and other forms of craziness. Thanks to DisInformation (http://www.disinfo.com), there's now a starting point for the disturbed side of the Web (Figure 15.5). Very highly recommended and fun!

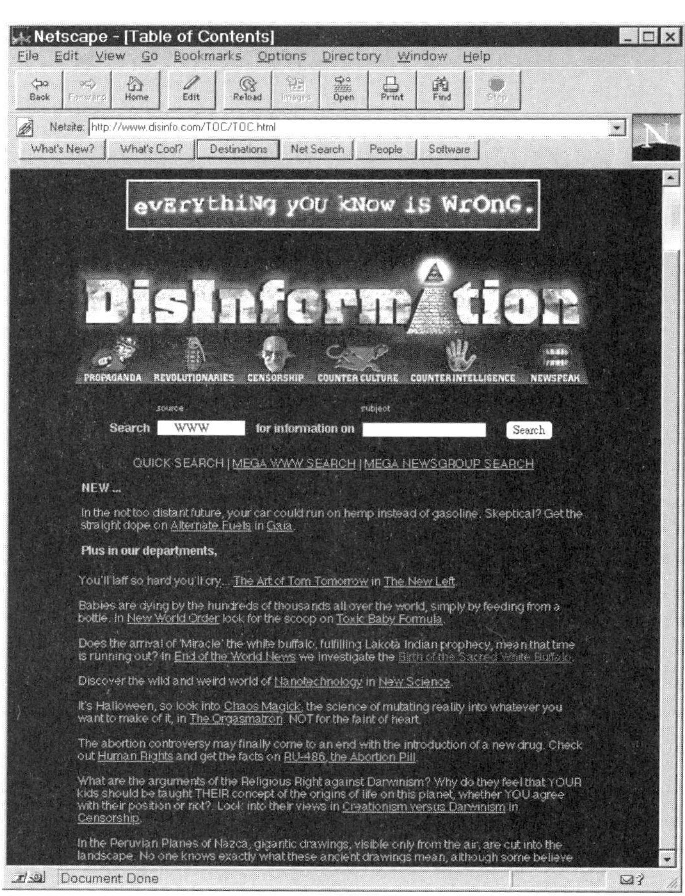

Figure 15.5 DisInformation indexes the zany side of the Web

iGuide

Here's a great starting points page for anyone interested in entertainment: It's called iGuide (http://www.iguide.com; Figure 15.6). You'll find links to the online version of TV Guide; reviews of books, films, and recent CDs; and a search engine for entertainment-related areas.

Figure 15.6 iGuide

More Starting Points Documents

Still looking for the perfect starting points document? Here are a few to try:

- **Spry's General Internet Page** (http://www.spry.com:80/internet.html) The home page of Spry, Inc., the makers of Air Mosaic. Lots of links to Internet guides and tutorials, and archives of connectivity software.
- **John December's Internet Index** (http://www.rpi.edu/~decemj/index.html) Lots of useful Internet information focusing on the analysis of computer-mediated communication. Lots of stuff focusing on John, too.
- **Internet Services List** (http://www.spectracom.com/islist/) Scott Yanoff's excellent subject tree listing links for every subject from geophysics to women's issues.
- **The WebCom Power Index** (http://www.webcom.com/power/index.html) A nice starting points selection: WWW information, pointers to search tools and subject indexes, and links to great sites in fields such as art, government, and education.

As a source of good starting points, don't forget personal home pages. These are essentially hotlists (bookmark lists) that certain individuals have made accessible to the public. Here are some great personal home pages:

- **Bazik** (http://www.cs.brown.edu/people/jsb/hotlist.html) Lots of stuff on commercial sites, random cool things, government sites, and lots, lots more.
- **Cybergrrl** (http://www.cybergrrl.com/title.html) Music, people, good causes, and a link to Grrls on the Web; some great women's/feminist links.
- **Karen** (http://www.cs.cmu.edu/afs/cs.cmu.edu/user/kcf/www/me/newhot.html) Very good entertainment links, plus a collection of cool home pages.
- **Lorrie** (http://dworkin.wustl.edu/pub/lorracks/home.html) Some good stuff on social issues facing the Internet.

- **Meng** (http://www.seas.upenn.edu/~mengwong/meng.html) The single most substantive page on the Web, if she does say so herself.
- **Ranjit** (http://moonmilk.volcano.org/playground.html) Toys for the amusement of travelers on the Information Superhighway.

You clown! You referred me to a home page—you said it was great—and it's not there anymore! That's the chance you take with personal home pages. Unlike companies, which tend to establish permanent Web presences, people move around, establishing pages on one server, then another, then disappearing from the Web altogether. This is especially true of college students, who still have a higher per capita home page count than any other demographic group. You can try using a search engine to search for the person's name, but, odds are, you're out of luck. Sorry.

Metapages

Metapages seek to sum up all the hyperlinks pertaining to a particular subject. Put together by volunteers who have personal interests in the area, they are gold mines of information. The following list provides some examples of useful metapages. Unfortunately, there's no real index of them; nobody's even sure what to call them (some people call them "home pages," while others call them "pointers pages," and still others call them "indexes"). You can try to discover a metapage in your area of interest by using the search techniques introduced in the next chapter.

- **Backcountry Home Page** (http://io.datasys.swri.edu/Overview.html) Fishing, hiking, backpacking, climbing—and the "distilled wisdom" of the experts.
- **Chronic Fatigue Syndrome** (http://metro.turnpike.net/C/cfs-news/) Tons of information about this disabling disease.
- **FedWorld** (http://www.fedworld.gov/) A very impressive list of U.S. government Web resources.

- **Games Domain** (http://www.gamesdomain.co.uk/) Everything you would ever want to know about computer games.
- **Human Languages Page** (http://www.willamette.edu/~tjones/Language-Page.html) A treasure trove of information about human languages, past and present.
- **Legal Links on the Internet** (http://ssnet.com/~james5/business.html) Emphasizing federal law and litigation.
- **Rockhounds Information Page** (http://www.rahul.net/infodyn/rockhounds/rockhounds.html) Everything on the Internet pertaining to rock collecting, including links to rock shops and photos of cool rock formations.
- **Science Fiction Links** (http://www.abdn.ac.uk/~u01rpr/sci-fi.html) Tons of links to *Star Trek*, *Star Wars*, and science fiction sites.
- **CineMedia** (http://www.gu.edu.au/gwis/cinemedia/CineMedia.tv.html) Grand Central Station for TV and film-related hyperlinks on the Web.
- **The Froggy Page** (http://www.cs.yale.edu/HTML/YALE/CS/HyPlans/loosemore-sandra/froggy.html) An unbelievable assortment of frog-related items: pictures, songs, sounds, links to scientific studies, lists of famous frogs. Wow!
- **The Web as a Learning Tool** (http://www.cs.uidaho.edu/~connie/interests.html) A very nice effort to bring together Web resources for K–12 education.
- **Ultimate Band List** (http://american.recordings.com/wwwofmusic/) Links to all the rock bands—over 1200 of them, from the 3D House of Beef and Cling to Trendy Wednesday and Weeping Tile—represented on the Web. There are some bands you've heard of here, too, somewhere.
- **Wine Home Page** (http://www.speakeasy.org/~winepage/wine.html) Dozens of links concerning wines, wineries, wine collecting, and wine accessories.
- **WWW Tennis Server** (http://www.cs.utoronto.ca/~cwong/tennis/tennis.html) Get the pun? Everything for the tennis fan, including ATP and WTA rankings, the code of tennis, and lots of tennis-related hyperlinks.

By far the best resource for subject-oriented metapages is the Virtual Library, a subject tree that is actually a compilation of volunteers' metapages. For more information on the Virtual Library, check out the next chapter.

What's Popular

Want to know what everyone else is doing with their Web browsers? Here's how to find out:

- **Most Popular Links at EINet Galaxy** (http://galaxy.einet.net/most-popular.html) EINet Galaxy is a subject tree/search engine hybrid. This page links the most popular sites directly accessed from Galaxy.
- **The WebCrawler Top 25** (http://webcrawler.com/WebCrawler/Top25.html) The top 25 most popular pages accessed by means of the WebCrawler search engine, discussed in Chapter 16.
- **WebCrawler Select Top 50** (http://www.webcrawler.com/select/top.new.html) The fifty most-accessed links in WebCrawler Select.
- **Yahoo What's Popular** (http://www.yahoo.com/popular.html) The most popular sites accessed from the Yahoo subject tree, also discussed in Chapter 16.

Best of the Web

What are the best sites available on the Web? Everyone has an opinion, but some have pages:

- **David Siegel's High Five** (http://www.highfive.com/) "The Carnegie Hall of Web Sites."
- **Best Webs of the World** (http://www.sct.fr/net/ubest.html) A French view, and a nice, succinct list.
- **Top 5% Sites** Lycos' rated list of Web pages worth a visit.

Cool Links

Frankly, I'm not sure what differentiates a "best" site from a "cool" site. You figure it out, and e-mail me (bp@virginia.edu), and I'll give you credit in the next edition. In the meantime, you're going to enjoy these pages:

- **Cool Site of the Day** (http://cool.infi.net/) Glenn Davis selects a new site every day for this coveted distinction. You can browse a voluminous list of previous cool sites.
- **What's Cool** (http://home.netscape.com/home/whats-cool.html) At least according to Netscape. I think this is verging on the "Best of the Web" territory. Or maybe it's a gallery of Netscape's business partners?
- **Yahoo Cool Links** (http://www.yahoo.com/Entertainment/COOL_links/) Definitely cool.
- **What's Hot and Cool on the Web** (http://kzsu.stanford.edu/uwi/reviews-l.html) A collection of cool sites, organized in a somewhat hard-to-figure-out table.

Worst of the Web

It had to happen. With all those "Best of the Web" pages, somebody, somewhere, would have had to come up with this idea.

- **Useless Web Pages** (http://www.go2net.com/internet/useless/) This is actually one of the Web's best sites. With additions made on a daily basis, you'll find plenty of hysterically funny stuff here. Latest editions: A penis length chart, a dissertation on barbecue potato chips, and a shocking exposé of the lesbian Barbie doll scene.
- **Enhanced for Netscape Hall of Sham**e (http://www.meat.com/netscape_hos.html) Too many blinks spoil the broth.

Weird Links

It's the fringe. The edge. And if you're looking for it, here are the starting points:

- **Anders' Weird Page** (http://www.nada.kth.se/~nv91-asa/weird.html) Discordiana, very substantial collection of links to the Church of the Subgenius, Geek-related mysteries, and more; you figure it out, you let me know, OK?
- **The Web's Edge** (http://kzsu.stanford.edu/uwi.html) This is apparently the leading edge of some kind of worldwide conspiracy.

What's New Pages

As if there weren't enough stuff on the Web to wade through, there are dozens—possibly hundreds—of new Web documents created daily. Here's how you can find out what's new:

- **Automatic News HREFs** (http://www.cs.cmu.edu/afs/cs.cmu.edu/user/bsy/www/auto_news/auto_news.0.html) URLs culled automatically from Usenet postings.
- **NCSA's What's New** (http://www.ncsa.uiuc.edu/SDG/Software/Mosaic/Docs/whats-new.html) Probably the best What's New resource. Includes a Pick of the Week.
- **What's New** (http://home.netscape.com/home/whats-new.html) Netscape's own list. Just click the "What's New" button on Netscape's button bar.

From Here

- Take advantage of subject trees and search engines to find information on the Web. Both subjects are covered in Chapter 16.

- Manage those Web documents—print 'em, save 'em, and cache 'em. Find out how (and what cache means) in Chapter 8.
- Put those helper applications to work! Chapter 10 documents all the multimedia helper applications included with this book.

Chapter 16

Find It on the Web!

Search Engines and Subject Trees

Looking for information on the Web? Let's start with the bad news. No single, up-to-date catalog of Web documents has ever been created. To do so would require a staff of hundreds of subject indexers working 'round the clock. Perhaps we'll see a Web Library someday, a service that would exhaustively catalog everything that's on the Web, but nothing like it exists right now.

Now here's the good news. To find information on the Web, you can make use of the following tools:

- **Subject Trees** A subject tree is an alphabetically organized list of selected Web resources that is usually organized with major headings such as Arts and Humanities, Business, Economy, Government, and the like. Within each category are found subheadings, which in turn

display pages listing specific hyperlinks. Because subject trees are manually updated, they cannot hope to cover all of the Web—these services aren't the Web Library, or anything close. But they are very useful because they are selective; they list only those documents that would likely prove useful to you.

- **Search Engines** A search engine enables you to search a database of Web documents using keywords (such as "frogs" or "wine"). The search engine ransacks a database of Web documents. Where does this database come from? In most cases, the databases are created by Web-roaming programs called *spiders*. These programs seek out new URLs and add them to the database. Searching one of these search engines will very likely produce a lot of useless, junk URLs, but you may find some gold amidst the gravel.

This chapter shows you how to construct an effective Web search using Netscape Navigator, subject trees, and search engines. If it's out there, you'll know how to find it after reading this chapter. You should use the information in this chapter with that in Chapter 15, which discusses trailblazer pages, metapages, and other subject-specific Web resources.

The distinction between subject trees and search engines is starting to erode, as you'll discover. InfoSeek Guide, one of the most technologically interesting and advanced search engines, tries to link your search terms with subject tree headings, which are displayed in a frame on the left of the retrieval list. If your search didn't work out very well, you can find some high-quality documents under these headings, one or more of which might be relevant to your interests.

Understanding Search Techniques

In both subject trees and search engines, you can make use of keyword searches. In subject trees, you search the subject tree entries. In search engines, you search a huge database of URLs. In either case, you will find it helpful to understand a few basic concepts:

- **Choosing Keywords** Try to think of one or more words that best describe the subject for which you're searching. The more general the term, the more likely it is that you'll find something useful.

For the Time-Challenged

- Subject trees try to classify Web documents according to subject. You can browse the subject tree. You can also search the subject headings and document titles. But bear in mind that subject trees classify only a small percentage of the total number of documents available on the Web.
- Search engines compile huge databases of Web documents, and you can search the databases using keywords. The trouble is, you'll retrieve a lot of junk amidst the useful documents.
- A good search strategy uses both subject trees and search engines. To make sure you've found all the useful documents in a given subject area, you should repeat your search in several subject trees and search engines.

- **Choosing Portions of the Document to Search** Some of the search tools discussed in this chapter let you specify which part of the document to search. For example, Yahoo enables you to search the document title, the URL, and the document description. It searches all three by default. You can perform a more focused search by restricting the search to the document title. This will eliminate irrelevant documents that just happen to include the keyword in their descriptions.
- **Case Sensitivity** Most of the search tools discussed in this chapter are case-insensitive, which means that they ignore the capitalization pattern you type. However, some offer the option of case-sensitive searching. If you choose this option, the search tool will match only those documents containing keywords with the capitalization pattern you typed (if you type "MRI," the software will match "MRI" but not "mri").
- **AND Operator** Most of the search tools you use will use the Boolean AND operator by default. If you type more than one keyword, the software will not retrieve a document unless it contains all of the words you type. This is a very restrictive search and may not produce good results. However, it's a good approach when your initial search produces too many documents.
- **OR Operator** Some search tools enable you to use the Boolean OR operator. If you type more than one keyword, the software will retrieve documents that contain any of the words you typed.

- **Contiguous Strings** A few search tools let you specify that the software should match the keywords you type only if they occur in the precise order you typed them, with no other words in between. For example, if you type "Mesoamerican archaeology," the software will retrieve only those documents that contain these two words in this exact order, without any other words between them.
- **Substrings and Whole-Word Searches** By default, most of the search tools discussed in this chapter search for substrings. A substring is a series of characters that might be embedded in a longer word. For example, if you search with the substring *very*, the software will retrieve documents that contain *every* as well as *very*. To restrict the search to whole words only (*very* only), you can sometimes choose a "whole word" or "complete word" option. If you choose this option, the search software will not retrieve documents in which the keyword appears as a substring.

If the search doesn't produce any results, click the Back button to redisplay the search page, and check your spelling! This is the most common cause of search errors. If the search retrieves too many documents, try using more specific keywords—and be sure to use the AND rather than the OR operator. To cut down on false drops, use whole-word searches instead of substring searches.

To access most of the Web's search services, including subject trees and subject engines, just click the Net Search directory button. You'll see a panel of subject tree and search engine offerings. From this panel, you can choose (currently) InfoSeek, Lycos, Magellan, Excite, or Yahoo. If you scroll down, you'll find links to the rest of the services discussed in this chapter (including Alta Vista), and many more.

A Guide to the Web's Subject Trees

There are several excellent subject trees available on the World Wide Web. Each has its own plusses and minuses, as you'll see in the pages to follow. We'll survey the top three: Yahoo, the Virtual Library, and WebCrawler Select.

Yahoo

Yahoo—short for Yet Another Hierarchically Odiferous Oracle—is the work of David Filo and Jerry Yang, two Stanford University graduate students who abandoned their Ph.D. work to make their subject tree the centerpiece of a private company. It's the best place to start your quest for Web information.

To access Yahoo, just click the Net Search directory button and click the Yahoo hyperlink, or enter the URL (http://www.yahoo.com/) directly. You'll see the Yahoo page, shown in Figure 16.1. Listed are Yahoo's main subject classifications, followed by second-level headings in each category. The word "Xtra" next to a subject classification signals the existence of a page of hyperlinked headlines pertaining to that category.

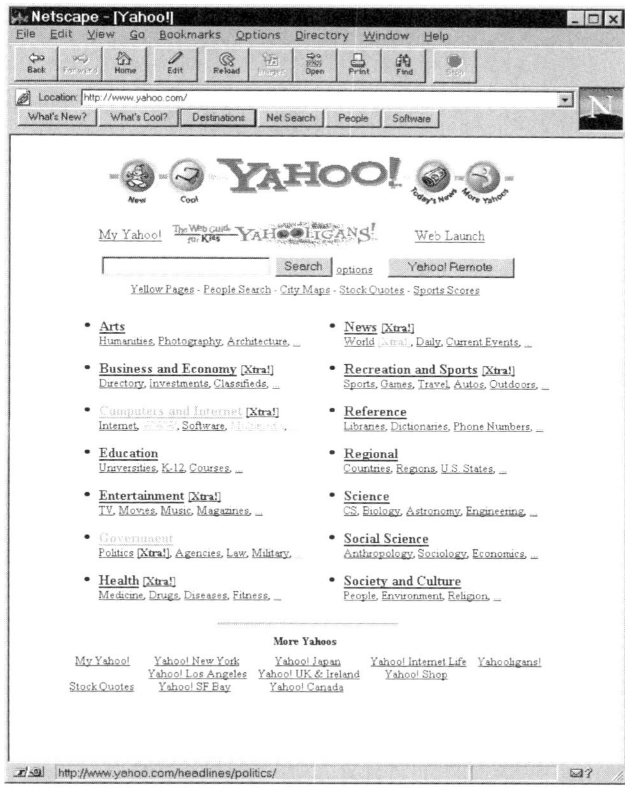

Figure 16.1 The main Yahoo page

What's up with all these academic sites becoming private companies? The Web started as an academic phenomenon—and then the general public caught on. It makes sense that the best academic resources break free of their academic incubators and make a go at it in the private sector, and that's what's happening. All the major academic search tools, including Lycos and WebCrawler, have "gone .com," and other resources are doing the same with regularity. It's part of the trend toward privatization on the Web.

Listing over 34,000 documents (at this writing), Yahoo offers a rich library of hyperlinks. To explore them, you can use two techniques, exploring the tree and searching.

Exploring the Tree The first way to use Yahoo is to navigate the subject tree by clicking on hyperlinks. To do so, just click on one of the subject classifications, such as "Entertainment." You'll see an additional page of second-level subject headings, such as the one shown in Figure 16.2. These headings are followed by the number of hyperlinks in each category in parentheses. The word "New" signals categories to which new hyperlinks have been added. If you keep clicking, you'll eventually reach a page that includes hyperlinks to Web documents. Unlike Yahoo's internal links, hyperlinks to Web documents aren't followed by a number, and many of them include descriptions (see Figure 16.3). To access a hyperlink to a Web document, just click it.

Look for hyperlinks that have a picture of a little pair of sunglasses next to them. These are the cool links—the ones that Yahoo recommends!

Yahoo's toolbar, positioned near the top of the screen, provides handy navigational aids. Here's what the options do:

YAHOO! Displays Yahoo's opening (top-level) page.

Displays the What's New At Yahoo page—the most recently added links.

Takes you to The Cool Links page.

Brings up Yahoo's Reuters news feed.

Displays the Yahoo Information and Help page.

Lets you suggest a URL to add to Yahoo.

Displays a page of more specific search engines, such as National and Metro Yahoos.

Searching for Information Another way to access the information in Yahoo is to perform a keyword search. To do so, go back to the Yahoo welcome

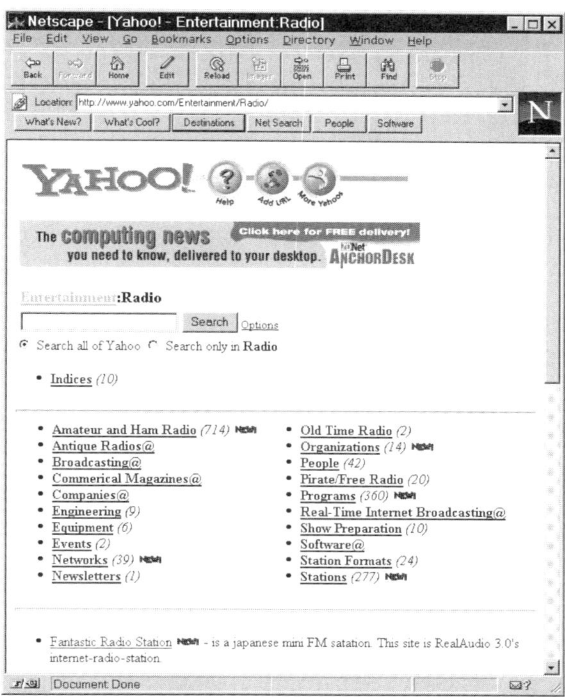

Figure 16.2 A page of second-level subject headings in Yahoo

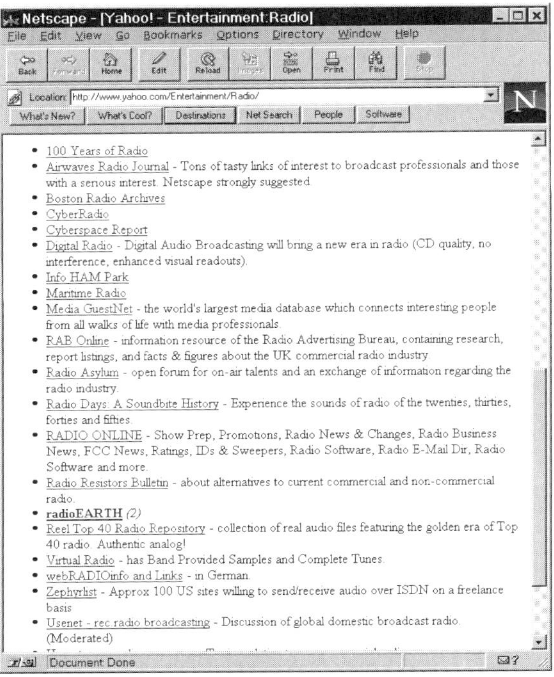

Figure 16.3 Descriptions of sites in Yahoo

page. You'll see a text box for entering keywords at the top of the page. That's a pretty basic search. If you need a more flexible search, click the Options hyperlink to the right of the search box. You'll see a complete search page, as shown in Figure 16.4. The instructions below explain how to use the expanded search page you see after clicking the Options hyperlink.

Yahoo offers excellent search capabilities, allowing all of the search options discussed in "Understanding Search Techniques," earlier in this chapter. To search Yahoo, follow these steps:

1. You should see the Yahoo search box on every Yahoo index page. If you don't see it—if, for example, you're looking at the Information page—click the large "Yahoo" at the top of your screen. To the right of the search box is the Options hyperlink. Click it to bring up the complete search page.

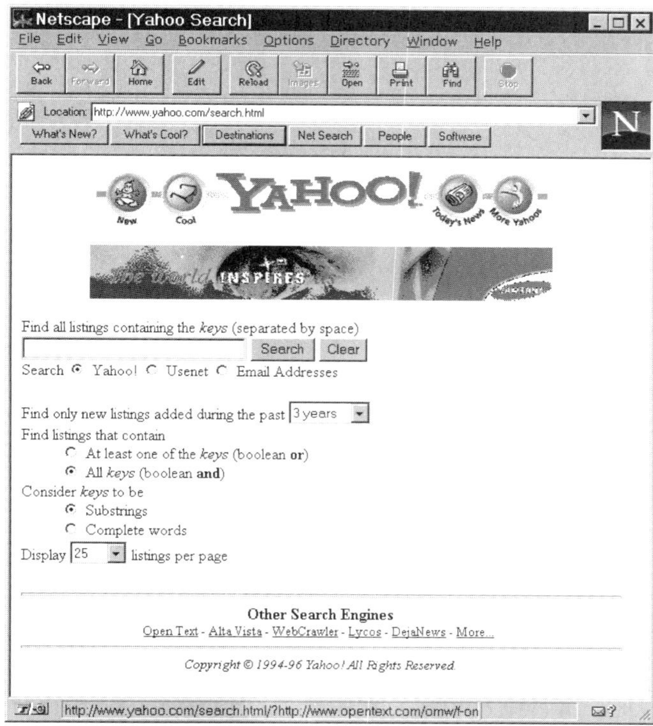

Figure 16.4 The Yahoo search page

2. In the text box, type one or more keywords. Check your typing and spelling carefully.
3. If you would like to restrict the search to Yahoo, click the leftmost radio button. By default, Yahoo searches its entire subject tree. You can also choose to search Usenet articles or e-mail addresses.
4. To perform a Boolean search, click the OR or AND button.
5. To perform a contiguous string search, click Substrings.
6. To perform a whole-word search, click Complete words.
7. To start the search, click Search.

The result of a Yahoo search is a list of Yahoo entries that match your keywords (Figure 16.5)—or, if there aren't any matches, a message that no match was found. You can browse the list and click the links as you please. To redo the search, click the Back button. Click the Clear button to clear the previous search and try again.

The Virtual Library

CERN, a center for particle physics research located in Geneva, Switzerland, is the birthplace of the Web. Among its many contributions to the Web is the Virtual Library, one of the first subject trees to be developed and still one of the most useful and comprehensive. The Virtual Library, in order to

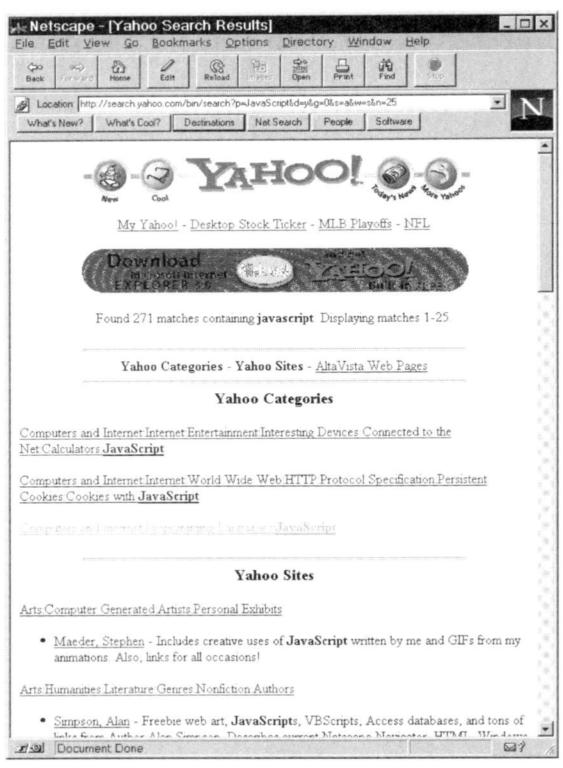

Figure 16.5 The results of a Yahoo search

allow CERN to focus on high-energy physics, is now maintained by the W3 Consortium.

Unlike Yahoo, whose administrators take upon themselves the arduous task of adding new URLs to the subject tree, the Virtual Library is a *distributed subject tree*. This means that the responsibility for maintaining the pages is distributed among individuals, each of whom possesses expertise in their area.

The Virtual Library's links point to pages maintained by these individuals, who have been chosen to maintain only the page for which they are responsible. Figure 16.6 shows the Anthropology page.

Many of the Virtual Library's pages got their start as metapages. They were incorporated into the Virtual Library after it became obvious that they had succeeded in achieving the most comprehensive collection of links in a given area.

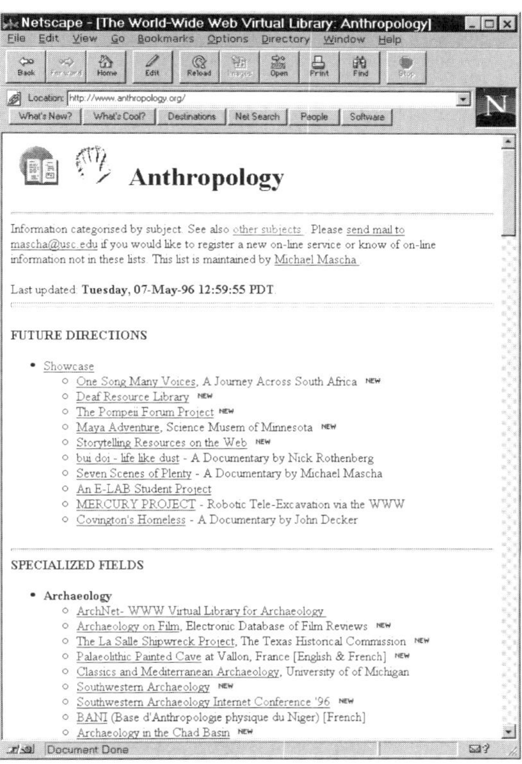

Figure 16.6 The Virtual Library Anthropology page

You can browse the list of subject headings in numerous ways. The default list is more compact and somewhat easier to browse. If you click the Category Subtree hyperlink, you see a lengthier list of subject headings and subheadings. The Category Subtree gives you more of a sense of the riches stored within the Virtual Library's hyperlinks. In addition, you can display the subject headings according to Library of Congress subject classifications (to do so, click the Library of Congress Classification hyperlink; see Figure 16.7). Alternative listings include Statistics, which orders subject fields according to their popularity, and Service Type, which orders the Library's resources by type of service (Web servers, Gopher, WAIS databases, etc.).

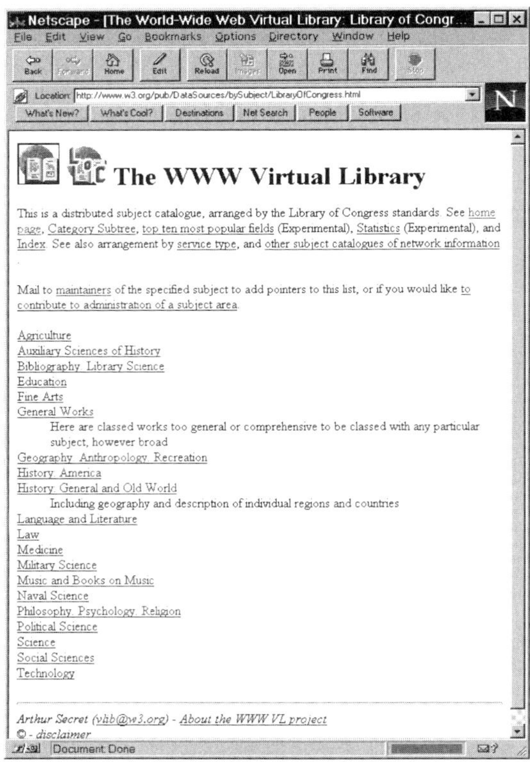

Figure 16.7 The Virtual Library listings arranged by Library of Congress classification standards

To access the Virtual Library, just click the Virtual Library icon in this book's home page (HOME.HTM), or use the following URL:

http://www.w3.org/hypertext/DataSources/bySubject/Overview.html

To access one of the pages in the Virtual Library, just click one of the subject hyperlinks.

Magellan

Another comprehensive subject tree is Magellan (http://www.mckinley.com), shown in Figure 16.8. One of the neat things about Magellan is that each site is rated using a four-star system, with the best sites appearing at the top of each list (see Figure 16.9 for an example).

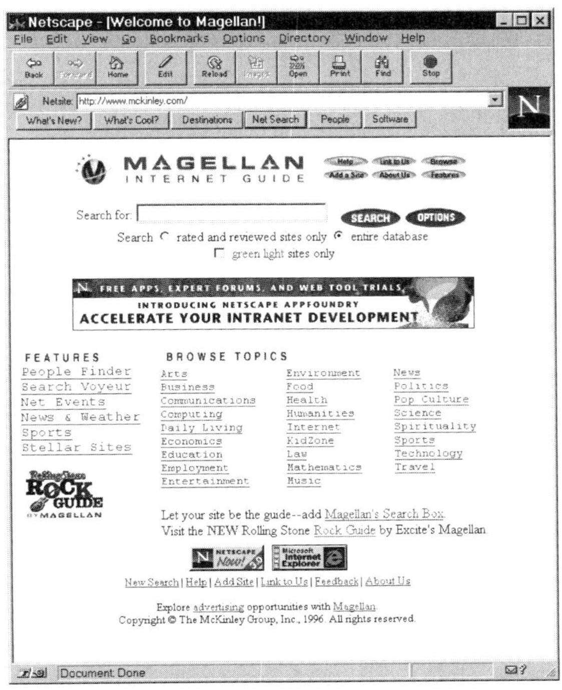

Figure 16.8 Magellan offers a searchable subject guide to the Web

Figure 16.9 Magellan reviews use a four-star system

Are your kids surfing the Net? Find kid-safe sites by looking for the green light in Magellan reviews. This indicates that the site doesn't contain adult content, such as nudity, adult language, violence, or sexual situations.

WebCrawler Select

One of the most impressive publishing phenomena of the 1990s was the success of Ed Krol's *The Whole Internet*, published by O'Reilly & Associates. Formerly a sleepy, strictly low-volume publisher of obscure books on obscure UNIX topics, O'Reilly hit the jackpot with Krol's excellent book. The revenue led to all sorts of ventures, and the Whole Internet Catalog—based on the useful appendix included in Krol's book—is one of them (Table 16.1). Now there's an on-line version (Figure 16.10), called WebCrawler Select, and you'll certainly want to make it part of your document-hunting strategy.

Like Yahoo, WebCrawler Select is maintained manually, but the staff doesn't even try to put in thousands of links. On the boundary between a starting points resource and a subject tree, the Catalog offers only about 2,000 links—but they're good links.

To access WebCrawler Select, just click the hyperlink in HOME.HTM, or use this URL:

http://webcrawler.com/select/

To access one of WebCrawler Select's subject pages, just click the hyperlink. You'll see a page such as the one shown in Figure 16.11.

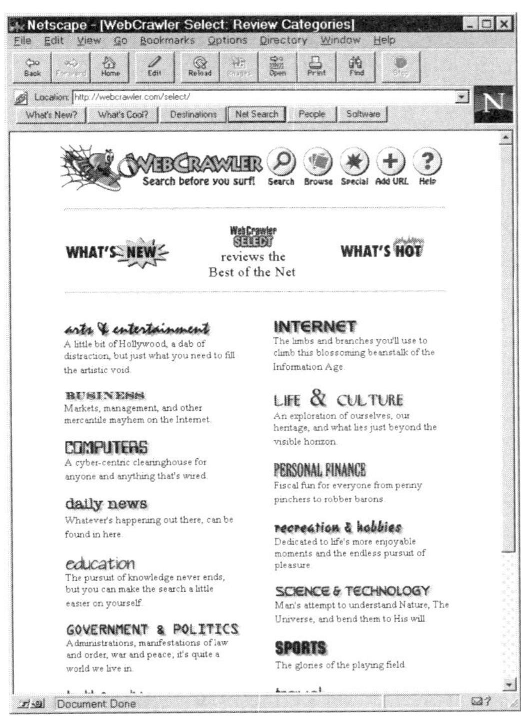

Figure 16.10 WebCrawler Select

Table 16.1 WIC Subject Classifications

Arts & Entertainment	Government & Politics	Personal Finance
Business	Health & Medicine	Recreation & Hobbies
Computers	Humanities & Social Sciences	Science & Technology
Daily News	Internet	Sports
Education	Life & Culture	Travel

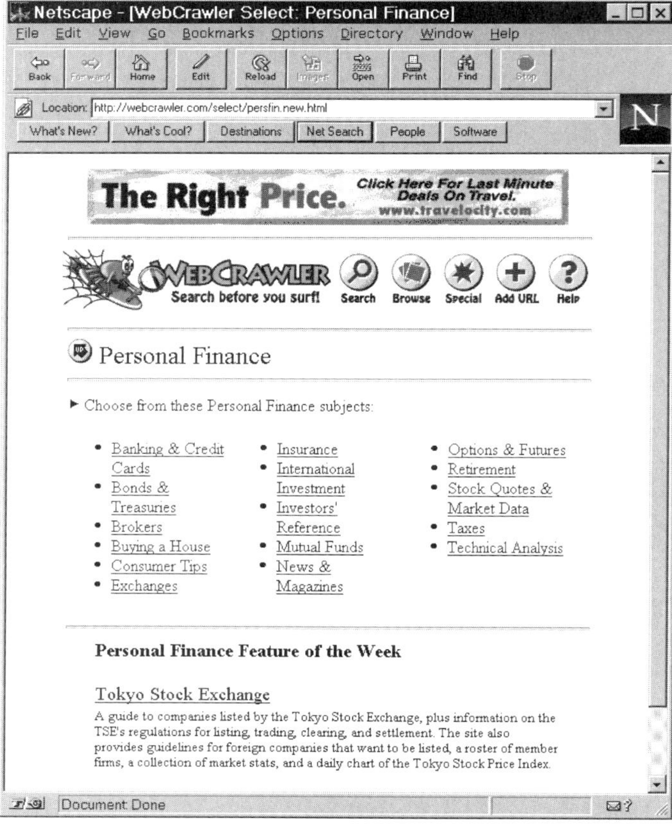

Figure 16.11 WebCrawler Select Personal Finance page

Search Engines

With more than two million documents on the Web and hundreds more arriving daily, there's no chance that Yahoo, the Virtual Library, or Web-Crawler Select can keep up. That's why your search strategy should include search engines.

Most search engines are based on robot-like programs called *spiders* (also called *worms*), which roam the Web looking for new URLs. Most of them do little more than catalog the words in the URL and the document's title and move on. Some spiders index the first few dozen words in the document itself, and a few index all the words in the entire document.

There's a tradeoff here. If the spider indexes only the title and words in the URL, it can index a lot of documents—the search goes quickly. But don't expect good results from your search. Web authors don't give much thought to their document titles, unfortunately, and URL words may have little or nothing to do with the document's content. Searching the database created by such a spider is sure to produce a lot of false drops, documents that aren't relevant to your interests. On the other hand, if the spider indexes the full text of the document, don't expect the database to include more than a few hundred thousand documents—the search takes a long time. However, searching the database produces better results. Now that you know about this tradeoff, you can make a more informed choice among the various search engines that are available.

Searching from the Location Box

New to Netscape 3 is a very cool feature that enables you to initiate a search from the Location box. To find something on the Web, simply type two or more search words, separated by spaces, within the Location box (the one that normally shows a URL), and press Enter. When Netscape has determined that what you've typed couldn't possibly be a domain name, the program sends the words you've typed to a search service, such as InfoSeek, Yahoo, or Magellan, and you see a retrieval list.

My Location box search didn't retrieve anything! When you use this new feature, Netscape selects a search engine at random—and it might not be the right one for your needs. For example, it's great to search Yahoo if you've typed general concepts (such as desktop publishing or Windows 95 shareware), but it's better to use Alta Vista or Lycos if you're hunting down something more obscure. If your Location

box search doesn't work out, try choosing the right search engine for your needs and access it directly.

Alta Vista

A service of Digital Equipment Corporation, Alta Vista indexes the full text of more than 16 million Web pages at this writing. It's one of the best major-league Web search engines.

To access Alta Vista, click the hyperlink on HOME.HTM, or use this URL:

http://altavista.digital.com/

You'll see the Alta Vista welcome page and search form, shown in Figure 16.12.

To search Alta Vista:

1. In the large text box at the top of the page, type your search terms.
2. Tell Alta Vista to search either Web documents or Usenet news by selecting an option from the list box.

Alta Vista offers one of the most customizable search interfaces out there. Here are some useful tips for Alta Vista searches:

- Putting words in quotes requires that the search engine find those words together, in sequence. A search for "scientific calculator," for example, would not return a site containing the words *scientific graphing calculator.*
- The plus symbol means AND; the minus sign means AND NOT. For example, a search for *cleveland+ohio-columbus* (without the italics) would return sites containing *cleveland* and *ohio*, but not *columbus*.
- Use the asterisk as a wildcard. A search for *fly* would return sites containing that word by itself; a search for **fly** would return *flypaper*, *flygirl*, and *barfly*.
- Use the modifier *title*: to specify words that must appear in a document's title. *title:Jones* would return sites with *Jones* in the title.

3. Opt for Standard, Compact, or Detailed (long) site descriptions.
4. Click the Submit button.

You'll see the results of your search on a new page, like the one shown in Figure 16.13. If you selected Standard output, the title of the site, hyperlinked to the site itself, appears at the top of its description. The URL, also hyperlinked to the site, appears at the bottom.

There's an advanced search form at Alta Vista, too. Access it by clicking the Advanced button on the toolbar on the Alta Vista welcome page. The advanced search form appears in Figure 16.14.

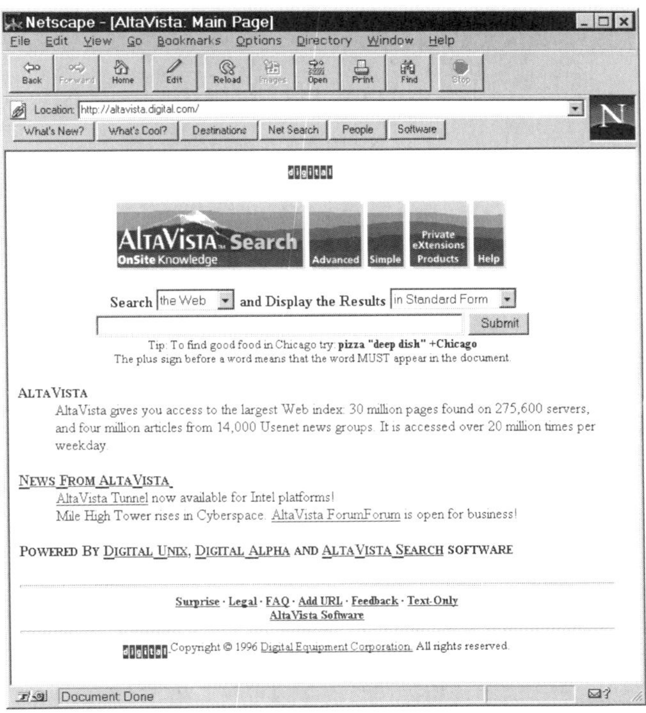

Figure 16.12 The Alta Vista search form

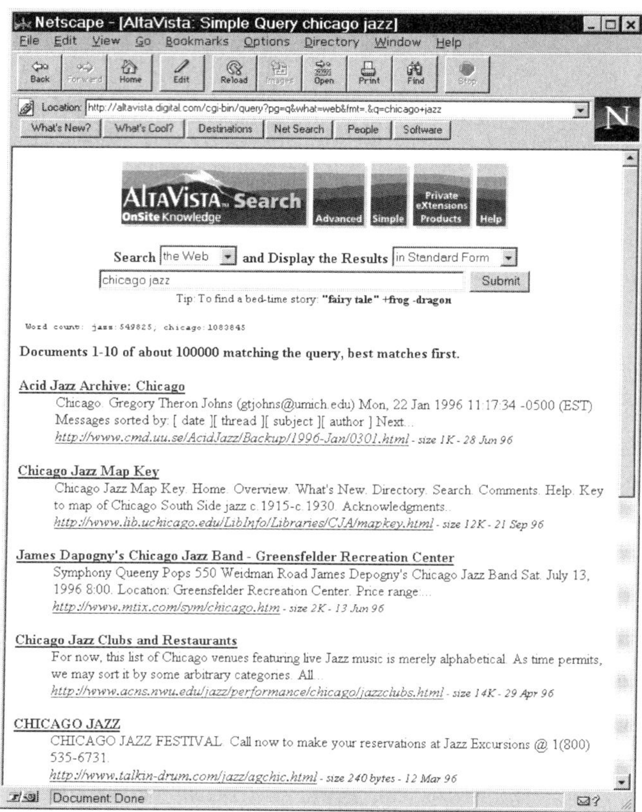

Figure 16.13 Results of an Alta Vista search

The advanced search form lets you construct searches with the Boolean operators AND, OR, NOT, and NEAR. NEAR specifies that one word must be within 10 words of another.

For example, an advanced search for the following:

grapes AND raisins AND NOT walnuts

would return a document containing the phrase, "How to make raisins from grapes," but would ignore one that contained the phrase "Grape-Raisin-Walnut Salad."

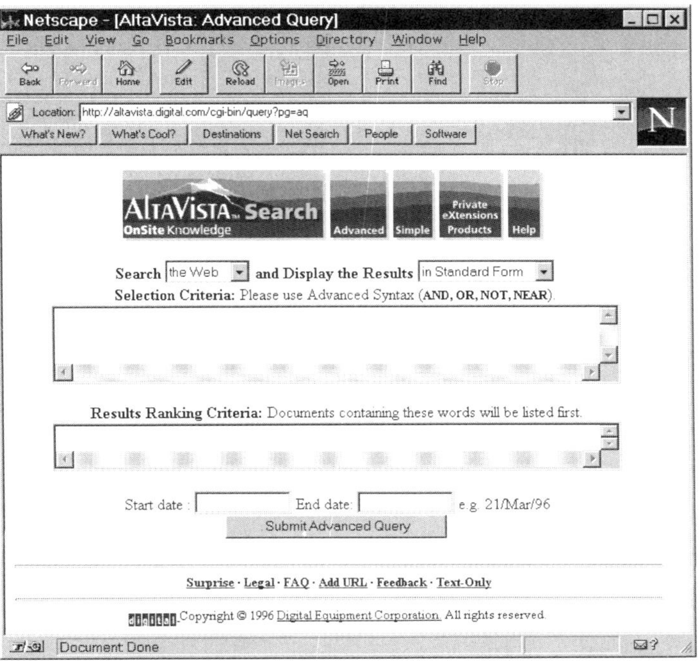

Figure 16.14 The Alta Vista advanced search form

The NEAR operator is useful in searching for someone's name. The search

richard NEAR jones

would return references to "Richard Jones," "Richard A. Jones," and "Richard Allison Jones, M.D." Unfortunately, that search would also return hits on documents containing phrases like "Richard Krinklemeyer and Joyce Jones are pleased to announce...," since "Richard" and "Jones" are within 10 words of each other in that phrase, too.

The advanced search form also lets you specify the order in which your search results appear. Enter the most important words in your search in the second text box. Alta Vista will rank documents containing these words ahead of documents that satisfy the search criteria but do not contain the words you put in the second box.

Infoseek

One of the easiest-to-use services on the web, Infoseek, doesn't have as large a database as Alta Vista, but it's a good way to get a fast idea of what's on the Web on a certain topic. The Infoseek page appears in Figure 16.15.

To access Infoseek, click the hyperlink in HOME.HTM or type the URL directly:

http://www.infoseek.com

Infoseek now has two search methods, Ultraseek and Ultrasmart. The latter method provides additional information in the area of your search, such as links to related topics and news stories. Ultraseek, on the other hand, generates a simple list of sites in a fast, streamlined fashion.

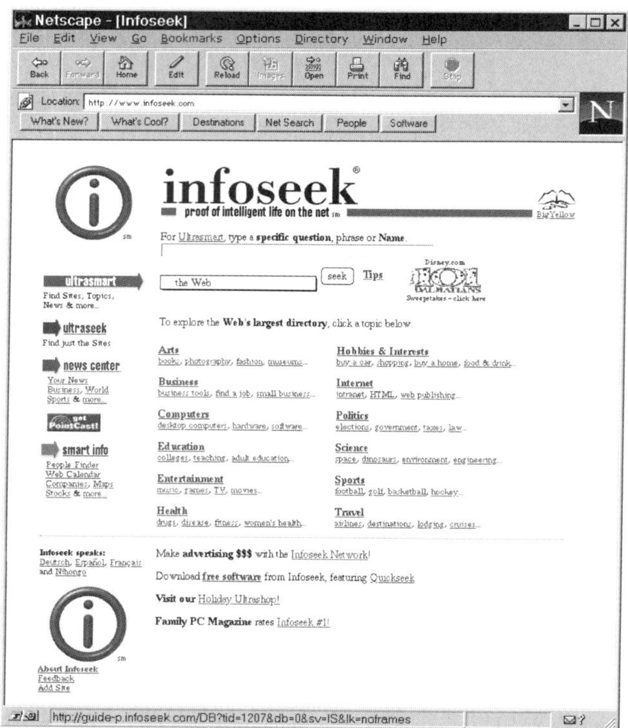

Figure 16.15 Infoseek

To search using Ultrasmart (the default method):

1. Type your search terms or query into the text box.
2. Specify, using the list box under the text box, whether you want to search Web pages, FAQs, or whatever.
3. Click the Seek button.

Infoseek will display the results of your query on a page like the one shown in Figure 16.16. Click the heading of a page's listing to jump to that page.

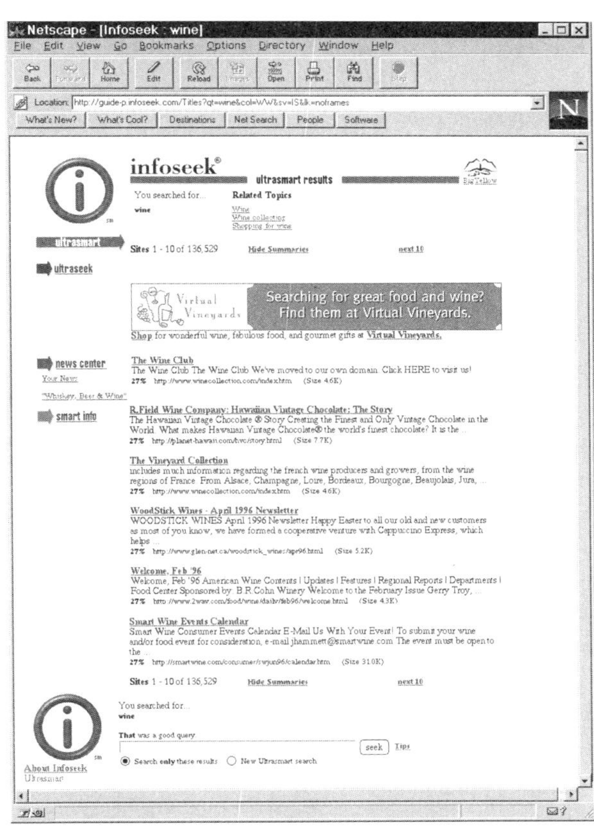

Figure 16.16 Results of an Infoseek Ultrasmart search

Infoseek offers advertisers a nifty bonus for advertising on Infoseek pages: When users enter a search term, the search software examines the list of advertisers and tries to match the search subject to a pertinent ad. Try searching for "Netscape." You'll almost certainly see an ad from Netscape Communications, Inc. Clever, huh? Advertisers pay more for this type of advertisment, since it's more likely to generate a response. In Figure 16.16, for example, a search for "wine" netted an ad for Virtual Vineyards. Personally, I think this is great. Virtual Vineyards is one of the best wine sites on the Web. If I didn't already know about it, I'd be delighted to discover it, thanks to the ad. Nice job, Infoseek!

Look at the top of the result page to see a list of Infoseek subject headings that are relevant to your search topic. If you see one that looks dead-on, click it to see a list of high-quality (reviewed) links. Look in the left panel for news stories related to your topic. As you can see, Infoseek combines a search engine and subject tree in a very appealing way.

At the bottom of the Ultrasmart result listing is another search box so that you can narrow the original search. For example, if you started searching by typing "wine," you could narrow the search by typing "California" in this box and clicking the "Search only these results" button. A new list of sites that include both search terms will be returned.

Lycos

The Web search engine that started it all, Lycos left Carnegie-Mellon University in 1995 to form the centerpiece of a private company. Though it competes with such wonderful search engines as Infoseek and Alta Vista, Lycos still offers excellent capabilities and belongs in everyone's search repertoire. Like Infoseek, Lycos is breaking down the boundaries between search engines and subject trees, thanks to the firm's acquisition of Point (which reviews the "top 5% of Web sites").

To access Lycos, just click the hyperlink on HOME.HTM, or use this URL:

http://www.lycos.com/

You can work with that simple form, or click the Custom Search hyperlink to see a search form like the one shown in Figure 16.17. These instructions deal with using the advanced form (the best choice for serious searching).

To search Lycos using this form:

1. From the list box next to "Search," choose whether to search the entire Web or Lycos' site list, or search directly for sound and image files on the Web using Lycos' multimedia index, Pictures & Sounds.
2. In the text box next to "for," type one or more keywords. If you wish, search with one of these options:

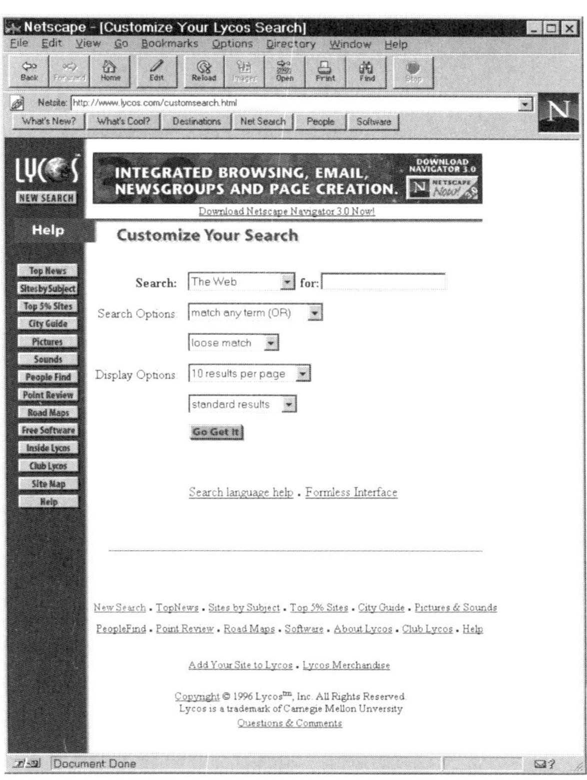

Figure 16.17 The Lycos advanced search form

- To exclude documents containing an unwanted word, type a minus sign followed by the word. For example, suppose you're interested in X Window software and you don't want to see documents about Microsoft Windows. Type the following keywords: X Window–Microsoft.
- To perform a whole-word search, type a period after the keyword (for example, "cat." retrieves "cat" but not "caterpillar," etc.).

3. Set options in the list boxes below the search box. You can link all your search terms with AND or OR, or specify the number of search terms the engine must match. You can also specify the exactness of the match (from "strong" to "loose"), the number of hits displayed per page, and the amount of detail displayed about each hit.
4. To initiate the search, click the Go Get It button.

The results of your Lycos search appear in a new window (Figure 16.18), unless the server is too busy (an all-too-frequent result, I fear). You see your keywords, plus a list of the words in Lycos' database that match the keywords you typed. Following are the hyperlinks that Lycos retrieved, if any. If you find an interesting hyperlink, click it—or click the Back button to revise your search strategy.

This document's at the top of the list, but it isn't relevant to my interests! Just because a document scores high in Lycos' ranking system doesn't mean that it's going to contain material of interest to you. This ranking is done by mindless computers, blindly following their programming. They can't read the documents or understand the content—they can just match characters. Sometimes the result is laughably off the mark.

WebCrawler

Owned by America Online, the spider-based WebCrawler doesn't have a very large database, but it amply compensates by indexing the full text of the documents it analyzes. As such, WebCrawler is much more likely to retrieve that valuable document in which the keywords appear only at the end of the document, buried deeply within the document's text. Even though its database isn't very big, you should still include WebCrawler in

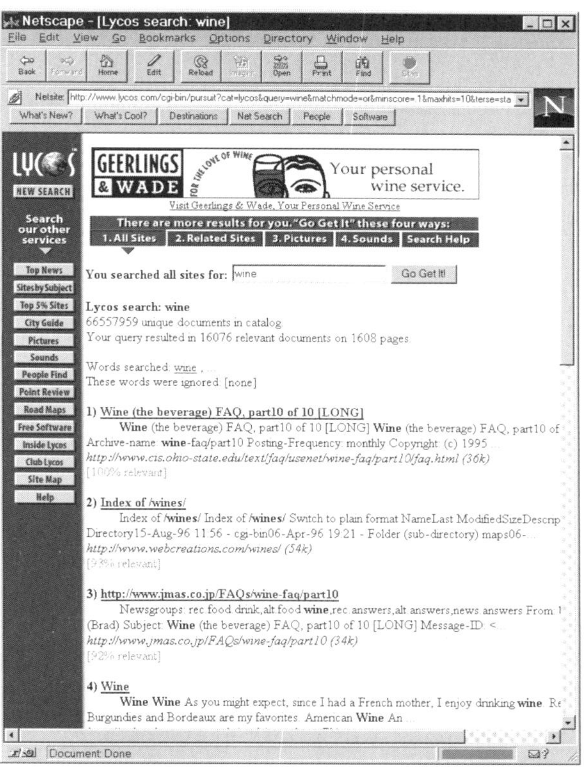

Figure 16.18 The results of a Lycos search

your search. To access WebCrawler, click the hyperlink in HOME.HTM, or use the following URL:

http://www.webcrawler.com/

You'll see the WebCrawler page, shown in Figure 16.19.

To search WebCrawler, follow these steps:

1. Type one or more keywords in the text box.
2. If you would like to perform a Boolean OR or AND search, include those terms with your search terms. For example, you can search for "beer or ale," or "netscape and plug-ins."

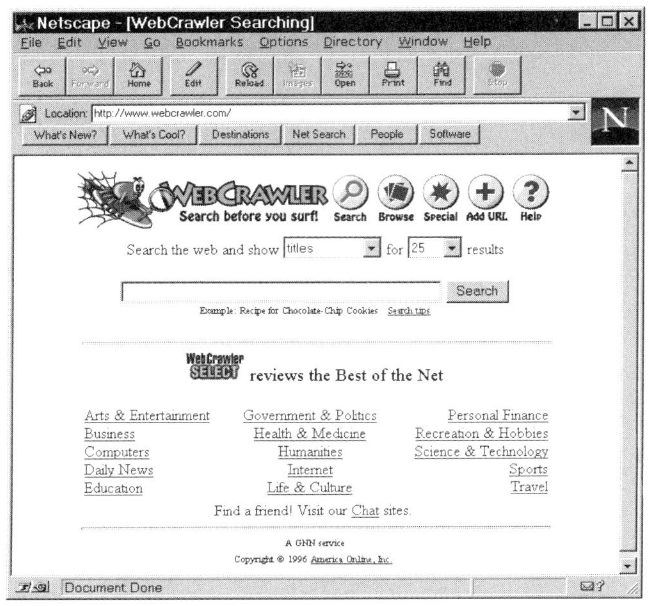

Figure 16.19 The WebCrawler welcome page

3. If you would like to see more than 25 documents, choose a larger number next to "results."
4. Click Search to initiate the search.

The result of your WebCrawler search is a page of hyperlinks, such as the one shown in Figure 16.20. Like the results of a Lycos search, the documents are ranked in order of relevance, with the top-scoring document at the top.

From Here

- If you've gotten this far in this book, congratulations! You're a darned good Netscapist by now, and what's more, you know how to

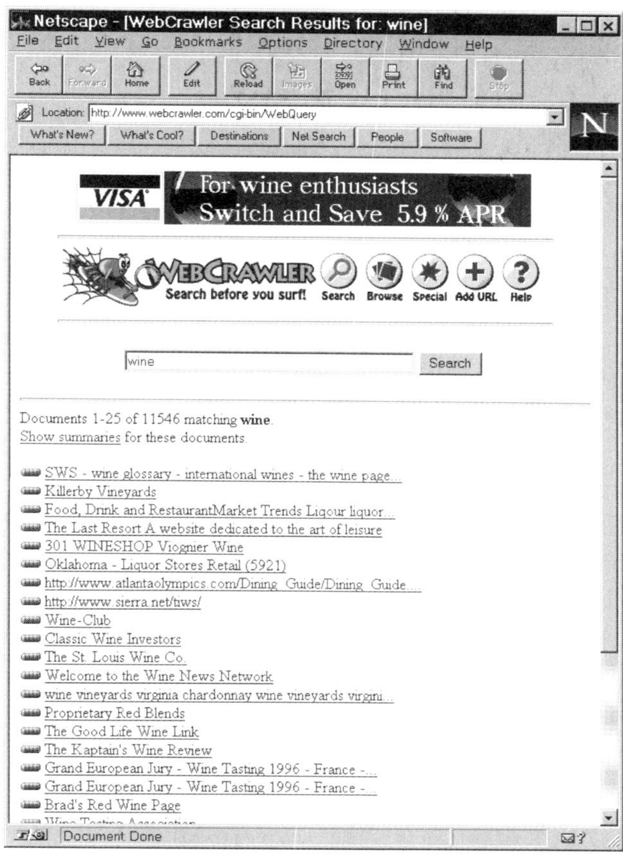

Figure 16.20 The results of a WebCrawler search

retrieve information in an orderly way. You'll be getting tons of useful documents, so you'd better learn how to share them with others by electronic mail, the subject of Chapter 17.

- What, electronic mail isn't fast enough for you? Learn about real-time chat with IRC in Chapter 18.
- Reach out and touch someone—but without paying long-distance charges! Find out how in Chapter 19.

Part V

Exploring the Internet with Netscape Navigator

Chapter 17

Sending and Receiving E-mail

Netscape Navigator is fast becoming the only tool you'll need to access just about everything on the Internet. You can use Netscape to send and receive electronic mail.

Introducing E-mail

When you establish an account with an Internet service provider (ISP), you'll get an electronic mailbox. This mailbox is stored on the ISP's *mail server*, an Internet-connected computer with special mail software and a very large hard disk. The mail server stores your mail temporarily until you log into the

system. At that time, Netscape looks for new mail—if there's any waiting for you, you'll see an exclamation point after the envelope on the status bar. (This envelope shows up in the browser as well as the Mail and News windows.) Think of the mail server as a temporary parking place for your mail.

When you compose and send e-mail to others, what happens is the reverse of the above process: Netscape sends your mail to the server, which relays it on to its Internet destination.

How do I know whether someone's read my message? Some e-mail programs enable you to send messages with receipt notification, but Netscape doesn't include this feature. If you don't get a reply from somebody, don't assume you're being ignored—the person may not have logged on! If you want others to have confidence in sending mail to you, be sure to log on to your server frequently and check your mail.

About E-mail Addresses

To exchange e-mail with someone, you'll need your own e-mail address, as well as the e-mail address of the person with whom you'd like to correspond. You'll receive your e-mail address when you establish an account with an Internet service provider.

Internet e-mail addresses have three parts:

- **User name** The first part of the e-mail address identifies your personal mailbox. For example, if your name is David Smith, you may be assigned a mailbox name of *dsmith*.
- **At sign (@)** The second part of the e-mail address is a separator: It separates the first part from the third part, so those dumb computers can tell the difference.
- **Mail server's domain name** The third part of the e-mail address gives the domain name of your e-mail server.

A complete, correct e-mail address looks like the following fictitious one:

dsmith@asteroid.chv.va.us

Please note that you can't place any spaces in an e-mail address.

If you're familiar with electronic mail, you're probably wondering how Netscape compares to other e-mail programs. If you're using Windows 95, you'll be pleased to know that Netscape's e-mail beats the default Windows e-mail client, Microsoft Exchange, hands down. However, Netscape has one drawback for a serious e-mail user: There's no provision for filtering messages automatically. With message filtering, you set up filters using keywords, such as a person's name or message text (such as "test" or "ignore"); when the program detects an incoming message that contains the specified text, it diverts the message to a folder of your choice—including the trash can, if you wish! With filtering, you're not bombarded with dozens of unwanted or low-priority messages. Instead, they're parked into folders where you can read them later, if you wish. Aside from this shortcoming, though, Netscape has some cool features—including the ability to thread mail messages, so you can see the relationship between the mail you've sent and the mail you've received.

E-mail addresses aren't case-sensitive, the way URLs are. Most people use lowercase letters for e-mail addresses, though, and it's a good practice because it prevents confusion (if you type part of your address in capital letters, people might think they need to do so).

For the Time-Challenged

- Netscape's e-mail capabilities are excellent and convenient. You'll need to configure the Mail window using information supplied by your Internet service provider.
- Create a signature containing your name, address, and phone numbers. Netscape will append your signature to the messages you send.
- Click To: Mail to compose a message.
- Click Re: Mail to reply to a message.
- Add e-mail addresses to the Address Book for convenient entry.

Configuring E-mail

To get started with Netscape's e-mail, you need to configure your copy of Netscape so that it knows where your mail server is located. Before you do this, call your ISP and ask the following questions:

- What is the address of the SMTP server for outgoing mail?
- What is the address of the POP-3 server for incoming mail?
- What is my user name?
- What is my mail password?

Often, the addresses for the outgoing and incoming mail are the same. Be sure to write all this information down, but keep your password from prying eyes.

To configure Netscape's e-mail:

1. From the Options menu in any Netscape window, choose Mail and News Preferences. You'll see the Preferences dialog box, shown in Figure 17.1.
2. Click the Servers tab. Figure 17.1 shows the Servers options.
3. In the Outgoing Mail (SMTP) Server box, type the Internet address of the computer that handles your outgoing mail.
4. In the Incoming Mail (POP) Server box, type the Internet address of the computer that handles your incoming mail.
5. In the Pop User Name box, type the user name that your ISP gave you.
6. The other options can be left as is, but consider whether you want to leave your messages on the server or have Netscape delete them when they're downloaded. The best option is to have Netscape delete them. This preserves disk space on the server. To choose this option, which I recommend, click the option button next to "Removed from the server."
7. You may also wish to have Netscape check your mail automatically at intervals you specify. To do so, click the Every option and type the interval, in minutes, at which you want Netscape to check for mail. I recommend 10 minutes.

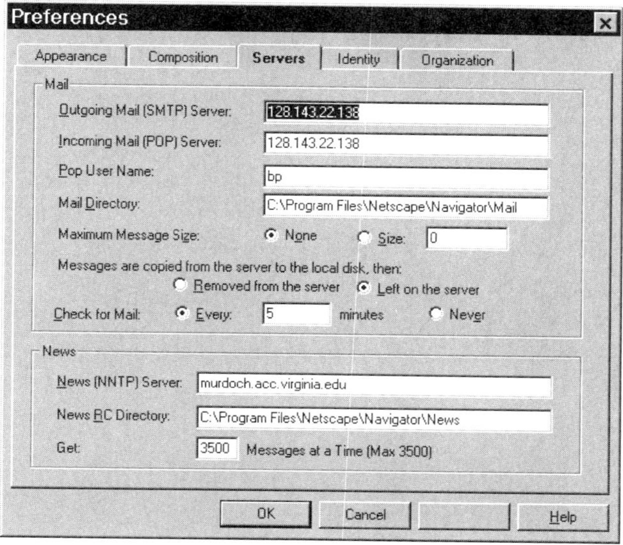

Figure 17.1 Servers page (Mail and News Preferences dialog box)

8. Click the Identity tab. You'll see the Identity page, shown in Figure 17.2.
9. In the Your Name box, type your name as you wish it to appear in other people's inboxes.
10. In the Your Email box, type your e-mail address exactly the way your ISP gave it to you.
11. Leave the Reply-To box blank, unless you want people to reply to an e-mail address other than your own.
12. In the Your Organization box, type the name of your organization (school or company), if you wish (this is optional).
13. Click the Organization tab. You'll see the Organization page, shown in Figure 17.3.
14. In the General area, click Remember Mail Password if you would like Netscape to remember the password that accesses your mail

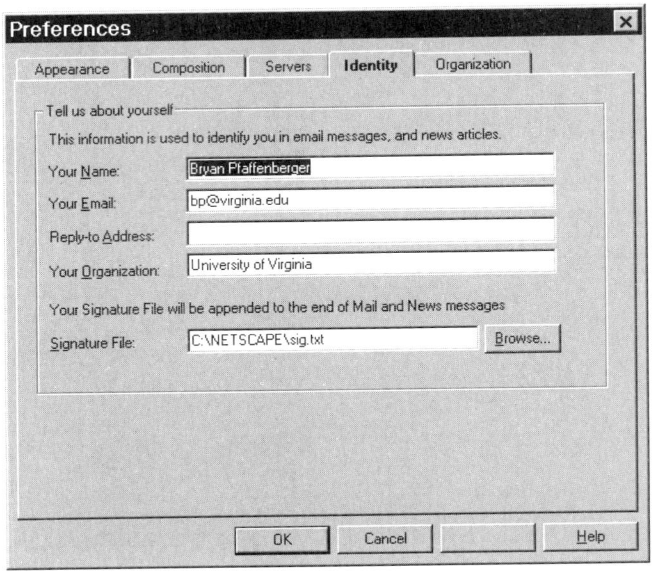

Figure 17.2 Identity page (Mail and News Preferences dialog box)

server. However, you should not do this if anyone besides yourself has access to your computer.

15. Netscape can "thread" e-mail messages the same way it organizes Usenet messages: replies are shown beneath the original message, so that you can see the "thread" of discussion. This is a very cool feature and I recommend that you enable it. To do so, click Thread Mail Messages.

16. In the Sorting area, you'll see that Netscape sorts e-mail by date, by default. With this sort order, you'll see the most recent messages first, which is the best way to sort your e-mail. As you'll see later on, you can re-sort the messages by name or subject, if you wish, without changing the default sort order. This comes in handy for finding a message that you received some time ago.

17. Click the Appearance tab. You'll see the Appearance page, shown in Figure 17.4.

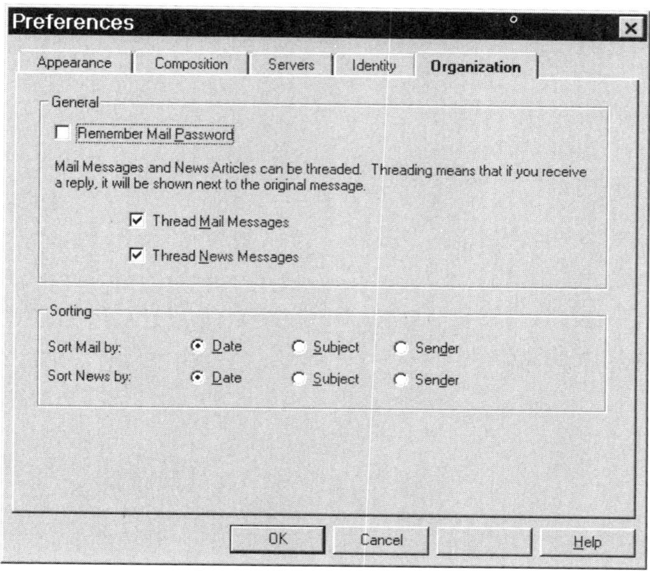

Figure 17.3 Organization page (Mail and News Preferences dialog box)

18. In the Message Styles area, you can choose to display messages with a fixed width font or a variable (proportional) width font. The fixed width option is actually better; many people send e-mail messages with spacing options that assume you're viewing the message with a fixed width font.
19. In the "Text beginning with > (quoted text)" area, choose a text style for quoted text, if you wish. The default is italic, which is fine. This shows up only in the copy of the message you're viewing with Netscape; your recipients won't see it.
20. In the Text Size area, choose a text size for quoted text, if you wish. The default is Plain; you can choose a bigger or smaller font size. This shows up only in the copy of the message you're viewing with Netscape (your recipients won't see it).
21. **Important**: Under the heading "When sending and receiving electronic mail," choose Use Netscape for Mail and News.

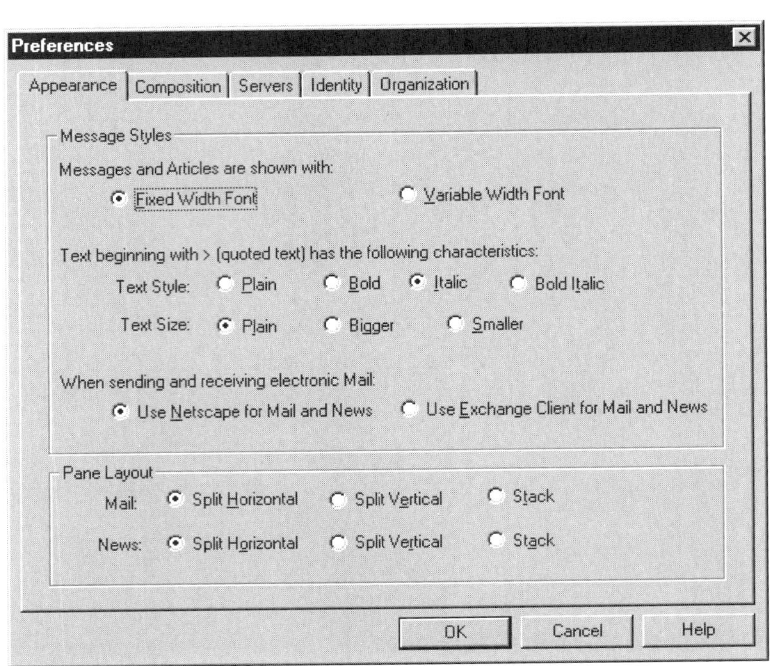

Figure 17.4 Appearance page (Mail and News Preferences dialog box)

22. Click the Composition tab. The default options are fine in this page (Figure 17.5). You need to fill in these areas only if you would like to copy all of your outgoing news and mail messages to someone. One option you may wish to consider is the quotation option on the bottom of the dialog box; if you click this, Netscape will automatically quote the text of every message to which you're replying. This is convenient, but it's not advisable: Not every reply message needs to contain a verbatim quotation of the original. If you leave this option blank, you can quote text in replies by clicking the Quote button—and that's what I'd advise you to do.
23. Click OK to confirm your options and return to Netscape.

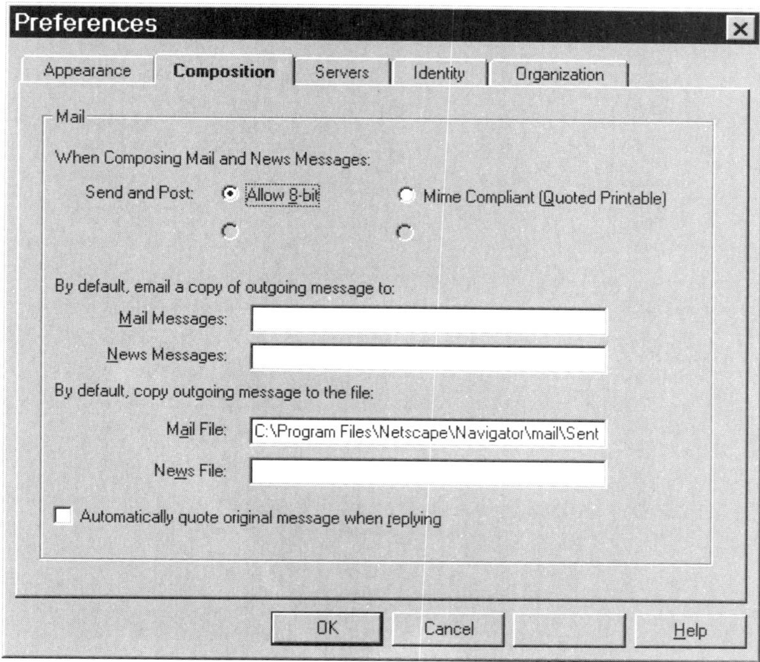

Figure 17.5 Composition page (Mail and News Preferences dialog box)

Understanding the E-mail Window

Now that you've configured Netscape for your e-mail account, it's time to open the e-mail window and log on to your server. Ask someone to send you some mail, so you'll have something to work with! In the meantime, you can get to know Netscape's Mail window.

Opening the E-mail Window

To open Netscape's e-mail window, open the Window menu and choose Netscape Mail. You'll see the Mail window, shown in Figure 17.6.

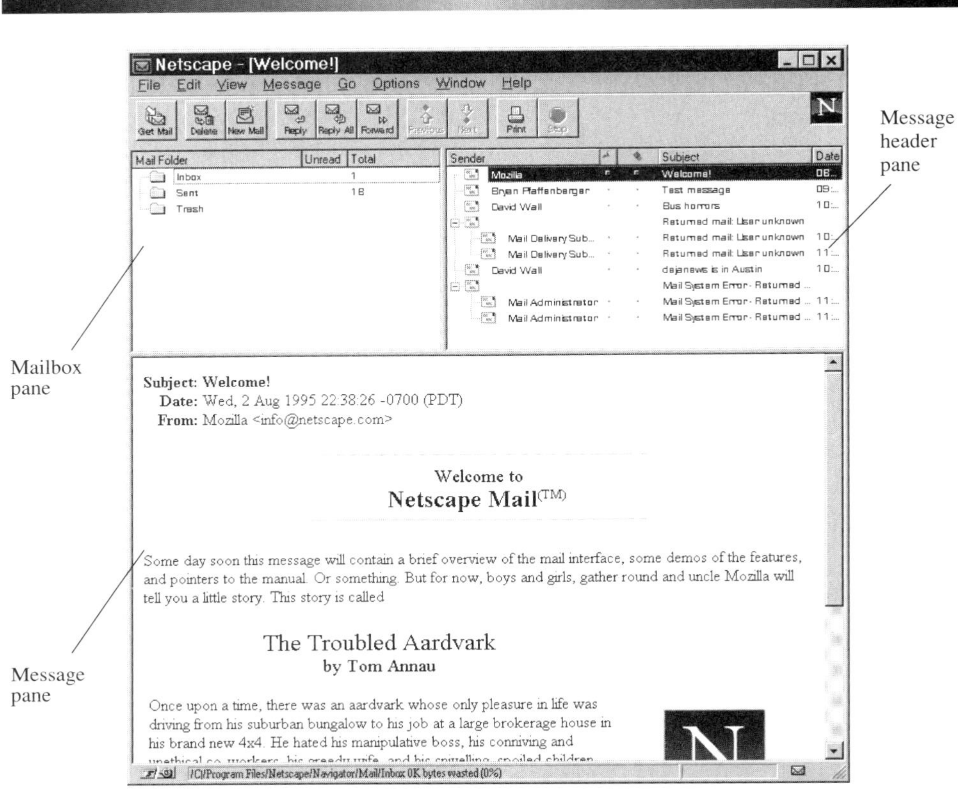

Figure 17.6 Mail window

The Parts of the Mail Window

The Mail window has its own menu and button bar, which we'll examine in a moment. For now, note that the window is divided into three panes:

- **Mailbox Pane** Here you see Netscape's default folders (mailboxes). The Inbox holds your incoming messages, while the Sent folder holds the messages you've sent. The Trash folder holds messages that you've deleted. (You can recover messages from the Trash until you've emptied it.)

- **Message Header Pane** Here you'll see the messages that you've received. You'll see the sender's name, the subject of the message, and the date received. You can also see whether you've flagged the message (if so, you'll see a red flag in the second column) and whether you've read the message (unread messages are shown in boldface and there's a tiny icon in the third column).
- **Message Pane** Here you see the text of the message that's currently selected in the message header pane.

With the mouse, you can adjust the size of the window panes. Just drag on the borders to do so. You might try decreasing the size of the mailbox pane—it doesn't need so much room—so that there's more room to display the message header pane.

New to Version 3 is an option that enables you to control the layout of the three panes. To see what the various options do, open the Options menu and choose Mail and News Preferences. Click the Appearance tab. In the Pane Layout area, you see three options for Mail: Split Horizontal (lays out the screen with a horizontal split), Split Vertical (lays out the screen with a vertical split), and Stack (stacks all three panes so that all three span the window width). Try each of these to see which one you like best.

The Mail Window's Menu Bar

The Mail window's menu bar differs slightly from the one you're used to seeing in the browser window. Missing are the Bookmarks and Directory menus; in their place, you'll find a Message menu. In addition, the menus contain many new options. You'll learn about them later in this chapter. For now, note that the commands and options you'll choose most often are accessible using the button bar, described in the next section.

The Mail Window's Button Bar

The Mail window's button bar enables you to choose frequently used options quickly. Here's a quick rundown of what these buttons do; you'll learn more about them later.

Click here to see if there are any new messages waiting for you on the server.

Click here to delete the message you're currently viewing.

Click here to compose a new message.

Click here to write a reply to the sender.

Click here to write a reply to everyone included in the message header, including people who receive "carbon copies" of the original message.

Click here to forward the message to someone.

Click here to display the previous unread message.

Click here to display the next unread message.

Click here to print the message.

Click here to stop downloading a lengthy, unwanted message.

Logging on to Your Server

To log on to your mail server, open the File menu and choose Get New Mail. Alternatively, press Ctrl + T or just click the Get Mail button.

If this is the first time you've logged on, you'll see a dialog box asking you to type your password. Do so, and click OK.

If nobody else uses your computer, and you're sure it's secure, you can avoid having to type your password every time you log on. Netscape will remember your password and supply it automatically. From the Options menu, choose Mail and News Preferences, and then click the Organization tab. Activate the Remember Mail Password option, and click OK. *Note*: Some ISPs regard this to be a security violation, since this setting would enable anyone who could gain access to your computer to log on to your account and send e-mail under your name. Don't choose this option unless you're sure that your system is secure and that it's OK with your ISP.

After you log on to the mail server, Netscape checks to see whether you've received any mail. If there's no mail for you—and at this point, there probably isn't—you'll see a dialog box informing you that no mail is waiting for you. Click OK to proceed.

If there is some mail for you, you'll see a new message header in the message header pane. To learn how to read and reply to your mail, see "Reading and Replying to Mail," after the next section.

Composing and Sending a Message

Now that you've configured Netscape Mail and logged on to your server, it's time to send a message! You've probably got somebody's e-mail address—but if not, you can send a message to yourself. Either way, try it out!

Creating a Signature

A signature (abbreviated "sig") is a brief return address (no more than four lines in length) that contains your name, e-mail address, and other information. Signatures are optional, but it's good manners to include it: Doing so makes it easier for people to reply to you.

Compose your signature using a text editor, such as the Windows Notepad utility. Make it brief and simple. Here's an example:

```
Suzanne Smith, M.S.
Environmental Engineering, Green Valley College
Green Valley, VA 22876
ssmith@speedy.greenv.edu
```

Save your signature. Now tell Netscape where your sig file is located:

1. From the Options menu, choose Mail and News Preferences.
2. Click the Identity tab.

3. In the Signature File box, type the location of your sig file, or use the Browse button to locate this file.
4. Click OK.

Composing Your Message

To compose your message, open the File menu and choose New Mail Message. Alternatively, use the Ctrl + M shortcut, or just click the To: Mail button. You'll see the Message Composition window, shown in Figure 17.7. If you've added a signature, as explained in the previous section, you'll see the sig text at the bottom of the message area.

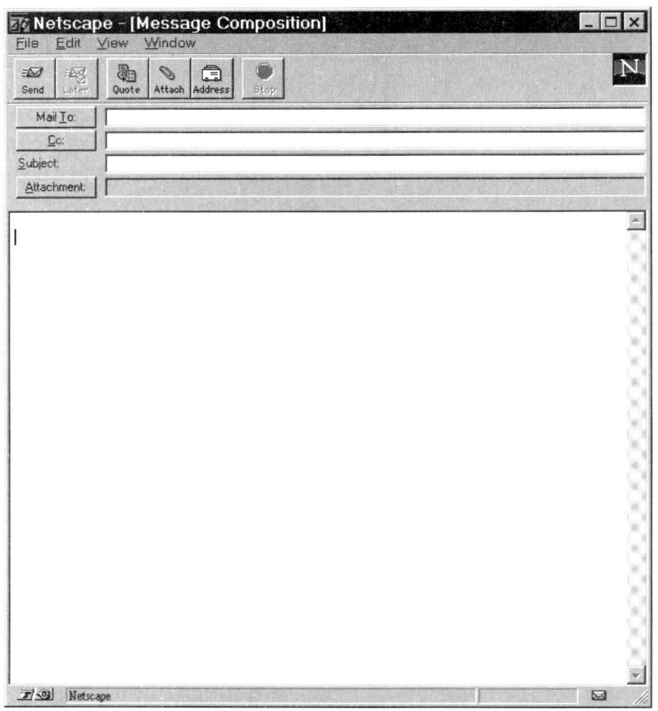

Figure 17.7 Message Composition window

To compose your message:

1. In the Mail To box, type the e-mail address of the person to whom you're sending the message. If you would like to send the message to more than one person, type additional e-mail addresses, separated by semicolons (as in this example: jn@snoopy.virginia.edu; rm683e@grumpy.green.edu).
2. In the Cc: box, you can optionally type the e-mail address or addresses of anyone whom you'd like to receive a copy of this message.
3. In the Subject box, type a subject line for your message. *Note*: Don't forget to do this. People get annoyed when they see messages without subjects.
4. In the message body area, type your message.

Would you like to send a blind carbon copy? (A *blind carbon copy* is a copy of your message that's sent to a third party without your recipient knowing that this person has also received the message.) To send a blind carbon copy, choose Mail Bcc in the View menu. In the Blind Cc box, type the e-mail address of the person to whom you'd like to send the blind carbon copy.

Adding an Attachment

Using established Internet standards, Netscape enables you to include an attachment with your e-mail message. An *attachment* is a file that's carried along with your message. The standards that support sending and receiving attachments are called the Multipurpose Internet Multimedia Extensions (MIME). Thanks to these standards, you can send just about any computer file your system can create—formatted word processing files, graphics files (including bitmaps, JPEG, and GIF images), compressed files of any type, and even computer programs.

Will your recipient be able to receive the attachment? That depends. To receive a message that contains an attachment, your recipient must be using a computer that's directly connected to the Internet. In general, people using on-line services (such as America Online) can't receive attachments, although they can receive Internet mail. In addition, the person must be

using a MIME-compliant mail program, such as Netscape Mail. Most decent mail programs are MIME-compliant.

To add an attachment, do the following:

1. In the Message Composition (New Mail) window, click the Attach button. You'll see the Attachments dialog box.
2. To attach a Web document, click Attach URL. You'll see a dialog box asking you to specify the location to attach. Type the URL that you want to attach. Click OK to confirm.
3. To attach a file, click Attach File. You'll see a dialog box asking you to enter the file to attach. Use this dialog box's navigation controls to locate and select the file you want to attach, and click Open.
4. In the Attachments dialog box, you'll see a list of the attachments you've added to your message. If you would like to delete one of them, select it and click the Delete button. For each attachment, you should make sure that the As Is option is selected; don't select Convert to Plain Text unless you really want Netscape to do this.
5. Click OK to confirm your attachment. You'll see the attachments you've added listed in the Attachment box of the Message Composition window.

If you're thinking about sending an attachment, bear in mind the capabilities of your recipient's system. Generally, it's pretty easy to send an attachment successfully to somebody who's using the same type of system and the same software you're using; problems occur, though, when Windows users send files to Mac users, and vice versa. A little advance planning can solve these problems. For example, if you're sending a Word for Windows document to somebody using a Macintosh and Microsoft Word 5.1, it might be wise to convert the file to the file format used by the Macintosh version of Word (Word for Windows can do this). The person to whom you send the file will then be able to open it with no problems.

Sending the Message

Before you send your message, check it carefully for grammatical and spelling mistakes. When you're sure that it's ready to go, think again!

I shouldn't have sent that message! Can I cancel it? Nope, you're out of luck. That's why we say Think first!

Lots of people get themselves into trouble—sometimes serious trouble, liking losing jobs or Internet privileges—by sending threatening or abusive e-mail. Remember that e-mail isn't secure—it can be easily intercepted and read en route by anyone with a modicum of Internet knowledge.

Please carefully consider the following before you click the Send button:

- Would you want your letter to wind up on your boss's desk the next morning?
- Would you want your mother to read it?
- Would you want it published in your hometown newspaper?
- Would you like to receive such a letter?

If your answer to any of these questions is "no," then *don't send the letter!* To abandon your letter, just click the close box; you'll see a dialog box informing you that the message has not been sent. To abandon the message, click No.

When you're sure that the message is OK, click the Send button.

Reading and Replying to Mail

Have you received some mail from someone? You'll know if you do. After you log on to your mail server, Netscape automatically begins downloading any messages you've received, and they'll be shown in bold in the message header area. In addition, you'll see icons in the Read column, indicating that the messages haven't yet been read.

If you've set up Netscape Mail as I suggested earlier, the program will automatically check for new mail at intervals you specify, such as every 10 minutes. You can also check for new mail whenever you wish. When you've got some new mail, you can read it, view the attachments (if any), reply to the mail you've received, forward the mail to others, flag messages for later attention, and print messages. The following sections discuss each of these procedures in detail.

If you switch to another Netscape window, Mail lets you know if a new message has arrived at your server. On the status bar, you'll see a mail envelope followed by an exclamation point. If you see an envelope without an exclamation point, Mail is telling you that there's a previously downloaded message that you haven't yet read.

Checking for New Mail

To check for new mail, open the File menu and choose Get New Mail. Alternatively, use the Ctrl + T shortcut, or just click the Get Mail button.

Reading Your Mail

If you've received a new message, select the new message in the message header pane. You'll see the message text in the message pane.

Did you receive more than one message? To read the next message, click the Next button. To redisplay the previous message, click Previous.

You'll soon find that your mailbox is filled with messages that you've already read. However, very few of them are worth keeping. Do yourself a favor and delete worthless messages right after you've finished reading them. To do so, click the Delete button. Note that this button doesn't actually delete the message—instead, it moves the message to the Trash folder, where you can recover it should you later decide that it wasn't so worthless after all.

Viewing Attachments

If you've received a message with one or more attachments, you can view the attachment in-line (you actually see the attachment within the mail message, if Netscape can figure out how to display it) or as a link (to see the attachment, you click the link). Unless the attachment is very small, it's much more convenient to view the attachment as a link.

To control the way attachments are viewed, open the View menu and choose one of the following: Attachments Inline (to view attachments in the same window as the message) and Attachments as Links (to view the attachment as a link).

Replying to Your Mail

To reply to a message, select the message in the message header pane, and click Re: Mail. You'll see a composition window. Netscape automatically filled in the sender's e-mail address (look at the Mail To box), and the program has proposed a subject (using Re: followed by the original message's subject line). You can change the subject, if you wish.

If you set up Netscape Mail to quote the original message's text automatically, you'll see the text in the window. If not, and if you'd like to quote the text, click the Quote button. You'll see the quoted text in the window. Note that each line is preceded by a greater than sign (>), and that's desirable: To experienced Internet users, these characters immediately convey that the following text is quoted.

Note that you don't have to use all the quoted text. If you prefer, you can edit the text down to just a line or two that you want to discuss.

To finish the reply, type your message, and proofread it carefully. As always, ponder the "think before you send" rules before you click that Send button!

Replying to All Senders

If you've received a letter from more than one sender, Netscape automatically sends the reply to the first sender only. If you would like to reply to all senders, begin your reply by clicking the Re: All button. Create and send your reply as described in the preceding section.

Forwarding Mail

To forward a message to someone, highlight the message in the message header panel, and click the Forward button. You'll see a message composition window. Note that Netscape has automatically included the message as an attachment.

Type text that explains why you're forwarding the message, and click Send.

If you're forwarding mail to somebody whose system can't handle attachments, you can forward the mail as quoted text. To do so, start the forwarding process by opening the

Message window, and choosing Forward as Quoted Text. This command automatically quotes the message you're forwarding instead of adding it as an attachment.

While you're working in the message pane, you can use the right mouse key to display a pop-up menu. From this menu, you can reply, reply to all, forward, forward quoted, and delete messages.

Marking and Flagging Messages

When you're reading your mail, you'll often say to yourself, "I don't want to answer this right now" or "I better remember to look at this again, later, and do something about it." With many e-mail programs, the messages you've read disappear into a long, lengthy list of read messages, and you forget about them. With Netscape, though, you can mark messages as unread (even if you've read them). The message then shows up in bold in the message header pane, encouraging you to look at it again. If that's not enough, you can also put a red flag next to a message.

To mark a message as unread (even though you've read it), highlight the message in the message header pane. Then open the Message menu and choose Mark as Unread. If you change your mind, open the same menu again and choose Mark as Read.

To flag a message, highlight the message in the message header pane. Then open the Message menu and choose Flag message. You'll see a red flag next to the message. To unflag the message, open the Message menu again and choose Unflag message.

To mark or flag items quickly, or to unmark or unflag them, click on the mark or flag column next to the item's name.

Printing Messages

You can easily produce hard copy (printed output) of one or more messages.

To print the message you're currently viewing, just click the Print button. To print more than one message, hold down the Ctrl key; in the message header pane, select all the messages you want to print. Then open the File menu and choose Print Message(s).

Creating an Address Book

As you'll surely agree after typing a few e-mail address, it's tedious to type all those funny characters, obscure user names, and funny computer names—and what's worse, your message won't reach its destination if you make a typing mistake. For these reasons, it's a great idea to build an Address Book. The Address Book will contain the e-mail addresses of the people with whom you frequently correspond. From the Address Book, you can quickly and accurately enter a recipient's e-mail address. The following sections show you how to take full advantage of this neat capability.

Adding Addresses to Your Address Book

The easiest way to add an address to your Address Book is to display a message that somebody has sent you. Point to the message within the message pane, and click the right mouse button—you'll see a pop-up menu with lots of reply and forwarding options. But what you're after is Add to Address Book. When you select this option, you'll see the Address Book dialog box, shown in Figure 17.8.

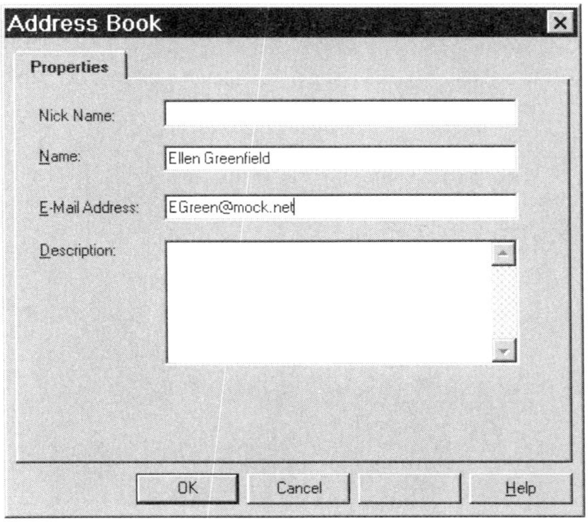

Figure 17.8 Address Book dialog box

To add an address to your Address Book:

1. In the Nick Name box, type a nickname for this person, if you'd like to use one. For example, if you type "ken," you can simply type "Ken" when you wish to address mail to this person, and Netscape will automatically fill in the full e-mail address. Note that nicknames must be one word and must contain nothing but lowercase letters.
2. Note that Netscape has automatically entered the person's name (if available) and e-mail address in the Name and E-Mail Address boxes. If you wish, type a short description.
3. Click OK to confirm the addition to your Address Book.

This guy's address has changed! How do I edit his entry? Simple. In the Address Book window, select the person's name. From the File menu, choose Properties. You'll see the Address Book dialog box with the person's current information. Edit this information, and then choose OK.

If you would like to add an address to your Address Book without right-clicking an existing address, choose Address Book from the Options menu. From the Item menu, choose Add User. You'll see the Address Book dialog box. You'll have to type the name and e-mail address manually.

Pasting an Address from Your Address Book

After you've added names to your Address Book, you can paste them into e-mail messages you're composing. To add an address to a message, click the Mail To button in the Message Composition window. You'll see the Select Addresses dialog box, shown in Figure 17.9. Select the address you want to add, and then click one of the following buttons:

To:	Click this button if you want to send the message to this person.
Cc:	Click this button if you want to send a copy of this message to this person.

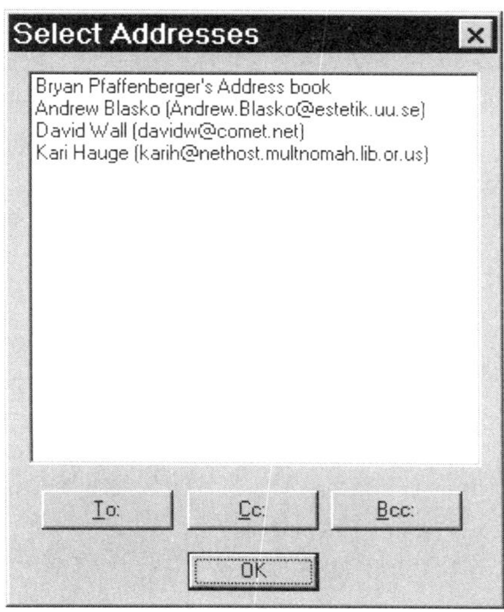

Figure 17.9 Select Addresses dialog box

Bcc:	Click this button if you would like to send a copy of this message to this person without the main recipient knowing.

Click the close box to close this dialog box.

You can add addresses in other ways, too. To start a new message from the Address Book window, select the person to whom you want to send a message, and choose Send New Message from the File menu (or just use the Ctrl + M shortcut). But the simplest way to add an address to your message is to type the person's nickname in the Mail To box (Message Composition window). If you didn't define a nickname for a person, you can do so by opening the Address Book window, selecting the person's name, choosing Properties from the File menu, and adding a nickname in the Nick Name box.

Creating a List of E-mail Addresses

Sometimes you will wish to send frequent e-mail messages to more than one person, such as a group of co-workers. To do so, you can use the Address Book to create a list of e-mail addresses all grouped under a single name. This greatly simplifies the task of sending e-mail messages to two or more people. You need only type the nickname of the list, or enter the list's name from the Address Book—Netscape takes care of the rest.

To create a list of e-mail addresses:

1. In the Address Book window, choose Add List from the Item menu. You'll see an Address Book window, but the e-mail address box is dimmed.
2. In the Nick Name box, type a lowercase, one-word nickname. You can enter this name in the Mail To box (Message Composition window) to send a message to all the people in the list.
3. In the Name box, type the name you want to use for this list.
4. In the Description box, type a description, if you wish.
5. To add e-mail addresses to the list, select the name of the list in the Address Book window.
6. Click Add User. You'll see an Address Book dialog box.
7. Add the information for this recipient.
8. Click OK.
9. Repeat steps 5 through 9 to add additional people to your mailing list.

I can't find so-and-so's e-mail address! Added a lot of names, huh? To search your Address Book, choose Find from the Address Book's Edit menu, or just press Ctrl + F within Address Book. You'll see a Search Headers dialog box. Type all or part of the person's name, and click OK. Netscape will find and select the person's name, if it's able to find it. If not, check your spelling and try again.

Organizing Your Messages

Before long, you'll have a lengthy list of e-mail messages. Searching for a message by hand can become a time-consuming process. However, Netscape has tools that enable you to search the messages, sort them in a variety of ways, delete unwanted messages, and move messages to folders. To save disk space, you can compress the folders—or just delete them.

Finding a Message

To find a message, choose Find from the Edit menu, or just press Ctrl + F. You'll see the Find dialog box, shown in Figure 17.10. This box enables you to search for text in the message headers (which include the sender's name, e-mail address, and subject). In addition, you can search the full text of the message that's currently selected in the Mail window.

To use the Find dialog box:

1. In the Find box, type the text for which you want to search.
2. In the Find In area, click Message Headers in This Folder if you want to search the message headers. If you want to search the full text of the currently selected message, click Body of This Message.
3. If you selected Body of Message, choose whether you want to search Up or Down by clicking the appropriate option button in the Direction area.
4. If you would like Netscape to match the case of the text you've typed, click Match Case. The program will ignore case if you leave this check box blank.
5. Click Find Next.

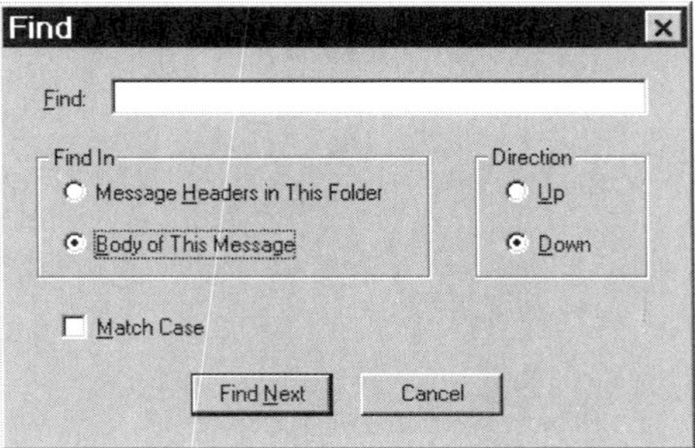

Figure 17.10 Find dialog box

If Netscape finds a match, the program displays the message. If not, you'll see a dialog box informing you that the search string was not found. Try again, and check your spelling.

Sorting Messages

Netscape enables you to sort the messages in a number of ways. First, you choose the sort criterion (Date, Subject, Sender, or Message Number). For example, if you choose to sort the messages by Sender, the program will organize the messages in alphabetical order sorted by the sender's name. To choose a sort criterion, choose Sort from the View menu, and then choose a sort criterion from the pop-up menu.

You can also choose whether you would like Netscape to thread the messages. This unique feature groups messages that share the same subject. For example, suppose you've received a message with the subject "Catalina sailboats." You reply, and then you receive another message entitled "Re: Catalina sailboats." With this option, Netscape will group these two letters together, rather than separating them. This makes it much easier to follow the "thread" of discussion that you've been having with somebody. This is the best sort option for most purposes. You can turn threading on or off independently of other sort options. To turn threading on or off, choose Sort from the View menu, and then choose Thread Messages from the pop-up menu.

You can also choose whether you'd like Netscape to sort the messages in ascending order. This doesn't make much sense, in my humble opinion, if you're sorting by Name or Subject, unless you really like reading lists in reverse alphabetical order. It's a great choice, though, if you'd like to sort by Date. With the Ascending option, you see your most recent messages at the top of the mail window.

To sort your list quickly, just click the Sender, Subject, or Date buttons at the top of the message header pane.

Deleting Messages

If you don't want to keep a letter, delete it so that it doesn't clutter up your message header panel. To delete the message you're viewing, just press the Delete key.

To delete more than one message, hold down the Ctrl key and click the headers of all the messages you'd like to delete. Then press the Delete key.

Oh no! I just deleted a really important letter! Don't worry—you're saved. Netscape didn't really delete the letter—it just moved the letter to the Trash folder. To open the Trash folder, click Trash in the folder panel. To restore the letter, drag its header back to the Inbox folder.

To really delete unwanted letters, you must empty the Trash folder. To do so, choose Empty Trash Folder from the File menu.

Creating New Folders

Once you've got an Inbox full of letters that you really want to keep, you may experience problems navigating through the list and finding letters (despite all of Netscape's neat finding and sorting tools). To keep your Inbox to a minimum, you should create additional folders for storing your messages. For example, I've got folders for messages pertaining to Sailing, Backpacking, Wine, and other hobbies of mine, and then of course I've got one (down at the bottom of the list) called Work.

To create a folder, choose Create New Folder from the File menu. You'll see a dialog box prompting you to type the new folder's name. Type the name, and click OK.

To add messages to the new folder, select the messages in the Inbox window and drag the messages to your new folder.

To delete a folder and all the messages it contains, select the folder and choose Delete Folder from the Edit menu.

Compressing Folders

The storage technique that Netscape uses for your mail is very inefficient, but it maximizes retrieval speed. That's great for the messages you're reading right now. If a folder contains a lot of messages that you don't plan to read very often, but want to store indefinitely, you can compress the folder. You'll still be able to acces the messages, but they'll open a little more sluggishly.

To compress a folder, select a folder and choose Compress Folder from the File menu.

From Here

- Don't like the time delay in e-mail? Talk to other Internetters in real time with Chat, discussed in the next chapter.
- Get into the swing of things on Usenet, and you'll get lots more electronic mail—not all of it friendly! Check out Chapter 22.

Chapter 18

Chat It Up!

Internet Relay Chat. It's the coolest thing on the Net—or the biggest waste of time, depending on your perspective. Tales are rife of the positive role played by eyewitness IRC reports of the downfall of the Soviet Union, the devastation of the Los Angeles earthquake, and the defeat of the Cleveland Indians. Tales are equally rife of idiotic, expletive-laden conversation, in which the overall maturity quotient seems to be in the early adolescent phase. You should be aware, too, that the IRC is a sort of playground for some of the most malicious computer hackers you'll ever run across.

Decide for yourself, and to do so, take a look at Internet Relay Chat, which usually goes by its acronym IRC. It's a real-time chat system of global scope, made possible by the Internet. And thanks to Netscape's Chat accessory, IRC takes on a new level of user-friendliness and functionality: As

For the Time-Challenged

- Netscape Chat enables you to join IRC conversations.
- After you join an IRC group, you can type messages that the whole group will see, or "whisper" to just one person.
- If you'd like, you can invite someone to join you in a private conversation.
- You can create your own IRC channel, if you wish.

you'll see, Chat enables you to send and display Web pages while you're chatting it up with other denizens of IRC.

This chapter introduces IRC and fully explores the Chat accessory, which transforms the rather quirky IRC interface into something that's actually a pleasure to use. You'll learn how to join conversations, whisper to individuals without anyone hearing, and how to start your own conversations. And throughout, you'll learn how to bring all of Netscape's functionality to your chat sessions. As you'll see, it's fun to send people the URL to your home page and to see other peoples' pages displayed while you're chatting to them!

My, what filthy language! Let's get this straight: IRC is strictly an *adult* pastime: There's a lot of discussion of every conceivable aspect of human sexuality, and many of the groups are frankly erotic in intent. It's definitely not for kids. Don't install Netscape Chat on a Net-connected computer that your kids are using! That said, there are plenty of non-erotic conversations to join, so don't write off IRC as another Internet playground for perverts. As with anything on the Internet, there's dross and there's gold.

What Is IRC?

IRC is an Internet-based chat network that enables you to engage in live conversations with real people—who might be located just about anywhere in the world. At any one given time, there are hundreds of distinct conversations going on in IRC, each with its own title. Within each conversation, you'll find one to dozens of people, chatting it up.

Looking at a Conversation

"Conversation" is a misnomer, since what's going on, really, is that you're typing and sending lines of text, and you see on-screen what you've typed and what others have typed. A conversation might look something like this:

```
<El Viejo> So where did you-all go to school?

<Furrmonger> Berserkely—degree in late Sixties

<Ju-ju> U of Texas

<Inconnubula> I dropped out
```

Starting a Private Conversation (Whispering)

If there are too many people in the conversation, you'll find it difficult to carry on a meaningful dialogue with a person. For this reason, it's possible to engage any single individual in a private conversation that the others can't "hear," as in the following example:

```
<El Viejo whispers to Furrmonger> I went there too! What was
your major?

<Furrmonger whispers to El Viejo> Biology. I'm a vet now.
What was yours?
```

Starting Your Own Conversation

After browsing around IRC for a while, you'll get the idea—correctly—that many conversations are private clubs, set up in advance by friends scattered hither and yon. Some are ongoing affairs, with regulars who know each other well; in these conversations, you'll need a lot of patience and time to feel that you're accepted into the clique. At the extreme, you might even get kicked out of a conversation that turns out to be a purely private affair (yes, it's possible to kick people out—if this happens to you, don't whine to your system administrator, just find a new conversation).

If you find the current conversations alienating or unfriendly, there's a ready cure: Start your own. Of course, there's no guarantee that anyone will show up, but I'll tell you this: There are a *lot* of lonely people out there!

As you'll see in the pages to follow, Netscape Chat makes it easy to perform all these actions. Before you know it, you'll be chatting away on IRC—who knows, maybe you'll get hooked.

Getting Started with Netscape Chat

Netscape Chat is downloadable from Netscape's FTP server, which you can access by clicking the Netscape Now! button on Netscape's home page. Once you've downloaded and installed Netscape Chat, you'll need to configure it for your copy of Netscape, the IRC server you're going to use, and your personal information. All these topics are explored in the sections to follow.

The new version of Netscape Chat available at this writing, 2.0, gives you lots of new features and increased usability. It eliminates some of the quirks of version 1.0. If you've previously downloaded version 1.0, be sure to obtain the newer version.

Obtaining and Installing Netscape Chat

Chat is currently available from Netscape's file servers. To obtain Chat, click one of the Netscape Now buttons you'll see just about everywhere on the Net, or click the Software button. Select Chat from the list of programs to download. Be sure to choose the right version for your system: Chat's available in 16-bit (Windows 3.1) and 32-bit (Windows 95 and NT) versions. Netscape will download the program as a self-extracting archive; use File Manager (Windows 3.1) or Windows Explorer (Windows 95) to locate and double-click the file. You'll see an installation program that will install Chat automatically. When the installation program is finished, you'll see Chat in the Program Manager (Windows 3.1) or Programs menu (Windows 95).

Starting Netscape Chat

To start Netscape Chat with Windows 3.1, open the Netscape Chat program group and double-click the Netscape Chat icon.

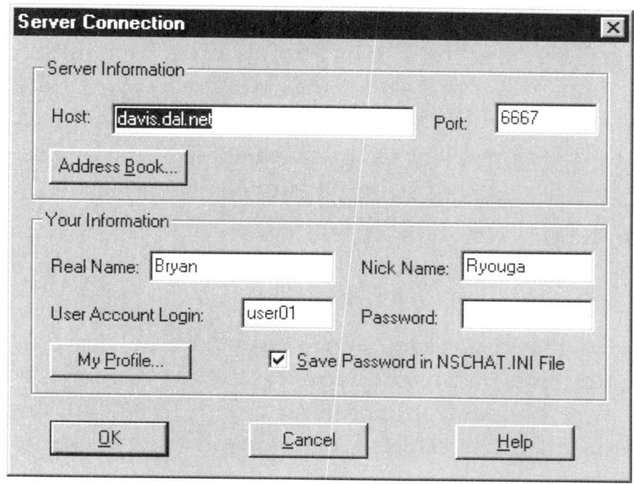

Figure 18.1 Server Connection dialog box

To start Netscape Chat with Windows 95, open the Start menu, click Programs, and click Netscape Chat.

Configuring Netscape Chat

The first time you start Netscape Chat, you'll see the Server Connection dialog box (Figure 18.1), which enables you to supply some needed information, including the name of the IRC server you want to use. An IRC server is a program that enables you to connect with other IRC users worldwide. Without accessing an IRC server, you can't use IRC.

Unfortunately, the number of IRC servers seems to be shrinking rather than growing, for the simple reason that IRC is perceived by most system administrators as a waste of Internet resources. By default, Netscape Chat is currently set up to access davis.dal.net.

For a list of publicly accessible IRC servers, see http://benso.com/irchjelp.servers.txt

To configure Netscape Chat, follow these instructions:

1. In the Server Information area's Host box, type the name of the IRC server you want to use. Chat is already configured to use the davis.dal.net, but this server may be down by the time you read this.
   Note the Address Book button. If you click this, you'll find several additional servers that you can try. You can also add the name of servers you discover on your own.
2. In the Real Name box, type a name. *Note*: This name is accessible to IRC users. If you don't want your real name to be known, type a pseudonym here—many people do.
3. In the Nick Name box, type the nickname that you want to use. This name will appear in conversations. If you're female, I'd suggest using a gender-neutral name—unless you really like being bombarded with tasteless come-ons. You can use up to nine characters, with no spaces.
4. The user account login, password, and e-mail address fields are optional. Fill them in only if the IRC server you're using requires these.
5. If you would like to make your personal information available to others in IRC—I don't recommend it—click the My Profile button, and fill in your personal information, such as your e-mail address and home page. Click OK to confirm.
6. To initiate the connection, click OK.

Assuming Netscape Chat is able to make a connection with the server you chose, you'll see the Quick Join dialog box (see Figure 18.2). This dialog box enables you to join an IRC channel (a "conversation room," in Chat's terminology) quickly and easily.

As you're using Chat, the Console window keeps a running record of your transactions with the server, and it also shows who's joined—and who's left—the conversation you will join (as described in the next section). You can ignore this information, unless you're insatiably curious to know what's going on behind the scenes.

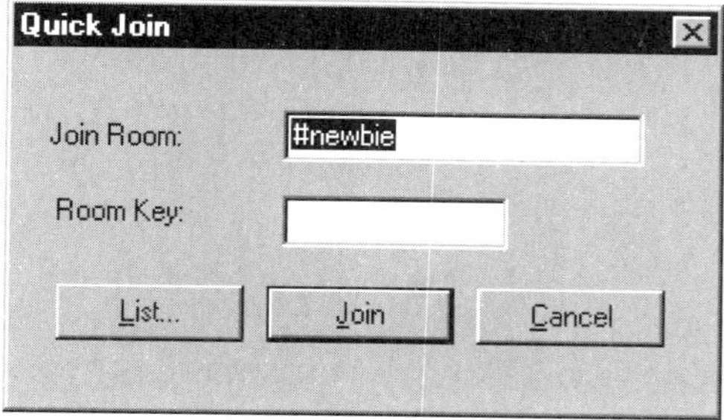

Figure 18.2 Quick Join dialog box

Joining a Conversation

If you know the name of the room (channel) you want to join, just type it in the Quick Join box and click Join. By default, Chat displays the last room you accessed (or #newbie, if this is your first outing with Chat).

If you don't know which conversation to join, or you'd like to browse through the list to see what's available, click the List button. You'll see the Conversation Rooms dialog box (shown in Figure 18.3). This window lists all the chat rooms that are currently operating. A *chat room* is a named conversation that you can join.

In the Users column, you'll see how many people are currently enrolled in a given chat room. As you'll see, there are lots of rooms with one person, while others have as many as several dozen. Try to find a room that's got from three to seven participants—you'll find some lively action, but not so much that it becomes overwhelming.

There are some really nice folks on IRC—you just have to know where to look. Try starting with a group called #irc-help or #ircnewbies; chances are you'll meet other newcomers like yourself, chatting away with some helpful IRC vets. Another suggestion: Try some of the age-grouped conversations (such as #40+), or those focused on an interest (such as a musical group or hobby). Stay away from groups that have sex-related or incomprehensible names.

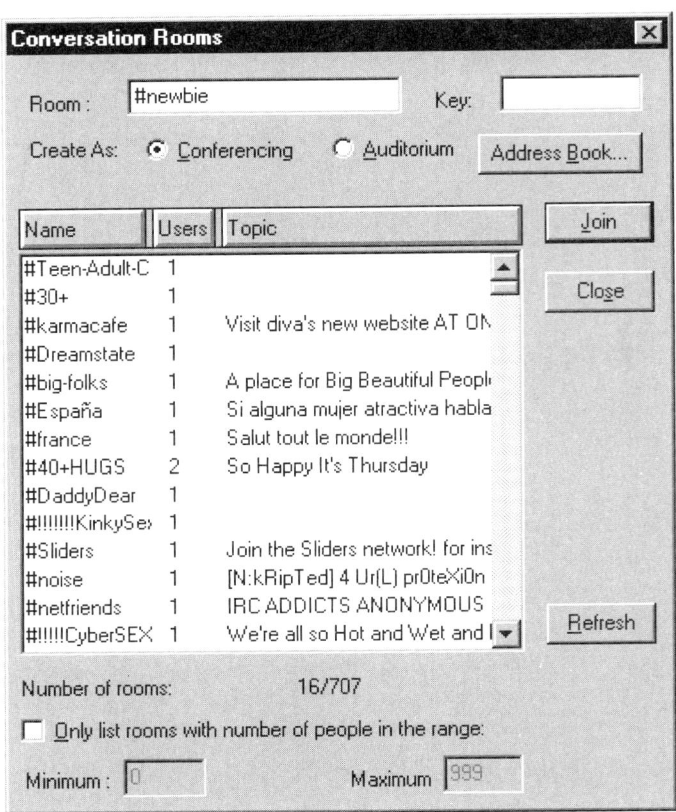

Figure 18.3 Conversation Rooms dialog box

To join a conversation, just highlight the conversation's name and click Join. You'll see a new Conferencing window, as shown in Figure 18.4.

After you've used Chat a few times, you'll find that the program has kept a list of the rooms you frequently visit. To join one of these rooms quickly, open the Edit menu and choose Frequent Channels. In the Frequent Channels dialog box, highlight the name of the room you want to join, and click OK. If you would like to remove a room's name, highlight the name and click Remove Selection.

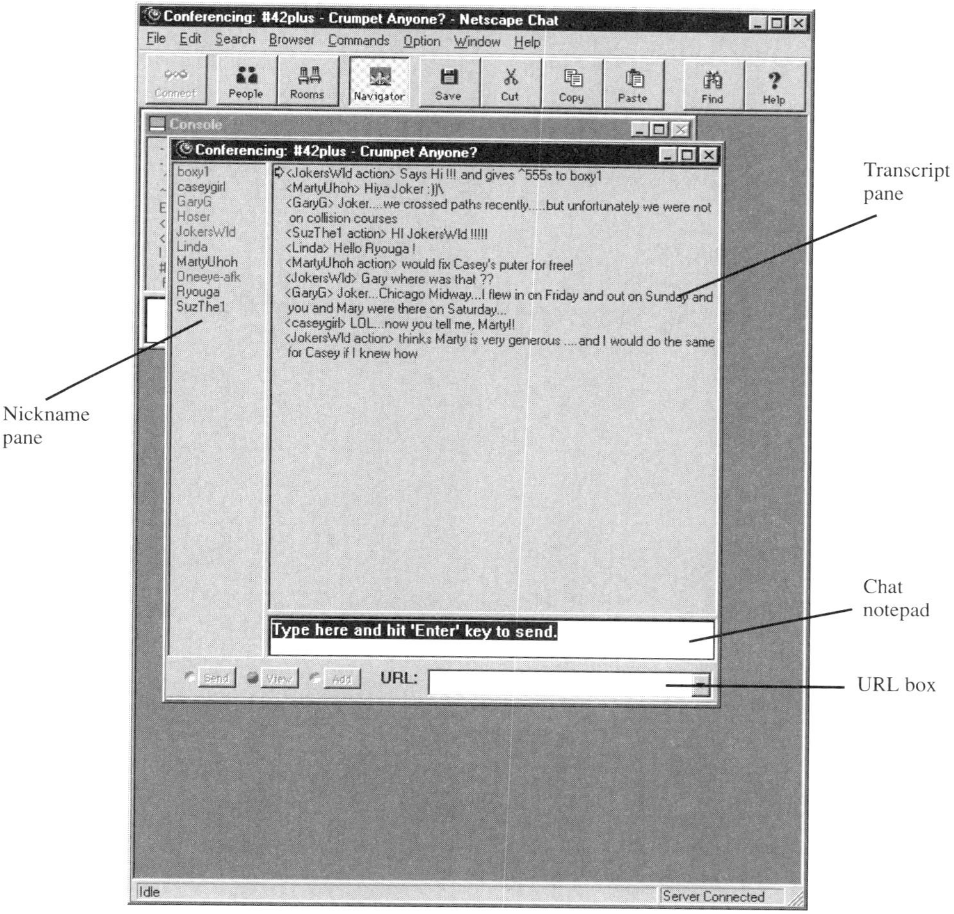

Transcript pane

Nickname pane

Chat notepad

URL box

Figure 18.4 Conferencing window

When you enter a conversation, the person who set it up will probably say hello. It's polite to answer—see "Sending a Message," later in this chapter—but you *don't* need to say hello to everyone who's present. Doing so is a considered a waste of IRC bandwidth and could even get you kicked out of a conversation.

Understanding the Conferencing Window

The Conferencing window displays what's going on in the chat room you're currently using. It contains the following sections (see Figure 18.4):

Nickname Pane This pane shows a list of the people currently enrolled in this conversation.

Transcript Pane Here's where you see a running transcript of the conversation you've joined. When you type a message and press Enter, you'll see your message in this pane. You also see the messages other people have sent. When you exit the conversation, you'll have an opportunity to save the transcript, if you wish.

Chat Notepad Here's where you type your messages and describe your actions, as described in the following section.

URL Box This box displays a URL list. When you display a Web page in the Navigator window, you'll see the URL in this box. Additional pages are added to a list, with the most recently added page shown first.

You'll soon become familiar with the Conferencing window, once you've worked with it a while.

Chatting It Up

After you've joined a conversation, it's time to chat! You should begin by reading the dialog for a while. Then you can send your own messages and get involved in the swim of things. You can whisper to someone, describe actions you're performing (virtually, of course), send Web pages, view Web pages, compile a list of Web pages to linked partners, and much more. The following sections describe all the actions you can perform during the time you're engaged in a conversation.

Reading the Dialog

When you first join a channel, you'll start seeing the messages that others are typing. In the Nickname pane, you'll see a list of the people currently enrolled in the conversation. Follow the conversation for a while until you grasp what's going on.

Sending a Message

If you've joined a friendly group, somebody will say "hi" to you. Here's your chance to type your first message. To send a message, simply type your message in the Chat notepad, and press Enter.

While you're working in the Chat notepad, you can use all the standard Windows editing commands (Undo, Copy, Cut, and Paste) to create and perfect the text you're writing.

I was just trying to be friendly, and they got mad! Don't say "hi" to everyone in the group, one by one. This is considered a waste of IRC bandwidth. Just say "Hi all."

Once you've got an idea of what's being discussed in the room you've selected, you'll soon find yourself in the swim of things.

As you'll soon find, IRC users employ abbreviations to cut down on the amount of text they type. Here's a quick rundown on the abbreviations you'll commonly find on IRC:

2	to	k	OK
bbiaf	Be back in a few minutes	lol	Laughing out loud
bbl	Be back later	m	male
brb	Be right back	r	are
c	see	re	Hi again ("repeat hi")
f	female	ttyl	Talk to you later
imho	In my (not-so) humble opinion	u	you
		y	why

If you're having a one-to-one conversation with somebody in the room, you may wish to converse privately, so that others don't see the exchange. For more information, see the section entitled "Whispering to Someone."

They're talking about "bots!" What's a bot? A bot, short for robot, is an automated program that pretends to be a person. Bots aren't welcome on most IRC servers. Although some bots perform useful functions, such as welcoming people to a conversation and explaining the ground rules, many more are downright nasty. The nasty ones are the playthings of the socially maladjusted types who are all too commonly encountered on IRC.

Whispering to Someone

If you're getting into a one-on-one conversation with somebody, you may prefer to *whisper* to the person. When you whisper, only the person to whom you're whispering can read your message. For this reason, it doesn't interfere with the group's ongoing dialog.

To whisper to someone, select the person's nickname in the Nickname pane. Then type and send your message. Your message will be seen only by the person whose name you've highlighted.

To stop whispering to the person, deselect the person's name. Now your messages will be seen by everyone in the group.

If a whispering session starts going great guns, consider starting a private conversation, as described later in this section. You'll have a one-on-one chat window without the distractions of the group's conversation. You can leave the group channel open while you're doing this, too.

Finding Out More about Someone

Like to know more about one of the people with whom you're conversing? From the File menu, click Personal Conversation. You'll see the Show People dialog box (Figure 18.5). Scroll down and highlight the person's name, and click Info. You'll see the Personal Info box for that person, showing the

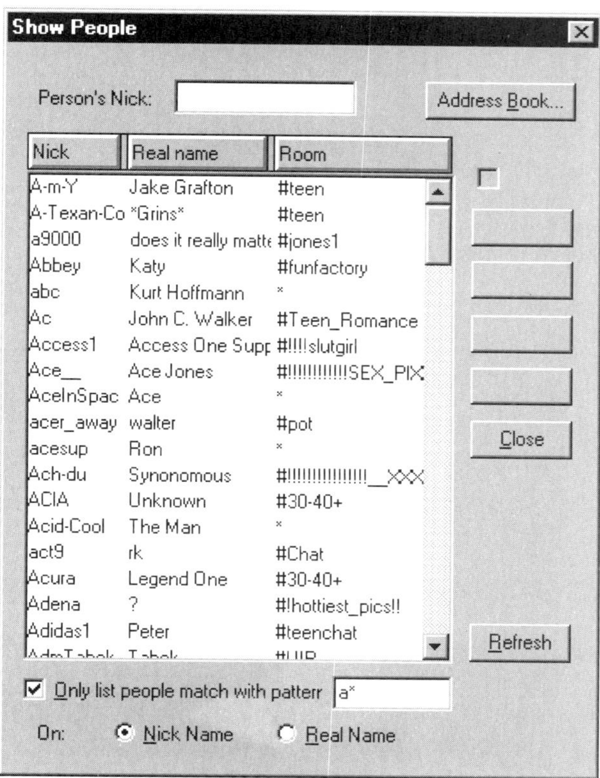

Figure 18.5 Show People dialog box

information that the person has chosen to make public. This may include the person's real name and e-mail address—but more than likely, it won't. Knowing that one can run into some pretty malicious people on IRC, most people like to keep their personal information private.

Starting a Private Conversation

If you find that you'd rather talk one-to-one with an individual rather than join in the room's conversation, you can whisper, as described above. But

it's difficult to track the conversation when so many other messages intervene. Happily, there's a solution: You can start a private conversation with someone.

To start a private conversation, follow these steps:

1. From the File menu, choose Personal Conversation. You'll see the Show People dialog box, shown in Figure 18.5.
2. Scroll down the list to find the name of the person to whom you'd like to chat privately.
3. Select the person's name.
4. Click Talk. Chat sends out an invitation to this person to join you in a private conversation. If he or she accepts, you'll see a new Chat window, and you can begin the one-to-one conversation (Figure 18.6).

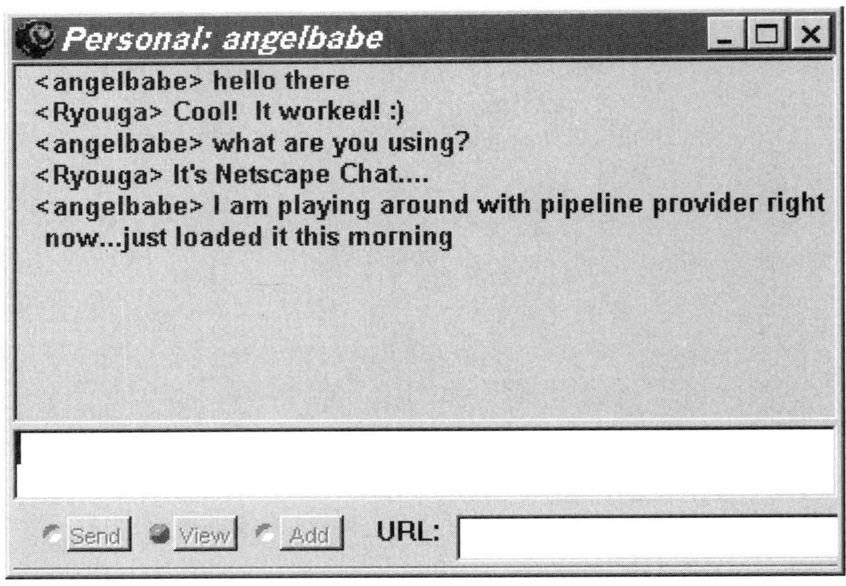

Figure 18.6 Personal conversation

When you successfully initiate a personal conversation with somebody, Chat automatically adds that person's nickname to your Personal Phone Book. To talk to this person again, open the Edit menu and choose Personal Phone Book. Highlight the person's name and click OK.

Performing an Action

You'll often see *actions*, which are written descriptions of somebody doing something:

```
<Lacy1> Lacy sidles up to the bar, and orders a glass of
chilled Chardonnay
```

To perform an action, type a slash mark in the Chat notepad, followed by *me*, and the description of the action you want to perform:

```
/me El Viejo sits down beside Lacy and orders an Anchor Steam
Beer
```

You'll see the results of your action in the conversation window:

```
<El Viejo action> El Viejo sits down beside Lacy and orders
an Anchor Steam Beer
```

Ignoring Someone

You may find that you're not really interested in the comments being made by an individual in the conversation—at the best, perhaps they're interfering, or

You can send any of the IRC commands that Netscape supports by typing a slash mark followed by the command, as in the /me example given above. For example, to change your nickname, type /nick followed by the new nickname you want to use. To change your nickname from Ryouga to Akane, for instance, type /nick Akane. To get information about somebody to whom you're talking, type /whois followed by that person's name (for example, /whois Laura displays information about the person using the nickname Laura).

not contributing; at the worst, you may find that you're being harassed by some infantile jerk. Happily, there's a cure: You can ignore him or her.

To ignore a person:

1. From the File menu, choose Personal Conversation. You'll see the Show People window.
2. Highlight the harasser's name.
3. Click Ignore On.
4. If you like, you can ignore additional people by repeating steps 2 and 3.
5. Click the Close button to close the Show People window.

Note that your ignore list isn't saved when you quit Chat.

If you would like to give the miscreant a reprieve, you can do so by following the instructions below.

To de-ignore a person:

1. From the File menu, choose Personal Conversation. You'll see the Show People window.
2. Highlight the name of the person you're ignoring.
3. Click Ignore Off.
4. If you like, you can de-ignore additional people by repeating steps 2 and 3.
5. Click the Close button to close the Show People window.

Compiling a List of Web Pages to Share

One of Chat's neatest characteristics is its close integration with Netscape. You can send Web pages to others, and if they're using Chat, they'll see the page in their copy of Netscape.

To send Web pages to others, you begin by compiling a list of one or more URLs to send.

To compile a list of URLs:

1. In Netscape, locate and display the first Web page that you want to send, or just type the URL in the URL box.
2. Repeat step 1 until you've finished your list. You'll find the URLs in the list box. You can display the list—and then choose any of the URLs you've collected—by clicking the down arrow.

Sending a Web Page to Someone

Once you've compiled a list of one or more URLs, you can send a Web page to other people in the channel you're using.

To send a Web page:

1. In the URL list box, select the Web page that you want to send.
2. If you would like to send the Web page to just one person, highlight that person's name in the Nickname pane. To send the page to everyone, just skip this step.
3. Click Send in the URL toolbar.

If any of the people you're chatting with are using Netscape Chat, they'll see the page you've sent displayed automatically in their copy of Netscape. (The automatic display of pages sent in this manner is controlled by the Auto Start option in Chat's Preference menu, which is activated by default. If this option is turned off, Netscape won't display pages conveyed via IRC.)

Printing a Transcript

If something memorable has happened while you're on IRC, you can print the transcript. To do so, click the Print button.

Exiting a Room

When you're finished chatting, it's polite to say goodbye. To exit the conversation, just click the Close box, or choose Exit Conversation from the File menu.

Starting Your Own Room

If you don't see a room that pertains to a subject you'd like to discuss, try starting one. There's no guarantee that anyone will join your conversation—in fact, there's no guarantee of *anything* on IRC! Try it and see what happens.

To start a room:

1. From the File menu, choose Group Conversation. You'll see the Conversation Rooms dialog box.

2. Choose Conferencing (the default) or Auditorium. In the Conferencing mode, anyone can speak to anyone. In the Auditorium mode, participants must get permission from the moderator to start speaking to the group. If you choose Auditorium, you become the moderator of the auditorium by default. If you would like to appoint others to be co-moderators, you can do so by selecting their names and choosing Grant Moderator from the Auditorium menu. You might wish to do this if you choose to leave a moderated channel you've created, because IRC will cancel an auditorium that doesn't have a moderator.
3. To start the room, just click Join. IRC creates the new room, and its name appears on the list of rooms that other IRC participants are viewing.

Using an Auditorium

If you're participating in an auditorium, you must ask permission to speak—and if you're a moderator, you must decide whether to grant it. You'll know when you're participating in an Auditorium—if you are, you'll see the Auditorium menu on Chat's menu bar.

To ask for permission to speak:

1. Select a moderator's name from the Nickname pane.
2. From the Auditorium menu, choose Request Microphone.
3. In the Chat notepad, compose your request and press Enter. This sends the message to the moderator you've selected.
4. Check the transcript pane for a message from your moderator.
5. If you're granted permission to speak, use the notepad to communicate with the audience.

To grant permission to speak:

1. Highlight the name of the person who has asked to speak.
2. From the Auditorium menu, choose Grant Speaker.

If you wish to remove permission to speak, highlight the person's name, open the Auditorium menu, and choose Revoke Speaker.

From Here

- Access Gopher archives with Chapter 20's help.
- Get free software from FTP archives; find out how in Chapter 21.
- Get into the fray in Usenet newsgroups in Chapter 22.

Chapter 19

You've Got a Call!

Using CoolTalk

The latest wrinkle on the Internet is Internet-based telephony, which is giving the long-distance phone companies fits. And for good reason: If you've got an Internet connection, you can call somebody for *free*. (A not-so-minor detail: You and the person on the other end will need a computer equipped with a sound card, speakers, a microphone, an Internet connection, and copies of CoolTalk, the Netscape program that makes all this happen.)

You probably already have a sound card and speakers, but what about the mike? You can use any microphone that can plug into your sound card's microphone input. Most sound cards are designed to accept the same small stereo plugs that

For the Time-Challenged

- CoolTalk is a complete real-time communication tool for the Internet. It includes not only an Internet telephone, enabling live two-way audio calls, but also the ability to exchange text files and to work collaboratively in a shared graphical whiteboard space.
- When you set up CoolTalk, the program will give you a CoolTalk "number" (which looks something like an e-mail address). The program also registers you with the CoolTalk server, which enables others to find your address.
- To place a call, you choose a number. You can do so by selecting a number from the server or by typing an address manually.
- While the call is in progress, you can exchange text using the Chat Tool. You can also work collaboratively in the Whiteboard, a shared graphical space.

fit into portable tape recorders; check your sound card's documentation to make sure. (I'm using the cheap little mike that came with my daughter's Macintosh LC.)

Internet telephony might be making the phone companies nervous, but right now they don't have much to worry about. The reason? There's no standard for Internet telephony. There are more than a dozen Internet telephony programs, and each uses its own proprietary compression/decompression (CODEC) and addressing techniques. If I have CoolTalk and you have Internet Phone, we can't talk. In order to connect with somebody, you both have to have the same program. Think what a mess the telephone system would be if there were a dozen different brands of telephones, and you could only call somebody who had the same brand you did!

This lack of standardization might be resolved through the creation of an open standard, which is precisely what Netscape Communications is hoping to achieve with LiveMedia. LiveMedia is a set of standards for real-time data delivery via the Internet, including Internet telephony. CoolTalk conforms to the LiveMedia standard. In all likelihood, though, the matter will be resolved by the brute-force method: After a period of fierce competition, one product will prevail over the others, and that product's telephony method will become the standard. Given the fact that CoolTalk is being distributed free with zillions of copies of Netscape, CoolTalk has an obvious advantage here.

CoolTalk looks a little different from what this chapter describes! This chapter is based on a pretty early beta version of CoolTalk, and some features weren't implemented or weren't working as this book went to press. I normally don't like to include a discussion of early versions of programs—they're bound to change as the developers iron out bugs—but CoolTalk is a fun and useful tool, and I'd like to encourage you to give it a try.

Introducing CoolTalk

Here's a quick overview of CoolTalk's features :

- Full-duplex audio conferencing enables both users to speak and hear at the same time.
- You can adjust the audio quality for the type of modem you're using (14.4 or 28.8 Kbps).
- A Chat Tool enables you to send and receive text, including entire files, while you're talking.
- A shared Whiteboard, replete with graphics tools, enables both users to think through ideas visually while they're talking. You can import a file (eight formats are supported) into the Whiteboard, and then mark it up with the graphics tools (which function on a separate layer, preserving the original file).
- An answering machine takes your calls and messages while you're out.
- The CoolTalk Watchdog enables you to accept CoolTalk calls even if CoolTalk isn't running.

- Your Business Card enables callers to receive your business information (company, address, phone number, fax number, and even a picture of yourself).

Can somebody listen to my conversation while it's en route? Not very easily. All CoolTalk conversations are sent in compressed form, which would be just so much gibberish if they were intercepted in some way.

Configuring CoolTalk

Before you start CoolTalk for the first time, make sure you've plugged in your speakers and microphone. You'll need them for various tests that the program makes to determine the optimum sound quality for your system.

The first time you start CoolTalk, you'll see the CoolTalk Setup Wizard (Figure 19.1), which walks you through the installation procedure. You'll be asked to fill out your Business Card (Figure 19.2), which you can make available to callers if you wish.

Figure 19.1 CoolTalk Setup Wizard

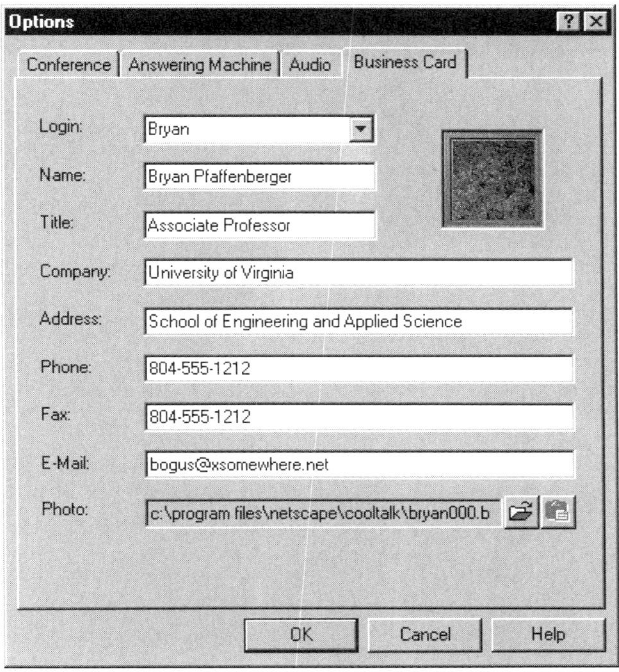

Figure 19.2 CoolTalk Business Card

WHAT'S IN THE COOLTALK WINDOW?

The CoolTalk window includes the following (see Figure 19.3):

- **Toolbar** The CoolTalk toolbar contains the most frequently accessed menu commands.
- **Recording Meter** This meter monitors recording. The red arrows represent the Silence Sensor, showing the level below which no audio is sent. To the right of the recording meter are volume adjustment controls. As you click the plus or minus signs, the status bar (at the bottom of the window) shows the recording sensitivity level.

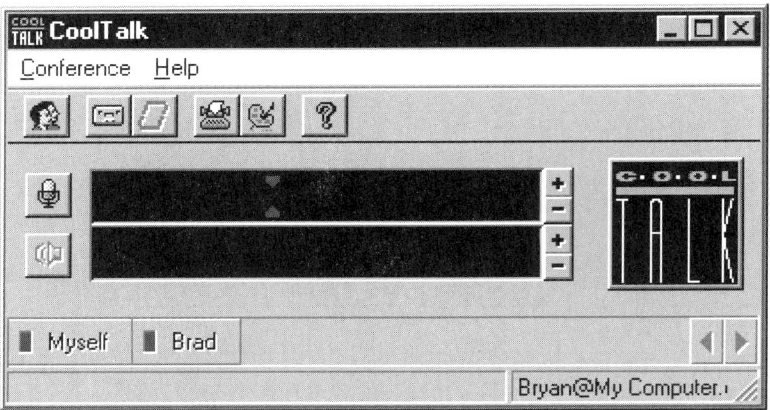

Figure 19.3 The CoolTalk window

- **Playback Meter** This meter monitors playback. To the right of the playback meter are volume adjustment controls. As you click the plus or minus signs, the status bar (at the bottom of the window) shows the recording sensitivity level.
- **CoolTalk Icon** Click here to see information about participants, the host system from which you're dialing, and the version of CoolTalk you're using.
- **Speed Dial** In this area, you'll find buttons for frequently called numbers.

Here's a guide to the tools you'll find on the Toolbar:

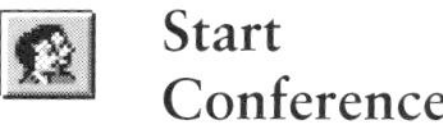

Start Conference Click here to display the Open Conference dialog box, where you can create a new conference participant or choose an existing one. You can also start a conference by clicking one of the Speed Dial buttons.

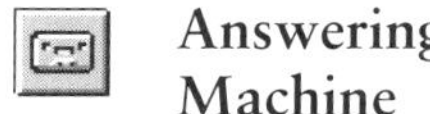

Answering Machine Click here to turn on the answering machine. Click again to turn it off.

	Read Messages	Click here to read messages left on your answering machine.
	Chat Tool	When you click this tool, you'll see the Chat Tool, which enables you to send text and text files.
	Whiteboard	Click here to display the Whiteboard, which enables you to draw and send pictures.

Understanding the IS411 Server

This section is a little technical, but it's needed so that you can understand how CoolTalk handles Internet "phone numbers." These aren't the same as e-mail addresses.

Here's the problem with Internet phone numbers. Many people using the Internet have direct connections (often through a local area network at the office), and these lucky individuals have *permanent IP addresses.* (An IP address is a number that uniquely identifies the location of a computer on the Internet. It's something like the address of your house or apartment.) It's no problem for CoolTalk or any other Internet telephony program to link with somebody who has a permanent IP address: You just get the person's address (which will look something like 128.15.299.52) and make the connection.

The problem is that many people use modems to connect to the Internet, and most of these people don't have permanent IP addresses. The modem does, but most Internet service providers have lots of modems—hundreds or thousands of them—and you can't control which one you're going to get. So your IP address is assigned temporarily, and differs from session to session.

To solve this problem, computer geniuses came up with the idea of a telephony server. Here's how it works. Your telephony program (such as CoolTalk) creates a unique name for you, a name that doesn't change (for example, "JJ-Chan@saotome.com." When you start your telephony program, the program contacts the server and says (in effect), "Hey, JJ-Chan's using such-and-such IP address for this session." If somebody wants to call JJ-Chan, they look up JJ-Chan in the server's phone number list and select this name. The server takes care of making the connection.

The telephony server, in sum, functions as a global telephone operator, keeping track of changing IP addresses so that somebody wishing to call you

can always get through. CoolTalk's server is called the IS411 server ("IS" is short for InSoft, the company that created CoolTalk).

I don't want to make my phone number public! What if some weirdo calls me? Remember that your CoolTalk "number" isn't the same as your telephone number. Also, you can configure CoolTalk so that it doesn't automatically accept incoming calls. If somebody's bugging you, you can set the program to refuse all incoming calls. Still, this is a concern. Later in this chapter you'll learn how you can bypass the IS411 server entirely and make direct calls.

Selecting a Number to Call and Placing the Call

To call somebody, you need to know the number. You can find out in two ways:

- **Look up the number in the IS411 server** To do this, click Start Conference, and select the IS411 Directory tab. In the Search Substring box, type part of the person's name so that you can narrow the search down. (*Note:* This portion of the program was still under development as this book went to press, and it's very likely that the IS411 Directory will look different, and operate differently, by the time you read this.)
- **Get a person's CoolTalk address by telephone or e-mail** Use this method if someone has given you a CoolTalk address. To enter the number into the Address Book, click Start Conference, and select the Address Book tab. In the text box, enter the address. If you would like to add this number to your Speed Dial list, click Add to Speed Dial. Click OK to confirm the new number (and place a call).

After you click OK, CoolTalk attempts to make the connection, and you'll hear the phone "ring" just as you would in a normal phone call. What's happening is that CoolTalk is attempting to invite the person you're calling to join a conference. The person on the other end of the "line" will see a

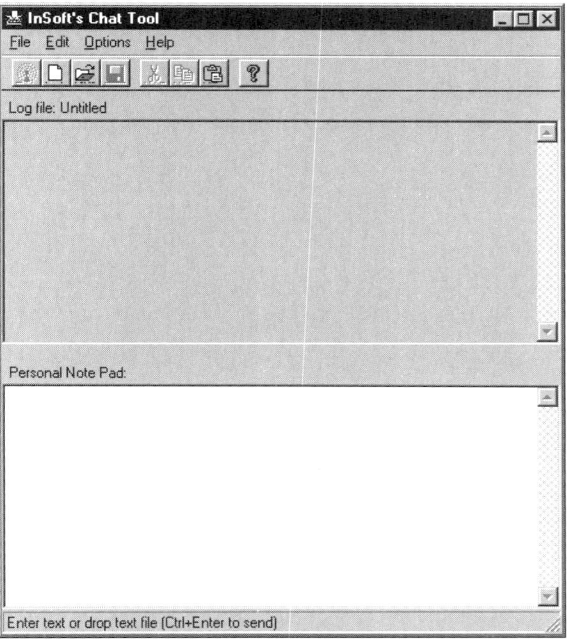

Figure 19.4 Chat Tool

dialog box that extends an invitation to join the conference. If the person's on-line and "answers," you can begin talking.

Using the Chat Tool

If you would like to send some text or a file to the person with whom you're speaking, click the Chat button on the toolbar. You'll see the Chat Tool, shown in Figure 19.4. At the top of the window, you see the Log File, which is seen by all conference participants. At the bottom of the window, you see the Personal Note Pad, where you can type text to send. Other participants don't see this text unless you click the Send button.

Here's a guide to the tools on the Chat Tool's toolbar:

	Send To	Sends the text that you've typed in the Personal Note Pad.
	New	Clears the Log File and starts a new, blank one.
	Include	Enables you to select a file to send. You can send any plain text (ASCII) file.
	Save	Saves the Log File to your hard disk for later review or use.
	Cut	This is the standard Windows editing tool (same as Ctrl + X).
	Copy	This is the standard Windows editing tool (same as Ctrl + C).
	Paste	This is the standard Windows editing tool (same as Ctrl + V).
	Help	Click here to see help screens for this window.

Using the Whiteboard

CoolTalk's nifty Whiteboard (Figure 19.5) enables you to create a collaborative illustration with conference participants. You can create your own picture using the graphics tools provided, or you can import an existing picture (CoolTalk recognizes nine popular graphics file formats). With the Whiteboard, you can discuss a project timeline, map, proposed illustration, or anything else that's graphic in nature, and conference participants can see what you're discussing.

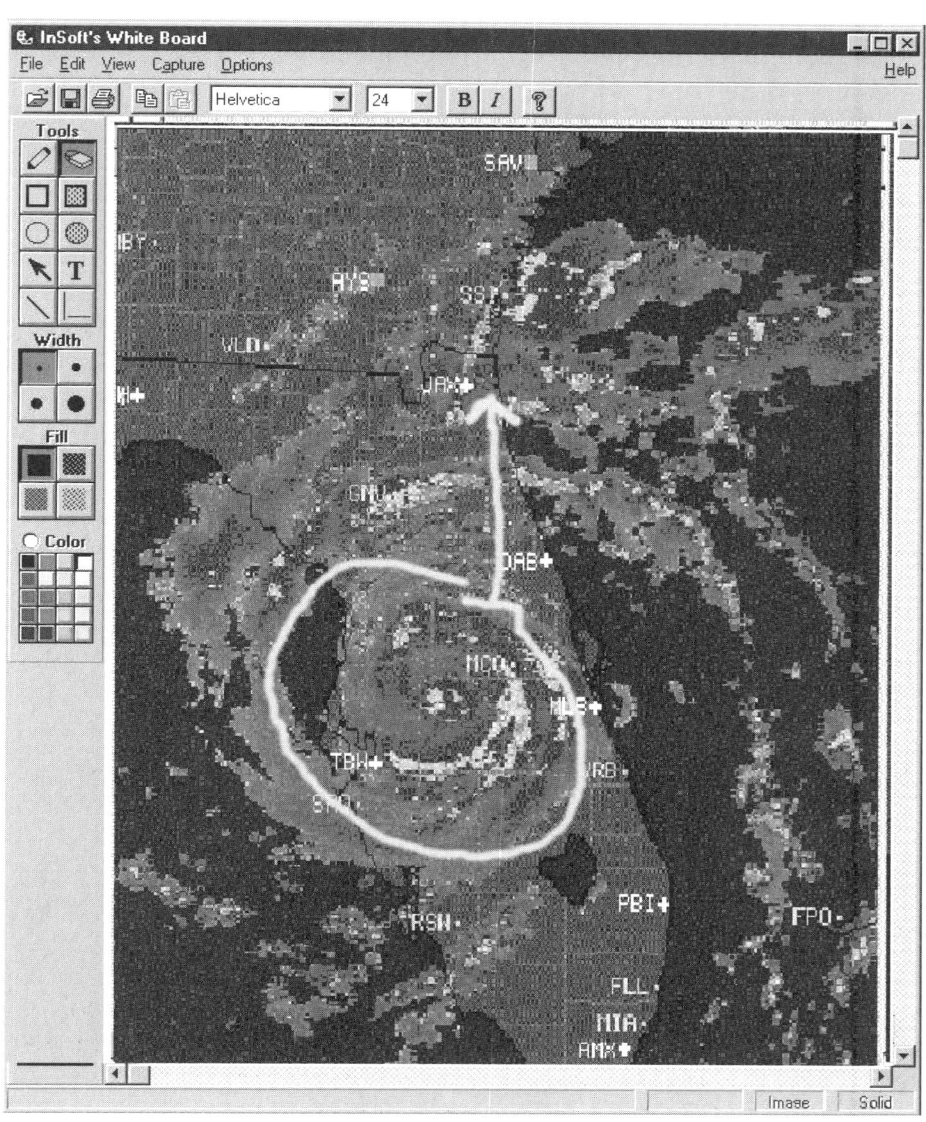

Figure 19.5 CoolTalk Whiteboard

From Here

Explore the rest of the Internet with Netscape as your guide. Here's what you'll find in the chapters to come:

- Learn how to find cool Gopher sites and navigate Gopher menus in Chapter 20.
- In Chapter 21, you'll learn how to download excellent freeware and shareware software using FTP, the File Transfer Protocol.
- Chapter 22 fully covers Netscape's excellent Usenet capabilities.
- Looking for data on a non-Internet computer? You can access it using Telnet and QWS3270, as explained in Chapter 23.

Chapter 20

Digging Around in Gopher

Gopher got its start as a campus-wide information system at the University of Minnesota, the mascot of which is—you guessed it. It enables people to access all kinds of different information with the same easy menu-based browsing system. Those nice University of Minnesota folks made the program freely available, and what do you know? Colleges and universities everywhere used Gopher to make information available. A few private organizations did, too.

Before the Web came along, Gopher was the Latest Best Thing for accessing Internet resources, and it grew wildly. But the Web's success has choked off Gopher's growth. Still, there are lots of useful resources available in Gopher menus, mainly because people haven't had the time to put them on the Web yet. But no matter; clever Netscape can navigate Gopher menus

For the Time-Challenged

- ♦ Gopher is a menu-driven information system that Netscape can access directly. Gopher menus may contain links to Gopher submenus, documents, binary files, graphics, or search utilities.
- ♦ If you've gone "down" into a Gopher submenu, click the Back button to get out of the "hole."
- ♦ Check out TradeWave Galaxy's Gopher Jewels list for some terrific Gopher sites.
- ♦ You can search Gopher directory titles and document names with Veronica, but you'd be wise to access this overloaded service in the wee hours of the morning.
- ♦ It isn't obvious from Veronica's search screen, but the software has some very sophisticated search capabilities.

directly. You can also use services called Veronica and Archie to find Gopher-based information.

This chapter covers the use of Gopher menus with Netscape. Although Gopher is easy to use, this chapter includes some yummy tips for locating great Gopher sites and searching Gopherspace effectively. Even if you've navigated Gopher already, you'll still want to skim this chapter.

Accessing Gopher Sites

To access a Gopher site, you have two options:

- **Click a Gopher hyperlink** A hyperlink to a Gopher site looks like any other hyperlink. After you click the link, you'll see a Gopher menu instead of a Web page.
- **Type a Gopher URL directly** A Gopher URL looks like a Web URL, except that it starts with gopher:// instead of http://, as in the following:

  gopher://gopher.well.sf.ca.us/

Understanding Gopher Menus

After you've accessed a Gopher site, you'll see a Gopher menu, such as the one shown in Figure 20.1.

As displayed by Netscape, a Gopher menu is a list of hyperlinks—but they're of different kinds. You may see one or more of the following items, each with its own icon:

 **Another Gopher menu** Click this item to display the items in this folder.

 **A document** If you click this link, you will see a plain-text document, which you can read on-screen.

 **A binary file** If you click this link, Netscape will begin downloading the file.

 **A graphic** If you click this link, Netscape will display the graphic.

Perform a search If you click this link, you'll see a search document. Type one or more keywords, and click the Search button to initiate the search.

 **Access a Telnet session** If you click this link, Netscape will start your Telnet helper application. For more information on Telnet, see Chapter 23.

When you've gone "down" into a Gopher submenu (otherwise known as a "Gopher hole"—get it?), you can go back "up" again to the menu you just viewed. To do so, click the Back button.

Figure 20.1 Gopher menu

Gopher Jewels

Looking for good stuff on Gopher? Check out Gopher Jewels, accessible via TradeWave Galaxy (http://galaxy.einet.net/GJ/). You'll see a list of hyperlinks to great Gopher sites, which are classified by subject; there are over 2,300 Gopher sites accessible in this way. Table 20.1 lists the subject categories currently found in the Gopher Jewels list. Have fun!

Table 20.1 Subject Categories in Gopher Jewels (TradeWave Galaxy)

Agriculture and Forestry	Internet Cyberspace Related
AIDS and HIV Information	Internet Resources by Type (Gopher, Phone, USENET, WAIS, Other)
Anthropology and Archaeology	Internet Service Providers
Architecture	Journalism
Arts and Humanities	Language
Astronomy and Astrophysics	Legal or Law Related
Biological Sciences	Library Information and Catalogs
Books, Journals, Magazines, Newsletters, and Publications	List of Lists Resources
Chemistry	Manufacturing
Computer Related	Math Sciences
Country Specific Information	Medical Related
Disability Information	Meteorology
Economics and Business	Military
Education (includes K–12)	Miscellaneous Items
Employment Opportunities and Resume Postings	Museums, Exhibits, and Special Collections
Engineering Related	News Related Services
Environment	Patents and Copyrights
Federal Agency and Related Gopher Sites	Physics
Free-Nets and Other Community or State Gophers	Political and Government
Fun Stuff and Multimedia	Products and Services—Store Fronts
Genealogy	Psychology
General Reference Resources	Radio and TV Broadcasting
Geography	Religion and Philosophy
Geology and Oceanography	Safety
Global or World-Wide Topics	Social Sciences
Grants	State Government
History	Technical Reports
	Technology Transfer
	Travel Information

Searching Gopher: Veronica

Veronica is a search engine that's designed to find resources in Gopherspace (the world of accessible Gopher items). To do so, Veronica scans an automatically compiled index of titles of Gopher directory titles and document names. Note that this index does *not* include words found within the text of these files. Jughead is essentially a version of Veronica that searches for directory titles only.

To access Veronica, click the Veronica hyperlink in HOME.HTM, or use the following URL:

gopher://gopher.ed.gov:70/11/other_gopher/veronica

Note that you can search two ways:

- **Directory Titles Only (Jughead)** This is a good place to start your search. If you're lucky, you'll find a Gopher menu that groups a lot of resources pertaining to the subject in which you're interested.
- **Searching All Gopherspace (Veronica)** This search examines Gopher document names as well as directory titles. You'll get a lot more items from this search, but much of it will be irrelevant junk.

To initiate the search, decide whether you're going to search directory titles or Gopherspace, and click a server name. You'll see a search page.

It says "Too many connections—Try again soon"! What, you're trying to search Veronica during the *day*? With so many gazillions of people using the Internet, Veronica has become an early-morning-hours service, unless you're very lucky.

Simplified Searching

On some Veronica servers, you'll see an item called "Simplified Veronica Search." This option uses automated techniques to find an available server. It gives you the best chance of actually getting something out of your Veronica search.

Interpreting the Results of the Search

If the search is successful, you'll see a Gopher menu containing the items the server has retrieved. You can navigate this Gopher menu just like any other Gopher menu.

If the search is unsuccessful, you'll see a message informing you that the server returned no data. Try again, using more general keywords.

Advanced Veronica Searches

Like many of the Internet's search services (see Chapter 16), Veronica searches are more capable than you'd think, looking at that simple search page. By default, Veronica performs a case-insensitive search; if you type two or more words, Veronica ANDs them (no document is retrieved unless all of the keywords are present in the document title). In addition, Veronica performs a whole-word search; if you type "cat," you'll get documents with the word "cat" in the title, but not "concatenate."

You can override Veronica's default search settings in the following ways:

- **OR Operator** To search with an OR operator so that Veronica retrieves documents that have any of the keywords in their titles, separate the words with OR ("cats or dogs").
- **NOT Operator** To exclude documents containing a certain word in their titles, type NOT followed by the word you want to exclude ("cats not dogs").
- **Parenthetical Statements** For a finely honed search, you can embed Boolean operators in parentheses. For example, a search for "recipes and (indian or thai)" retrieves Indian as well as Thai recipes, but nothing else pertaining to India or Thailand.
- **Searching for Resources of a Certain Type** The -t operator enables you to restrict the retrieval list to certain types of documents. For example, the following retrieves graphics (GIFs) and sounds pertaining to Star Trek: Star Trek -tgs. To restrict the search in this way, type -t followed by a code and the text you're searching for. For a list of the -t codes, see Table 20.2.
- **Specify the Maximum Number of Hits** By default, Veronica retrieves 200 hits. To increase this number, use the -m operator. The following retrieves 1,000 Star Trek documents: Star Trek -m1000. (You can combine this code with the -t code, if you wish: Star Trek -m1000 -tg retrieves 1,000 Star Trek GIFs, which is assuredly more than you'll ever need.)

Table 20.2 Codes for Restricting Veronica Searches with the -t Operator

0	Text file	s	Sound
1	Directory	e	Event (not in 2.06)
2	CSO name server	I	Image (other than GIF)
4	Mac HQX file	M	MIME multipart/mixed message
5	PC binary	T	TN3270 session
7	Full Text Index (Gopher menu)	c	Calendar (not in 2.06)
8	Telnet session	g	GIF image
9	Binary file	h	HTML, Hypertext Markup Language

From Here

- Hunt down some files with FTP; you'll find the lowdown in Chapter 21.
- Join the tumult on Usenet newgroups with Netscape's excellent newsreading and mail capabilities; check out Chapter 22 for the details.
- See Chapter 23 for information on using Telnet with Netscape.

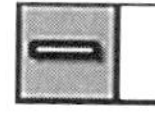

Chapter 21

Ransacking FTP File Archives

FTP is short for File Transfer Protocol, and its full name pretty much describes what it does. Using FTP, you can exchange program or text files with anyone connected to the Internet. Netscape gives you partial FTP capabilities—specifically, to get files. (You can send files with Netscape's mail capabilities, as discussed in Chapter 17, but that is mail, not FTP—there is a difference.)

You can't just browse around in anyone's computer in search of files. Normally, you need an account and a password to access someone else's computer on the Internet. But some kind people have created publicly accessible file archives. This is also called "anonymous FTP," since you had to log into these computers as "anonymous" when you were using one of those old, clunky FTP programs (which are still needed to upload files to FTP sites). Netscape logs you in to anonymous sites automatically.

For the Time-Challenged

- ♦ Netscape accesses anonymous FTP file archives smoothly, showing you a graphical version of server file directories. Just click the items you want. To go back up to a parent directory, be sure to use the hyperlink, not the Back button.
- ♦ Archie searches a database of thousands of FTP archives. With Netscape, you can access Archie through a gateway such as ArchiePlex.
- ♦ shareware.com provides an easy way to obtain software from the largest and best shareware archives. Don't miss it!

Most of the files in these publicly accessible file archives are programs, including tons of Microsoft Windows programs. You can obtain these and soup up your computer to just an incredible degree. (Mine shows a picture of the Starship Enterprise on start-up, plays the theme from Star Trek, and then you hear a "beam-me-up" transporter sound. OK, it's dumb, but it's more fun than looking at the Windows logo.) These programs are either freeware (copyrighted but freely copiable as long as you don't sell them) or shareware (you really ought to pay that registration fee, you know). The moral: Use FTP to get your hands on extremely cool programs, and they're free (or really cheap). Netscape gives you wonderful tools for browsing FTP file archives and the WinZip software included with this book automatically decompresses the files after you download them.

If you're interested in obtaining software from the Internet, this chapter's for you!

Accessing Anonymous FTP File Archives

FTP is smoothly integrated with Netscape. You can access anonymous FTP file archives in two ways:

- **Clicking an FTP hyperlink** You see an FTP file directory.
- **Typing the URL directly** To access an anonymous FTP archive, you can type ftp:// followed by the archive's name, such as ftp://ftp.virginia.edu/.

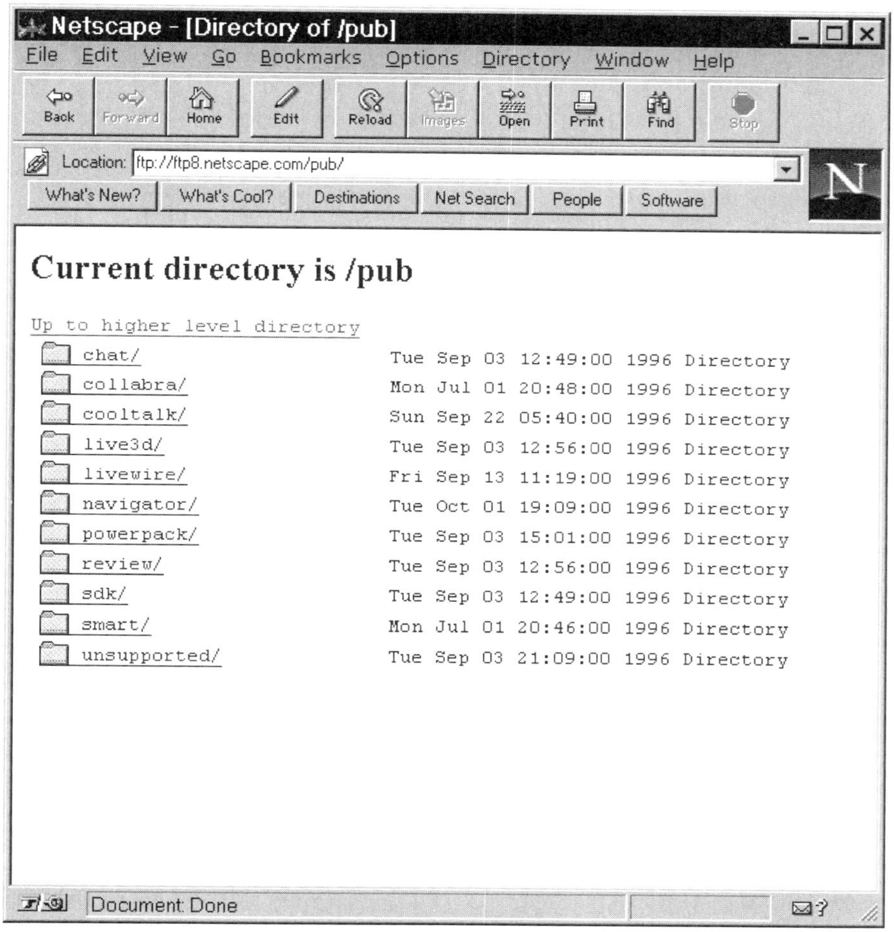
Netscape - [Directory of /pub]
File Edit View Go Bookmarks Options Directory Window Help
Back Forward Home Edit Reload Images Open Print Find Stop
Location: ftp://ftp8.netscape.com/pub/
What's New? What's Cool? Destinations Net Search People Software
Current directory is /pub
Up to higher level directory
chat/ Tue Sep 03 12:49:00 1996 Directory
collabra/ Mon Jul 01 20:48:00 1996 Directory
cooltalk/ Sun Sep 22 05:40:00 1996 Directory
live3d/ Tue Sep 03 12:56:00 1996 Directory
livewire/ Fri Sep 13 11:19:00 1996 Directory
navigator/ Tue Oct 01 19:09:00 1996 Directory
powerpack/ Tue Sep 03 15:01:00 1996 Directory
review/ Tue Sep 03 12:56:00 1996 Directory
sdk/ Tue Sep 03 12:49:00 1996 Directory
smart/ Mon Jul 01 20:46:00 1996 Directory
unsupported/ Tue Sep 03 21:09:00 1996 Directory
Document: Done

Figure 21.1 An FTP archive viewed with Netscape

Navigating FTP Directories

As a Windows user, you've surely plowed around in lots of MS-DOS directories. If you have, you're already familiar with UNIX directories, since DOS was modeled on UNIX. Netscape makes it even easier by providing a highly graphical interface, as shown in Figure 21.1.

To navigate within FTP directories, do the following:

- To open a subdirectory, click one of the folders.
- To go back to the parent directory (the next directory up in the directory tree), click "Up to higher level directory," a hyperlink you'll find at the top of the file list. Do not click the Back button. If you do, you'll get disoriented and lose track of the directories' hierarchical arrangement.

What's in the Files?

Netscape uses little icons to tell you which kind of file you're viewing. Here's a handy guide:

	A text document	Click here to read the document. If it's called README, chances are it contains important and useful information about the files in this directory.
	A graphic	Click here to download the graphic.
	A document or file that Netscape couldn't identify	Click it and see what happens.
	A movie or animation	Click here to download an MPEG or QuickTime movie.
	A program	Click here to download the software.
	A compressed file	Click here to download and decompress the file.
	A sound	Click here to hear the sound.

A subdirectory Click here to see another directory of files, and possibly additional subdirectories.

They're demanding my e-mail address! To cut down on vandalism, many FTP sites require you to enter your e-mail address as your password when you log on via anonymous FTP. If you feel comfortable doing this, Netscape can do it automatically. From the Options menu, choose Network Preferences, and click the Protocols tab. Select the option Send Email Address as Anonymous FTP Password, and click OK.

Looking for Shareware with shareware.com

One of the coolest sites on the Web is shareware.com, a service of c|net. Offering an excellent search interface, shareware.com gives you access to more than 150,000 shareware and freeware programs, which you can directly download.

To access shareware.com, use the following URL:

http://www.shareware.com

You'll see shareware.com's welcome screen, shown in Figure 21.2.

To search for files in shareware.com, choose Quick Search or click the "other search options" hyperlink on the welcome page. Your options are as follows:

Quick Search Gives you a simple but useful search form—usually all you'll need. You can specify a platform or category to search by selecting an option from the drop-down list box.

Power Search Lets you tailor your search extensively with an elaborate form. The power search form appears in Figure 21.3.

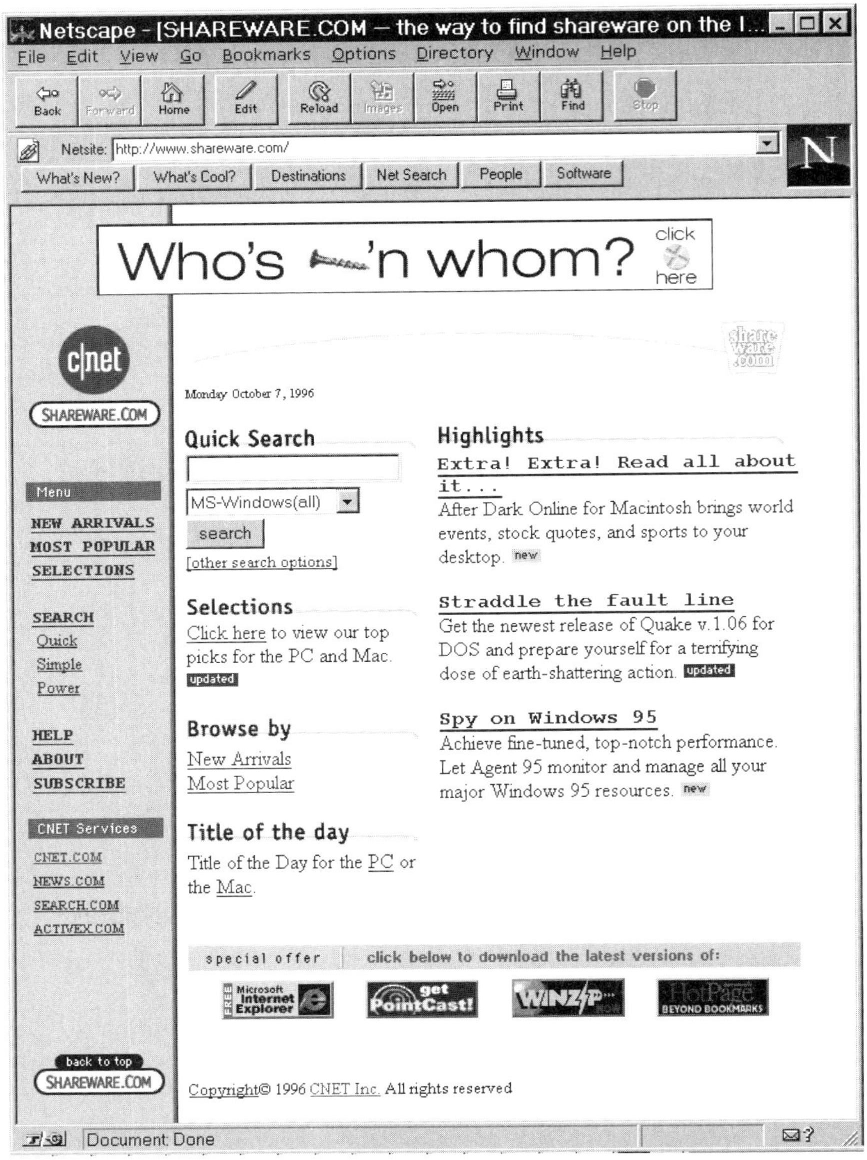

Netscape - [SHAREWARE.COM — the way to find shareware on the I...
File Edit View Go Bookmarks Options Directory Window Help
Back
Forward
Home
Edit
Reload
Images
Open
Print
Find
Stop
Netsite: http://www.shareware.com/
What's New?
What's Cool?
Destinations
Net Search
People
Software
Who's 'n whom?
click here
c|net
SHAREWARE.COM
Monday October 7, 1996
Menu
NEW ARRIVALS
MOST POPULAR
SELECTIONS
SEARCH
Quick
Simple
Power
HELP
ABOUT
SUBSCRIBE
CNET Services
CNET.COM
NEWS.COM
SEARCH.COM
ACTIVEX.COM
back to top
SHAREWARE.COM
Quick Search
MS-Windows(all)
search
[other search options]
Selections
Click here to view our top picks for the PC and Mac.
updated
Browse by
New Arrivals
Most Popular
Title of the day
Title of the Day for the PC or the Mac.
Highlights
Extra! Extra! Read all about it...
After Dark Online for Macintosh brings world events, stock quotes, and sports to your desktop. new
Straddle the fault line
Get the newest release of Quake v.1.06 for DOS and prepare yourself for a terrifying dose of earth-shattering action. updated
Spy on Windows 95
Achieve fine-tuned, top-notch performance. Let Agent 95 monitor and manage all your major Windows 95 resources. new
special offer
click below to download the latest versions of:
Microsoft Internet Explorer
get PointCast!
WINZIP
HotPage
BEYOND BOOKMARKS
Copyright© 1996 CNET Inc. All rights reserved
Document: Done

Figure 21.2 shareware.com

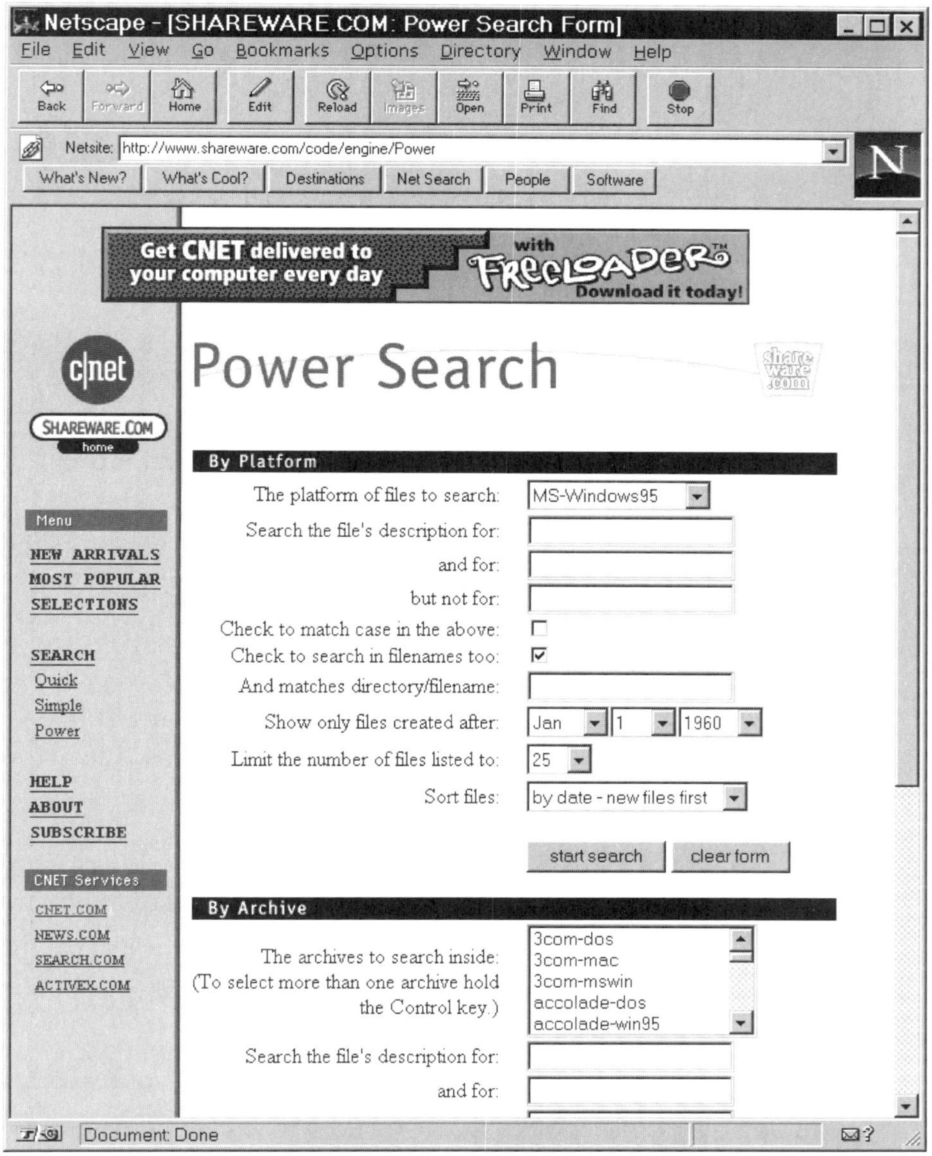

Figure 21.3 The shareware.com Power Search form

Simple Search	Slightly more detailed than Quick Search, the Simple Search lets you use boolean AND or OR operators and specify the number of results to be displayed.

These instructions describe how to use the Power Search form.

1. In the "platform of files ..." list box, choose the operating system for which you want software. You'll want to choose either MS-Windows(all), MS-Windows 3.x, MS-Windows95, or MS-Windows NT, but, as an indicator of shareware.com's comprehensiveness, note that Atari and Amiga are options, too.
2. In the text box labeled "Search the file's description for," type the first word you want to match.
3. If you would like to perform an AND search, type a second keyword in the "and for" box. This service will retrieve a file only if it matches both the keywords you have typed.
4. If you would like to exclude files with certain words in their descriptions, type the unwanted word in the "but not for" box.
5. If you want to perform a case-sensitive search, click the "match case" check box.
6. If you want to search file names, as well as descriptions, for your search terms, click the "Check to search in filenames too" check box.
7. Unless you know exactly which directories you want to search, leave the "And matches directory/filename" box blank.
8. To search for files of a certain age, enter a month, day, and year in each of the three date list boxes.
9. To increase the number of files retrieved, choose a larger number in the "Limit the number of files listed to" list box.
10. You can tell the search engine to sort the results of your search by date or by directory path by choosing an option from the "Sort files" list box.
11. You can specify particular software archives that you want to search by selecting them from the scrolling list in the By Archive section of the search form.
12. Click the Start Search button.

You'll see a new page reporting the results of your search (Figure 21.4). If shareware.com couldn't find any files, you won't see any file names. If you do see file names, click the one that looks like it meets your needs. You'll see another page of hyperlinks for downloading the file; click the one nearest you to begin downloading.

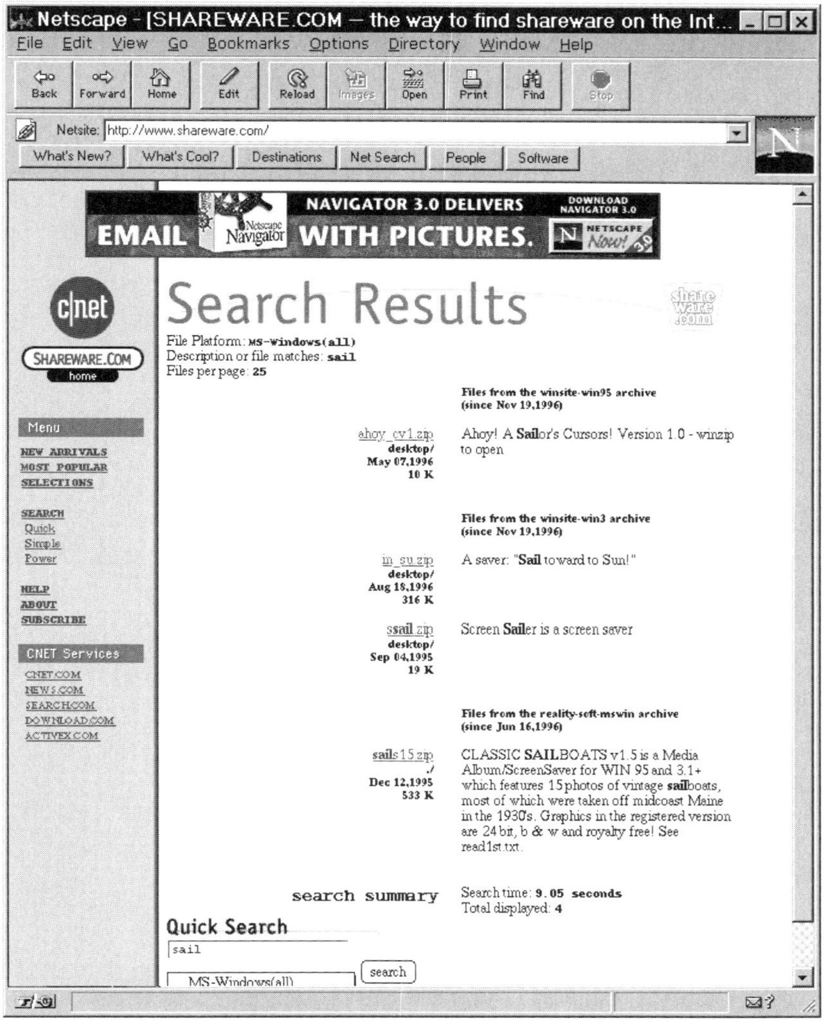

Figure 21.4 The results of a shareware.com search

Finding FTP Resources: Archie

There are thousands of anonymous FTP file archives out there—but how do you find them? A service called Archie enables you to search for a file, but there's a rub—you pretty much need to know the name of the file for which you're looking. Suppose someone tells you about a file called uudecode.exe that you just have to have. Since you know the name, Archie can help you find an anonymous FTP file archive that contains it, if there is one.

Archie is a UNIX program, but there are lots of Web gateways that enable Netscape and you to communicate with Archie. One of the best is the ArchiePlex gateway, at the following URL:

http://pubweb.nexor.co.uk/public/archie/archieplex/archieplex.html

After accessing ArchiePlex, you'll see the page shown in Figure 21.5.

If you haven't already read Chapter 16, take a look at the section called "Understanding Search Techniques." It will help you use ArchiePlex more effectively.

To use ArchiePlex, follow these steps:

1. The easiest way to use ArchiePlex is with the interface that takes advantage of Netscape's forms capability. Click the "ArchiePlex Form" hyperlink on the welcome page. One of the other two search facilities is for browsers without forms capability; the other isn't very flexible. The ArchiePlex form appears in Figure 21.6.
2. In the Search For box, type the name of the file you want to retrieve. If you don't know the whole name, that's OK—type as much as you know for sure. The default search setting, Case Insensitive Substring Match, is a good one for Archie. It allows you to get hits on, say, "EasyWriter," if you typed "Easywriter" in the Search For box.
3. If you wish, change the default output sort order (click By Date to see the most recent version of the file first).
4. Next to "Several Archie Servers can be used," pick the Archie server nearest you, geographically.

5. Choose other options, if you wish, although the defaults are fine. In particular, be Nice to other users.
6. Click Submit. If you made a mistake, click Reset and start over with step 2.

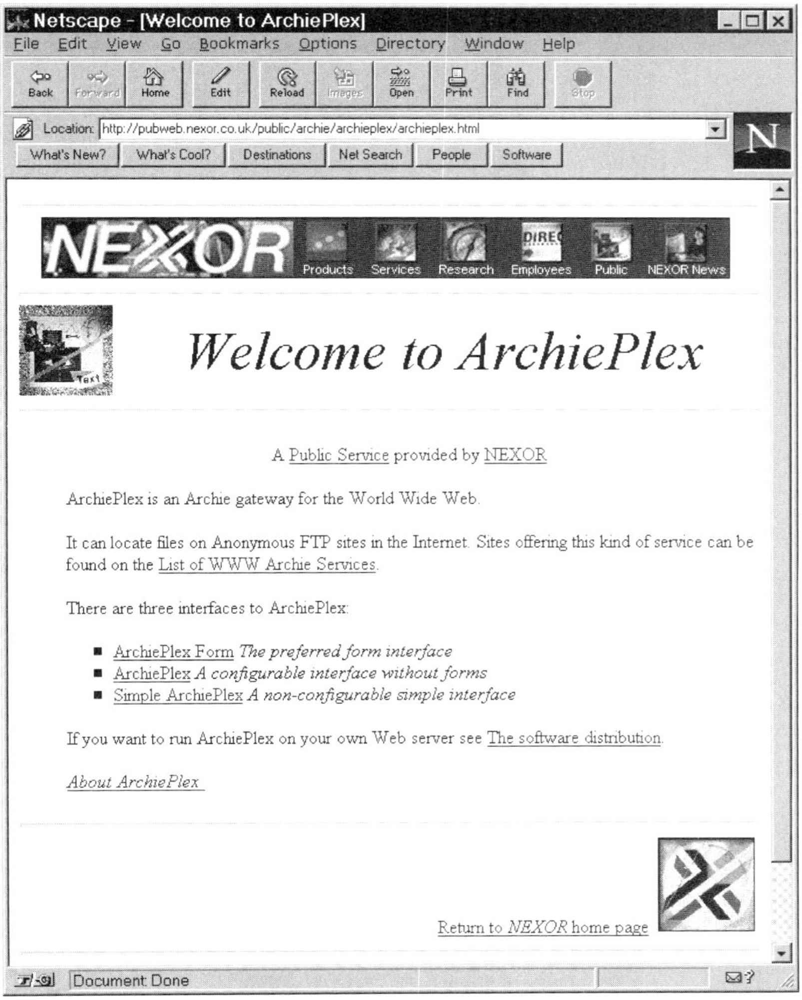

Figure 21.5 The ArchiePlex welcome page

Netscape - [ArchiePlex Form]

File Edit View Go Bookmarks Options Directory Window Help

Back Forward Home Edit Reload Images Open Print Find Stop

Location: http://pubweb.nexor.co.uk/public/archie/archieplex/doc/form.html

What's New? What's Cool? Destinations Net Search People Software

NEXOR Products Services Research Employees Public NEXOR News

ArchiePlex Form

A Public Service provided by NEXOR

This ArchiePlex form can locate files on Anonymous FTP sites in the Internet. Other servers can be found on the List of WWW Archie Services.

Search for: [ ] Submit Reset

There are several types of search: Case Insensitive Substring Match

The results can be sorted (•) By Host or ( ) By Date

Several Archie Servers can be used: United Kingdom (Imperial College London)

You can restrict the results to a domain (e.g. "uk"): [ ]

You can restrict the number of results to a number < 100: 95

The impact on other users can be: Nice

Document: Done

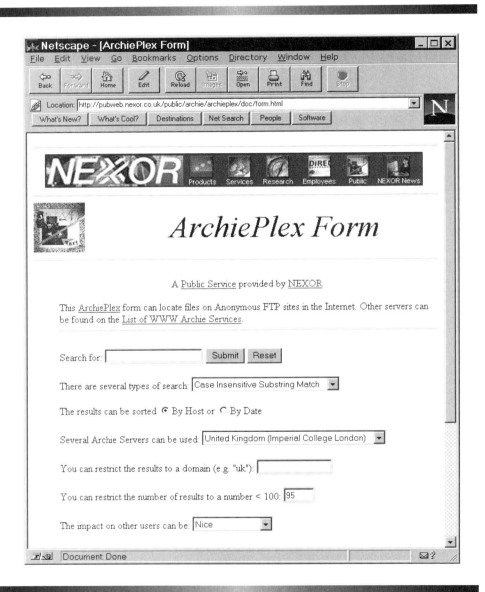

Figure 21.6 The ArchiePlex form

If Archie finds any files matching your request, you'll see a new page listing the anonymous FTP sites that have the file for which you're looking.

It says "Server timed out"! Welcome to the club. Here, unfortunately, is yet another of those overloaded Internet services that is becoming increasingly difficult to access. If the server is busy, you're likely to see this message. As the saying goes, "try again later". . . like at 3:30 AM.

From Here

- Feeling brave? Venture into the wilds of Usenet, with Netscape as your helper. See Chapter 22.
- Don't forget you can access Telnet sessions with Netscape, as you'll learn in Chapter 23.

Chapter 22

Ranting and Raving in Usenet Newsgroups

Usenet is a computer-based discussion system that's widely distributed on the Internet. The idea underlying Usenet is devilishly clever: The Usenet software works behind the scenes, copying and relaying the messages users contribute, so that in time every participating computer (called a *Usenet site*) has an exact copy of every message contributed to the network. The software knows how to organize these messages into topical categories, called *newsgroups*, which you can read. In addition, you can contribute your own messages to these newsgroups. With more than 160,000 Usenet sites connected to the network worldwide, more than 15,000 newsgroups, and an estimated 7 million regular users, contributing to Usenet may be the ultimate act of self-publishing—or self-immolation, if you break any of Usenet's none-too-explicit rules or guidelines. Whatever else you do with Usenet, read newsgroups for a good while before attempting to post your own messages.

Usenet got its start in 1979 as a method of sharing information about UNIX computer systems, and the network still plays a major role in providing computer support. From its earliest days, though, participants showed even more interest in discussing social and political issues, including controversial ones such as abortion and the death penalty. Since then, Usenet has grown wildly, but the growth has not been without controversy. Usenet's strong points lie in the discussions of computer hardware and software, hobbies, entertainment, and recreation. But many people have concluded that Usenet is not very well suited for the discussion of controversial social issues. It's just too easy for obnoxious twerps to ruin the discussion, leading to a "low signal-to-noise ratio," as experienced Usenet hands term it. I'll promise you one thing: After reading Usenet for a while, your estimate of the number of obnoxious twerps in the world will go up by a very substantial percentage.

One of Usenet's worst problems is its own success. Every day, Usenet contributors post the equivalent of 80,000 pages of text—the days are long gone, obviously, when anyone could hope to read all or most of the newsgroups. Most people follow just one or two of them and ignore the rest—but even so, many newsgroups receive dozens or hundreds of messages per day.

Still, Usenet is a wonderful resource. Many newsgroups offer intelligent discussion, particularly the moderated ones, in which all submissions must pass the scrutiny of a human moderator, who checks to see whether they are relevant to the newsgroup's goals. Generally speaking, the technically oriented newsgroups are of the greatest value; there's a real spirit of information exchange and resource sharing. One of the best things about Usenet are the FAQs (Frequently Asked Questions), which attempt to provide answers to the questions people are most likely to ask. There are hundreds of these, and some of them are among the best sources of information on a topic that you can obtain anywhere.

To read and contribute to Usenet newsgroups, you need software called a *newsreader*. But don't go out on the Net hunting down FTP sites—you already have one of the best newsreaders available: Netscape. Whether you want to join in the hue and cry or just access FAQs, Netscape provides wonderful tools for accessing Usenet. You can read messages, post your own messages on a new subject, or reply—either by a follow-up post or an e-mail message—to messages others have left. Compared to the most powerful newsreading programs, Netscape lacks only a few advanced functions. It's the perfect tool for reading Usenet on a daily basis. This chapter thoroughly explores Netscape's Usenet capabilities.

For the Time-Challenged

- To get started with Usenet, you must name your NNTP server in the Mail and News Preferences dialog box.
- To download the newsgroup names, click Show All Newsgroups in the Options menu.
- To read a newsgroup, click its name in the Subscribed Newsgroups window. You'll see a list of current article titles. To read an article, click its title.
- Netscape organizes articles so that you can see the "thread" of discussion; original articles are listed with their replies.
- Use the Next and Previous buttons to navigate through the articles, or just click the article you want to read.
- Don't even think about posting until you fully understand the rules of netiquette.
- Create your signature file before posting.
- To post an article, click the To: News button at the newsgroup's article title level.
- Consider posting an e-mail reply instead of posting a follow-up message to the group. To post a reply to the group, click Re: News. To post an e-mail reply, click Re: Mail.

The new version of Netscape offers vastly improved newsreading capabilities, as you'll find in this chapter. Netscape's now as good as most of the stand-alone newsreader programs available today.

They flamed me! To be "flamed" means to receive a lot of unfriendly e-mail letters. If you break the rules of Usenet "netiquette," flaming may be the result. Please do not post messages to a Usenet newsgroup until you fully understand the newsgroup's purpose and the range of acceptable discussion subjects. Most of all, please do not post questions that have already been answered in the newsgroup's FAQ (Frequently Asked Questions), if there is one (not all newsgroups

have FAQs). This chapter shows you how to access Usenet FAQs; please read this section carefully and obtain the FAQ for any newsgroup to which you're thinking of posting a message. Carefully observe the rules of netiquette, which boil down to good manners, basically: be polite, don't "shout" (using all capital letters), give credit where credit is due, and don't post anything in anger.

Introducing Usenet Newsgroups

With at least 15,000 Usenet newsgroups available from most servers, some kind of organization is needed to make sense of the lengthy list of newsgroup names. This organization is hierarchical, and works in the following way:

- Every newsgroup is part of a top-level hierarchy, such as comp (computer-related subjects), rec (recreation), or soc (social newsgroups).
- Every newsgroup has at least one other part to its name, with the parts separated by dots (such as misc.test or alt.censorship).
- Many newsgroups are further subdivided by adding additional names, as in the following examples:

  alt.fan.tolkien
  alt.fan.woody-allen
  comp.sys.ibm.pc.games.action
  comp.sys.ibm.pc.games.adventure

Newsgroups are organized into two broad categories:

- **Standard Newsgroups** These newsgroups have been established by a formal voting procedure. Every Usenet site is expected to carry the standard newsgroups; not all do, however, owing to problems with disk storage space.
- **Alternative Newsgroups** Anyone who knows the correct UNIX command can create a newsgroup in the alternative (alt.*) hierarchy—but no Usenet site is obligated to carry it. However, many sites offer all or many of the alt newsgroups, which range from important and useful (alt.censorship) to completely silly (alt.barney.dinosaur.die.die.die).

The standard newsgroups fall into the following hierarchies:

bionet	Biology and the environment
biz	Business discussions and advertising
ClariNet	A do-it-yourself on-line newspaper consisting of feeds from major wire services, such as UPI and AP
comp	Computers and computer applications
K12	Primary and secondary education
misc	Anything that doesn't fit into the other categories
news	Newsgroups about Usenet itself
rec	Hobbies and sports
sci	The sciences generally
soc	Social issues and socializing
talk	No-holds-barred controversy, flaming, verbiage—and occasionally, interesting discussion and debate

Usenet may be among the world's most ephemeral communications media: Every article is set to expire after a certain period (usually, two weeks), in which case the message simply disappears from the Net. With hundreds of megabytes of new articles streaming in daily, many Usenet sites have no choice but to decrease the expiration period down to as little as 24 hours. If you don't read the newsgroup regularly, then, you'll miss the action—and you won't have a clue about why a certain topic has become the day's cause célèbre.

What's in a Newsgroup?

A newsgroup consists of articles that have been contributed by Usenet's participants. They fall into two categories:

- **Posts** An original message, with a new topic, that somebody contributed.
- **Follow-up Posts** A reply to the original message, which usually contains some quoted text from the original message. The title of a

follow-up post usually echoes the original post's title, with the addition of "re:" at the beginning of the title.

To enhance your ability to follow the thread of discussion, Usenet software can organize posts and follow-up posts into groups (called *threads*). Not all newsreaders are threaded, though, in which case they throw the messages at you in chronological order. Happily, Netscape can thread the messages—and that makes it an above-average newsreader. Other features take it into the "very good" category, as you'll see in the pages to follow.

Why won't Usenet work? To access Usenet, you need access to an NNTP server, a program that makes Usenet newsgroups accessible to newsreading software. Generally, access to an NNTP server is included with Internet service subscriptions. If you're not sure, call your service provider, and be sure to get the NNTP server's domain name. The next section shows you how to tell Netscape which server to use.

Configuring Netscape to Access Usenet

To configure Netscape to access Usenet, you supply the program with the domain name of your NNTP (Usenet) server. To tell Netscape which NNTP server to use, follow these steps:

1. From the Options menu, choose Mail and News Preferences.
2. Click the Servers tab. You'll see the Servers page, shown in Figure 22.1.
3. In the NNTP server box (News area), type the domain name of your NNTP server.
4. Click OK.

Understanding the News Window

The News window is very similar to the Mail window discussed in Chapter 17—in fact, if you've already learned how to send and receive e-mail with Netscape, you know a lot of how to get into the swing of things on Usenet.

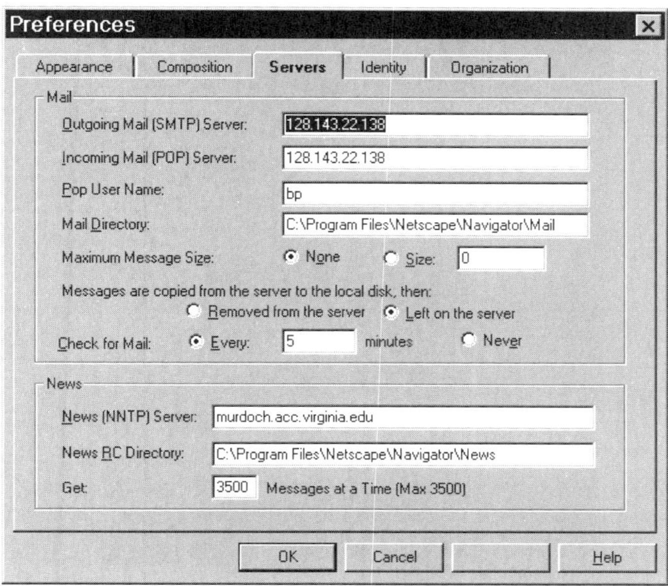

Figure 22.1 Servers page of Mail and News Preferences dialog box

The window is divided into three panes (see Figure 22.2):

- **Newsgroup Pane** In this window, you see the newsgroups to which you are currently subscribed. By default, you'll be subscribed to newsgroups helpful to new Usenet users. Learn Usenet by reading these first. If you enlarge this window slightly by dragging the right frame border, you'll see the number of current unread and total messages for each newsgroup.
- **Message Header Pane** In this window, you see the author and title of the messages currently available in the newsgroup that's selected in the newsgroup pane. Each item has several items of information, organized in columns. First is the sender's name, followed by a "Hot Item" flag that you activate (if you wish), a read/unread icon, the message's subject, and the date the message was written.
- **Message Pane** This window shows the text of the message currently displayed in the message header pane.

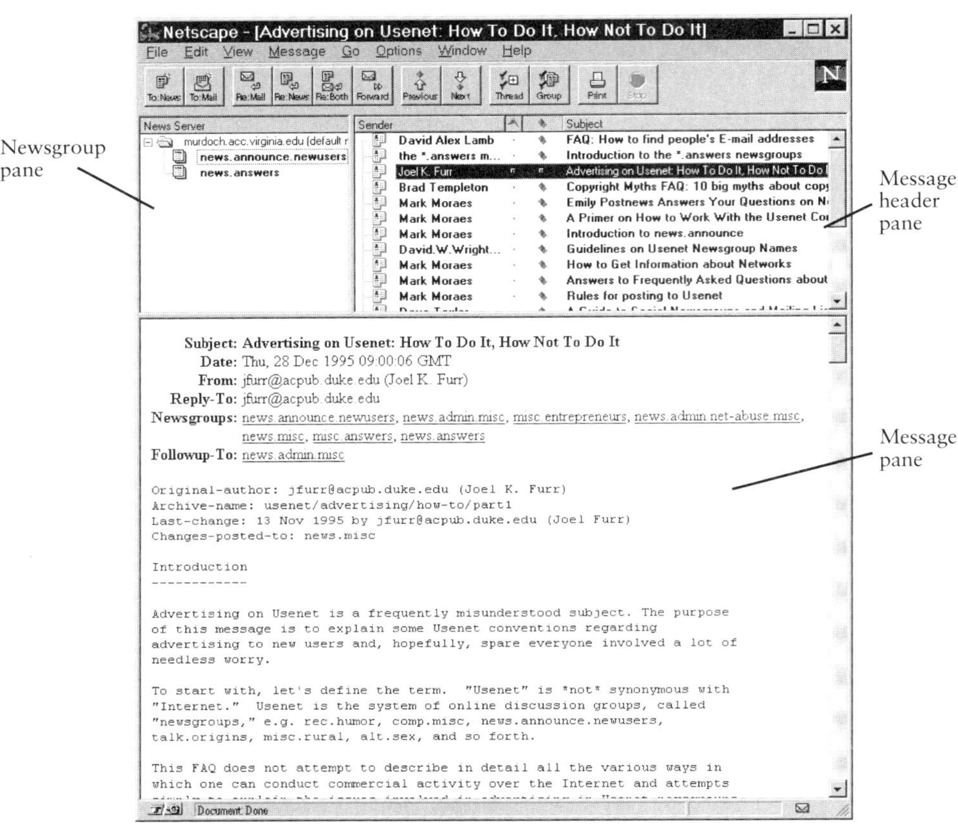

Figure 22.2 The three panes in the News window

The News window also has its own button bar. Here's a guide to the buttons you'll find:

To: News Click this button to post a new message to the newsgroup that's currently selected in the newsgroup pane.

To: Mail Click this button to mail a message to someone.

Re: Mail Click this button to send a reply via e-mail to the person who wrote the message that's currently displayed.

Re: News Click this button to post a follow-up article to the message that's currently being displayed.

Re: Both Click this button to send a reply via e-mail and post a follow-up article at the same time.

Forward Click this button to forward the current article to someone's e-mail address.

Previous View the previous message.

Next View the next message.

Thread Mark entire thread as read. You won't see this thread the next time you open the newsgroup.

All Mark entire newsgroup as read. You won't see any of the current messages the next time you open the newsgroup.

Print Print the current message.

Stop Stop downloading the current message.

Understanding Threading

By default, Netscape sorts the messages by *threads*. The term thread comes from the phrase "follow the thread of a discussion." In thread sorting, original message are grouped with their replies.

Here's an example. Suppose I post a message asking people in rec.boats which marinas they recommend in the Deltaville area of the Chesapeake Bay. Soon, several people reply. The message header pane looks like this:

```
Suggestions for marinas near Deltaville?
   Re: Suggestions for marinas near Deltaville?
   Re: Suggestions for marinas near Deltaville?
```

Now suppose somebody responds to one of the Re: messages. Netscape will add the message as follows:

```
Suggestions for marinas near Deltaville?
    Re: Suggestions for marinas near Deltaville?
    Re: Suggestions for marinas near Deltaville?
      Re: Suggestions for marinas near Deltaville?
```

Threading is a great feature. You're going to love it. Without threading, you'd have to search through the message list to find replies—and that really takes the fun out of Usenet.

About Crossposting

One of the things you'll notice in Usenet is that some messages are posted to more than one newsgroup. This is called *crossposting*. You'll see a lot of flames about crossposting, a fact that's attributable to new users' misconceptions about it. So let's get this straightened out right now.

Crossposting isn't a bad thing in itself. Often, it makes sense to crosspost. For example, suppose I'm describing marinas in Virginia. I might want to post my message to rec.boats.cruising and crosspost it to a local Virginia newsgroup. Nobody would object to that.

What gets people in trouble with crossposting is overdoing it. People who abuse Usenet—for example, by posting irrelevant advertisements in newsgroups on completely unrelated subjects—tend to crosspost wildly, sometimes crossposting to dozens or even hundreds of newsgroups. There have been several infamous incidents of crass individuals trying to post ads to every newsgroup in existence.

What's in the Header?

For each message, you'll see a *header*, which contains a lot of information about the message you're viewing, including the message's subject, date, the

If you try crossposting to too many newsgroups, you're sure to get flamed. Worse, you could become the Cancelmoose's next target. The Cancelmoose is a shadowy figure, whose identity is thought to be known to Usenet gurus but is carefully hidden from the public and the media. Cancelmoose busies himself by running a secret, hacked program that seeks out and cancels messages posted by people who have been known to abuse Usenet. It isn't very ethical to cancel somebody else's message—in fact, it's not even supposed to be possible—but nobody's complaining. Think of the Cancelmoose as something like the Lone Ranger, and you'll have the idea.

e-mail address (and sometimes the name) of the person who contributed the message, and the newsgroups to which the message was posted. Sometimes you'll see additional information, including the following:

- **Reply To** This field indicates the e-mail address to which you should reply, if you wish to do so.
- **Followup-To** If the message was posted to more than one newsgroup, this field indicates the group to which you should send the reply.
- **References** If you're viewing a reply, the references identify the original messages. These are links; if you click the first reference (number 1), you'll see the original message, if it's still available (it might have been deleted by the server).

Downloading the Newsgroups List

Your next step is to download the full newsgroups list from your news server. Depending on how many newsgroups your server carries, this may take a minute or several minutes.

To download the newsgroups list: From the Options menu, choose Show All Newsgroups. Netscape downloads all the newsgroup names, and you see them listed in the newgroups pane (Figure 22.3).

The newsgroup list is arranged into folders and subfolders, making it easy for you to navigate. That's a good thing, because there may be as many as 13,000 names in this list! To see the newsgroups within a folder, click the

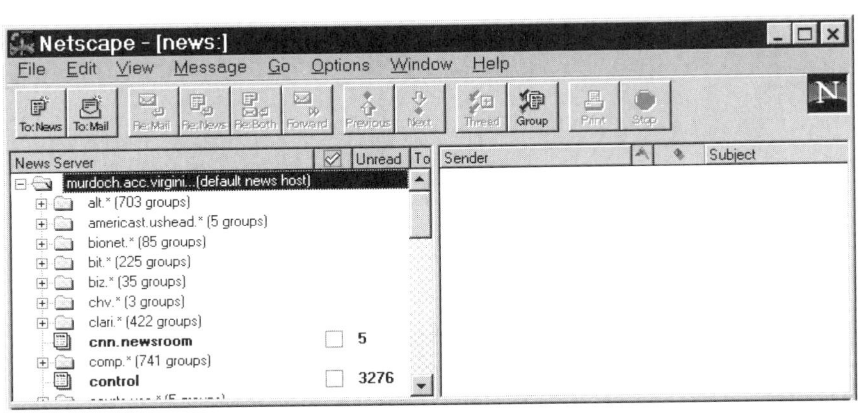

Figure 22.3 Newsgroups pane after downloading all the newsgroup names

plus sign next to the folder. You'll see folders within folders, which helps even more to keep the list organized.

Browse around in the newsgroup list for a while until you get the hang of how it's organized. Next, you'll subscribe to the newsgroups that you want to read on a regular basis.

Subscribing to Newsgroups

Once you've downloaded the newsgroups list, as described in the previous section, it's time to select the newsgroups that you think you'll want to read on a regular basis.

The term "subscribe" is something of a misnomer, since it doesn't affect anything at the server level. On the contrary, it's a setting that's local to your system. After you've subscribed to some of the newsgroups in the total list, you can change the list display so that the newsgroup panel displays only those newsgroups to which you've subscribed. That's convenient.

To subscribe to a newsgroup, select the newsgroup's name in the newsgroup pane and click the check box. You may need to move the right border frame to bring the check box into view (Figure 22.4).

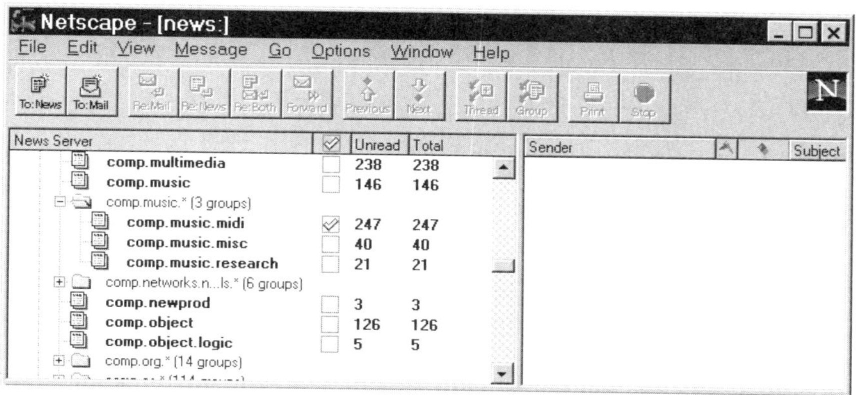

Figure 22.4 Subscribing to newsgroups

To display only the newsgroups to which you've subscribed, choose Show Subscribed Newsgroups from the Options menu. I recommend this option; in the newsgroups pane, you'll see only the newsgroups to which you've subscribed, saving you the trouble of having to hunt them down in the long, huge list.

Reading the News

To read the articles in a newsgroup, click its name in the newsgroups pane. To read an article, just click the article's subject header in the header pane.

I read this cool article the last time I logged on to this newsgroup, but now it's gone! There are two possible reasons for this. First, the article may have expired (most Usenet servers keep articles for only a couple of weeks). Second, Netscape always hides the articles you've already read. To redisplay the read messages, choose Show All Messages from the Options menu.

As you read the news, you'll commonly perform the following actions:

- **Go to the next article** Click the Next button.
- **Go to a previous article** Click the Previous Article button.
- **Read the article that started all this ruckus** If you're reading a follow-up article, look in the header for a References field, and click the first number you see. The original article may have expired, though.
- **Mark an article as read** When you read an article, Netscape removes the little green icon next to the article's name in the message header pane. This indicates that the article has been read. You'll still see the article for the rest of this session, but it won't appear the next time you access this newsgroup (unless you choose Show All Articles from the Options menu). To mark an article as read without reading it, just click the little green icon so that it disappears. Netscape will also remove the bold from the article's subject header. You won't see this article the next time you access this newsgroup.
- **Bag all the articles in this thread and go on to the next thread** Click the Thread button. Netscape marks the entire article as read and displays the first article in the next thread. You won't see the marked articles the next time you log on to this group.
- **Mark every current article as read** If there's nothing of interest, mark all the articles as read so that you won't have to page through them the next time you access the newsgroup. To mark every article as read, click the Group button.
- **Leave this newsgroup entirely and choose another newsgroup** Click another newsgroup name in the newsgroup pane.
- **Subscribe to another newsgroup** If you're displaying only the newsgroups to which you've subscribed, as the previous section recommended, choose Show All Newsgroups from the Options menu. Subscribe to the newsgroups you wish to read.
- **See if there are any interesting new newsgroups** From the Options menu, choose Show New Newsgroups. You can subscribe to any of these.

Many graphic images are posted to the alt.binaries.pictures.* newsgroups—and not just the naughty ones you've heard about. There are plenty of fun and perfectly legal pictures, too (while browsing alt.binaries.pictures.animals, I found a really cute picture of some kittens—and it's now my Windows wallpaper). Netscape can display these images, as long as they're posted in one part (look for 1/1 in the subject line). If the image is posted in two or more parts, Netscape can display only the first part.

Printing a Message

You can print the text of any Usenet post you see. Just open the File menu and choose Print. Alternatively, you can press Ctrl + P or click the Print button.

Posting Your Own Messages

After you've read a newsgroup for a while, you may wish to try posting your own messages. But please be sure you know what you're doing before posting.

Netiquette

Before you post to Usenet, you should make sure you know what you're doing. If you don't, you may find yourself on the wrong end of lots of angry posts and e-mail messages. Usenet people aren't difficult to get along with—as long as you follow the rules. Here's a quick overview:

- Don't crosspost (post to more than one newsgroup) unless there's a compelling reason to do so. Since you're a beginner, you wouldn't know any such reasons, so don't do it.
- Make sure you are posting to the right newsgroup.
- Read the newsgroup for at least two weeks before posting.

- Read the FAQ (Frequently Asked Questions) for the newsgroup. Don't ask questions that have already been answered in the FAQ. To locate the FAQ for a newsgroup, use Infoseek or one of the other search engines discussed in Chapter 16, and search for the newsgroup's name and FAQ.
- Do not criticize anyone's spelling or grammar. Lots of people who post to Usenet speak English as a second or third language.
- Keep your cool. Never post in anger.
- Ignore messages that contain obvious inaccuracies ("Francis Ford Coppola directed *Star Wars*"). These messages may be a trap (called a *troll*) to tempt you to make a fool out of yourself.
- Do not post a follow-up message if an e-mail reply will do.
- Don't post anything you wouldn't want to see on your boss's desk tomorrow morning—or your mother's.
- Do not post "test" messages to an ordinary newsgroup. There are newsgroups for this purpose, such as alt.test.

Creating Your Signature

It's not strictly necessary, but you may wish to create a *signature*, a text file containing your name, address, phone, and fax numbers, so that people can find out how to contact you (other than through e-mail).

To create a signature file, follow these steps:

1. From Program Manager (Windows 3.x) or the Start menu (Windows 95), open the Accessories program group.
2. Double-click the Notepad accessory.
3. Type a signature of no more than four lines. Include your name, title, organization, city, state, zip, phone, and fax. Don't get cute.
4. From the File menu, choose Save, and save the file using the name sig.txt. Make a note of where you've saved the file.
5. In Netscape, open the Options menu and choose Mail and News Preferences.
6. Click the Identity tab.

7. In the Signature File area, type the location and file name of your signature file.
8. Click OK.

Posting an Original Message

Assuming you've carefully read the "Netiquette" section above and you're confident you know what you're doing, you can use Netscape to post a message to Usenet. For your first post, use alt.test.

To post your message:

1. Open the newsgroup to which you want to post.
2. Click the To: News button. You'll see a window that's identical to the one you use to create e-mail (see Chapter 17), shown in Figure 22.5. If you created a signature file, Netscape automatically adds it. In addition, the program has automatically placed the current newsgroup's name in the Newsgroups box.
3. In the Subject area, type a brief but descriptive title for your document. This is what people will see in the newsgroup's article title list. Don't type "Help" or "A Question." Titles such as this will be ignored. Be specific.
4. Type the message.
5. Carefully proofread your post for spelling and typographical errors. You can't get it back once it has been sent!
6. Click Send. Netscape posts your message.

I don't see my message on the article list! Don't worry, everything's OK with your post. Usenet software has a low priority for processing; the posts you contribute are kept in a storage area until there's enough computer capacity to take care of them. This might be minutes, or even hours, from the time you actually post the message.

Replying by E-mail

If you want to reply to somebody's post, consider sending an e-mail reply rather than posting to the group. Suppose, for example, that somebody has

posted a question and you know the answer. Do you think the whole group would be interested? If so, then post a follow-up reply, as explained in the next section. If you think only the person asking the question would be interested, then send an e-mail reply.

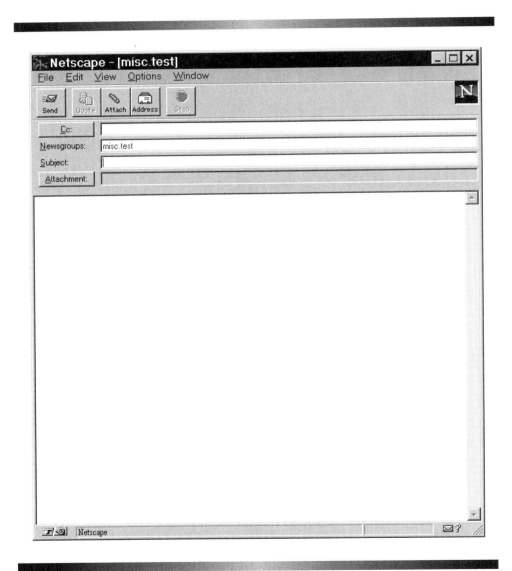

Figure 22.5 Posting an article

To send an e-mail reply, follow these steps:

1. Display the article to which you want to reply.
2. On the Netscape button bar, click Re: Mail. You'll see the message window, like the one shown in Figure 22.5. Netscape has echoed the person's e-mail address in the To box.
3. If you would like to quote the text of the document to which you are replying, click Quote. By all means edit this text down to just the part to which you want to respond. In particular, edit out the person's signature.
4. Type your reply. You can insert this within the quoted text, if you like.
5. Carefully check your typing and spelling, and make sure that you've deleted the newsgroup name from the Newsgroups field.
6. Click Send.

I changed my mind! I don't want to send this! No problem. Just click the close box. You'll see a message asking if you really want to abandon the message. Click Yes.

Posting a Follow-up Message

Post a follow-up message only if you're sure you want the whole newsgroup to see your reply. It's OK to post such a message, as long as you really think that it's worth reading and that it falls within the newsgroup's guidelines.

To post a follow-up message, follow these steps:

1. Display the article to which you want to reply.
2. Click the Re: News button. You'll see the message window, like the one shown in Figure 22.5. Netscape has echoed the subject and placed "Re:" before it.
3. If you would like to quote the text of the document to which you are replying, click Quote. By all means edit this text down to just the part to which you want to respond. In particular, edit out the person's signature.

4. Type your reply. You can insert this within the quoted text, if you like.
5. Carefully check your typing and spelling.
6. Click Send.

Searching Today's Usenet Postings

If you're looking for specific information on Usenet, you can easily go nuts trying to search manually through the thousands of postings that appear each day. Why not let the computer do it for you?

There are several services on the Web that enable you to search Usenet posts. You can access them by clicking the Net Search button. All of these services enable you to view the articles retrieved by the search. Here's a quick overview:

- **Infoseek** To search newsgroups, select Usenet Newsgroups from the list box. Type the words for which you want to search, and click Seek.
- **Alta Vista** Click the Alta Vista link. In the Alta Vista page, choose Usenet from the drop-down list box after Search. Type the words for which you want to search, and click Submit.
- **DejaNews Research Service** In the Search Categories area of Netscape's Internet Search page, click the Newsgroups link, which leads to a page of search services specializing in Usenet searches. Click the DejaNews link. In the DejaNews page, type the words for which you want to search, and click Find.

Searching Usenet FAQs

To make sure you don't post a question that others have asked before, you should read the FAQ for a newsgroup to which you want to post. Not all newsgroups have FAQs, but you should make an effort to find one in case there is.

Happily, it's easy to search for Usenet FAQs. Just click Netscape's Net Search directory button. In the Search Categories area, click Newsgroups. You can choose the List of FAQs link, or search Infoseek's FAQ database.

From Here

- There's only one portion of the Internet you've yet to traverse: Telnet. Flip to the next chapter to complete your training!

Chapter 23

Surviving Telnet and 3270 Sessions

Some computers cannot connect to the Internet. Among the worst offenders are IBM mainframe computers, which don't speak the same language that most other computers do. Fortunately for you if you need information stored on one of these dinosaurs, Telnet (and the similar 3270) lets you access information stored on mainframes via your Web browser. In addition to mainframe computers, the roster of Telnet sites includes thousands of bulletin board systems (BBSs) all over the world, and a good sprinkling of freenets (community information services). All in all, there's a lot of interesting stuff out there, as long as you're willing to forgo multimedia—Telnet is strictly text-only.

In order to access the information stored on Telnet resources, you'll need a Telnet and a 3270 helper application, as discussed in Appendix C. Basically, a Telnet helper application turns your computer into a primitive,

For the Time-Challenged

- By means of Telnet and 3270 links, you can access the resources of thousands of mainframe computers, bulletin board systems (BBSs), and freenets worldwide. But it's strictly text-only.
- When you click a Telnet hyperlink, Netscape starts NCSA (National Center for Supercomputing Applications) Telnet for Windows. Watch for a dialog box telling you how to log on. If nothing happens, press Enter. To quit the Telnet session and return to Netscape, double-click the Control menu icon or click the close button.
- When you click a 3270 hyperlink, Netscape starts QWS3270. You may be able to use your computer's function keys (F1 through F10) to perform certain functions. The application may paint the screen with vivid colors and text-based graphics. To exit, choose Close and then Quit from the File menu.

dumb VT100 terminal, which allows you text-only access to mainframe computer data. A 3270 session is virtually the same species of beast, save that your computer is taught to emulate an IBM 3270 terminal. Like Telnet, 3270 sessions are text-based, but 3270 sessions can include text of varying color (wow!) and even primitive ASCII-style graphics.

This chapter isn't of much value unless you really need to access a Telnet resource, such as a university library card catalog. If so, read on, and good luck.

Using NCSA Telnet for Windows

When you see a hyperlink that leads to a Telnet session, you can access the data contained in this resource. To do so, follow these instructions:

1. Click the Telnet hyperlink. You may see a dialog box telling you what to type after your Telnet client starts. If you do, click OK to proceed.
2. After NCSA Telnet for Windows appears on-screen (Figure 23.1), you may need to press Enter once or twice before things start happening.

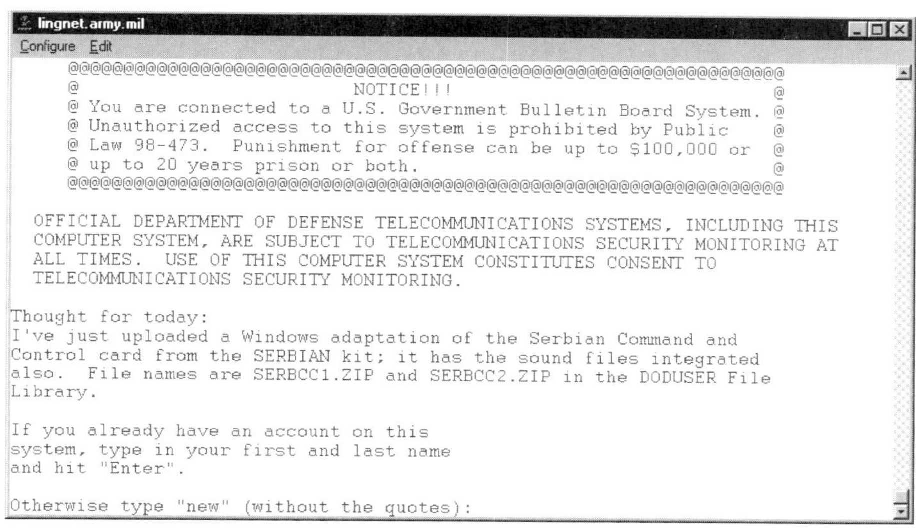

Figure 23.1 NCSA Telnet for Windows in action

3. If you were instructed to type something special to log on (see step 1), do so now.
4. If the Telnet server asks you what type of terminal you are using, type VT100 and press Enter.
5. To end your Telnet session, just double-click the Control menu icon (the large hyphen in the left corner of the application's title bar). If you're using Windows 95, click the Close button (the one with an X in it) on the title bar. When the program asks if you want to close the Telnet session, click the OK button.

In most Telnet sessions, you can type a question mark (?) and press Enter to see an on-screen list of your options.

From now on, you're at the mercy of the mainframe programmer who created the application you're using. Like MS-DOS applications, each Telnet session you encounter will have its own unique user interface, which might be very good or very bad. Figure 23.2, for example, shows the Telnet screen of PALS, the catalog at the State University of New York at Fredonia's Reed

```
LIBRARY.FREDONIA.EDU
Configure  Edit

BEGIN SESSION ON      PALS 01-05-96 21:49:31 ID/WA: P00004/041  VSN: 8R1.00

 The Basic Search Command forms are:

     AU Last-name First-name Middle-name         (Search by Author)
     TI First 4 Title words                      (Search by Title)
     TE Word <BO> Word <BO> Word ...             (Search by Term/Topic)
        *Where <BO> is a boolean operator (AND, OR, or NOT)
     SU First 4 Subject Heading words            (Search by Subject)
     CO Author-last-name First-title-word        (Search by Combination)
     CA Call Number                              (Search by Call Number)
     BR <IN> Name-or-Word                        (Browse Catalog Indexes)
        *Where <IN> is an Index Symbol (AU, TI, TE, SU, CO, or CA)

     Send messages by pressing the RETURN, ENTER or NEWLINE key
     Use the BACKSPACE or BS key to backup and type over mistakes
CATALOG-FRE=>_
```

Figure 23.2 The PALS library catalog at SUNY-Fredonia—a typical Telnet session

Library. PALS' user interface is reasonably easy to use; the commands you need to know appear on a menu, and help screens are provided.

Here are some things to remember about Telnet sessions:

- If the screen is blank, press Enter.
- If you need to correct a typing mistake, you can usually do so by pressing the Backspace key to rub out what you've typed. If this doesn't work, open the Configure menu and activate the Backspace option.
- If you get lost or confused, just quit the session by double-clicking the Control menu icon or the close box. You'll see the Web page containing the Telnet hyperlink; you can start over, if you wish.

Using QWS3270 (3270 Telnet Sessions)

3270 sessions closely resemble their Telnet brethren, save that your computer emulates an IBM 3270 mainframe terminal. Generally, that's good news—you'll see colored text and even some primitive graphics, which may make the application easier to use. As in all things Telnet, though, that depends on the programmer's skill.

If you click a hyperlink to a 3270 session, Netscape starts QWS3270, (you can learn to install this application in Appendix B). You'll see the QWS3270 screen, as shown in Figure 23.3. You can't see the colors very well in this book's screen shot, admittedly, but it's much better than garden-

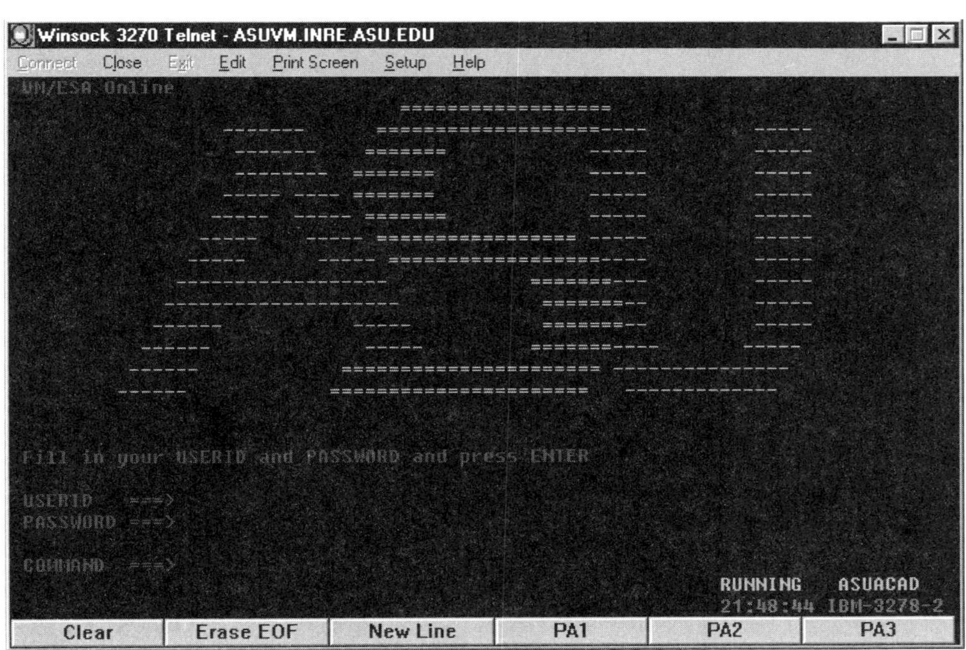

Figure 23.3 A typical 3270 session—this one's at Arizona State University. The text appears in various colors.

variety Telnet: red and bright blue against a black background, which all adds up to an easier-to-use interface. In addition, you'll see a row of buttons along the bottom of the application's window. You can click these buttons to perform special tasks (just what they do depends on how the programmer set up the application you're accessing). Otherwise, QWS3270 looks and works pretty much the same way NCSA Telnet does.

Here are some things to remember about 3270 sessions:

- If the interface tells you to press a PF key to do something, press the corresponding function key on your keyboard. For example, PF1 corresponds to F1.
- If the interface tells you to press a PA key to do something, click the corresponding PA button at the bottom of QWS3270's window.
- If you need to correct a typing mistake, you can usually do so by pressing the Backspace key to rub out what you've typed.
- To delete the word to the right of the cursor, hold down the Ctrl key and press Del.
- To erase everything you've just typed, click the Erase Input button.
- You can move the cursor by pressing the arrow keys on your keyboard.
- If the screen display doesn't look right, click the Clear button.

Searching for Telnet Resources with HyTelnet

What's out there in Telnet-land? To find out, you can search a database of Telnet and 3270 gateways called HyTelnet. To access HyTelnet's search page, use the following URL:

http://galaxy.einet.net/hytelnet/HYTELNET.html

You'll see the search page shown in Figure 23.4.

The result of a HyTelnet search is a Web page that lists Telnet sites that include your search words in their descriptions. To access one of these sites, click the hyperlink; you'll see another Web page with the Telnet site's

Figure 23.4 The HyTelnet search page. Enter your search terms in the box at the bottom of the page.

description. Included in the description page is a Telnet or 3270 session link.

From Here

- Now that you're an experienced Web surfer, why not create your own Web page? It's easy using Netscape Gold's Editor. Check out Part VI for details about creating high-impact Web documents.

- You've surfed the Web and explored the Internet. So what's left? How about the future? Check out Part VII for information about the exploding world of on-line commerce, which you can access by means of Netscape's secure protocols.

Part VI

Creating High-Impact Web Documents

Chapter 24

Web Publishing Quick Start

The very, very quickest way to create your own Web page is to use the Netscape Page Wizard, a Web site that guides you through the creation of a simple page. If you're wondering whether you can really create a Web page, give this a try—it's a great confidence booster. After you've created the page in the Wizard, you can open and embellish it with the Editor, or just use it as is.

The Wizard, spiffy as it is, isn't really part of Gold. It's a Web site, actually, that makes extensive use of JavaScript.

This chapter walks you through the process of creating your first page with the Page Wizard. In the next chapter, you'll learn the basics of Netscape Editor, which you can use to open and embellish the page you create in this chapter.

For the Time-Challenged

- The Netscape Page Wizard isn't part of Gold, actually; it's a Web page on Netscape's server that uses JavaScript to help you build your first Web page.
- The Wizard guides you through the process of creating a simple page, replete with a title, introduction, some hot links, a conclusion, and an e-mail address.
- You can choose a look for your page, including color combinations, background colors or graphics, and animated bullets and rules.
- After you build your page, it isn't done until you've opened and saved it with Netscape Editor.

Getting Started with the Netscape Page Wizard

To get started with the Netscape Page Wizard, make sure you're connected to the Net—you'll need to be, in order to contact Netscape's server. That's where the Wizard is located—hiding behind a thick curtain, presumably.

Once you're logged on, click File on the menu bar, and choose New Document. From the pop-up menu, choose From Wizard. You'll see a page that introduces the Wizard.

To continue with the Wizard, click the Start button. You'll see the first page of the Netscape Page Wizard, shown in Figure 24.1.

It says I'm not running JavaScript! You need to turn JavaScript on in order to use the Netscape Page Wizard. (Some users like to keep JavaScript off because it's full of security holes.) To turn JavaScript on, click Options, and choose Network Preferences. Click the Languages tab, and make sure that the Enable Java and Enable JavaScript options are selected.

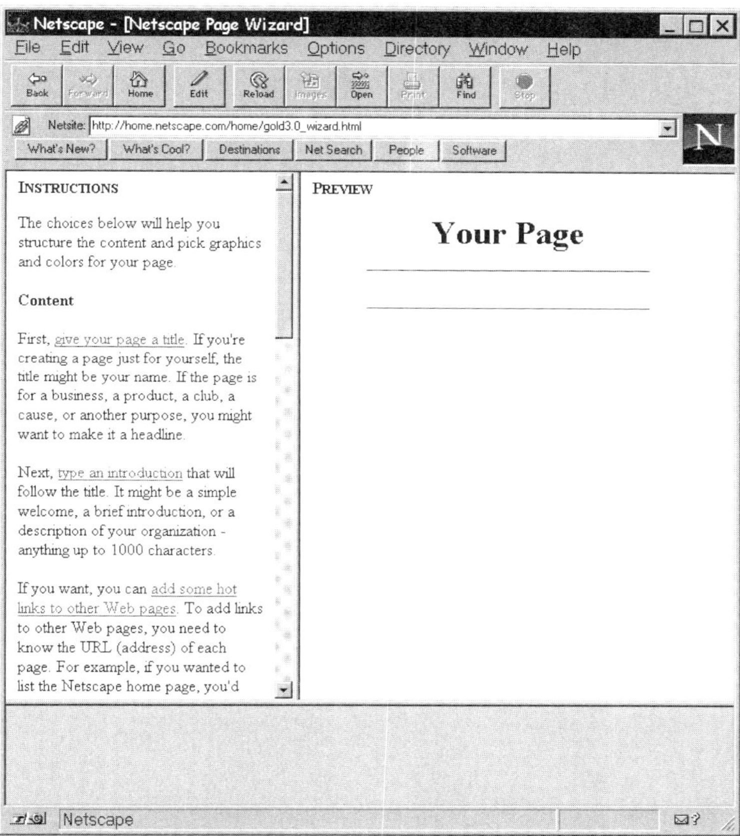

Figure 24.1 The first page of the Netscape Page wizard gets you started

Giving Your Page a Title

Let's start by giving your page a title. This title will appear at the top of your page. Click the "give your page a title" hyperlink. You'll see a Choices list box in the bottom frame panel. Delete the text in the box, and type your title. After you click Apply, you'll see your title in the right panel (Figure 24.2). Easy, huh?

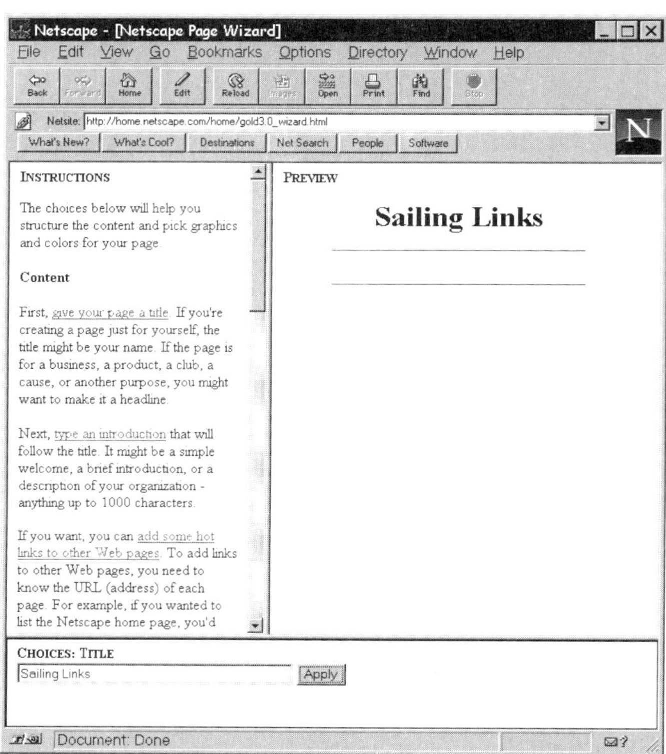

Figure 24.2 The Wizard adds your title to the page design in the right panel

Adding Introductory Text

Next, click the link that enables you to add some introductory text. This text should describe the purpose of your page; you may also want to say something about your intended audience. Figure 24.3 shows the results.

I made a typing mistake but didn't notice it before I clicked Apply! Don't worry about it for now. You'll learn how to correct it later, when you open the page with Editor (see Chapter 26, "Working with Text").

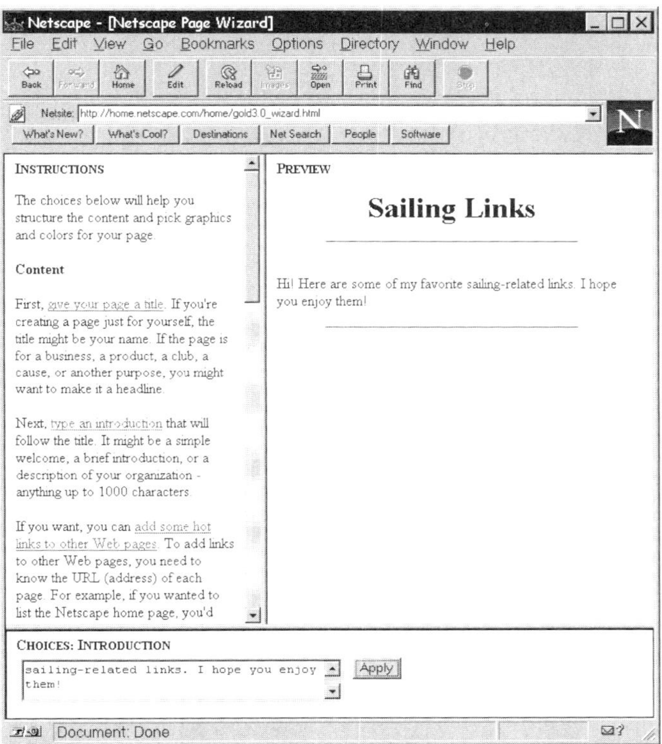

Figure 24.3 Here's how the page looks after adding an introduction

Adding Links

Now for the fun part. Below the introduction, the Wizard will create a section called Hot Links. You can add your favorite URLs here. (For a brush-up on URLs, see "What's in a URL," in Chapter 1.)

To add a link, click "add some hot links." You'll see Choices: Hot Links in the bottom panel. In the Name box, type the text that you want to see on your page. (This will be formatted in blue color with underlining, indicating that it's a hyperlink.) In the URL box, type the URL—or better, copy it from the Web browser, as the following tip explains.

Try to avoid typing URLs as much as possible since they're hard to type correctly. If you make the tiniest little mistake, your link won't work. Here's a cool trick: In the Netscape browser window, right-click the hyperlink you want to add. From the pop-up menu, choose Copy Link Location. Switch to the Wizard window, position the cursor in the URL box, and press Ctrl + V (or choose Edit/Paste). You'll see the URL in the text box—and it's perfect.

You can add more than one URL just by repeating the process, as shown in Figure 24.4.

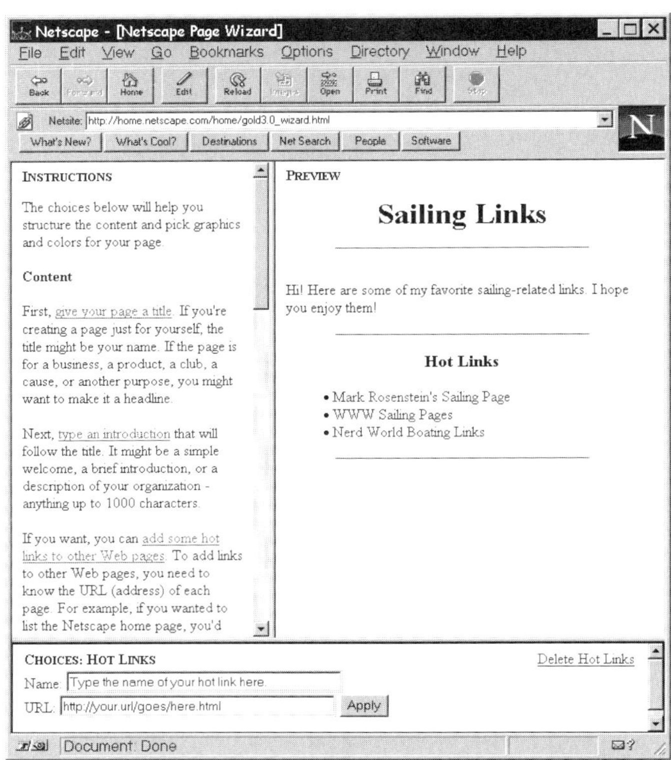

Figure 24.4 Page with URLs added

Adding a Conclusion

Want to add some more text? Click the link that enables you to add a paragraph of text to serve as a conclusion. You can add up to 1,000 characters. (This is just a limitation of the Wizard; you can expand this later, when you polish up your page using the Editor.)

Adding Your E-mail Address

It's a custom among Web authors to "sign" pages by adding their e-mail addresses. Thoughtful readers will let you know if a link is incorrect; others will contact you if they have any suggestions to make. Every once in a while you get a complaint or something rude—people say things in e-mail that they would never say to your face!—but a sympathetic, cooperative reply almost always elicits an apology.

To add your e-mail address, click "add an e-mail link." You'll see the Choices: EMail Link box in the bottom panel. Type your e-mail address, and click Apply. You'll see your e-mail address after the text, "If you have comments or suggestions, email me at...". Figure 24.5 shows what the page looks like at this point.

Changing the Look of Your Page

Now that you've finished adding your text, it's time to choose a look. You can choose a look for any of the following:

- **Color Scheme** Choose from among more than a dozen preset color combinations, which include background color, text color, and link color.
- **Background Color** This is the color of the document's background.
- **Background Pattern** This is a background graphic. If it's too busy, your readers won't be able to read your text!
- **Text Color** This is the color of ordinary text. By default, it's black.
- **Link Color** This is the color of hyperlinks. By default, it's blue.
- **Visited Hyperlinks** This is the color of a visited hyperlink. By default, it's a light purple.

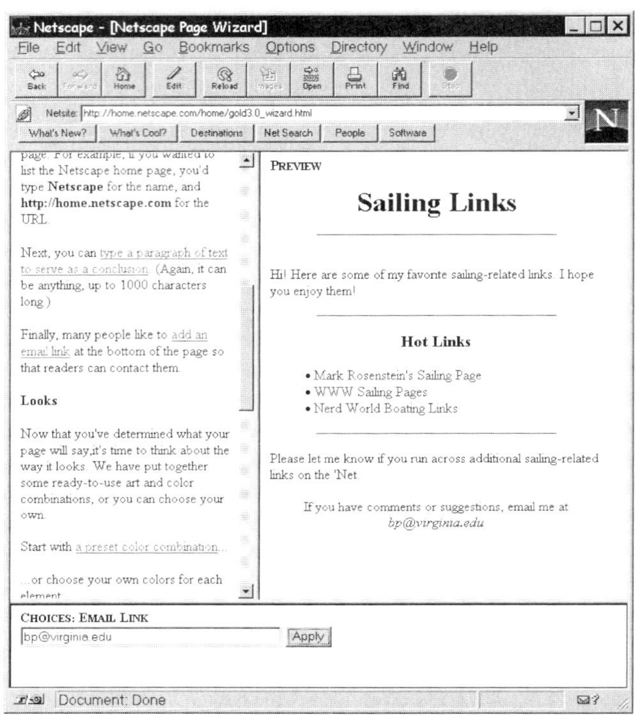

Figure 24.5 Page after adding conclusion and e-mail address

- **Bullet Style** This is the style that's applied to bullets in a bulleted list. Some of the provided bullets include cool animation!
- **Horizontal Rule Style** You can substitute a graphic for the default rule (the line that separates portions of the page).

Try choosing lots of these options to see how your page looks with a variety of different colors, bullets, and rules. The preset color schemes are worth a close look, since they're well thought-out; you may wish to use one or more of these schemes for your own pages.

Building Your Page

When you're done, click Build. You'll see your page in the browser window, as shown in Figure 24.6—complete with a Netscape logo!

Note that your page isn't saved yet. It's not even on your computer yet! It only exists in cyberspace. To save your page to your hard disk, just follow these steps:

1. With your Wizard-built page displayed in the browser window, click the Edit button. You'll see the Save Remote dialog box.

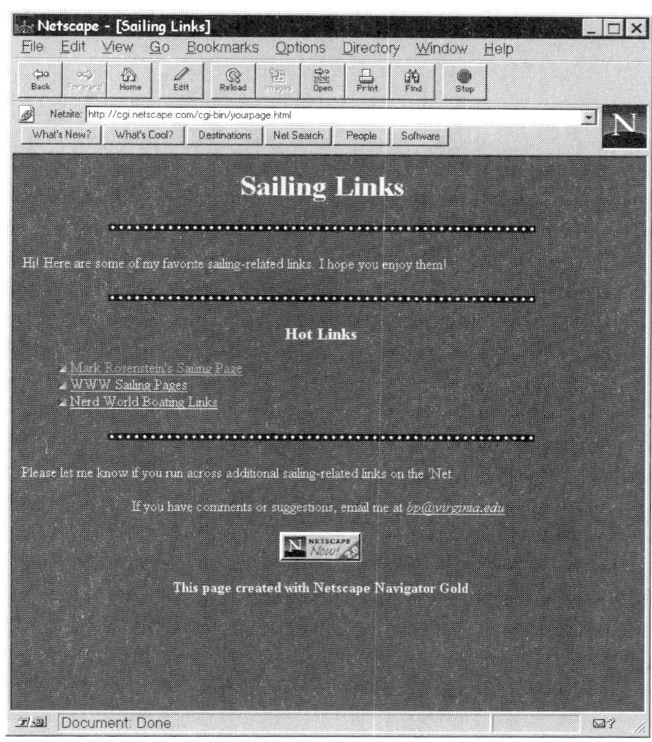

Figure 24.6 This page was created by the Wizard in about 5 minutes!

2. You'll learn more about this dialog box (and its options) in the next chapter. For now, just click Save.
3. In the Save As dialog box, choose a location for your page and click Save. Note that Netscape Editor downloads and saves not only your page, but all the graphics associated with it! This is just one of Netscape Editor's many conveniences.
4. Choose File/Exit to close Netscape Editor.

From Here

- Learn the basics of Netscape Editor in Chapter 25.
- Add some text to your page! See Chapter 26.
- Develop your page with headings, lists, and indents; it's all explained in Chapter 27.
- Get fancy with characters and fonts, as explained in Chapter 28.
- Add background graphics and other cool effects, as explained in Chapter 29.
- Put some more hyperlinks into your document! Learn how in Chapter 30.
- Add some graphics to your page! Chapter 31 shows you how.
- To learn how to publish your page so that others can access it, see Chapter 34.

Chapter 25

Netscape Editor Fundamentals

Netscape Editor provides the environment you need to create winning HTML pages. Best of all, you don't need to learn HTML (see the sidebar on page 411.)

The cool thing about Gold's Editor is that your Web page looks like it does when it's viewed in Netscape's browser window (although, as you'll see, there are a couple of exceptions to this—for example, you can't see text wrapped around a graphic). This is a seriously cool thing, since previously you had to code the HTML and then switch to a browser to view your work, which was a time-consuming pain. For the most part, you see your changes immediately while you're working with Netscape Editor, and your page looks like it does in the browser.

This chapter gets you going with Netscape Editor by introducing all the Editor fundamentals.

For the Time-Challenged

- Netscape Editor enables you to prepare winning Web pages without knowing HTML. However, it doesn't do quite everything, and some formats can't be displayed until you view them in the browser.
- To publish your pages, you first create them with Netscape Editor, and then copy them to a computer that's running a Web server.
- Begin by choosing initial preferences, including supplying your name.
- The menus are useful, but the most frequently accessed commands are more conveniently accessed on the toolbars.
- The toolbars include commands for character formatting, paragraph formatting, filing operations, and editing tasks.
- You can create a new blank document, or you can build one using the Wizard. Alternatively, you can open and modify a template.

Getting Oriented: The Gold Publishing Process

Publishing great-looking Web pages with Netscape Gold is a two-step process.

Step One: Creating Your Page with Netscape Editor

First, you create your page using the Editor. You can start with the Netscape Page Wizard, one of Netscape's templates, or a blank document. (A *template* is a sample Web page that you can download and modify for your own purposes.)

After you finish your page, it's stored on your hard disk, which means it isn't accessible to anyone.

Step Two: Publishing Your Page

For other people to access your page via the Web, you *publish* your page. To publish your page means to make it accessible to a *Web server*, a program

HTML—And Why You Don't Need to Learn It

In a recent interview, Web founder Tim Berners-Lee expressed amazement that people were still using HTML to create their Web pages. HTML was never intended for prolonged use, Berners-Lee said; its creators expected programs to come along that would generate the HTML code as the user manipulated text and images in a "what-you-see-is-what-you-get" environment.

Short for HyperText Markup Language, HTML enables Web authors to code text so that browsers (such as Netscape) will recognize the text to be a certain part of a document, such as a title, a heading, or a hyperlink. It's pretty tedious to use. In fact, it's a lot like the formatting codes that writers had to use during the early years of word processing. To make text bold, for instance, you had to type @BOLD(here is the text to be boldfaced). With HTML, the code looks like this: <B>here is the text to be boldfaced</B>. Both are prone to error: If you forget the closing symbol (in HTML, </B>), you get bold all the way to the end of your document. Nuts!

With Netscape Gold 3.0, the long-awaited automatic HTML may have finally arrived. I say "may," because Gold can't quite do everything. For example, frames—something that Netscape Communications themselves introduced—can't be created without manual coding. And there are a few tags here and there that Netscape Gold 3.0 doesn't enable you to insert unless you're willing to type the HTML yourself. That's why Netscape Gold includes a command that enables you to type HTML code directly. In the chapters to come, look for tips concerning some cool HTML that you can plug in here and there!

that knows how to accept incoming requests from the Internet and dole out the requested documents. Unless you have a Web server running on your own computer, you'll need to upload your page to the server's computer. It's easy to do this with Gold's extremely cool one-button publishing, as explained in Chapter 34.

I don't have anywhere to publish my page! Maybe you do and don't know it. Many Internet service providers (ISPs) give you some Web space—up to 5MB's worth, sometimes—for your Web publishing efforts. This is usually included as a freebie with your Internet subscription. Check with your ser-

vice provider to find out whether you've got some Web publishing space already. Otherwise, it might be time to look for a new ISP!

Choosing Initial Preferences

Before you get started with Netscape Editor, work through some initial preferences and options. Doing so now will help you work with Editor much more productively.

To begin choosing preferences, display the Editor Preferences dialog box (Figure 25.1) by choosing Options/Editor Preferences. This command is available in both the Editor and browser windows.

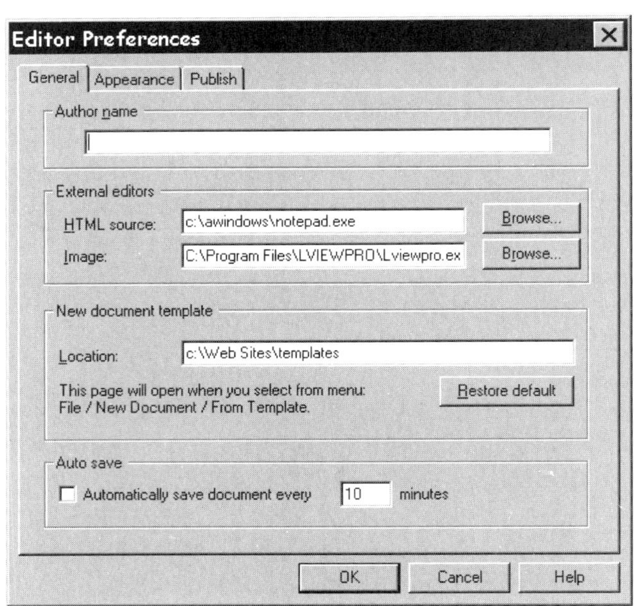

Figure 25.1 Editor Preferences: General options

Click the General tab, if necessary, to display the General page, and do the following:

1. In the Author Name area, type your name. Netscape will automatically add your name to all the documents you publish. The name won't appear in your documents, but search engines will be able to access it, and they'll index your documents under your name.
2. In the External Editors boxes, use the Browse button to locate the text and graphics editors that you would like to use. These come in handy when you're doing some direct HTML editing or sizing graphics. For a text editor, I recommend the Windows Notepad utility. For a graphics editor, I recommend Lview Pro, a shareware program that's widely available for downloading from the Net.
3. The New Document Template area shows the current place where Netscape Editor looks for documents when you choose File/New Document/From Template (see "Opening Documents," below). By default, this location is a page on Netscape's server. Leave this alone for now.
4. If you would like Netscape Editor to automatically save your document, check the box under Auto Save and type a time interval. This is highly recommended!

There are two other pages in the Editor Preferences dialog box, but they'll be discussed later (Chapters 29 and 34).

About the Menus

Netscape Editor's menu bar is very different from the browser window's, so you might want to take a few moments to get familiarized. Here's a very quick overview of the menus and what they do.

The File Menu

Here you'll find commands for creating new Web documents, opening existing documents, saving documents, publishing documents on the Web (see Chapter 34), mailing documents, and printing documents (Figure 25.2).

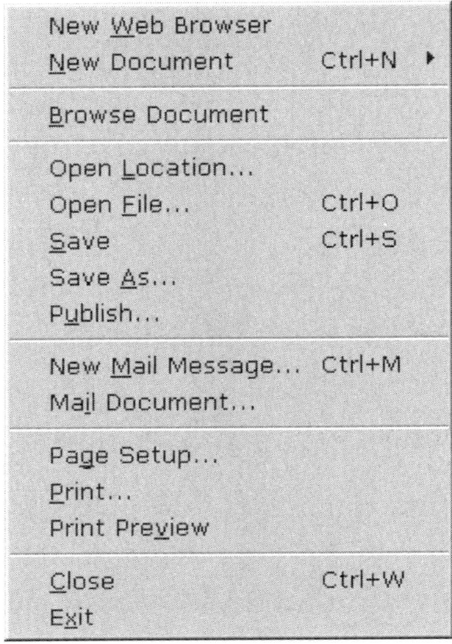

Figure 25.2 The Editor File menu

The Edit Menu

This menu, shown in Figure 25.3, contains the usual commands for copying, cutting, and pasting via the Clipboard. In addition, you'll find commands that let you select and delete tables (see Chapter 32), search for text in your document, and automatically remove all the existing links.

The View Menu

In this menu, shown in Figure 25.4, you find the same commands that you see on the browser window's View menu, including Reload, Load Images, Refresh, and View Document Source. In addition, you can edit the document source; this comes in handy when you want to go mano-a-mano with the underlying HTML. Additional commands enable you to show paragraph marks (the places where you hit the Enter key) and tables.

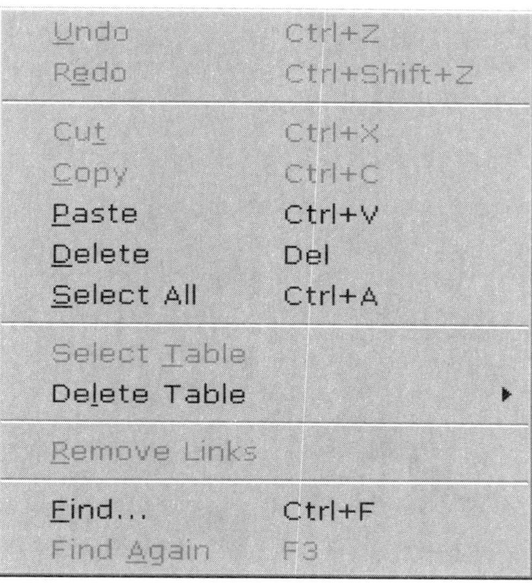

Figure 25.3 The Edit menu contains commands for selecting and editing

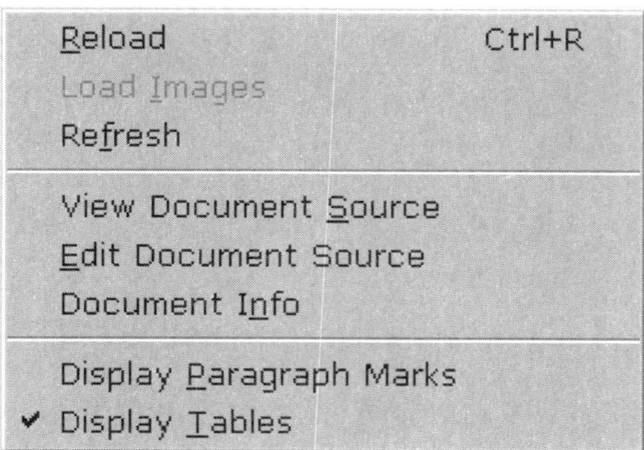

Figure 25.4 The View menu lets you look at your document in different ways

Unless your computer is really slow, make sure Display Tables is selected. You probably don't want to look at the paragraph marks, though, since they're distracting and ugly.

The Insert Menu

This menu (see Figure 25.5) enables you to add lots of Web features to your document, including hyperlinks, images, tables, and lines. However, you can also access these commands by clicking buttons on the toolbar, so you probably won't use this menu much. At the bottom of the menu are commands for line breaks (see Chapter 26), breaks below images (see Chapter 31), and nonbreaking spaces (see Chapter 26).

The Properties Menu

This menu, shown in Figure 25.6, enables you to define the properties for document elements you have already entered, including text, hyperlinks, images, tables, and lines. However, you can access and edit these properties more quickly by selecting the element and clicking the Object Properties tool. This menu also contains commands that enter formats for characters, font size, and paragraphs.

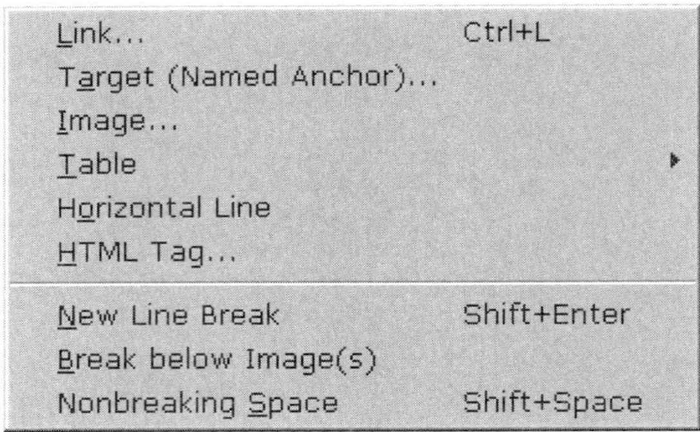

Figure 25.5 The Insert menu contains lots of commands that are more quickly accessed using the toolbar

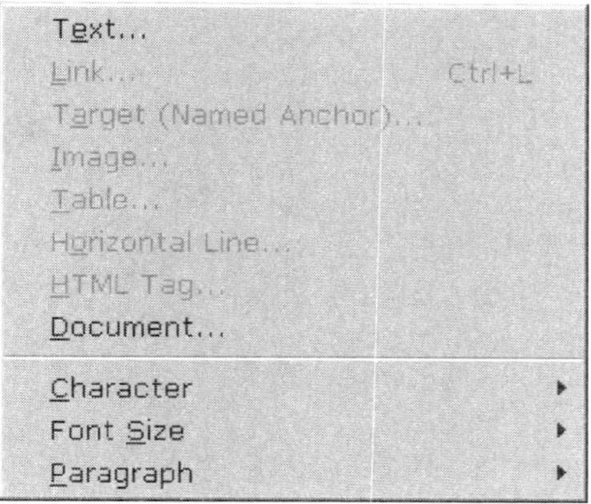

Figure 25.6 The Properties menu lets you change elements you've already entered

The Options Menu

This menu (see Figure 25.7) is essentially the same menu that you see in the browser window, except that it enables you to display or hide the toolbars.

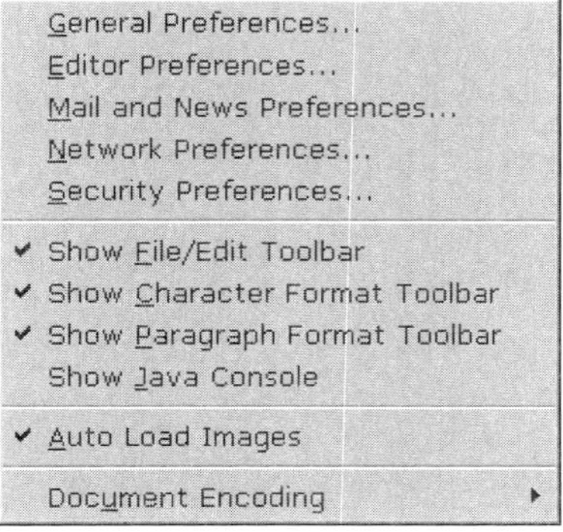

Figure 25.7 The Options menu

Work with all three of the toolbars displayed. They're really helpful.

The Window Menu

The Window menu (see Figure 25.8) is just like the one you see in the browser window. You can use this menu to switch to other open documents or windows quickly.

The Help Menu

The Help menu, shown in Figure 25.9, is identical to the one you see in the browser window. The Web Page Starter option is the same as choosing File/ New Document/From Wizard (see "Opening Documents," later in this chapter).

Using the Toolbars

Netscape Editor comes with three toolbars: the Character Format, the File/ Edit, and the Paragraph Format toolbars (see Figure 25.10). You'll find these toolbars very helpful and you'll want to keep them on-screen.

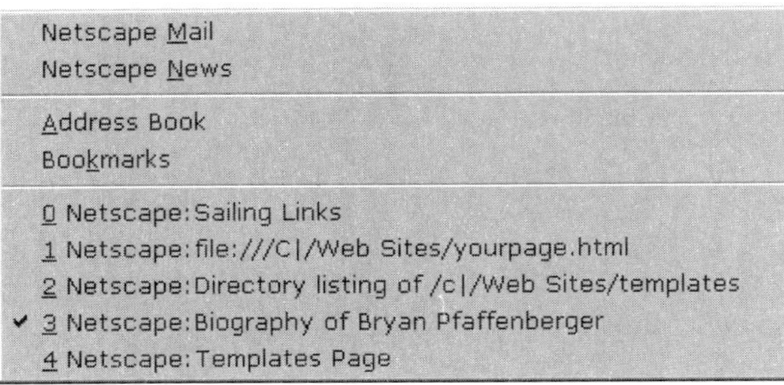

Figure 25.8 The Window menu

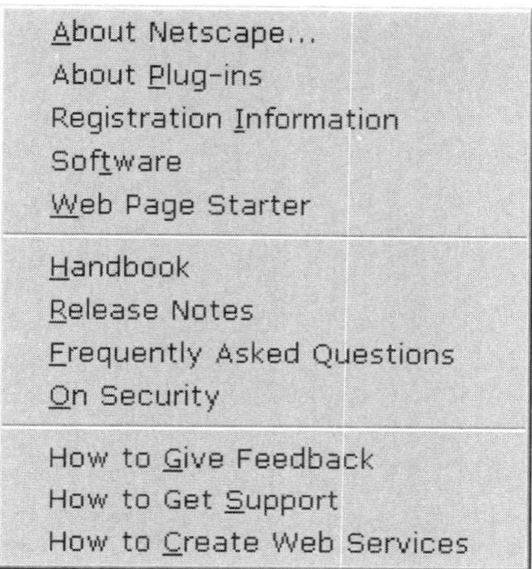

Figure 25.9 Netscape Editor's Help menu

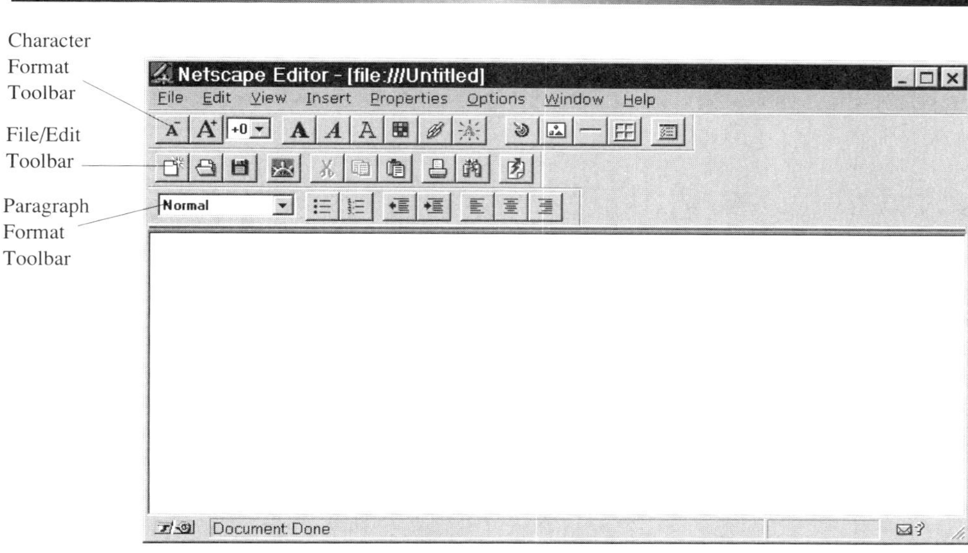

Figure 25.10 Toolbars in Netscape Editor window

This section introduces the tools briefly; you'll learn more about what each of them does in the chapters to follow. You'll also find this section handy for quick reference. Don't try to memorize what all of them do; a quick skim is all that's required for now.

If you forget what one of the tools does, just move the mouse pointer to the tool and wait a second or two. You'll see a help box that names the tool.

Using the Character Format Toolbar

The Character Format toolbar contains the following tools:

Tool	Name	Description
A⁻	**Decrease Font Size**	Changes the selection to the next lower font size.
A⁺	**Increase Font Size**	Changes the selection to the next higher font size.
+0	**Font Size**	Choose a font size from the list box (relative sizes range from –2, the smallest, to +4, the largest).
A	**Bold**	Changes the selection to boldface type.
A	**Italic**	Changes the selection to italic type.
A	**Fixed Width**	Changes the selection to a monospace (typewriter) font.
	Font Color	Enables you to choose a color for the selected text.
	Make Link	Inserts a hyperlink at the cursor's location.

	Clear All Styles	Removes all character formats from the document.
	Insert Target (Named Anchor)	Inserts a target for internal hyperlinks at the cursor's location.
	Insert Image	Inserts a graphic at the cursor's location.
	Insert Horizontal Line	Inserts a horizontal line (a rule) at the cursor's location.
	Insert Table	Inserts a table at the cursor's location.
	Object Properties	Displays the Properties dialog box for the selected object.

The File/Edit Toolbar

The File/Edit toolbar contains the following tools:

	New Document	Displays the Create New Document dialog box, which enables you to choose Blank Document, From Template, or From Wizard.
	Open File to Edit	Displays the Open dialog box.
	Save	Displays the Save dialog box.
	View in Browser	Displays the current Editor document in a Netscape browser window.
	Cut	Cuts the selection to the Clipboard.

Copy	Copies the selection to the Clipboard.
Paste	Pastes the selection from the Clipboard.
Print	Prints the current document.
Find	Displays the Find dialog box.
Publish	Sends the document to a Web server site so that it can be accessed by others. *Note:* This button doesn't work until you've filled out the Publish page of the Editor Preferences dialog box, as explained in Chapter 34.

The Paragraph Format Toolbar

The Paragraph Format toolbar contains the following tools:

Paragraph Style	From this list box, you can choose a variety of paragraph styles. The default for body text is Normal. These options are also available by choosing the Properties/Paragraph command.
Bullet List	Creates a bulleted list at the cursor's location. Bullets are entered automatically.
Numbered List	Creates a numbered list at the cursor's location. Numbers are entered automatically.
Decrease Indent	Decreases the indentation of the selection.

	Increase Indent	Increases the indentation of the selection.
	Align Left	Aligns the selection along the left margin.
	Center	Centers the selection within the margins.
	Align Right	Aligns the selection along the right margin.

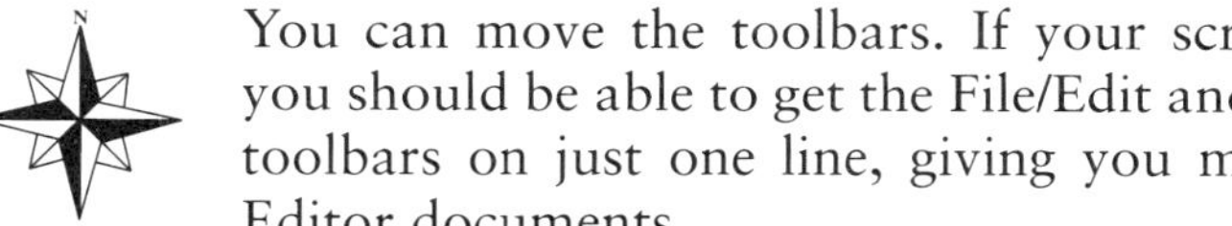

You can move the toolbars. If your screen's wide enough, you should be able to get the File/Edit and Paragraph Format toolbars on just one line, giving you more room for your Editor documents.

Creating New Documents with Netscape Editor

When you choose File/New Document or press Ctrl + N, you'll see a pop-up submenu that gives you three choices:

Blank Document You see a new, blank Web document. This is the best choice when you want to start your page from scratch.

From Template When you choose this option, Netscape accesses the template location that's currently listed in the New Document Location area of the Editor Preferences dialog box (General page). By default, this location is a page on Netscape's server, which gives you access to lots of templates. After you've chosen a template and opened it, you can modify it and save it to your hard disk.

From Wizard This option accesses the Netscape Page Wizard, discussed in Chapter 24. It's a great way to create the fundamentals of a good-looking page in very

short order. You can then embellish the page by opening it in Netscape Editor (see the next section).

Opening a File from Your Disk

If you would like to open an existing file that's stored on a disk drive in your system, you use the File/Open command.

In the browser window, choose File/Open File in Editor. You'll see an Open dialog box, which enables you to locate the file. After you click Open, you'll see the file in an Editor window.

In Netscape Editor, choose File/Open File or press Ctrl + O. You'll see an Open dialog box. Locate your file, and click Open.

Templates

A quick way to create a Web document is to begin with a template, which is a generic Web document that you can open and modify. You'll find lots of templates on Netscape's server; they're expressly available for your use and modification without any need for asking permission.

He says he's mad because I stole his work! Please be aware that it's a violation of copyright to open and save someone's page without their permission. Although Netscape Gold enables you to open *any* page on the Web, save it to your disk, and use its text and graphics in your own creative efforts, that doesn't mean it's right! *Always* ask for permission before you use anyone's textual expression (including the sequence in which ideas are presented) or graphics. Gold provides this capability so that you can open and edit your *own* pages that you've previously stored on a remote server's Web storage space. (For more information on publishing your Web documents, see Chapter 34.)

The big advantage of a template is that it enables you to begin with a page that already has a bunch of complicated formats entered. These pages have some text already entered, but you can easily replace this text with your own. Another advantage of using templates is that they were written with good Web page design practices in mind. Since you don't know what these practices are all about just yet, it's wise to use templates.

Figure 25.11 shows one of the templates available from Netscape. It's for a windsurfing page, but you could use it for almost anything.

Figure 25.11 You can modify this template to your heart's content

Before proceeding, you may wish to create a directory on your hard disk to store your Web creations. Call this directory something like WebPages.

Opening a Template

To open a template, choose File/New Document, and choose From Template from the pop-up menu. You'll see the dialog box shown in Figure 25.12. This dialog box is telling you that you must save a copy of this document on your own computer system in order to edit it.

Note that this dialog box contains a couple of options, and they're both selected, by default:

- **Adjust links to assist in remote publishing** Leave this option selected. If you download the graphics associated with this page, Gold will adjust the hyperlinks so that the graphics work when you display the page on your own system. They'll also work correctly when you publish your page, as explained in Chapter 34.
- **Save images with document** Leave this option selected so that Gold will download your page's graphics.

To save the document on your hard disk so that you can edit it, click Save. You'll see a warning about copyright. If you understand why you shouldn't steal someone else's work, click "Don't display this message again." Click OK to proceed. It's OK to use Netscape's templates—they're expressly in the public domain.

Next, you'll see the Save As dialog box. Save the page to the directory where you want your Web pages to be stored.

Hey! These links don't work! That's right. The links included with the template pages are there just for the purposes of illustration. You'll need to replace them with real links. See Chapter 30.

Modifying a Template

Once you've downloaded the template, you can modify it as you please. You can remove the existing text and add your own. You can also add hyperlinks and graphics.

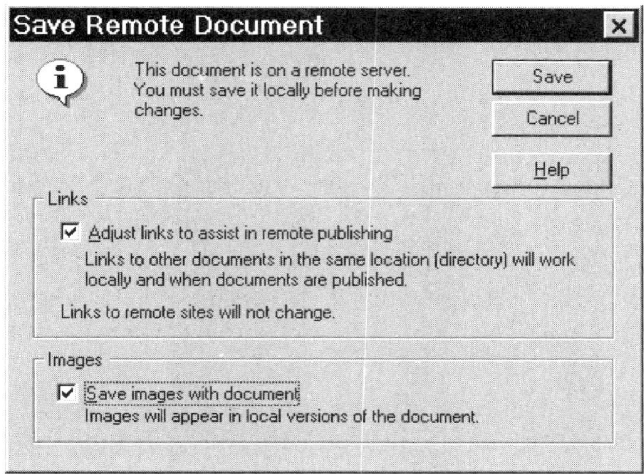

Figure 25.12 This dialog box appears when you open a remote page in the Editor

The big challenge, though, is to avoid messing up the predefined formats. You'll need to be careful when you replace the existing text. Before you try to modify a template, be sure to read the next chapter, "Working with Text."

Setting up a Directory for Your Own Templates

Soon, you'll learn how to create your own Web page designs, which you may wish to re-use as you add additional pages to your site. (It's a good idea to establish a consistent design for a presentation that involves several linked pages, and to use this design on each and every page.) First, create the directory where you want to store your templates. Then, in the Editor, choose Options/Editor Preferences, and click the General tab. In the New Document Template area, enter the location of your templates directory in the Location box (for example, c:\Web Sites\Templates). Click OK to confirm your choices. Now you'll see a directory listing for this folder or directory when you choose File/New Document/From Template.

From Here

- Learn the basics of text entry and editing in Chapter 26.
- Add headings, lists, and indents, as shown in Chapter 27.
- Control character and font formatting with Chapter 28 as your guide.
- Add cool-looking colors and backgrounds in Chapter 29.
- Add hyperlinks and graphics, as explained in Chapter 30.
- Publish your document on the Web! See Chapter 34.

Chapter 26

Working with Text

Writing with Netscape Gold is very much like writing with a word processing program. You work in a "what-you-see-is-what-you-get" environment. If you're already familiar with a good word processing program, such as Microsoft Word for Windows, you already know much of what you need to know in order to create and edit text with Netscape Editor. This chapter surveys the basics, including positioning the cursor, adding new text, selecting text, copying and moving text, and deleting text.

Positioning the Cursor

To enter and edit text with Gold's Editor, you need to move the cursor around. You can do this with the mouse; just click where you want the cursor

For the Time-Challenged

- You can position the cursor with the mouse, but Netscape Editor also responds to the cursor-movement keys used by popular word processing programs.
- Body text is entered using the Normal paragraph style.
- To start a new paragraph and enter a blank line at the same time, press Enter.
- To start a new paragraph without entering a blank line, press Shift + Enter.
- To select a word, double-click it. To select a line, click just to the left of the line's first letter.
- If you deleted something by mistake and want it back, choose Edit/Undo or press Ctrl + Z.

to appear. If you'd prefer to move the cursor with the keyboard, you can use any of the keys listed in the following table.

To move the cursor:	Press this key:
One character left	Left arrow
One character right	Right arrow
One word left	Ctrl + left arrow
One word right	Ctrl + right arrow
To the beginning of the line	Home
To the end of the line	End
One line up	Up arrow
One line down	Down arrow
To the beginning of the document	Ctrl + Home
To the end of the document	Ctrl + End

About the Normal Paragraph Format

To add body text to your document, you use the Normal paragraph format. To do so, choose Normal from the Paragraph Styles list box (in the Paragraph Formats toolbar), or choose Properties/Paragraph/Normal from the menus. In the next chapter, you'll learn how to enter text in other paragraph formats, including lists and headings.

ADDING TEXT

It's easy to add text with Gold's Editor. Just position the cursor where you want the text to apppear, and start typing.

You don't need to press Enter at the end of every line—the program automatically "wraps" text down to the next line.

Keep the following in mind:

- To start a new paragraph (with a blank line before it), press Enter.
- To start a new paragraph without adding a blank line, press Shift + Enter. You can also choose Insert/New Line Break. Figure 26.1 shows the difference between paragraphs started with Enter and Shift + Enter.
- To get rid of a paragraph break, place the cursor at the beginning of the second paragraph and press Del.

Writing for the Web

Every well-written document is adapted to its medium. You wouldn't put a business report into a newsletter, or a poem into a scientific article! Similarly, you should adapt your writing for the Web. The best Web writing is, above all else, concise. Get right to the point straightaway: Describe your page's purpose and audience at the inception. Write personally, and focus on your reader—use what business writers call the "you" orientation. Wherever possible, break up the text on the page using headings, bulleted lists, and white space. Highlight the terms that convey your document's key subjects: your reader should be able to grasp your page's scope in a quick visual scan.

- Paragraph breaks are marked by symbols, which you can see if you wish. They're ugly, but some people find it easier to edit their documents if they can see the symbols. To display them, choose View/Display Paragraph Marks. Figure 26.2 shows the paragraph marks; note that Enter marks are larger than Shift + Enter marks.
- If you would like to keep two words together on a line so that they're never separated by a line break, enter the space by pressing Shift + Space, or choose Insert/Nonbreaking Space.

I added lots of blank lines but Netscape won't let me see them! They show up in the Editor too, but, frustratingly, they don't show up when you view the page in the browser. Why? Here's a very important rule that you need to learn: Web browsers always ignore extra spaces and extra line

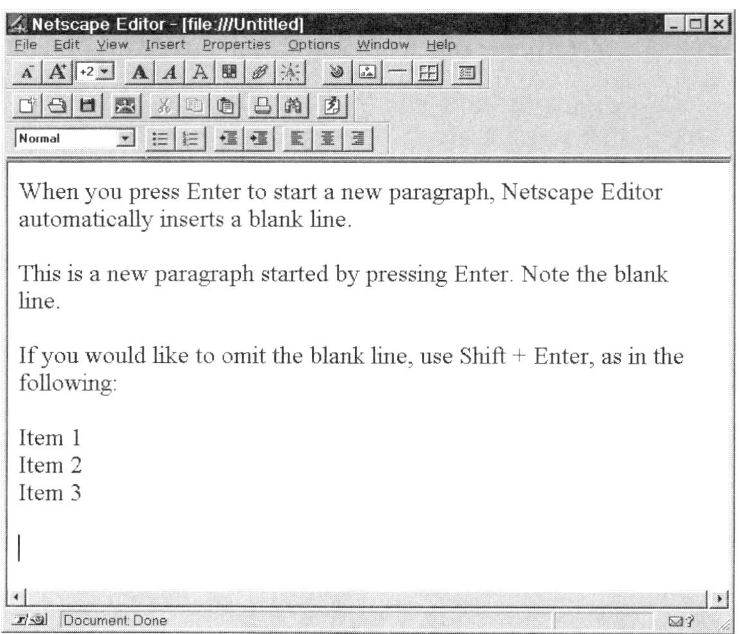

Figure 26.1 Paragraph breaks entered with Enter and Shift + Enter

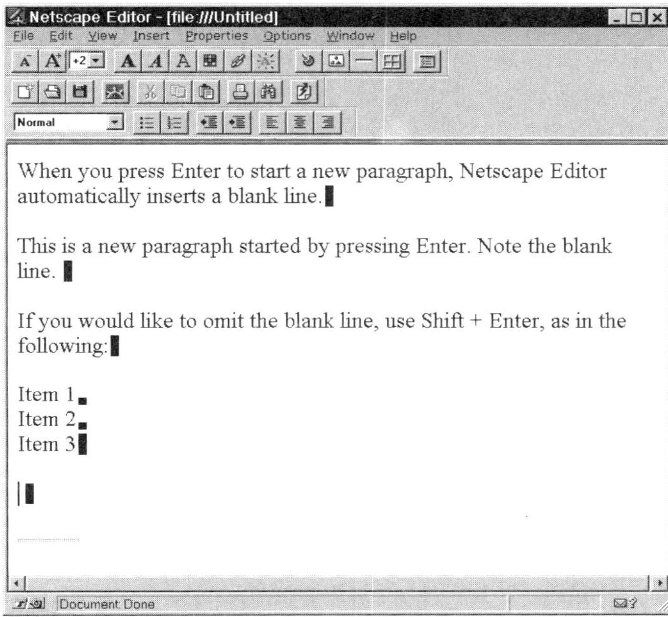

Figure 26.2 You can view the Enter and Shift + Enter paragraph marks if you wish

breaks. You can add all the spaces you want by pressing the spacebar, but your browser only shows one. You can add all the line breaks you want by pressing Enter gazillions of times, but the browser only shows one. You'll have to handle spacing by using commands other than manually entered spaces and Enter keystrokes, as this and the following chapters explain.

Selecting Text

The easiest way to select text is to drag over it with the mouse. Click where you want the selection to start, and then hold down the left mouse button

and move the pointer to the end of the text you want to select. If you don't like dragging, click where you want the selection to start, and then move the pointer to the place where you want the selection to end. When you hold down the Shift key and click, Gold automatically selects all the text between the first and second places you clicked.

Here are some cool text-selection tricks:

- To select an entire word, double-click the word.
- To select an entire line, move the cursor just to the left of the line's first letter, and click the left mouse button.
- To select an entire paragraph, move the cursor just to the left of any line in the paragraph, and double-click the left mouse button.
- To unselect text, just click elsewhere.
- To select the entire document, press Ctrl + A. You can also choose Edit/Select All. Be careful about doing this, though, since it's easy to delete the entire document while everything's selected!

Why isn't there a spell checker? The Web is full of atrocious spelling—and it's easy to see why. Web production tools don't include spell checkers! Unfortunately, Netscape Gold doesn't have one either. You'll need to hand-check your spelling. Alternatively, create your text in a word processing program that *does* have spell checking. Once you've proofread it, copy the text into Gold's Editor using the Clipboard. (To do this, select the text in your word processing program's window, and press Ctrl + C; then switch to the Editor window in Gold, position the cursor where you want the text to appear, and click Ctrl + V.)

Copying and Moving Text

You can also move text around in the Editor, just as you would in a word processing program.

- To copy text, select the text and press Ctrl + C or choose Edit Copy. Position the cursor where you want the copied text to appear, and press Ctrl + V (or choose Edit/Paste).

- To move text, select the text and press Ctrl + X (or choose Edit/Cut). Position the cursor where you want the text to appear, and press Ctrl + V (or choose Edit/Paste).

Deleting Text

If you've made an error, or if you would like to get rid of some generic text in a template, you can delete it using any of the following techniques:

- To delete text to the left of the cursor, press Backspace.
- To delete text to the right of the cursor, press Del.
- To delete the selection, press Del, or just type over it.

I just deleted something by accident! Can I get it back? Sure you can. Just press Ctrl + Z, or choose Edit/Undo. Note that you can only undo your last editing action. If you find that the deletion really deserved to be deleted, choose Edit/Redo to redo your last action.

Tips for Editing Templates

If you're modifying the text in a template, note that you can replace existing text just by selecting it and typing over it. However, this works best for normal paragraph text. (You can tell if you're working with normal paragraph text quite easily—just position the cursor within the text and look at the style selection box on the toolbar. If it's normal paragraph text, you'll see "Normal" in this box.) Exercise caution when changing headings or list items so that you don't lose the formatting; it's better to type your new text and then carefully delete the old text. Also, don't try to type over link text directly; it won't work. You'll need to delete the template's unwanted links and add new ones, as explained in the next section. Be careful not to press Backspace at the beginning of a section of distinctively formatted text, or Del at the end; if you do, you may wipe out hidden formatting information. To restore a format you've messed up, press Ctrl + Z or choose Edit/Undo.

From Here

- Learn how to enter text in heading and list formats. They're surveyed in the next chapter.
- Add character formatting, such as styles (e.g., boldface) and fonts. Learn how in Chapter 28.
- If you'd like to arrange your text in a table, see Chapter 32.

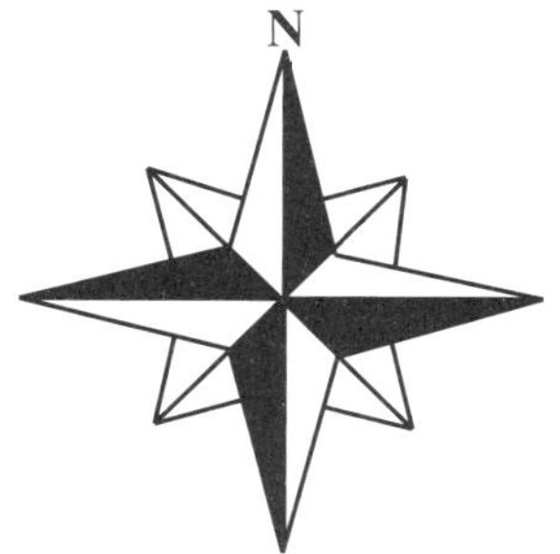

Chapter 27

Adding Headers, Lists, and Indents

One key to effective Web writing is to break up the text on the page as much as possible. Use headings and lists to provide visual cues to your readers. In this chapter, you'll learn how to add titles, headings, and a variety of lists, as well as how to indent and align text. These tools will help you create eye-catching, readable documents.

Giving Your Document a Title

On the Web, a document *title* doesn't actually appear within the document. It appears on the browser's title bar. A lot of Web authors ignore the title for this reason, but they do so at their peril: the browser may display such pages

For the Time-Challenged

- Your document's title shows up on the title bar. Don't forget to add a title or your document will show up in search engines' lists with the heading "No Title."
- Netscape Editor lets you enter up to six levels of headings, each with its own distinctive format, but few Web authors use more than three levels. Heading 1 text is used for a title that shows up in the document (unlike the true title, which appears on the browser's title bar).
- You can align text flush left, center, or flush right by clicking one of the alignment tools on the toolbar.
- Bulleted lists are useful for setting items apart from the text. You can choose from three default bullet styles.
- Netscape numbers the items in a bulleted list automatically, but you don't see the numbers until you switch to the browser.
- Description lists look nice, but they're tedious to enter; you can achieve the same effect by indenting normal text.
- Block quotes are useful for extended quotations and for emphasizing passages of text.
- You can create an outline with Roman numerals, but it's a lot of work.

with the word "Untitled" on the title bar. What's more, if somebody retrieves these documents using a search engine, it will probably list the document under a "No Title" or "Untitled" heading. Either way, it looks unprofessional!

To title your document, choose Properties/Document from the menu bar. You'll see the Document Properties dialog box. Click the General tab, if necessary, to display the page shown in Figure 27.1.

Do the following:

1. In the Title area, type your document's title. Be as descriptive as possible; indicate the general subject as well as the specific topic of your page ("Recreational Sailing: The Chesapeake Bay").
2. If you set Netscape Editor's initial preferences as the previous chapter suggested, you'll see your name in the Author box. If not, type

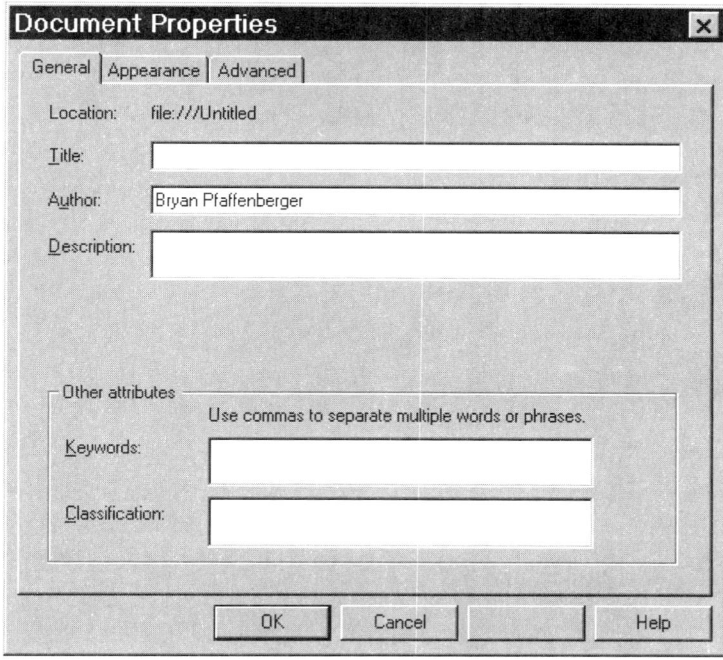

Figure 27.1 Enter your document's title here

your name. This doesn't show up in the browser window, but it will be seen by search engines.

3. In the Description box, you can type some information about the document. Like the author's name, this information won't be seen by browsers, but it will be taken into account by search engines.
4. In the Other Attributes area, you can type keywords and a document classification to improve your document's retrievability by search engines. This is strictly optional. Like the author and description, this information won't show up in the browser, but it will be seen by search engines.
5. Click OK to confirm your title.

After you've entered your title, you'll see it on the title bar of the Editor and browser windows. In the Editor window, the title is accompanied by the file name and location of the document on which you're working, as shown in Figure 27.2.

Although the title, strictly speaking, is the text that appears on the title bar, you still need to give your document something that will *look* like a title when people read your page. You do this by adding a Level 1 heading, as described in the next section.

Adding Headings

You can add up to six levels of headings to your document, each with its own distinctive formatting (Figure 27.3). You can use these headings to add what appears to be a document title (Level 1), major headings (Level 2), and subheadings (Level 3). Very few Web authors use the other levels.

Do you have to use the headings? Why not just add text using the Normal paragraph format and choose the formats you want? Go ahead, if you like, but bear in mind that most search engines give extra weight to terms found in heading

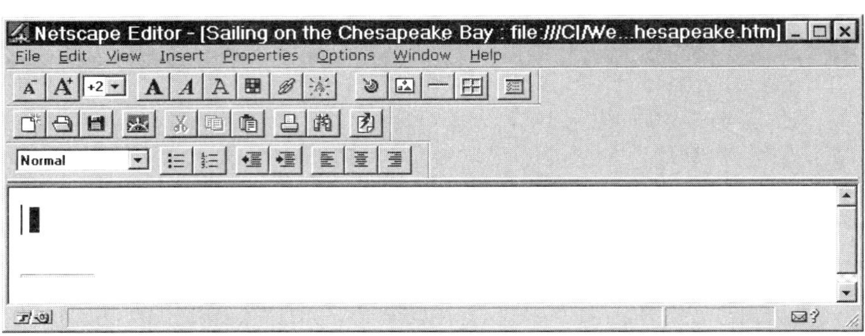

Figure 27.2 Your document's title appears on the title bar

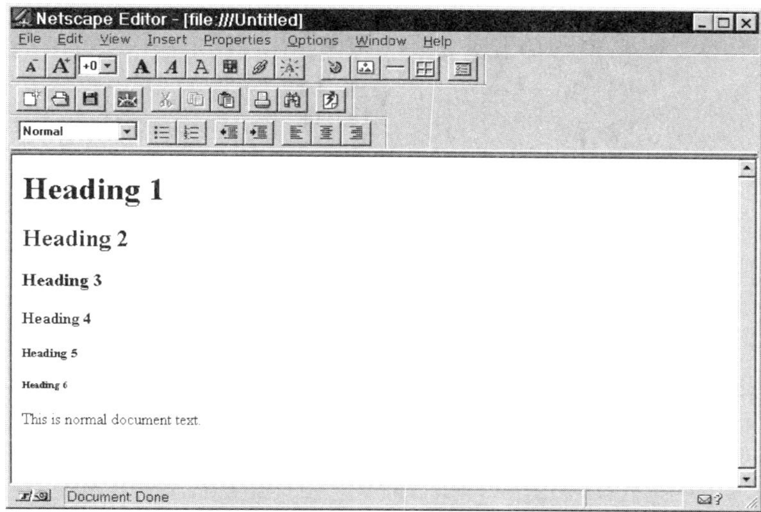

Figure 27.3 Each heading level has its own distinctive format

> formats. If you would like to maximize your document's retrievability, use headings.

To give your document a title that's visible in your document, not just the title bar, use a Heading 1 paragraph format, as shown in Figure 27.4.

Aligning Text

You can align a heading (or any other text you enter) by just selecting the text and clicking the appropriate tool on the Paragraph Format toolbar. Figure 27.5 shows the effect of clicking the Center tool, while Figure 27.6 displays text aligned flush right with the Align Right tool.

If you'd prefer to use the menus, you can align text by selecting it and choosing Properties/Text/Paragraph, and then choosing Left, Center, or Right from the Align area. Click OK to confirm.

Figure 27.4 Use a Heading 1 format to provide an apparent title for your document

You can press Tab or Shift + Tab to indent or unindent the selected text.

Creating Lists

To improve your document's readability, break up the text on the page. Netscape Editor gives you several list formats from which you can choose: bulleted lists, numbered lists, menu lists, directory lists, and description lists.

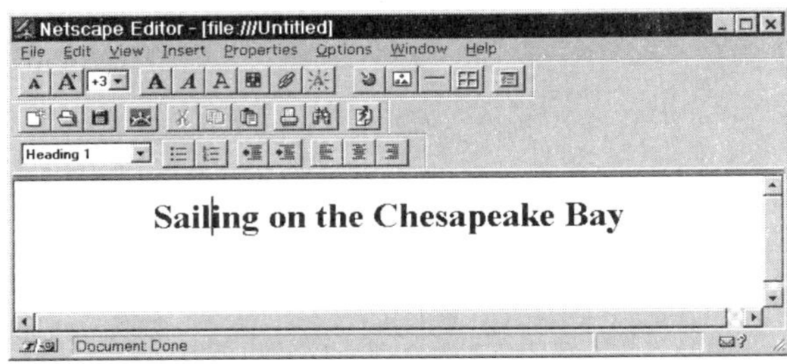

Figure 27.5 Text centered with the Center tool

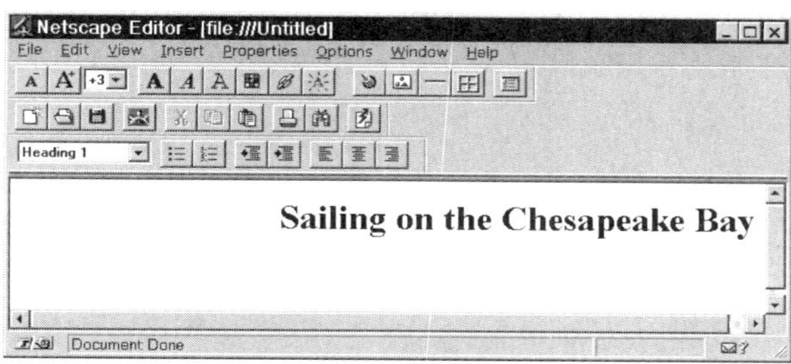

Figure 27.6 Text aligned flush right with the Align Right tool

As you'll see, you can combine list formats to produce precisely the effect you're looking for. The following sections describe each of these options.

Adding a Bulleted List

When you would like to list a number of items without implying that they're in a particular sequence, use a bulleted list. The bullets call attention to the items, as if to say, "These are all important." The eye naturally gravitates to a bulleted list.

To create a bulleted list, position the cursor where you want the list to begin, and click Bullet List. Alternatively, type the list, select it, and choose Bullet List. Netscape Editor adds the bullets automatically, as shown in Figure 27.7.

To stop typing in a bulleted or any other list format, press Enter to start a new line, and then choose Normal from the paragraph styles list box.

Changing the Bullet Style

By default, Netscape Editor adds a solid circle in front of each bullet list item. However, you can choose from two other formats: an open circle (see Figure 27.8) or a solid square (Figure 27.9). To change the bullet style, select the list items and choose Properties/Text. Click the Paragraph tab, and choose a bullet style in the Bullet Style list box. Click OK to confirm.

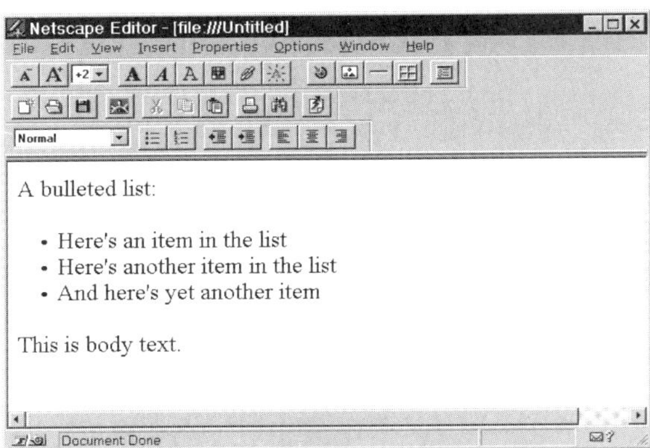

Figure 27.7 Bulleted list created with the Bullet List tool

Instead of creating a bulleted list, you may wish to create an unbulleted list and add small graphics that look like bullets. You'll find out how in Chapter 31.

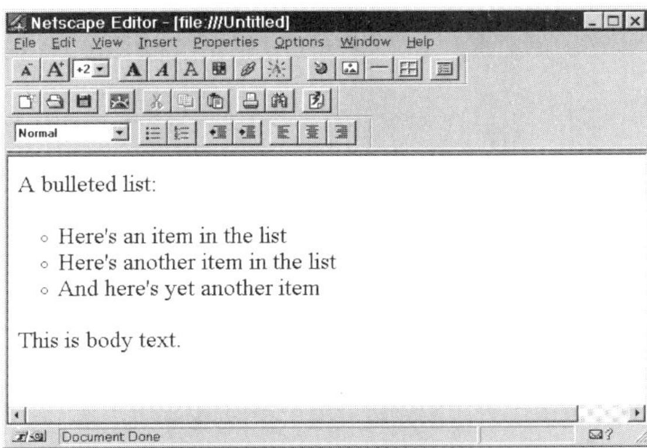

Figure 27.8 Bulleted list using open circles as the bullet style

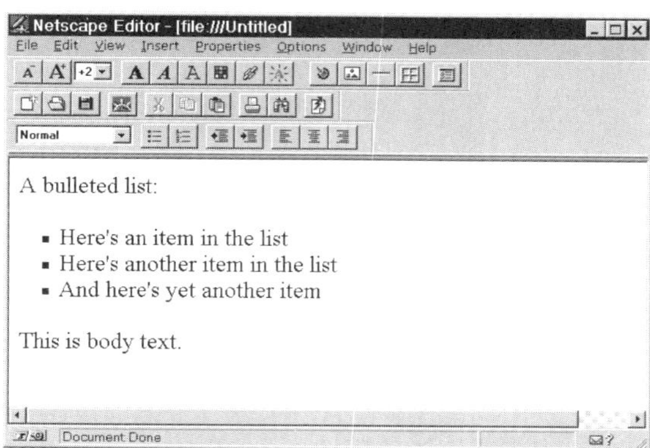

Figure 27.9 Bulleted list using solid squares as the bullet style

Adding a Numbered List

To create a numbered list, type the items but don't type any numbers! Your browser will number the items for you. When you're done typing the list, select the list and click the Numbered List tool.

I don't see any numbers! You won't see the numbers in Netscape Editor—all you'll see are # symbols. To see the numbers, click View in Browser. You'll see the numbers there (see Figure 27.10).

Adding a Description List

A description list, or glossary list, is often used to list and define terms, as shown in Figure 27.11. Such a list consists of two formats:

Description Item This format is used for the term.

Description Text This format is used for the definition. As you can see in Figure 27.11, it's indented.

It's somewhat tedious to create a description list. To enter the first description item, you choose Description Item from the paragraph style box

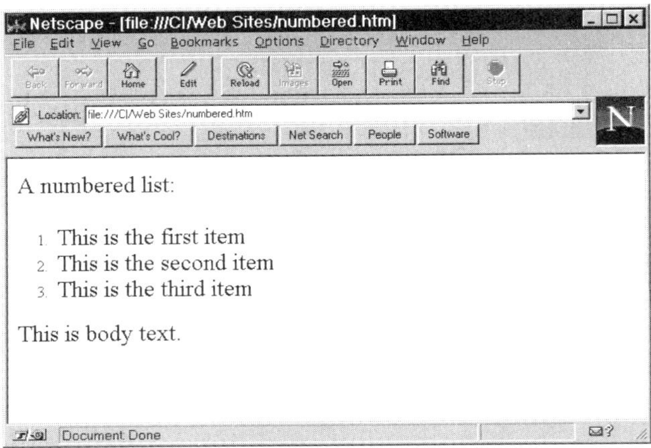

Figure 27.10 To see the numbers in a numbered list, you must switch to the browser view

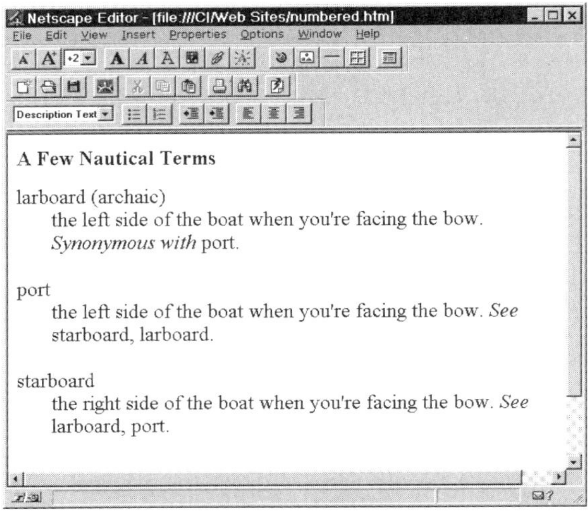

Figure 27.11 Description lists are useful for glossaries of key terms

and type the item. To enter the definition text for this item, you choose Description Text and type the text. You have to repeat these commands for each item you enter.

If you're creating a lengthy list, consider using the Normal text style plus indents to do the job. It's easier to enter the formats because you can just click the Increase Indent tool to indent the description text. However, you must leave a blank line between the description item and the text, as shown in Figure 27.12.

It says I can create menu lists and directory lists, but these just look like bulleted lists! That's right. These two formats stem from the early days of HTML, and they aren't often supported in most browsers—including Netscape! You'll see these two options in the Paragraph Properties dialog box, but just ignore them.

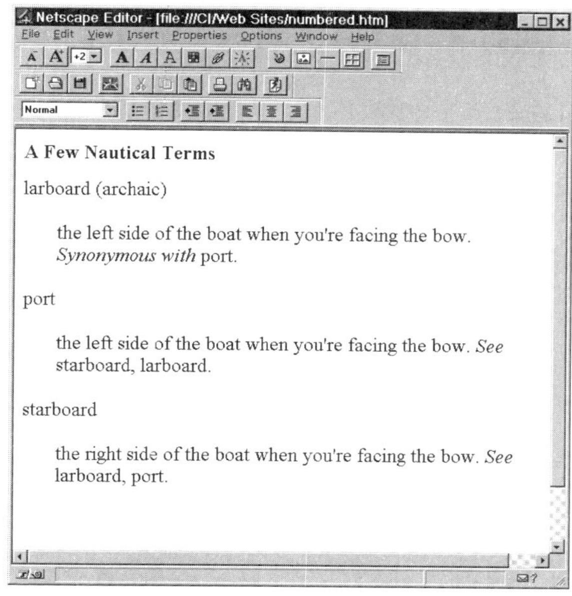

Figure 27.12 Description list created with indents

Creating Block Quotes

When you insert an extended quotation in your text—we're talking about three or four lines here—you should indent the text so that it's set apart from the body text. You can use the Block Quote format for this purpose (see Figure 27.13)

To create a block quote, press Enter to create a new line, and choose Normal from the paragraph styles box. Then choose Properties/Text, click the Paragraph tab, and choose Block Quote in the Additional Style area. Click OK to confirm. (You can also do this after typing the paragraph.)

The Block Quote format is useful for purposes other than typing extended quotations. For example, it's a great way to set important text off from the rest of the text. In Figure 27.14, you see a Block Quote format that's been set apart from the body text with horizontal lines; it's an effective way to call attention to something really important.

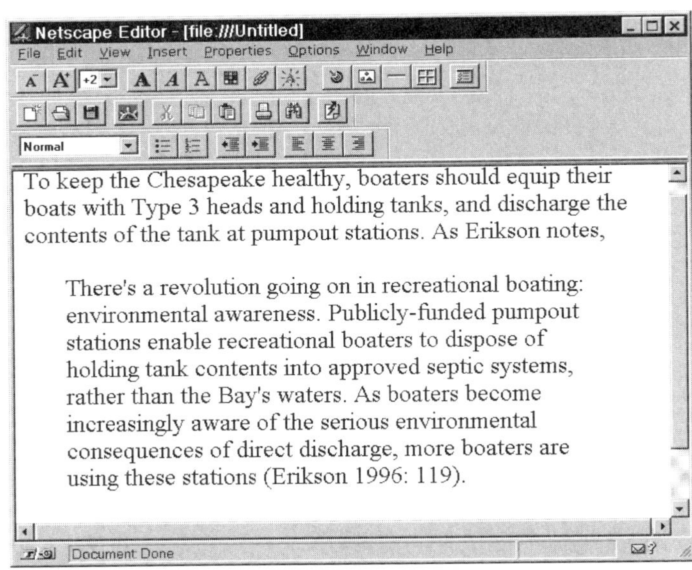

Figure 27.13 Block Quote format is used for extended quotations

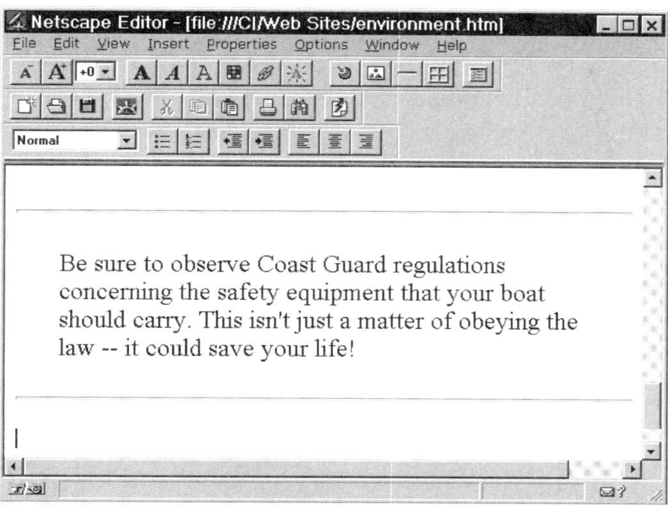

Figure 27.14 Block Quote format used with horizontal lines for emphasis

Indenting Text

It's easy to indent text using the Increase Indent and Decrease Indent tools. Try entering a paragraph of normal text, and click these tools to see what they do. When you click Increase Indent, the text moves about a half-inch right; clicking Decrease Indent moves the text back to the margin.

When you finish typing in some formats (such as Block Quote), the only way you can get back to the true Normal (body text) format is to click Decrease Indent. That's because the indent is separate from the paragraph style.

Creating an Outline

By combining indents with numbered list formats, it's possible to create a school-type outline, replete with Roman numerals. It isn't easy, though.

To start your outline, type all the major items, the ones that get capital Roman numerals (I, II, III, etc.). Select the whole list, and choose Properties/Text. In the Paragraph page, choose big Roman numerals (I, II, III...) in the Number Style box, and click OK.

To add the second level of headings, the ones that start with capital letters, press Enter after one of the first-level headings. *Important*: Click the Increase Indent tool. You must indent this heading or you can't give it a different number style. After you've indented the heading, choose Properties/Text. In the Paragraph page, choose capital letters (A, B, C...) in the Number Style box, and click OK.

Continue adding more headings by indenting, where necessary, and choosing the number format from the Properties/Text/Paragraph dialog box. You don't see the numbering in the Editor window, except that the program uses large and small X marks to denote Roman numerals, while it uses large and small A marks to denote letters (see Figure 27.15). You don't see the numbering until you view your document in the browser (Figure 27.16).

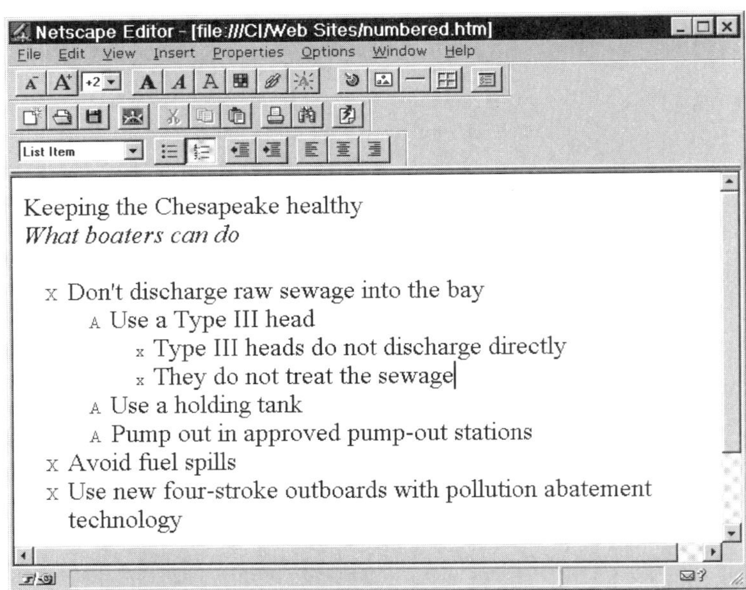

Figure 27.15 Outline viewed in Netscape Editor

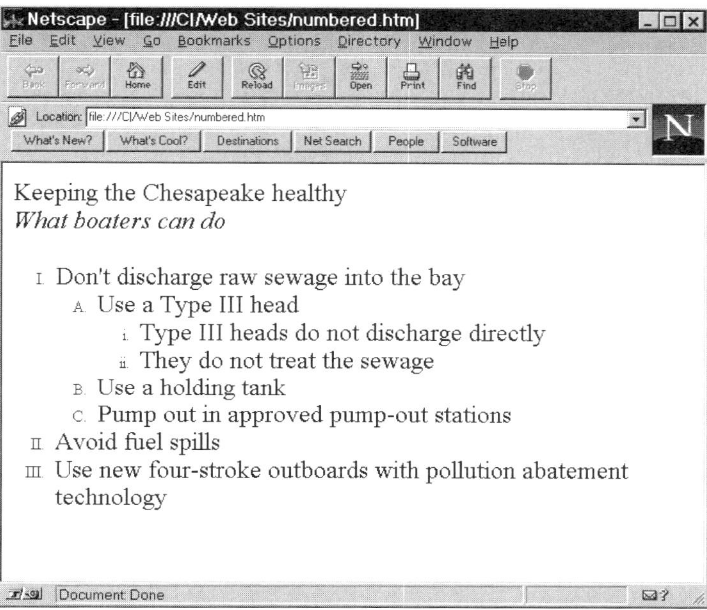

Figure 27.16 Outline viewed in Netscape Navigator

Writing Numbered Instructions with Explanatory Text

When you write instructions, you may wish to separate the numbered instructions from explanatory text, as shown in Figure 27.17. This is easy to do. After you've typed a numbered list item, press Enter to start a new paragraph. Then click Increase Indent, and disengage numbering by clicking the Numbered List tool so that it's no longer selected. Type the explanatory text. Press Enter, click Increase Indent, and click Numbered List to restart the numbering.

As before, you don't see the numbers in the Netscape Editor window. To see the numbers, view your document in the browser.

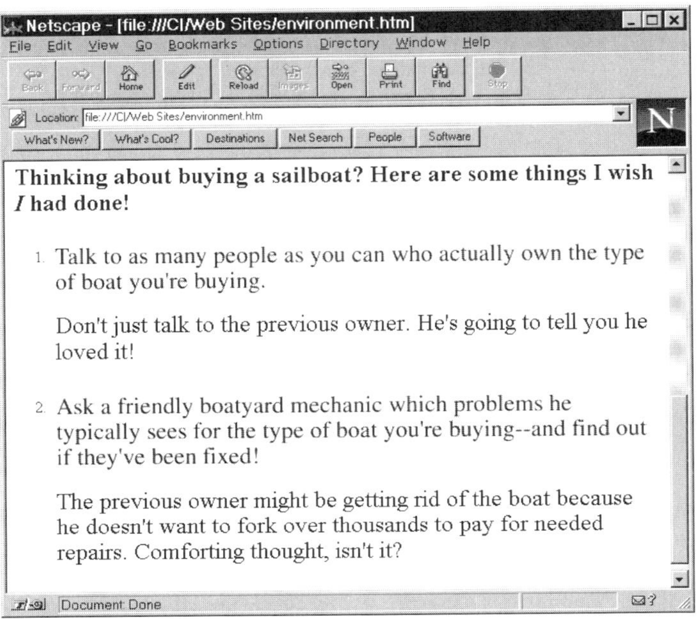

Figure 27.17 Instructional list with explanatory text

From Here

- You've mastered paragraph formats; let's tackle characters and fonts. On to the next chapter!
- Like to play around with fancy backgrounds? See Chapter 29.
- If you'd like to learn how to create bulleted lists with small graphics instead of bullets, flip to Chapter 31.

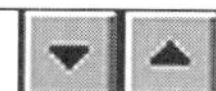

Chapter 28

Working with Characters and Fonts

To jazz up your document a bit, you may wish to add character styles (such as bold or italic), font colors, and varying font sizes. It's also possible nowadays to specify font typefaces, such as Helvetica, Garamond, or Times Roman, since the two leading browsers (Netscape Navigator 3.0 and Microsoft Internet Explorer 3.0) can both read and respond to your typeface choices. This chapter tells you everything you need to know to make your characters and fonts look attractive.

Adding Character Styles

Character styles (such as boldface and italic type) can add emphasis and meaning to your document—as long as they're not overused. Figure 28.1 goes

For the Time-Challenged

- You can add bold and italic quickly by selecting text and pressing Ctrl + B (bold) or Ctrl + I (italic). Other character styles—including superscript, subscript, strikethrough, and the dreaded blink—can be chosen from the Properties/Character menu.
- You can add color to selected text by clicking the Font Color tool, but you might want to wait until you've decided on a color scheme for your document (see Chapter 29).
- To size selected text, click Increase Font Size or Decrease Font Size, or use the Font Size list box.
- You can add distinctive typefaces to your document by inserting the <FONT FACE> tag directly into your document.

overboard, if you can pardon the pun. The character formatting really isn't necessary because the paragraph formats guide the eye sufficiently.

Still, there are valid reasons for using bold and italic, and it couldn't be easier to apply these formats with Netscape Editor. To add bold, for example, select the text you want to format, and click the Bold tool. If you prefer, you can choose Properties/Character/Bold from the menus, or press Ctrl + B.

You can add character styles while typing, if you prefer. For example, to start typing something in bold, click the Bold tool and type away. When you want to switch back to normal text, click the Bold tool again to turn bold off.

In addition to bold, Netscape Editor enables you to add the following character styles to your document:

Italic Click the Italic tool, choose Properties/Character/Italic, or press Ctrl + I.

Underline Click the Italic tool, choose Properties/Character/Underline, or press Ctrl + U. *Note:* Not many

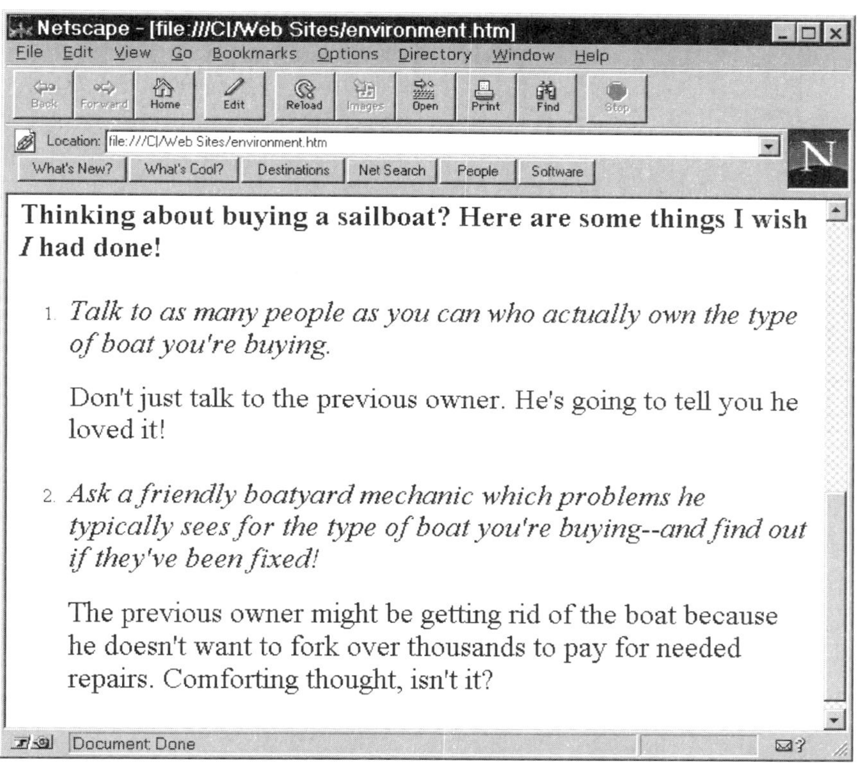

Figure 28.1 A bit too much character formatting

	browsers recognize underlining, for the simple reason that underlined text might be confused with a hyperlink.
Superscript	Choose Properties/Character/Superscript.
Subscript	Choose Properties/Character/Subscript.
Strikethrough	Choose Properties/Character/Strikethrough.
Blink	Choose Properties/Character/Blink.

If you went overboard in your character formatting, you can clear all the styles from a selection with just one click. Select the over-formatted text and click the Clear All Styles tool.

Figure 28.2 shows the appearance of each of these formats in the Editor (except that we can't really show the Blink format in this medium—no great loss!).

This guy flamed me for using Blink! Frankly, the blink character style isn't too popular, largely because it was overused when first introduced. Use it only when it's absolutely necessary to call attention to something really, really important—and use it only once in a document.

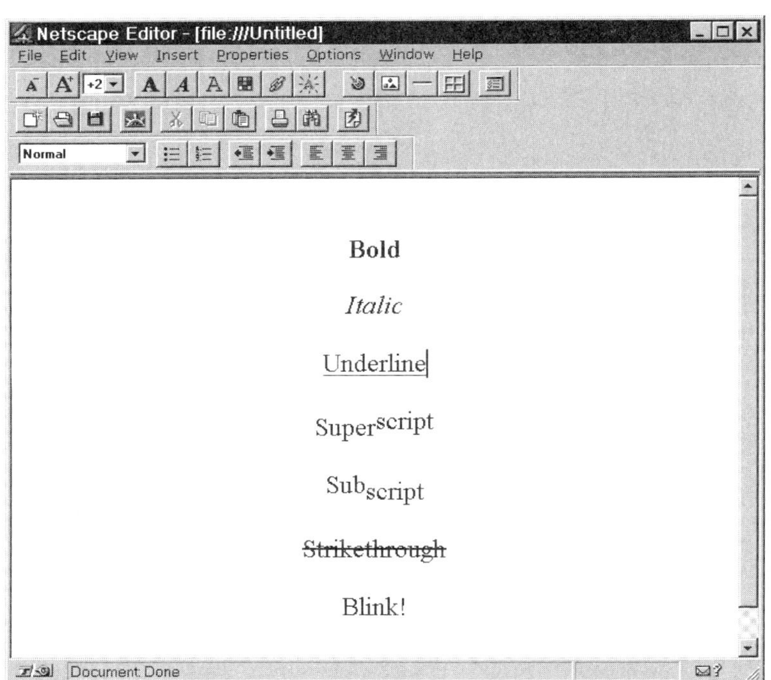

Figure 28.2 Character styles

Adding Color

You can add color to your text. Since many people browsing the Web are using color monitors, this is a great way to add emphasis and meaning to your text.

Before adding color willy-nilly to your text, you may want to think through the color scheme for your whole document. Get the lowdown in Chapter 29.

To add color to your text, select the text and click the Font Color tool. You can also choose Properties/Character/Text Color. You'll see the Color dialog box, shown in Figure 28.3. Just click a color and click OK.

If you're not happy with the colors you see in the Basic Colors or Custom Colors lists, you can create a new custom color by clicking Define Custom Colors, in the Color dialog box. This produces an expanded dialog box. To define a custom color, drag the color cursor around until you've found the

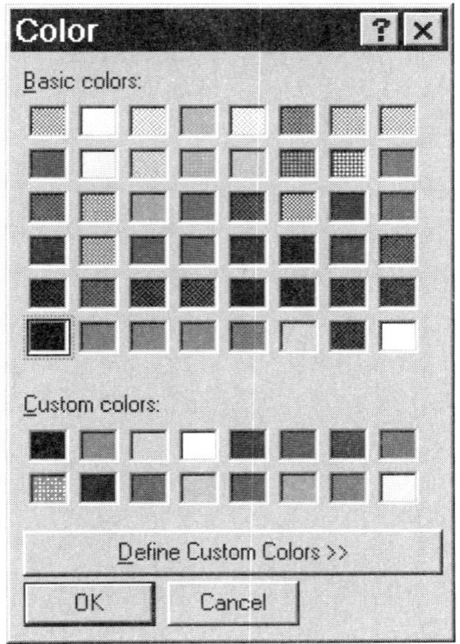

Figure 28.3 Use the Color dialog box to add color to your text

hue you want, and then drag the slider up and down to control the amount of white and black in your color. When you've finished choosing your color, click Add to Custom Colors.

Controlling Relative Font Sizes

You can enlarge or decrease the size of selected text by means of the Font Size list box, located in the Character Format toolbar. You can also change the size of selected text by clicking the Increase Font Size and Decrease Font Size tools, which are in the same toolbar. These controls enable you to choose a *relative* size for your text. It's up to the browser to determine just how large or small the text actually looks on-screen. By default, all text is set to the size +0. You can choose sizes up to +4, the largest size, or down to –2, the smallest. Figure 28.4 shows how Editor displays these font sizes.

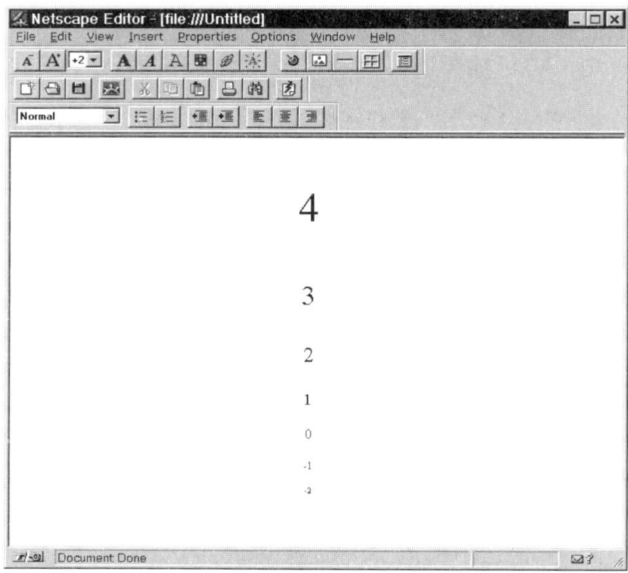

Figure 28.4 Relative font sizes (+4 to –2)

Using the Fixed Width (Typewriter) Font

In standard HTML, your font choices boil down to two:

- **Proportionally spaced type** This is the type of font used for body type. In a proportionally spaced typeface, each letter's width is proportional to its size (a "w" gets more horizontal space than an "I").
- **Fixed-width type** This type of font resembles typescript. Each letter gets the same width.

Figure 28.5 shows the difference. Normally, your document is formatted in proportionally spaced type; the exact font (such as Times Roman) is chosen by the user, who configures the browser to display this type using one of the typefaces installed on the user's system. You may wish to use the fixed-width font to show an example of computer code. Some Web designers like to use it for special effects.

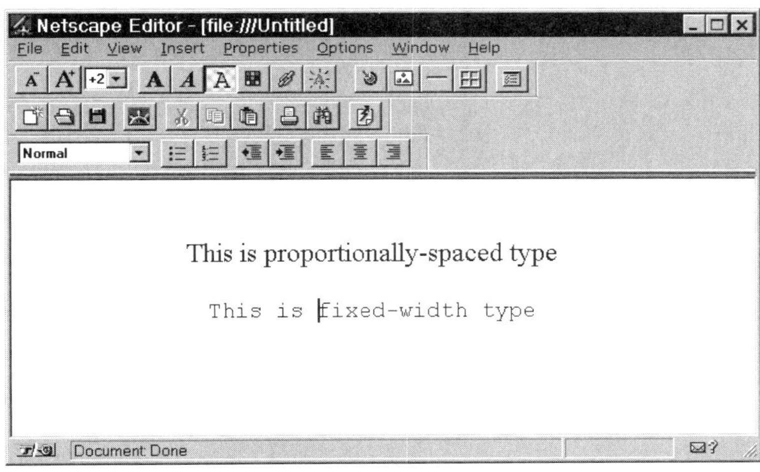

Figure 28.5 Proportional vs. fixed-width type

Specifying Fonts with HTML's <FONT FACE> Tag

Netscape Gold 3.0 is a bit behind the curve in one respect. Fonts have come to the Web; both Netscape Navigator 3.0 and Microsoft Internet Explorer 3.0 can read the font tags that Web authors can now embed in their documents. But there's no Netscape Editor commands for inserting this tag.

Here's where you might want to try a little HTML. You can use the Insert HTML Tag command to place the <FONT FACE> tag in your Editor document.

Most HTML tags are *containers*. This means that they contain some text between a start tag and a stop tag, so that all the text between the two takes on a distinctive appearance.

To code text so that it appears in a distinctive font:

1. Place the cursor at the beginning of the text you want to format, and choose Insert/HTML Tag. You'll see the HTML Tag dialog box, shown in Figure 28.6.
2. In the text box, carefully type the start tag using the following pattern:

   <FONT FACE="typeface_name">

   If you want to format the text in Helvetica, you would type <FONT FACE="Helvetica">. Make sure the font name you type is one that's installed on your system.
3. Click Verify to make sure you typed the tag correctly. This button checks for minor errors that could keep the tag from working.

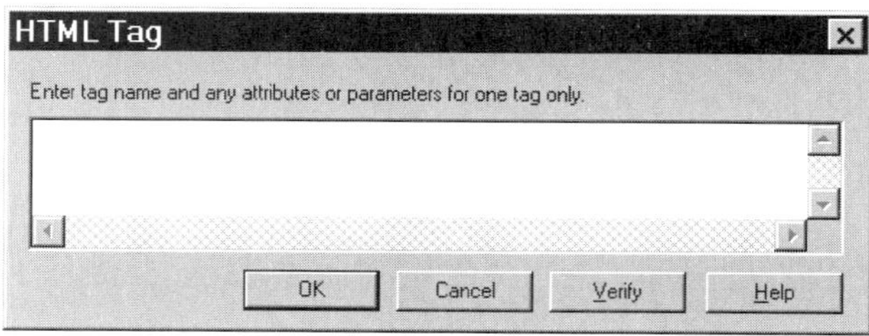

Figure 28.6 HTML Tag dialog box

4. If you don't see an error message, click OK to insert the tag in your document. You'll see a yellow icon that marks the beginning of the HTML tag you've entered.
5. Move the cursor to the end of the text you want to format, and choose Insert HTML Tag again.
6. In the text box, carefully type the following stop tag:

   </FONT>

   This ends the <FONT FACE> formatting. Click Verify to make sure you typed the tag correctly.
7. If you typed the tag correctly, click OK to insert the tag in your document.

In Figure 28.7, you see how the formatted text looks in the Editor: You see the start and stop tag symbols, but you don't see the fonts. To see the fonts, switch to the browser (Figure 28.8).

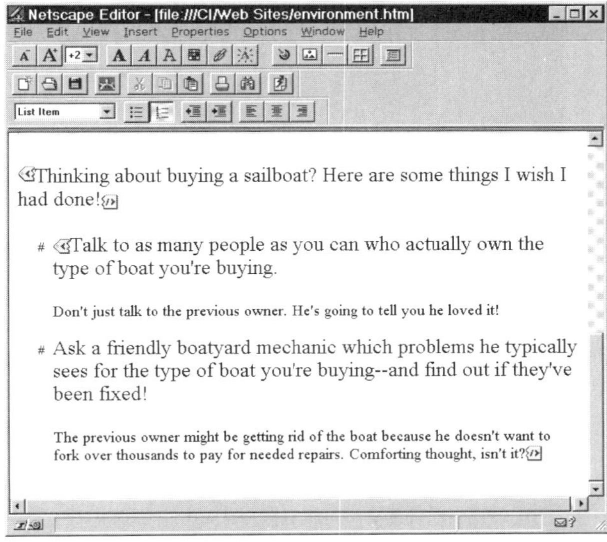

Figure 28.7 The beginning and ending symbols mark the places where you inserted the start and stop tags

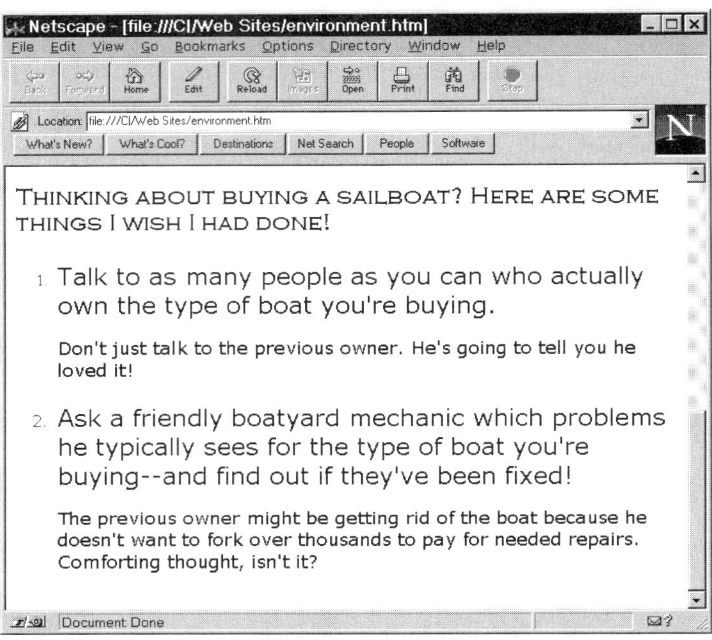

Figure 28.8 You can see your font choices in the browser

I added the font, but it doesn't show up! The drawback to using the <FONT FACE> tag is that the font won't appear if the font isn't installed on the user's system. Most Windows and Macintosh computers have Times Roman, Helvetica, and Courier, but these are about the only ones you can count on. If the user's system doesn't have the font you've requested, the browser just ignores your request and uses the default proportionally spaced font instead.

Don't like the font you used? You can change it easily. Just double-click the start tag symbol. You'll see the HTML Tag dialog box. Carefully change the font name, making sure you don't erase the quotation marks or misspell the font name. Click OK to confirm.

From Here

- It's time to work out your document's color scheme. For the low-down on this and other document formats, see Chapter 29.
- Add some hyperlinks, already! Find out how in Chapter 30. And how about some graphics, while you're at it? See Chapter 31.

Chapter 29

Choosing a Color Scheme

To put together a good-looking Web page, you need to devote some thought to color. You can choose distinctive colors for normal text, link text, visited link text, and backgrounds. Ideally, these colors will work harmoniously together. And if they do, you can use them on all the pages of your site, lending your creative efforts a level of consistency that users will appreciate.

This chapter shows you how to use one of Netscape's predefined color schemes-and how to create your own, if you wish. It also covers background graphics.

Using Predefined Color Schemes

You've already spent some time browsing the Web, and I'm sure you've been shocked by some of the weird color combinations you've seen, such as green

For the Time-Challenged

- Netscape's predefined color schemes are tasteful and, well, pedestrian.
- You can create your own color scheme, but please make sure that the text is legible against the background.
- If you create a color scheme you really like, you can make it the default for every new page you create.
- You can add a background graphic, but once again, please make sure that the text is legible.

text on purple backgrounds or blood-red type on a sickly lurid yellow. Often, there's not enough contrast between the text and the background, making the documents hard to read as well as repulsive. Yuk!

Perhaps aware of the need to provide some gentle guidance here, Netscape has set up Editor with a selection of nice-looking color schemes, all of which have commendable contrast.

To choose a color scheme for your document, do the following:

1. Choose Properties/Document, and click the Appearance tab. You'll see the Appearance options (shown in Figure 29.1).
2. In the Color Schemes box, choose a color scheme. You'll see what the color scheme looks like. You may wish to change the text and link colors (see "Choosing Text and Link Colors," in the next section) but give these a try, for now.
3. Click OK to confirm your choice.

Choosing Your Own Text, Link, and Background Colors

Now that you've chosen a responsible color scheme—a conservative, well-designed, respectable color scheme, mind you—you surely want to experiment a little. Perhaps you've got something a little wilder in mind?

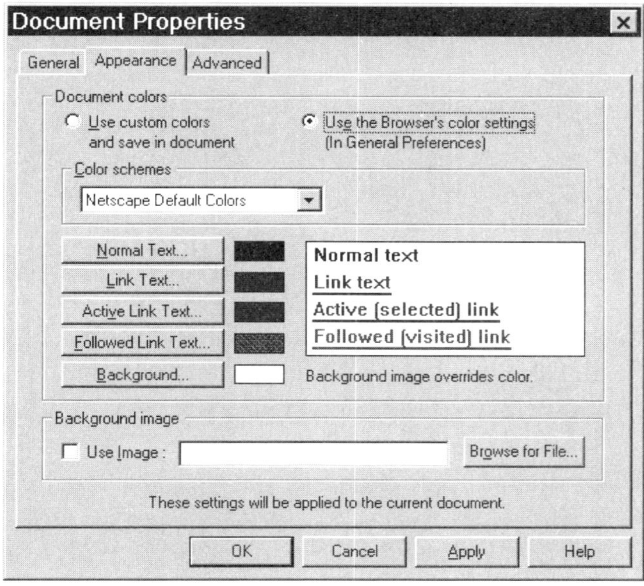

Figure 29.1 Appearance page of Document Properties dialog box

You can choose your own text, link, and background colors. But please, try to choose colors that work well together. Above all, make sure your page is readable. If there's too little contrast between the text and the background, your page will be hard to read.

To choose text, link, and background colors for your document, do the following:

1. Choose Properties/Document, and click the Appearance tab. You'll see the Appearance options (shown in Figure 29.1).
2. Click the Background button. You'll see the Color dialog box, shown in Figure 29.2.
3. If you'd like to choose a custom color, click Define Custom Colors, and move the hue control and black/white slider until you've created the color you want. Click Add to Custom Colors to add your

color to the custom color list. When you've decided on your color, click OK. You'll see your color choice. You will probably need to choose new text colors now!

4. Click Normal Text, and choose a color using the same Color or Custom Color dialog box that you used in step 3.
5. Make color choices for Link Text, Active Link Text, and Followed Link Text. Your Link Text choice should be brighter than your Followed Link Text choice.
6. Choose OK when you've finished making your choices.

Found a color scheme you really like? You can make it the default for every new Editor document you create. To do so, choose Options/Editor Options, and click Appearance. You'll see a dialog box that looks exactly like the one you just used—the only difference is that your choices here apply

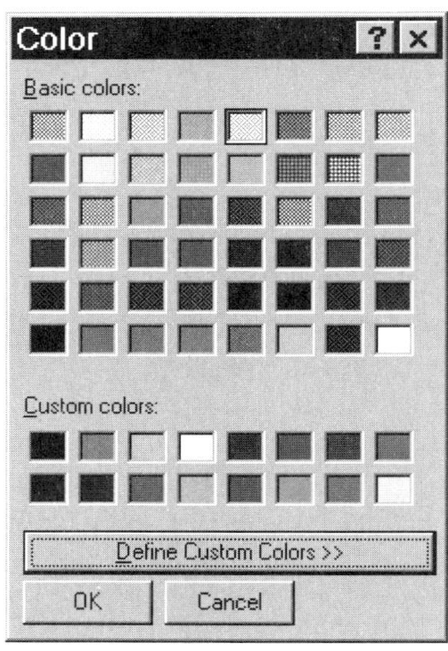

Figure 29.2 Color dialog box

to all the new documents you create (not just the current one). Make the same color choices and click OK.

Adding a Background Graphic

Instead of a solid color, you may wish to display a tiled background graphic. Such graphics are actually rather small—typically, the files are just a few kilobytes in size—but the browser automatically places them side by side until they fill the whole screen.

Before you add a background graphic, though, think about all the pages you've seen that were hard to read because the background graphic was so busy.

Let's look at some good backgrounds before proceeding. In Figure 29.3, you see what happens when a busy background graphic almost completely

Figure 29.3 Horrible background graphic

obscures the text. Ugly! Figure 29.4 shows a much better choice—it's a low-key yellow fabric that doesn't obscure the text at all. In fact, it adds legibility.

To add a background graphic to your document, do the following:

1. Choose Properties/Document, and click the Appearance tab.
2. In the Background Image area, click Use Image, and use the Browse button to locate your background graphic.
3. Click OK to confirm your choice.

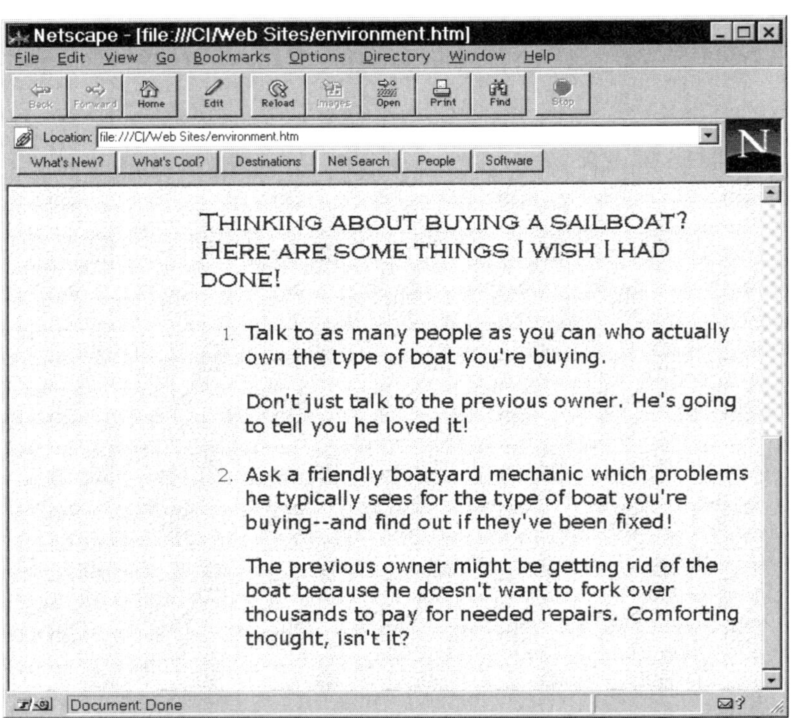

Figure 29.4 Beautiful background graphic

Looking for background graphics? You'll find tons of them on the Web. Assuming you ask permission to do so, you can copy a background to your hard disk—and use it in your pages—by right-clicking the background in the browser, and choosing Save Background As. You'll also find lots of sites that collect background graphics; one of the best is Pattern Land (http://www.netcreations.com/patternland/). For more great links, check out Yahoo's Backgrounds page (http://www.yahoo.com/, and search for Backgrounds). Texture Woild (http://www.websharx.com/~ttbrown/txtwoild.html) has lots of beautiful background graphics. If you hate my advice about tasteful backgrounds, please go directly to Jeffrey Zeldman's remarkable Jeffrey Zeldman Presents (http://www.zeldman.com), which is loaded with background graphics that go very far off the deep end.

From Here

- Enough with the aesthetics—let's get down to business. Add some hyperlinks! Learn how in Chapter 30.
- And how 'bout some graphics? Become a master of in-line images in Chapter 31.

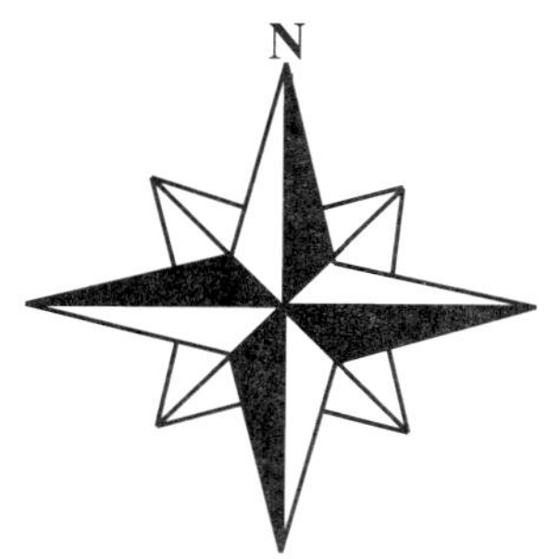

Chapter 30

Adding Hyperlinks

A *hyperlink* is a distinctively formatted word or phrase that, when clicked, takes the user to another document (or another location within the same document). Graphics can be hyperlinks, too. In this section, you'll learn how to add hyperlinks to your document.

Adding Hyperlinks Using the Properties Dialog Box

To add a hyperlink to your document, position the cursor where you want the hyperlink to appear, and click Make Link on the toolbar (it looks like

part of a chain). Alternatively, choose Insert/Link, or press Ctrl + L. You'll see the Properties dialog box, shown in Figure 30.1, with the Link page displayed.

Follow these instructions to add a link using the Link Properties dialog box:

1. In the Link Source box, type the text (called the *link text*) that you want the user to see.
2. In the Link To box, type the URL.
3. Click OK to add the hyperlink to your document. To see if it's working OK, click View in Browser on the toolbar, or choose File/ Browse Document.

If you prefer, you can type the link text in your document, and select it. When you click Make Link, you'll see that Netscape Editor has automatically entered this text in the Link Properties dialog box.

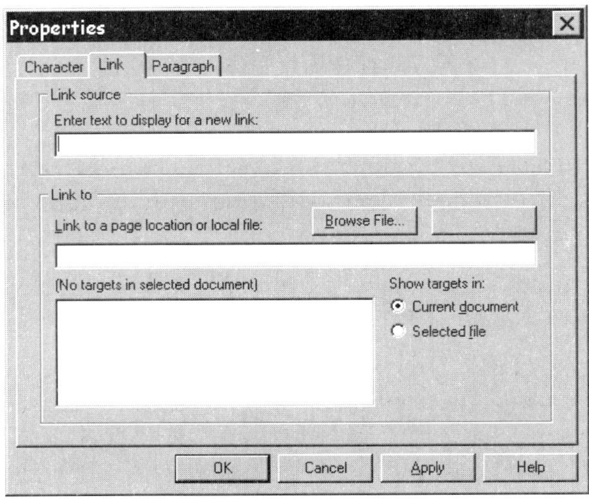

Figure 30.1 Use this dialog box to add new hyperlinks to your document

It doesn't work! You switched to the browser window and clicked your link—but it doesn't work! What went wrong? Lots of possibilities here:

- Probably, you typed the URL wrong. Note that URLs are case-sensitive; you have to duplicate the capitalization pattern exactly. Also, don't leave any spaces within URLs. Be sure there are two slashes and a colon after "http." Edit the hyperlink (see "Editing Hyperlinks," later in this chapter).
- The page may have moved or no longer exists. If it's moved, edit the link with the page's new location (see "Editing Hyperlinks," later in this chapter).
- Last but not least? Maybe you're not connected to the Internet. Log on!

Adding Links Using Drag-and-Drop

Windows 95 users can add hyperlinks just by dragging the link from a browser page to the Editor page. This enables you to build up a list of links very quickly!

You can use this technique to add a link on your page to the page currently displayed in the browser window:

1. Display the browser window as well as the Editor window. In the browser window, display the document to which you want to link.
2. In the Editor window, position the cursor where you want the new hyperlink to appear. If you want the hyperlink to appear on a new line, press Enter or Shift + Enter.
3. Drag the chain link icon (next to the Location box) from the browser window to the Editor window, and release the mouse button. Gold adds the link to your document at the cursor's location.

To test your hyperlinks at any time, click View in Browser (on the toolbar) or choose File/View Document from the menu bar. If you haven't saved your page, you'll be

prompted to do so—and you should. You'll then see your page in a Netscape browser window. Log on to the Net, if you haven't done so, and click your hyperlinks to test them.

Follow these instructions to add a link within a displayed page:

1. Display the browser window as well as the Editor window. In the browser window, locate a document that contains the link you want to include in your Editor document.
2. In the Editor window, position the cursor where you want the new hyperlink to appear. If you want the hyperlink to appear on a new line, press Enter or Shift + Enter.
3. Drag the hyperlink from the browser window (see Figure 30.2). As you do, you'll see that the pointer changes shape to indicate that you're "carrying" a hyperlink. When the pointer reaches the Editor window, release the mouse button. You'll see the new hyperlink at the cursor's location.

Creating Internal Links

Internal links enable users to move to a specific location within a document. In order to create internal links, you must first define *targets*, which are named places within a document. Targets serve as destinations for internal links.

Here's an example. Suppose you're creating a lengthy document that contains a lot of text. You could place a table of contents at the beginning, one that listed the major headings in the document. You could then define each of the major headings as a target, and make each entry in the table of contents serve as an internal link. Readers can then click an item in the table of contents, and they'll jump right to the section they want.

In the following sections, you learn how to create targets and how to link to targets using internal links.

Defining Targets

It's easy to define targets in your document. Wait until you've finished writing it and then do the following:

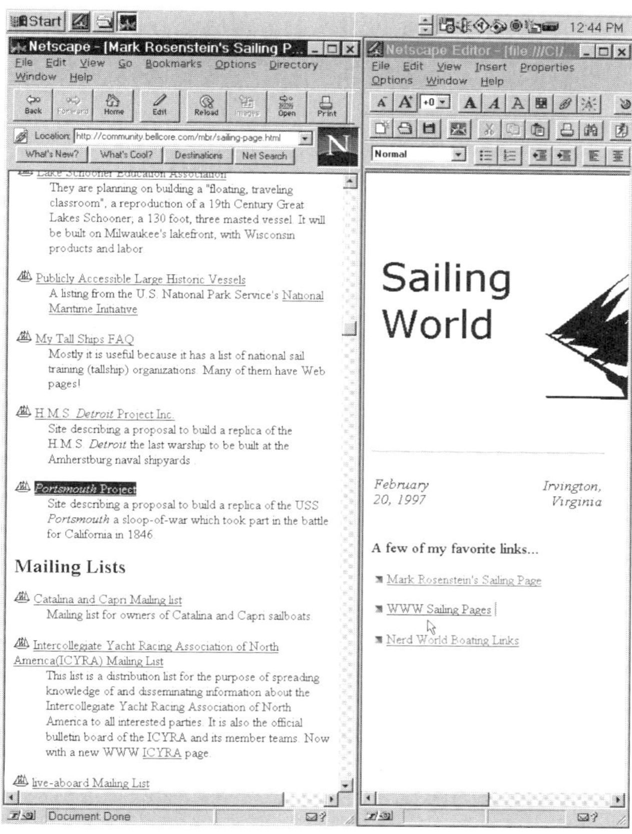

Figure 30.2 Dragging and dropping a hyperlink

1. Select a word at the beginning of the text that you want displayed when your reader selects the internal link. This word will be positioned at the top of the screen when your users jump to this target.
2. Click the Insert Target (Named Anchor) tool, or choose Insert/Target (Named Anchor) from the menu bar. You'll see the Target Properties dialog box, which automatically contains the text you've highlighted. In Figure 30.3, the word "previous" had been selected

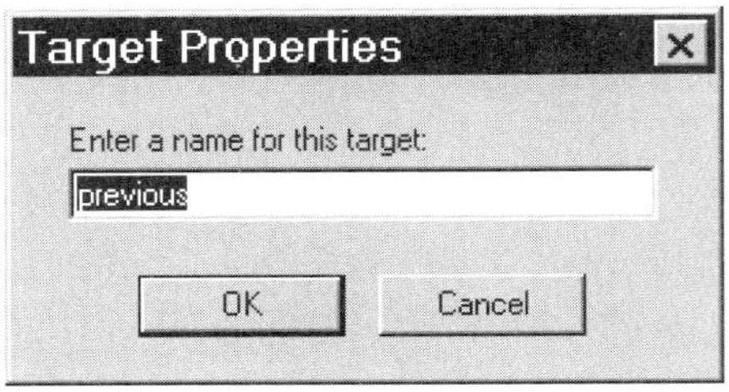

Target Properties

Enter a name for this target:

previous

OK Cancel

Figure 30.3 Defining a target

to serve as the target, and that's what appears in the Target Properties box.

3. Repeat step 2 to define all the additional targets that you want to create in this document.

After you define targets, Netscape Editor shows you where you've placed them by means of a little icon (see Figure 30.4).

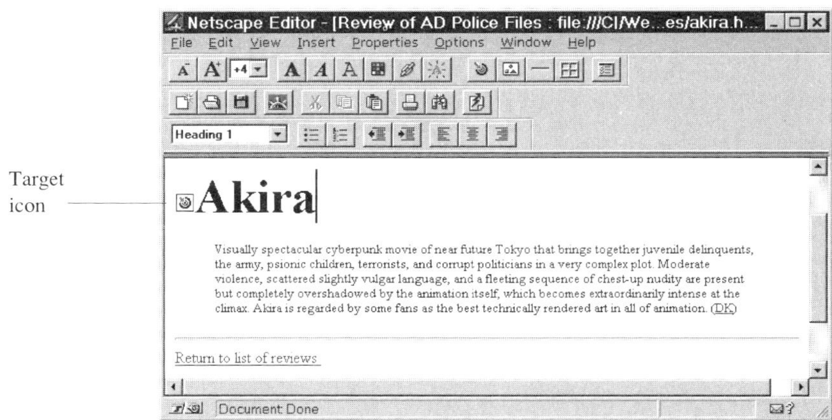

Figure 30.4 The icon shows you where you've entered a target

Creating Links to Targets

Now that you've created targets in your document, it's easy to create links to them. Do the following:

1. Type and select the text that you want to serve as the linking text.
2. Click Make Link. You'll see the Link Properties dialog box. Note that all the targets in your document are listed (look at the area called "Select a named target in current document"; see Figure 30.5).
3. Select the target to which you want to link.
4. Click OK.

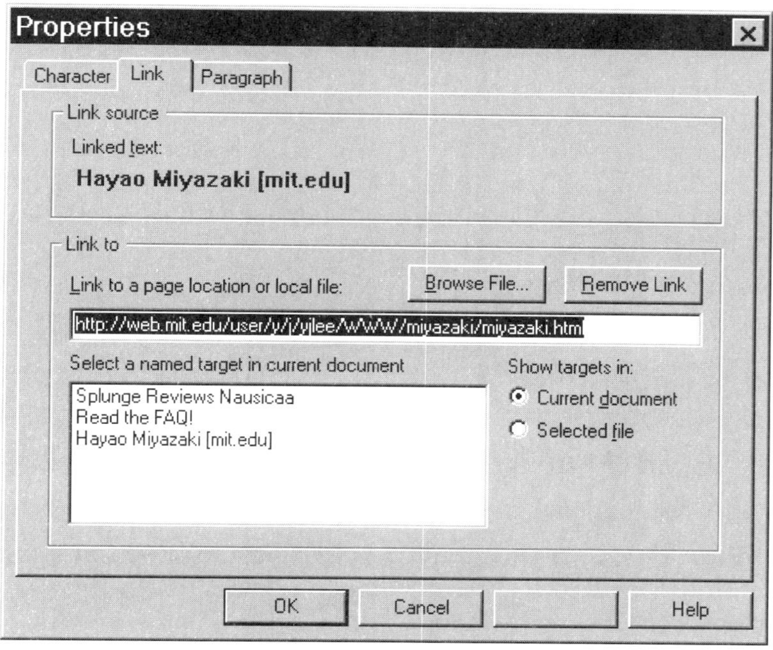

Figure 30.5 After you define targets, you'll see the target names in the Link Properties dialog box

Linking to a Target on a Different Page

You can also link to targets in another document. To do so, follow these instructions:

1. Type and select the text that you want to serve as the linking text.
2. Click Make Link. You'll see the Link Properties dialog box.
3. In the Link To area, use the Browse button to select the file that contains the targets.
4. Under the area called "Show targets in," click Selected File. You'll see the target names.
5. Select the target to which you want to link.
6. Click OK.

Adding a Mailto Hyperlink

Chances are you'll want to hear from the people who access your page; they may make suggestions, tell you about dead links, or just tell you how much they enjoyed your page! You can add a link, called a *mailto hyperlink,* to your page that automatically brings up a mail window if the user is using a reasonably up-to-date browser. The mail window automatically contains your e-mail address in the To box.

To create a mailto hyperlink, follow these instructions:

1. Type and select the text that you want to serve as the linked text. Normally this is your e-mail address. This will enable people who don't have mail-capable browsers to see your e-mail address.
2. Click Make Link. You'll see the Link Properties dialog box.
3. In the Link To box, carefully type *mailto*: followed by your e-mail address, with no spaces, as in the following:

    mailto:julia-bear@nowhere.net

4. Click OK.

Editing Hyperlinks

If you've already entered a hyperlink and it doesn't work (or the site's moved), you can edit the URL. To do so, select the hyperlink and then click Object Properties on the Toobar, or choose Properties/Link, or click Ctrl + L. You'll see the Properties dialog box. Edit the URL, and click OK.

From Here

- You've got the links. Now get the pix! Find out how in the next chapter.
- Want to achieve the ultimate in Web page design? Learn how to use tables and frames, as explained in Chapter 32.

Chapter 31

Adding Images to Your Page

Enough text! You want pictures! Well, you came to the right place. In this chapter, you'll learn how to jazz up your page by adding images. Like hyperlinks, images can be added in two ways: with the Image Properties dialog box or by dragging and dropping. Before getting to the specifics, though, let's take a quick look at the sorts of images you'll be adding, including how you can obtain them if they're freely available.

For the Time-Challenged

- You can insert GIF or JPEG graphics into your page. GIF graphics are best for small, geometric graphics with up to 256 colors, while JPEG graphics are best for photographic-quality images.
- If you've located some public domain art, or you have permission to copy some art, you can download a graphic by right-clicking the graphic in Netscape's browser and choosing Save Image As from the pop-up menu.
- When you add images, be sure to add alternate text for the benefit of those who have switched off graphics or use text-only browsers.
- The easiest way to add graphics to your Netscape Editor page is to drag them from a browser window!
- Once you've added a graphic to your document, you can align it, copy it, move it, or delete it. You can also choose how you want text positioned relative to the graphic, including text wrapping, and you can add white space or a border around it.

A Quick Introduction to Web Graphics

Graphics are stored in lots of differing file formats. For Web publishing, though, there are really only two kinds of graphics in wide use:

GIF	This graphic file format stores images in up to 256 colors. It's best used for graphics with a limited range of colors and geometric shapes.
JPEG	This graphic file format can store millions of colors. It's best used for photographic-quality graphics.

Where can you obtain graphics for your Web page? Lots of places, but make sure the image isn't copyrighted before using it on your page. Just because somebody makes a graphic available on the Web doesn't imply that the graphic can be freely reused elsewhere! That said, there are lots of image archives, and some of them are expressly in the public domain.

A great source of free graphics is Laurie McCannas' Free Art Website (http://www.mccannas.com). Laurie is the author of *Creating Great Web Graphics*, published by MIS Press. The site offers some particularly beautiful icons and bullets.

Getting Graphics with Netscape

If you've located a graphic that you want to use, and you're sure you can do so without violating copyright, you can save it to your hard disk. Later, you can add the image to your page using Editor.

The Virtual Image Archive (http://imagiware.com/via/) lists hundreds of links to image archives on the Web. Note that many of these images are copyrighted and can't be reused without permission; others are in the public domain. If you have any question about whether you can use any of the images accessible through this archive, contact the person who maintains the page containing the image.

To save an image to your hard disk, use the browser to display the page containing the graphic. Then hold down the right mouse button and choose Save Image As. In the Save As dialog box, choose the directory that contains the Web page on which you're working, and click OK.

Do you have access to a scanner? It's another great source of graphics. To learn how to get the most out of a scanner for Web publishing purposes, check out Sullivan's Scanning Tips Online (http://www.hsdesign.com/scanning/tipswelcome.html). It's a truly great site.

Adding Images Using the Properties Dialog Box

To add an image to your document with the Image Properties dialog box, follow these instructions:

1. Position the cursor where you want the image to appear.
2. On the toolbar, click Insert Image, or choose Insert/Image from the menu bar. You'll see the Properties dialog box, with the Image page displayed (see Figure 31.1).

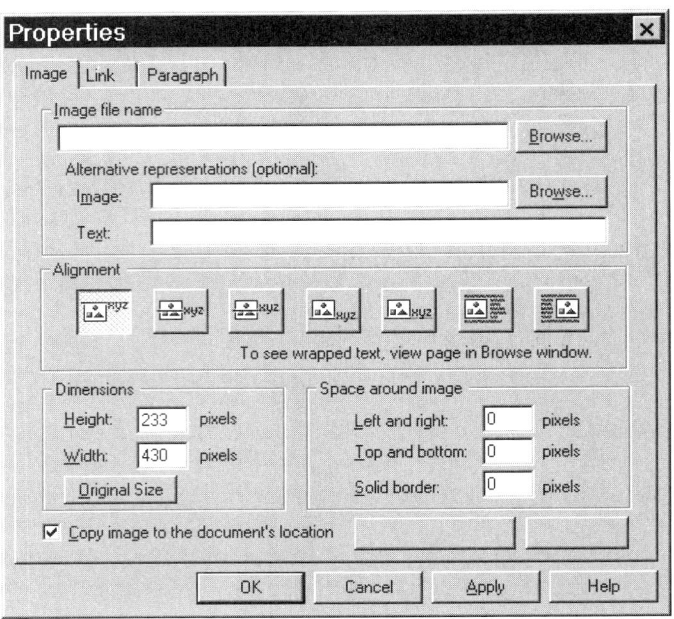

Figure 31.1 Image Properties dialog box

3. In the Image File Name area, type the location and name of the image file, or use the Browse button to locate the file.
4. *Important:* In the Alternative Representations area, use the Text box to type the text you would like to appear if the user has switched graphics off (this is common). This text is also visible to people using text-only browsers.
5. Select "Copy image to document's location." This will ensure that the graphic is located in the same directory as your Web page.
6. Click OK.

You'll see your graphic in your Web page (for an example, see Figure 31.2). For information on sizing the graphic and specifying its relationship with surrounding text, see "Sizing Graphics and Aligning with Text," later in this chapter.

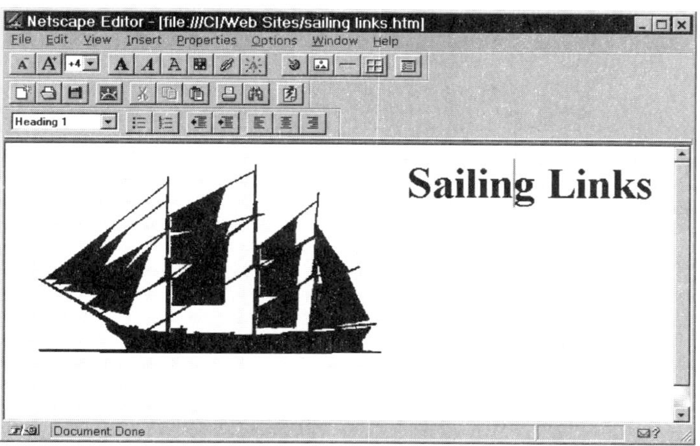

Figure 31.2 Graphic added to Wizard-produced page

Adding Images Using Drag-and-Drop

By far the easiest way to add images to your page is simply to drag them from a browser window into your Editor document. Adjust the two windows (the browser and Editor) so that you can see both the source graphic and the general area where you want the graphic to be positioned. In the Editor window, position the cursor where you want the graphic to appear. Drag the source graphic into the Editor window and release the mouse button. Gold automatically copies the source graphic to the Editor document's location.

Editing Graphics

Once you've added a graphic to your page, you can copy it, move it, or delete it.

Copying a Graphic

If you've just entered a graphic in a document and would like to use it more than once, you can copy it and paste as many copies as you like. This is exactly what you'll do when you insert a small graphic to serve as a bullet (see "Using Graphics as Bullets," later in this chapter). Just select the graphic and press Ctrl + C to copy the graphic to the Clipboard (you can also choose Edit/Copy from the menu bar, if you wish). Position the cursor where you want the graphic to appear and press Ctrl + V (or choose Edit/Paste).

Moving a Graphic

If you don't like the graphic's position, you can move it. Just select the graphic and press Ctrl + X, or choose Edit/Cut. Move the cursor to the place in which you would like the graphic to appear and press Ctrl + V, or choose Edit/Paste.

Deleting a Graphic

If you'd like to delete a graphic you've inserted, just select the graphic and press Del.

Positioning and Sizing Graphics

Once you've entered a graphic in your document, you can align it left, center, or right. You can also specify the relationship to the surrounding text and even "wrap" text around a graphic for a cool desktop-publishing effect.

Aligning Graphics

You can align your graphic simply by selecting it and clicking the Left, Center, or Right icons on the toolbar. In Figure 31.3, you see a graphic that's been aligned flush right.

Specifying the Relationship to Surrounding Text

If you would like to position one line of text next to your graphic, you can align it at the top, middle, or bottom of the graphic. By default, text appears

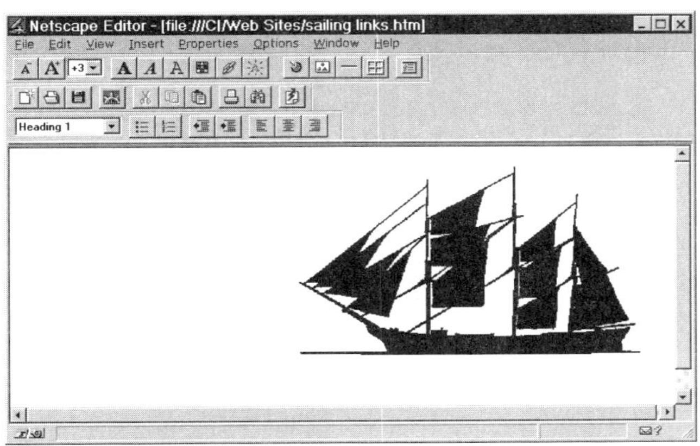

Figure 31.3 Right-aligned graphic

to the right of the graphic, no matter how you've aligned the graphic. Figure 31.4 shows the text positioned at the top of the graphic, while Figure 31.5 shows text aligned at the middle and Figure 31.6 shows text aligned at the bottom.

Note that for the middle and bottom positions, you can choose to position the text so that the text is either aligned with or above a line drawn through the graphic's middle or the graphics's bottom line. (You can't see the difference unless you display the page in the browser.)

To choose an alignment option, click the appropriate icon in the Alignment area of the Image Properties dialog box.

Wrapping Text around a Graphic

If the graphic is positioned next to a paragraph of text, you can wrap the text around it, as shown in Figure 31.7. To wrap text left or right around the graphic, click the appropriate icon in the Alignment area of the Image Properties dialog box.

The text wrapping won't work! You have to switch to the browser window to see the wrapped text. To do so, click View in Browser.

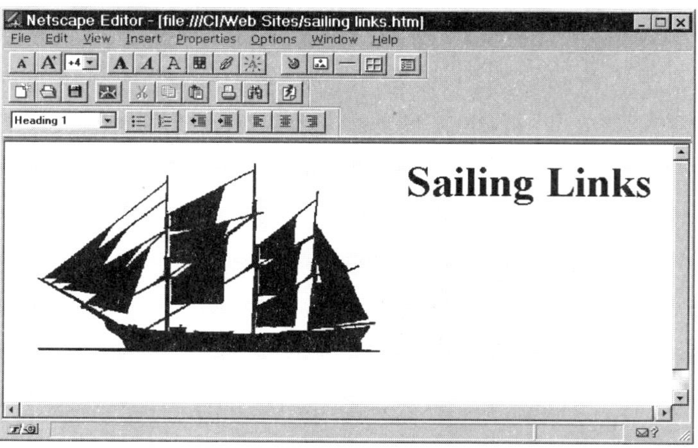

Figure 31.4 Text positioned at top of left-aligned graphic

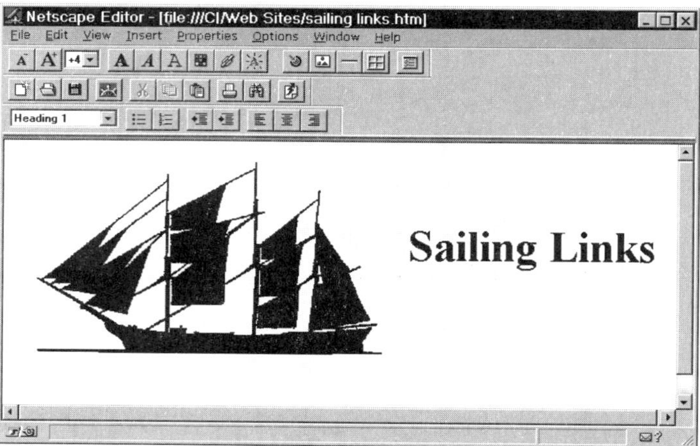

Figure 31.5 Text positioned at middle of left-aligned graphic

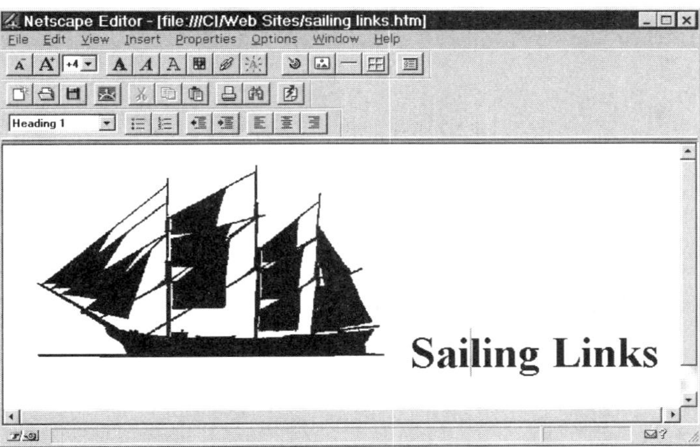

Figure 31.6 Text positioned at bottom of left-aligned graphic

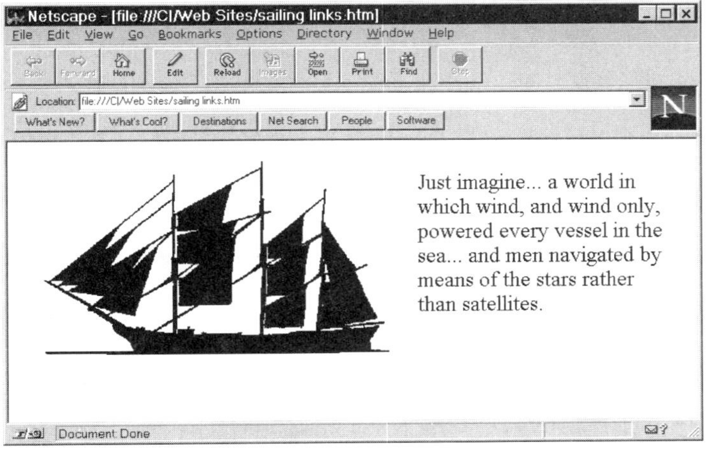

Figure 31.7 Text wrapped around left-aligned graphic

If you want to add some text below the graphic that isn't wrapped, choose Insert/Break Below Images from the menu bar. Then start typing the text. This text won't be included in the wrapped text. In Figure 31.8, note the text "A few of my favorite links" below the graphic; this text is preceded by Break Below Images.

Sizing Your Graphic

By default, Gold uses the graphic's original size, in pixels. However, you can specify a different size, and both the Editor and most browsers that access your page will size the graphic accordingly. To change the size, type a new height and width in the Dimensions area of the Image Properties dialog box, but be sure to preserve the original graphic's aspect ratio (the height divided by the width). Or better yet, skip sizing your graphic entirely.

I changed the size and now it looks terrible! You probably changed the aspect ratio. It's a much better idea to resize the graphic using a graphics program such as Lview Pro. Note

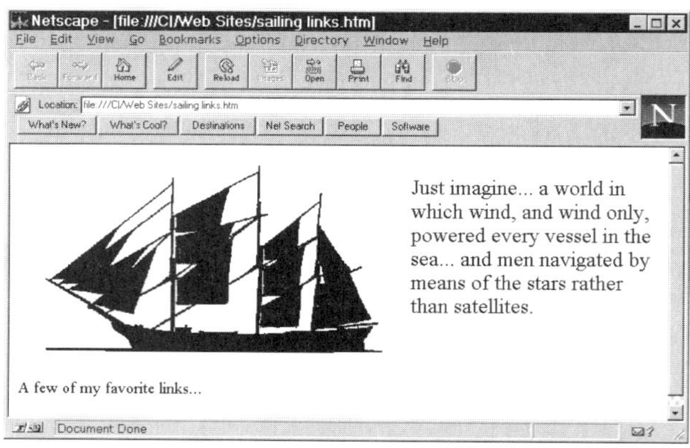

Figure 31.8 The Insert Break Below Images command enables you to stop text wrapping below a graphic

that there's a link to a graphics program in the Images Properties dialog box. You can use this link to open a graphics editor, such as Lview Pro, in which to resize the image correctly.

Adding a Border

If you would like to place a border around your graphic, specify the width in the Solid Border box of the Image Properties page. Try 2 pixels, if you like. Frankly, I think most graphics look better without borders.

Adding Space around the Image

If you don't add any space, the text can be positioned right up against the image, which might not look good. To increase the space, add 1 or 2 pixels to the "Left and right" or the "Top and bottom" boxes, which you'll find in the Space Around Image area of the Image Properties dialog box.

Adding Horizontal Lines

In publishing, a *rule* is a line that's used to separate text areas. You can easily add horizontal rules with Netscape Editor. Too easily, perhaps—it's easy to get carried away. Use horizontal lines like a spice: just a little does it!

Adding a Rule

To add a rule to your document, position the cursor where you want the rule to appear, and click Insert Horizontal Line on the toolbar, or choose Insert/Horizontal Line from the menu bar.

Choosing Rule Options

To change the appearance of the rule, select the rule, click the right mouse button, and choose Horizontal Line Properties. You'll see the Horizontal Line Properties dialog box, shown in Figure 31.9.

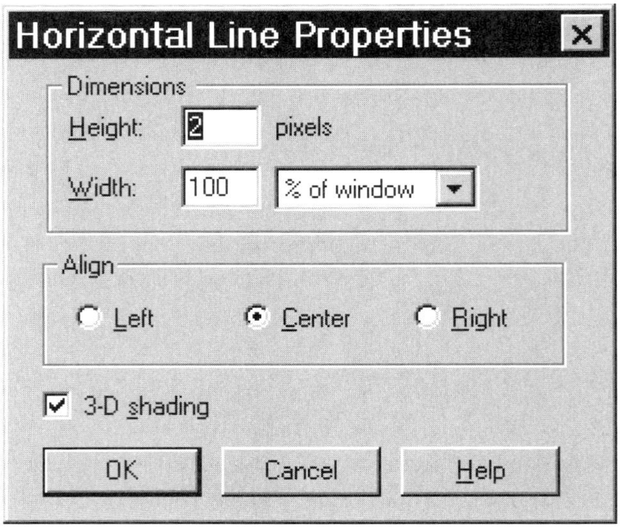

Figure 31.9 Horizontal Line Properties dialog box

In this dialog box, you can choose the following options:

Height — The default line is 2 pixels high. Try changing this number to see the effect of narrower or wider rules.

Width — By default, the line spans 100% of the window. You can specify the exact width in pixels or specify a different window width percentage.

Align — Lines are centered by default. Your page design might work with left or right alignment.

3-D Shading — Selected by default, this option produces a mannered line that calls attention to itself. Try turning it off!

Using a Graphic as a Rule

You can use a graphic as a rule—it's simple. You just add a rule graphic in the same way that you'd add any other graphic. There are lots of places on the Web where you can find graphics to suit every taste, or lack of taste.

Looking for cool rules? You'll find a nice collection at The Clip Art Collection (http://www.acy.digex.net/~infomart/clipart/) and most of them are in the public domain.

Using Graphics as Bullets

The bullets inserted into your document by Netscape Editor's Bullet List command are pretty boring. You've seen them zillions of times around the Net. To spice up your pages, it's better to use small graphics instead of those boring old default bullets. For an example, see the list in Figure 31.10.

Looking for bullets? Look no further than Bullets by Jen (http://ww2.cynernex.net/~jen/webpages/bullets/bullets.html). You'll find hundreds of graphics for every conceivable use. They're free for individual publishing or non-profit use. What will you find? Everything from the ace of spades to the yin-yang symbol.

To create a bulleted list with graphics serving as bullets, type the list in a Normal paragraph format. Press Shift + Enter at the end of each item, unless you would like to separate the items by blank lines. Add the first graphic by positioning the cursor at the beginning of an item and choosing Insert Graphic.

Consider adding some space on the left and right of the graphic so that it doesn't look so crunched-up at the beginning of the line. To add space, double-click the graphic; you'll see the Image Properties dialog box. In the "Space around image" area, try 5 pixels in the "Left and right" box. Click OK to confirm.

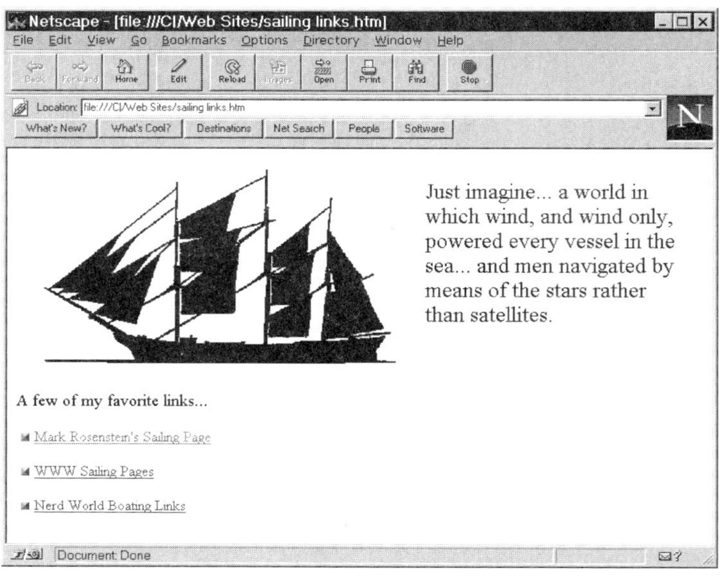

Figure 31.10 Small graphics make nice bullets

After inserting the graphic, you can copy it to the Clipboard and insert it at the beginning of each line.

This graphic has an ugly border around it! To get rid of the border, double-click the graphic so that the Image Properties dialog box appears. In the "Space around image" area, make sure the Solid Border box contains 0, and then click OK.

Making a Graphic a Hyperlink

You can convert any graphic into a hyperlink. To do so, simply select the graphic and click Make Link. You'll see the Link Properties dialog box. Specify the page to which you want to link, and click OK. That's all there is to it!

Can I Create an Imagemap with Netscape Editor?

You can't create one with Editor, but you can easily insert one. An *imagemap* is a graphic that contains multiple URLs. Just where you go when you click depends on precisely where the mouse pointer is positioned. Imagemaps used to be a pain to create, requiring all kinds of programming. Now it's easy to make them, but you'll need additional software to do it. A great program for creating imagemaps is Map This, which is available from the Map This home page (http://galadriel.ecaetc.ohio-state.edu/tc/mt). Map This enables you to open a GIF graphic, define "hot spots" that are associated with specific URLs, and paste the requisite code (automatically generated by the program) into your HTML source. It's really easy, and the results are spectacular.

After you define a graphic as a hyperlink, users won't have any way of knowing that it's a link unless they move the mouse pointer over the graphic. Then, the pointer changes to a hand shape, indicating that the user can click there to jump to a different document. But this may take a bit of explaining, if the picture doesn't say it all.

From Here

- Tables and frames add organization and visual interest to your page. Netscape Gold doesn't work with frames, but you can create tables. Find out how in Chapter 32.
- Jazz up your document with animated GIFs, JavaScript, and other bells and whistles. See Chapter 33.
- Publish your document on the Web! See Chapter 34.

Chapter 32

Creating Tables

Before Gold, creating a table with HTML was a mind-numbing exercise; you had to use table tags that were actually never designed for human use—something like Gold was envisioned from the beginning. Now that Gold is here, you can easily add a table to your Web page.

This chapter fully covers Gold's table capabilities, which are pretty impressive. You'll learn how you can use tables for layout purposes as well as for organizing information. You'll learn how to insert and add text to tables and how to modify a table's structure after you've created it.

For the Time-Challenged

- You can use tables for more than organizing information in a tabular form. They're also fantastic tools for layout purposes.
- Plan your table's layout of rows and columns before starting.
- By default, your table is sized dynamically as you type. You may wish to fix the size for special applications, such as a page design with a thin vertical column of navigation aids.
- You can choose a variety of appearance options for your table, including borders, cell spacing, cell padding, colors, and alignments.
- You can add a caption above or below your table.
- If you need to add rows, columns, or cells after creating your table, it's easy to do so. You can also delete rows, columns, or cells—and even the whole table. To create banners, you can define a cell so that it spans two or more rows or columns

What Are Tables For?

Tables provide a convenient way to organize material (see Figure 32.1). Here, borders make the information easy to follow.

Clever table design provides a means to provide layout control (see Figure 32.2), producing desktop-publishing-quality Web page designs. You can turn the borders off to achieve cool-looking layout effects.

Planning Your Table

Although it's possible to alter the structure of your table after inserting it, you will save time and trouble if you do some planning first. Begin by deciding how many rows and columns your table will have.

Rows are horizontal; they go across the table. *Columns* are vertical. Where a row and a column come together, they form a *cell.* At the top of each column, you can define the cells as *header cells*, if you wish. Header cell

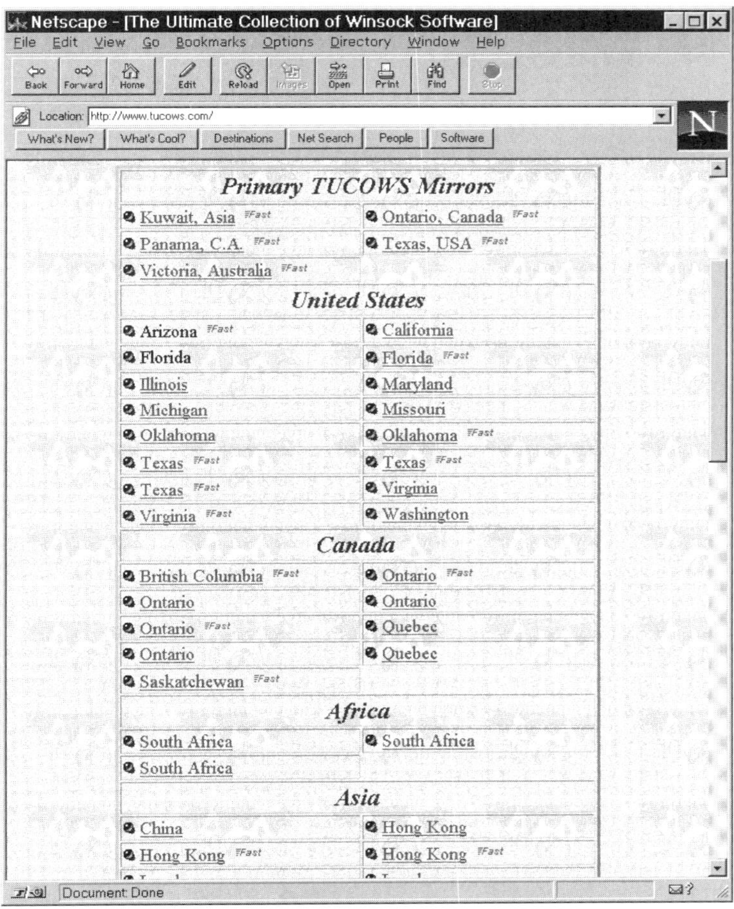

Figure 32.1 Tables can be used to organize material on-screen

text appears in bold. Figure 32.3 shows the basic table layout. Sometimes tables have rows or columns that *span* two or more cells (see Figure 32.4).

Take a few moments now to plan your table. For your first table, don't include row or column spanning—learn the basics first. You'll get to spanning later in this chapter.

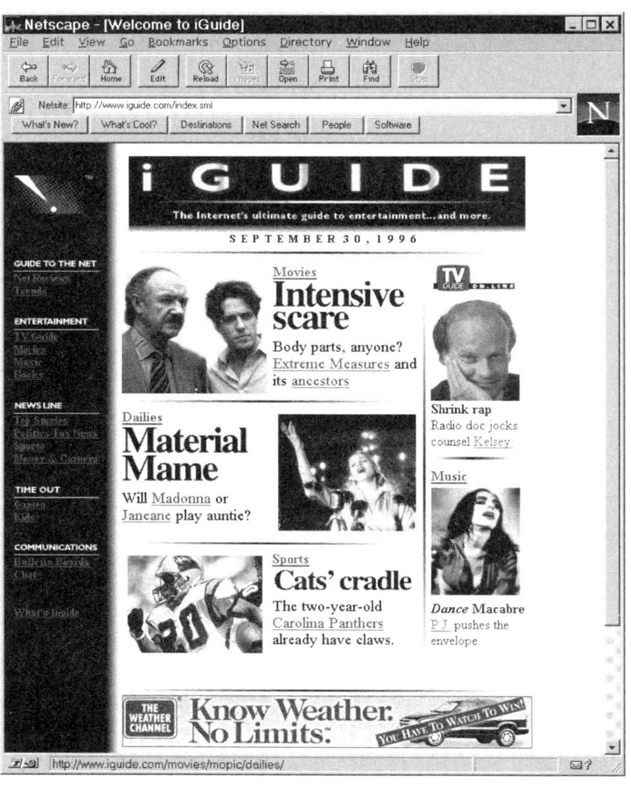

Figure 32.2 Tables can also be used for layout control

Inserting a Table

To create your first table, choose File/New Document/Blank to create a new Editor document. Press Enter a couple of times, and choose Insert/Table/Table from the menu bar. You'll see the New Table Properties dialog box, shown in Figure 32.5.

This dialog box has lots of options, but the only ones you should worry about now are the number of rows and columns you want. Try creating a table with three rows and columns. Type 3 in the Number of Rows box and in the Number of Columns box, and click OK.

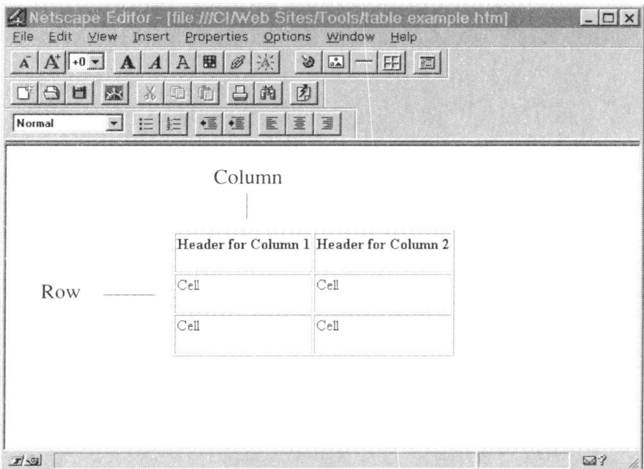

Figure 32.3 A table consists of rows, columns, and cells

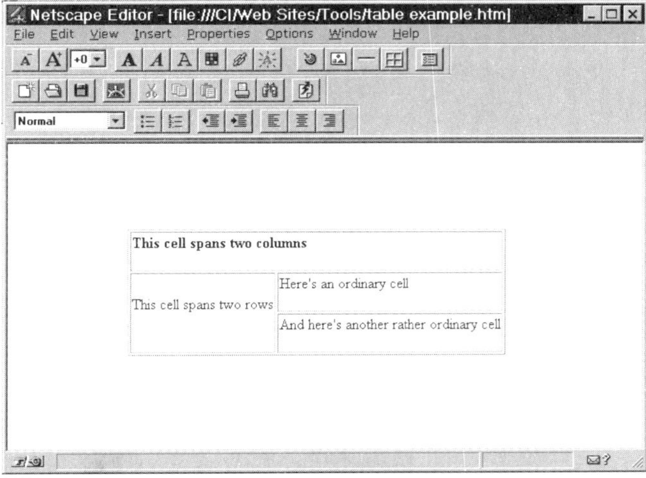

Figure 32.4 Cells can span rows or columns

Figure 32.5 New Table Properties dialog box

The table doesn't look like much after you insert it (see Figure 32.6). That's because you haven't added any text yet.

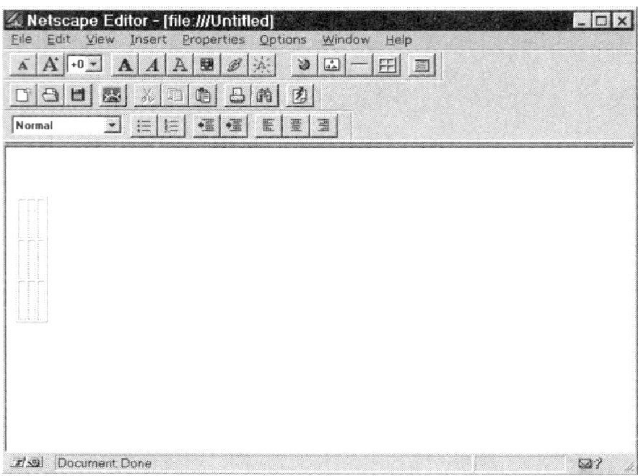

Figure 32.6 Table before adding any text

Adding Text to a Table

Now try adding some text to your table. To select a cell, just click in it. Figure 32.7 shows a table with some text added.

Typing in a table is a little disconcerting, since Netscape Editor expands the cell dynamically to accommodate your typing. By default, the program sizes the cells to fit the longest line you type, except that the whole table won't expand beyond 100% of the window width.

You can press Enter and Shift + Enter within cells to break lines. In Figure 32.7, Shift + Enter was used to create a line break after "Off-season rates" and "Rates in the high season."

I tried pressing Tab and Shift + Tab to move from cell to cell, but it didn't work! If you're used to moving from cell to cell in a spreadsheet by pressing these keys, you need to unlearn this habit. In Netscape Editor, you press Tab to indent text, and Shift + Tab to unindent. If you accidentally indented some text, just select the cell and press Shift + Tab.

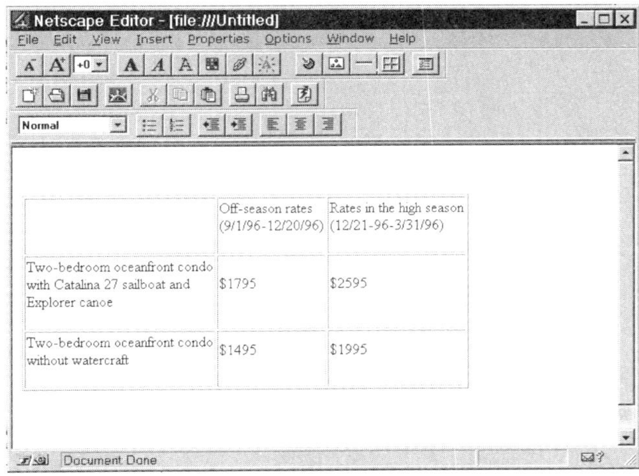

Figure 32.7 Table with text added

Changing Your Table's Look

Now that you've created your table, you can take advantage of commands that change your table's appearance. For example, you can turn off table borders. Figure 32.8 shows how much more attractive the example table looks with borders turned off.

You can choose appearance options for the entire table, for individual rows, or for individual cells. The following sections explain these options.

Appearance Options for the Entire Table

To change appearance options for the entire table, place the cursor within the table, and choose Properties/Table and click the Table tab. You'll see the Table Properties dialog box, shown in Figure 32.9.

You can change the following:

- **Borders** Type the width of the table border in pixels. To remove borders, type 0.

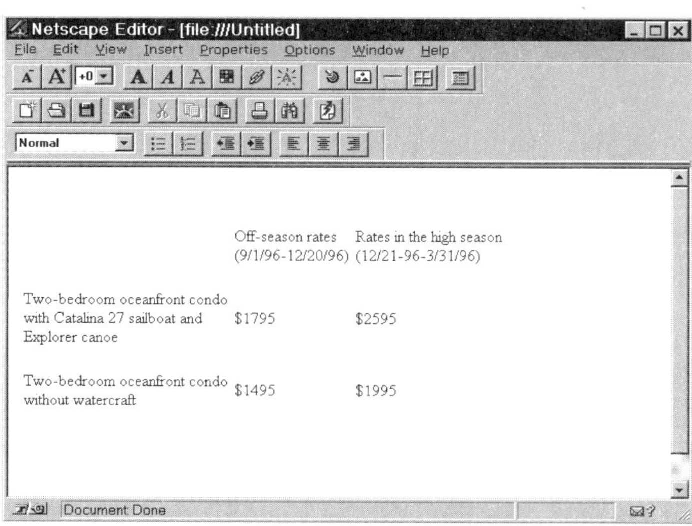

Figure 32.8 Table with no borders

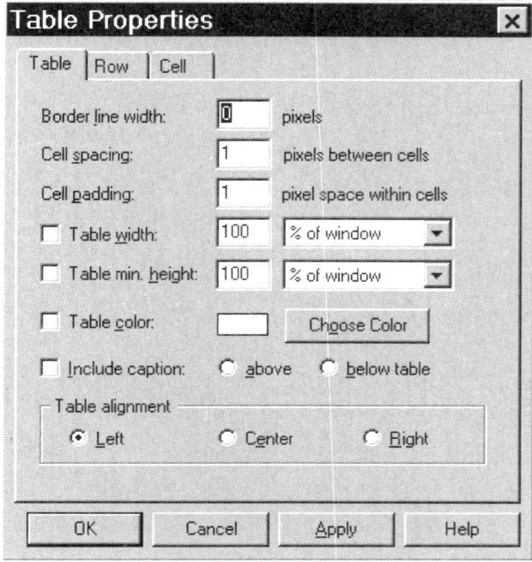

Figure 32.9 Table Properties dialog box

- **Cell Spacing** This controls the amount of white space that is inserted between cell boundaries.
- **Cell Padding** This controls the amount of white space that is inserted within the cell, between the text and the cell boundary.
- **Table Color** You can choose a background color for the whole table. *Note:* You can also choose colors for rows and individual cells. To choose a color, click the Table Color check box and choose a color by clicking the Choose Color button.
- **Table Alignment** Here, you choose a default text alignment for the whole table (left, center, or right).

To see what these options do, try playing around with them and clicking Apply. This leaves the dialog box open so you can experiment more, but you see the changes in the table. (If you can't see the table, adjust the location of the Table Properties dialog box so that you can.)

In addition to the formatting options in the Table Properties dialog box, you can format the text with font sizes, styles (such as bold or italic), and font colors. For more information on these options, see Chapter 28.

To choose formatting options for the whole table, choose Edit/Select Table from the menu bar. This selects every cell. Now you can choose alignment, font, font size, and style options that will affect the whole table.

Adding a Caption

To add a caption to your table, click Include Caption in theTable Properties dialog box, and click Above or Below table. After you click OK, you'll find that Netscape Editor has created a format for a table caption; just click above or below the table and start typing. Figure 32.10 shows the example table with a caption added. The caption is centered by default. The figure shows the caption's appearance with increased font size and bold added.

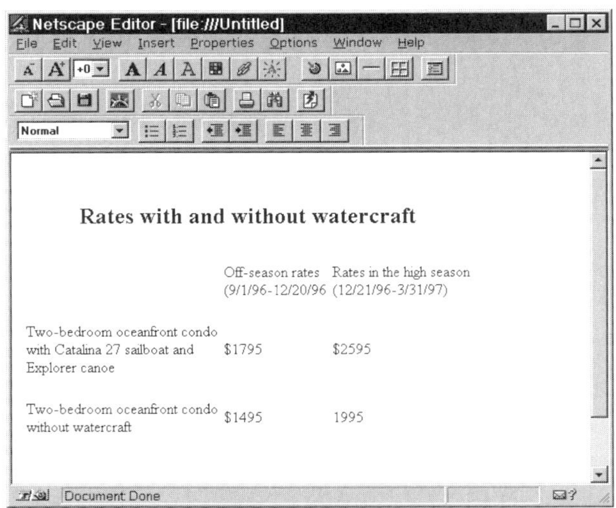

Figure 32.10 Table with caption added

Choosing Row Options

To choose row appearance options, position the cursor within one of your table's rows, choose Properties/Table, and click the Row tab. You'll see the Row page, shown in Figure 32.11. Here, you can choose the following:

- **Horizontal Text Alignment** This option enables you to choose text alignment for each cell in the row. If you choose an option other than Default, your choice here overrides the default alignment. You can choose Left, Center, or Right.
- **Vertical Text Alignment** This option enables you to position the text vertically within each cell in the row. By default, text is positioned according to the browser's default settings You can also choose Top, Center, Bottom, or Baselines (text is aligned so that the baselines of text are even).

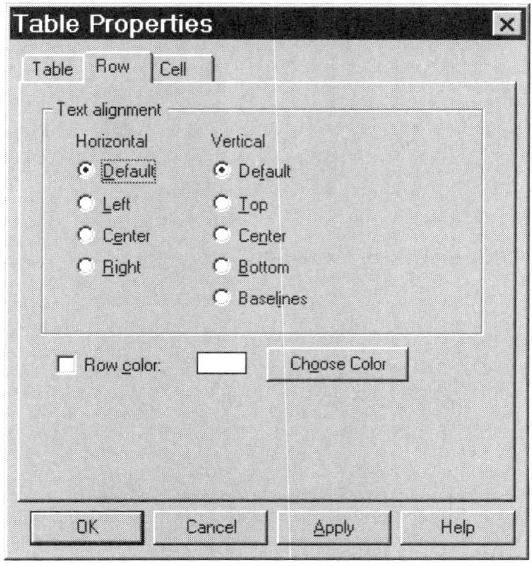

Figure 32.11 You choose row appearance options here

- **Row Color** This color choice affects the whole row. To choose a color, click the Color checkbox and choose a color by clicking the Choose Color button.

Choosing Cell Options

To choose cell appearance options, position the cursor within one of your table's cells, choose Properties/Table, and click the Cell tab. You'll see the Cell page, shown in Figure 32.12. Here, you can choose the following:

- **Horizontal Text Alignment** This option enables you to choose an alignment option for the current cell only. If you choose an option other than Default, your choice here overrides the default alignment. It also overrides any choice you might have made for the row in which the cell is positioned. You can choose Left, Center, or Right.
- **Vertical Text Alignment** This option enables you to choose vertical alignment options for the current cell only. By default, text is positioned according to the browser's default settings. If you choose an option other than Default, you override the row alignment setting.

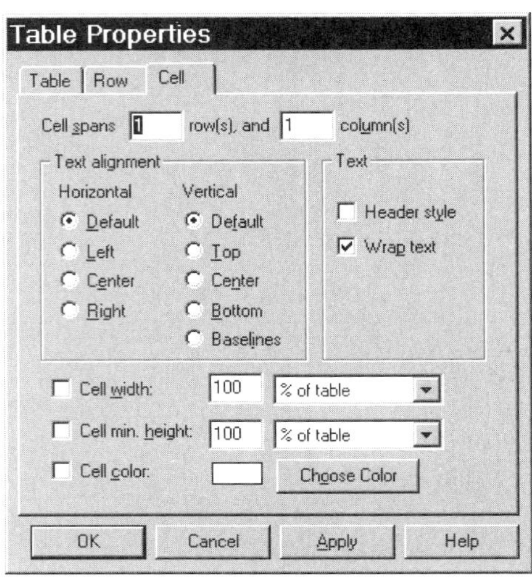

Figure 32.12 Cell appearances page of Table Properties dialog box

You can also choose Top, Center, Bottom, or Baselines (text is aligned so that the baselines of text are even).

- **Text** To define a cell as a header cell (with bold, centered type), click Header Style. By default, text is wrapped within cells—which is good, since people might display your table using a narrow window. Leave this setting as it is.
- **Cell Color** This color choice affects only the current cell. To choose a color, click the Color checkbox and choose a color by clicking the Choose Color button.

Figure 32.13 shows the example table after choosing a number of table, row, and cell appearance options, including row and cell colors and vertical and horizontal alignment options. The two cells in the top row are formatted with the Header Cell option.

Note that the table in 32.13 actually has nine cells. However, the blank cell doesn't show up because borders are turned off and it has no color. This cell would show up, though, if

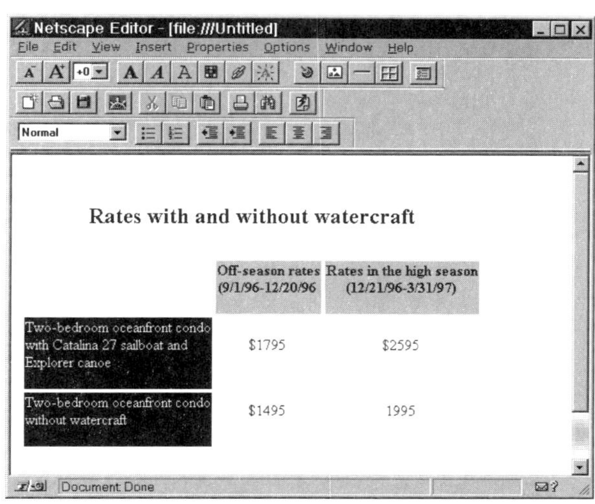

Figure 32.13 Table after choosing appearance options

you used borders—in which case you'd need to get rid of it. To delete an unwanted cell, position the cursor in the cell and choose Edit/Delete/Table Cell.

Sizing Your Table

By default, Netscape Editor dynamically sizes your table. For most purposes, that's fine. When people view your table with a browser, the browser will also dynamically size it, adjusting the table and cell width according to the window width that the user has chosen. With the default sizing setting, you'll know that all portions of your table will remain visible, although it might look funny if somebody chooses a ridiculously narrow window width.

But you may wish to specify the exact width of your table or of individual cells within it. For example, you can set the width of a column by specifying a fixed width for all the cells in the column. In Figure 32.14, for example, there's a very simple table—it only has one row and two columns—and the

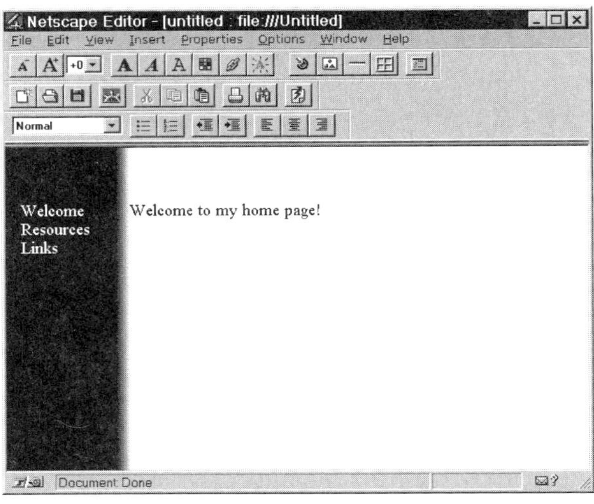

Figure 32.14

Creating a Page with a Vertical Row of Navigation Buttons

The secret to creating a page such as the one shown in Figure 32.14 is to use a background graphic like the one shown in Figure 32.15—very long and thin! You can easily make such a graphic using any good graphics program. Cool, huh?

left column is sized so that its contents fit within the dark part of the background graphic.

You can control the size of your table in the following ways:

- **Table Properties** In the Table page of the Table Properties dialog box, you can choose a table width or a minimum table height. You can specify the width or minimum height in a percentage of the window or in pixels.
- **Cell Properties** In the Cell page of the Table Properties dialog box, you can choose a cell width and a minimum cell height. You can specify these in a percentage of the table width or in pixels.

Changing the Table Structure

Need more columns or rows? You can insert them. Got some extras? You can delete them. And as this section shows, you can also span columns or rows.

Figure 32.15

Inserting Rows, Columns, and Cells

To insert a row into your table, position the cursor one row above where you want the row to appear (you must position it somewhere within the table) and choose Insert/Table Row. The new row will appear below the cell in which you positioned the cursor.

To insert a column into your table, position the cursor one cell to the left of where you want the new column to appear and choose Insert/Table Column. The new column will appear to the right of the cell in which you positioned the cursor.

You can insert cells in any row, even though the number of cells in that row exceeds those of other rows. To insert a cell, position the cursor one cell to the left of where you want the new cell to appear, and choose Insert/Table Cell. The new cell will appear to the right of the cell in which you positioned the cursor.

Deleting Rows, Columns, and Cells

You can delete rows, columns, or cells. Just position the cursor in the cell you want to eliminate and choose Edit/Delete/Table. From the pop-up menu, choose Row, Column, or Cell.

Deleting the Whole Table

If your table didn't work out, you can delete the whole table. Just position the cursor somewhere within it, and choose Edit/Delete/Table/Table.

Spanning Rows and Columns

To span a row or column, you format a cell so that it spans a specified number of rows or columns (for an example, see Figure 32.16). It's simple to format a cell so that it spans columns, but doing so will push the other cells in the row or column out of the way—you'll have to delete them using the Edit/Table/Delete Cell command.

To format a cell to span two or more rows or columns, position the cursor in the cell that you want to do the spanning, and choose Properties/Table. Click the Cell tab, if necessary, and type a number greater than 1 in the "Cell spans X rows" or "Cell spans X columns" box. Click Apply to make sure this makes sense; if not, change the settings. Click OK to confirm.

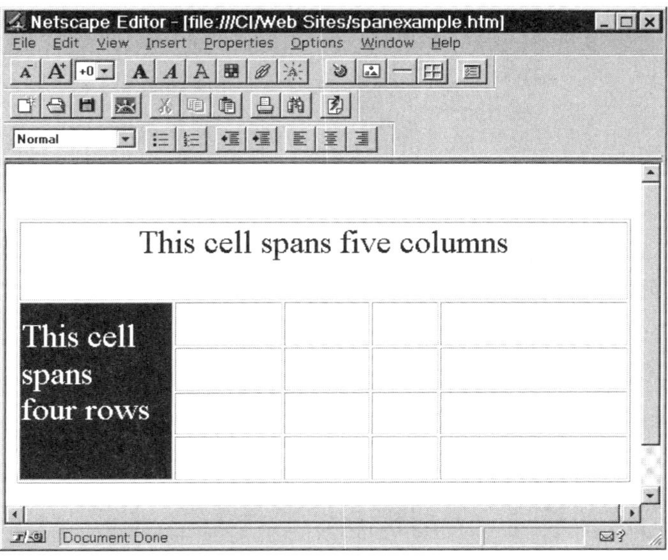

Figure 32.16 Table with cells spanning multiple rows and columns

Awesome Table Tricks

Experienced Web designers use tables to pull off all kinds of things that aren't possible with ordinary HTML—and you can do them, too.

Ever wanted to place your document's title to the *left* of a graphic? You can't do it with ordinary HTML, but you sure can with a simple two-cell, no-border table. Get it? Take a look at Figure 32.17.

Publishing an on-line newsletter? You may want to include a *banner*, which indicates the date and place of publication. Ideally, this would be a single line of text that mixes alignment (flush left and flush right). You can't do that with ordinary HTML, but you can do it with a one-row, two-column table, as shown in Figure 32.18.

See why Web designers love tables?

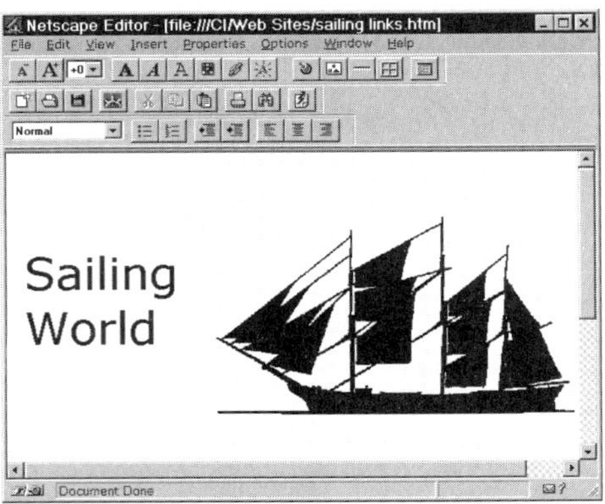

Figure 32.17 This document's title and graphic are positioned within a two-column table with no borders

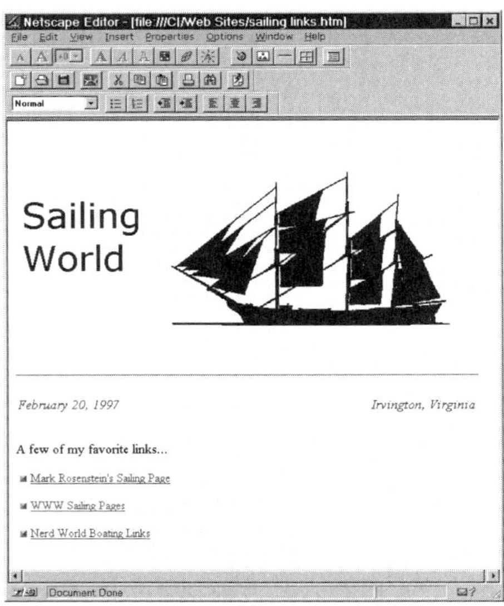

Figure 32.18 This newsletter's banner was created with a one-row, two-column table

From Here

- You're just about done with Gold! In the next chapter, "Bells and Whistles," you'll learn how to add links to multimedia and other live content, including Java applets.
- Chapter 34, "Publishing Your Page," shows you how to publish your page using Gold's fantastic one-button publishing.

Chapter 33

Bells and Whistles

If you're like most aspiring Webmasters, you want your page to come alive—specifically, with live action (such as animations and movies), sounds, and Java programs. This chapter shows you how to incorporate these "bells and whistles" (cool, advanced features) into your pages.

This chapter doesn't try to teach you how to create animated GIFs, record sounds, digitize movies, or write JavaScript or Java programs. Those are subjects that would require a book in themselves (or several!). Instead, it focuses on incorporating these features into your pages. As you'll discover, you'll find thousands of animated GIFs, sounds, movies, JavaScript scripts, and Java applets available on the Web, many of

For the Time-Challenged

- Even if you're not a whiz at graphics, sound recording, or programming, you can find active content all over the Web and incorporate this content into your document.
- You can easily add animated GIFs to your Web documents. Just copy one from a site that makes these GIF files freely available and add it to your document just like you'd add any other GIF.
- To make a sound or movie file accessible from your document, you simply make a hyperlink to the sound or movie file, just like those you would create to link to a document. There's a neat and easy trick you can do that makes a sound play in the background automatically when the user opens your document.
- JavaScript is a programming language that can make things happen on a Web page, such as displaying a clock, calendar, or scrolling banner. Without learning any JavaScript, you can copy and paste JavaScript code snippets into your documents, as this chapter explains.

which are free for the downloading. Simply by downloading these files and incorporating them into your pages following this chapter's instructions, you'll look like you're an absolute whiz at multimedia production!

Adding Animated GIFs

A quick 'n' easy way to add impressive animation to your site is to download and insert an *animated GIF.* In brief, an animated GIF is a graphic that contains several variants on a picture, together with information about the order in which they are to be displayed and the timing between frames. The leading browsers can display animated GIFs without any trouble, and they're equally easy to add to your document—you just add them as if they were any other graphic!

You'll find many animated GIFs on the Net, but bear in mind that not all are free for unrestricted use. Many of the artists who make animated GIFs available state that they want you to ask permission via e-mail, provide a link back to their site, or pay a modest fee.

To add an animated GIF to your page, simply insert the graphic into your document as you would an ordinary GIF or JPEG graphic: Click Insert Image on the toolbar, or choose Insert/Image from the menus. That's all there is to it!

A great place to see what people are doing with animated GIFs is the 1st Internet Gallery of GIF Animation, located at

http://www.r4eiworld.com/royale/galframe.htm

Please note: These aren't for downloading or reuse without permission.

For the latest free animated GIFs on the Web, see Yahoo's animated GIFs page (Computers and Internet:Graphics:Computer Animation:Animated GIFs:Collections), which you can access from Yahoo's home page (http://www.yahoo.com). One of the linked sites is the GIF Animation Site (http://www.cswnet.com/~ozarksof/), shown in Figure 33.1. You'll find dozens of animated GIFs on Debby's Animated GIFs page, located at

http://www.hooked.net/~jpadilla/animate.htm

For information on creating GIF animations, check out Scot Hacker's GIF 89a: Creating Dynamic Web Imagery and Animations Without Fancy Tools (http://www.zdnet.com/aci/articles/gif89a.html).

Adding a Link to a Sound or Movie

Adding a sound or movie file to your page is as easy as adding a hyperlink—in fact, you add it in exactly the same way!

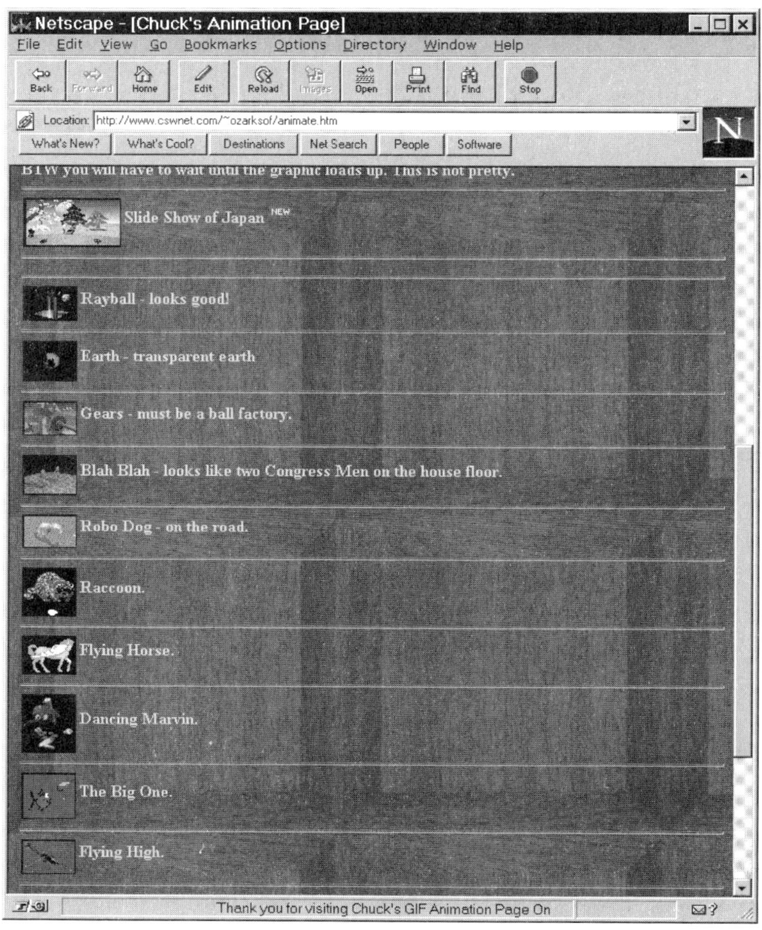

Figure 33.1 The GIF Animation Site has lots of cool animated icons.

When you're adding a link to a sound or movie, it's good manners to tell your users how large the file is (in K, such as 564K or 1024K). Some users have very slow connections, so they might want to skip the file if it's too large. By the same token, they're more likely to click the link if they know the file is fairly small (200K or less).

If you've obtained a sound or movie file and want to add it to your page, do the following:

1. Place the sound or movie file in the same directory as your Web page.
2. Open your Web page in Netscape Editor.
3. Select the text or graphic that you would like to serve as the linked source visible in your Web page.
4. Click Make Link, or choose Insert/Link from the menu bar, or just click Ctrl + L.
5. Click the Browse File button, and locate the sound or movie you want to add.
6. In the Files of Type box, choose the type of file you want to add. (For the types of sound and movie files you can use, see the sidebar.)
7. Select the sound or movie you want to use, and click Open.
8. Click OK.

For tons of sounds you can download and add to your site, see Yahoo's Sound Archives page (Computers and Internet:Multimedia:Sound:Archives), accessible from http://www.yahoo.com.

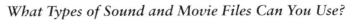

What Types of Sound and Movie Files Can You Use?

You can add the following sound and movies files to your Netscape Editor documents: QuickTime for Windows movies (*.mov files), Sun/NeXT sounds (*.au files), Silicon Graphics/Apple sounds (*.aiff files), Windows WAV sounds (*.wav files), MIDI music files (*.mid and *.midi files), and Video for Windows (*.avi files).

Playing a Sound in the Background

Here's a cool trick that you'll enjoy—and so will the people accessing your page. You can use the HTML <EMBED> tag to place a sound in the background of your document. It will begin playing automatically when your page opens. You can add a Windows WAV sound (*.wav), Sun/NeXT sound (*.au), or a Silicon Graphics/Apple sound (*.aiff).

This tag requires a browser that recognizes the <EMBED> tag. Not all do, including Netscape 1.0! Also, some of the advanced functions require a browser equipped with a sound-playing plug-in or helper program. Netscape Navigator 3.0 and Microsoft Internet Explorer 3.0 can handle the <EMBED> tag just fine.

To play a sound in the background, do the following:

1. Copy the sound file to the directory or folder containing your Web page. Make a note of your sound file's exact name, such as hello.wav.
2. Click in an empty area of the page, near the top.
3. From the menu bar, choose Insert/Tag.
4. In the HTML Tag dialog box, type the following carefully, but substitute your sound's file name in place of the example (hello.wav):

   <EMBED SRC="hello.wav" autostart = true hidden = true>

   If you would like the sound to loop endlessly, add a loop = true statement, like this:

   <EMBED SRC="hello.wav" autostart = true hidden = true loop = true>
5. Click OK to insert the tag.

Adding JavaScript to Your Page

JavaScript is a Netscape-developed *scripting language* that enables Web authors to make things happen on their pages. JavaScript resembles HTML in that you type various commands, which aren't visible to the person reading the page. However, JavaScript is a true programming language, unlike HTML. JavaScript enables an amateur programmer to create simple programs, such as an on-screen clock that displays the current date and time, a scrolling banner, or a calendar. (Java, in contrast, is a professional programmer's language that requires considerable expertise to learn.)

It's beyond the scope of this book to teach JavaScript, but it's easy to learn how to copy snippets of JavaScript code and paste them into your pages! (A *snippet* is a mini-program that does something, such as displaying an on-screen banner.)

Finding and Selecting a Snippet

If you find a page that has a JavaScript snippet that's been made available for downloading, choose View/Document Source (or, if you're viewing a framed document, select the frame and choose View Frame) to display the document in your default source viewer. (If you haven't selected a source viewer, choose Options/General Preferences, click the Apps tab, and use the Browse button next to the View Source box.)

You'll see that confusing HTML code in your source viewer, as shown in Figure 33.2. What you're looking for is everything between the <SCRIPT language = "JavaScript"> and closing </SCRIPT> tags. Select all of this text, including the <SCRIPT> and </SCRIPT> tags, and copy this text to the clipboard by pressing Ctrl + C.

Inserting the Code into your Gold Document

To insert the code into your Netscape Editor document, choose View/Edit Document Source. Go through your HTML code until you find the place where you want the applet's product (such as a clock or calendar) to appear. Press Ctrl + V to paste the code from the Clipboard. Then choose File/Save and click the close box to close this document.

When you return to Netscape Editor, you'll be asked whether you want to save the document. Choose Yes.

Testing the Script

To see whether your script is working right, click View in Browser.

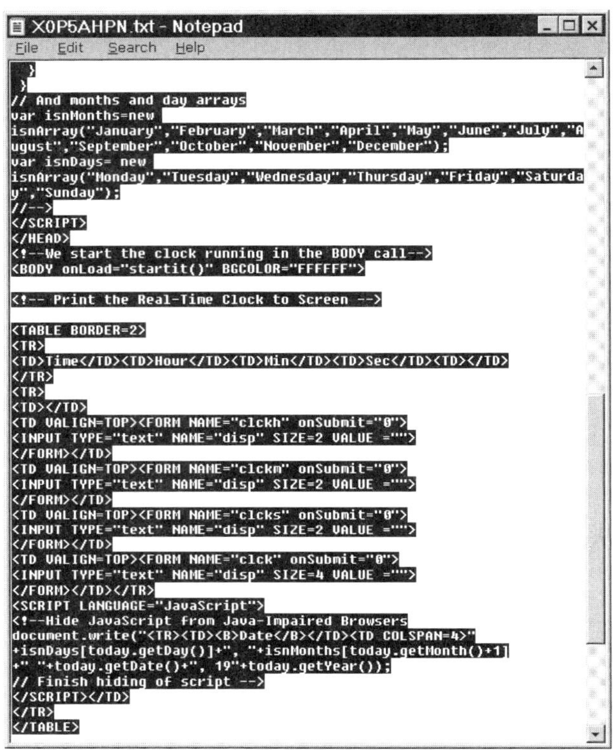

XOP5AHPN.txt - Notepad

File Edit Search Help

```
  }
 }
// And months and day arrays
var isnMonths=new
isnArray("January","February","March","April","May","June","July","A
ugust","September","October","November","December");
var isnDays= new
isnArray("Monday","Tuesday","Wednesday","Thursday","Friday","Saturda
y","Sunday");
//-->
</SCRIPT>
</HEAD>
<!--We start the clock running in the BODY call-->
<BODY onLoad="startit()" BGCOLOR="FFFFFF">

<!-- Print the Real-Time Clock to Screen -->

<TABLE BORDER=2>
<TR>
<TD>Time</TD><TD>Hour</TD><TD>Min</TD><TD>Sec</TD><TD></TD>
</TR>
<TR>
<TD></TD>
<TD VALIGN=TOP><FORM NAME="clckh" onSubmit="0">
<INPUT TYPE="text" NAME="disp" SIZE=2 VALUE ="">
</FORM></TD>
<TD VALIGN=TOP><FORM NAME="clckm" onSubmit="0">
<INPUT TYPE="text" NAME="disp" SIZE=2 VALUE ="">
</FORM></TD>
<TD VALIGN=TOP><FORM NAME="clcks" onSubmit="0">
<INPUT TYPE="text" NAME="disp" SIZE=2 VALUE ="">
</FORM></TD>
<TD VALIGN=TOP><FORM NAME="clck" onSubmit="0">
<INPUT TYPE="text" NAME="disp" SIZE=4 VALUE ="">
</FORM></TD></TR>
<SCRIPT LANGUAGE="JavaScript">
<!--Hide JavaScript from Java-Impaired Browsers
document.write("<TR><TD><B>Date</B></TD><TD COLSPAN=4>"
+isnDays[today.getDay()]+", "+isnMonths[today.getMonth()+1]
+" "+today.getDate()+", 19"+today.getYear());
// Finish hiding of script -->
</SCRIPT></TD>
</TR>
</TABLE>
```

Figure 33.2 Selecting a snippet of code in the source viewer

It doesn't work! If you see an error box, something must have gone wrong in the cutting and pasting. From Netscape Editor, redisplay the source, delete the JavaScript, and resave your document. Then repeat the whole process, making sure that you select the original script correctly.

A fantastic place to find JavaScript snippets is JavaScript Planet (http://www.geocities.com/SiliconValley/7116/), shown in Figure 33.3.

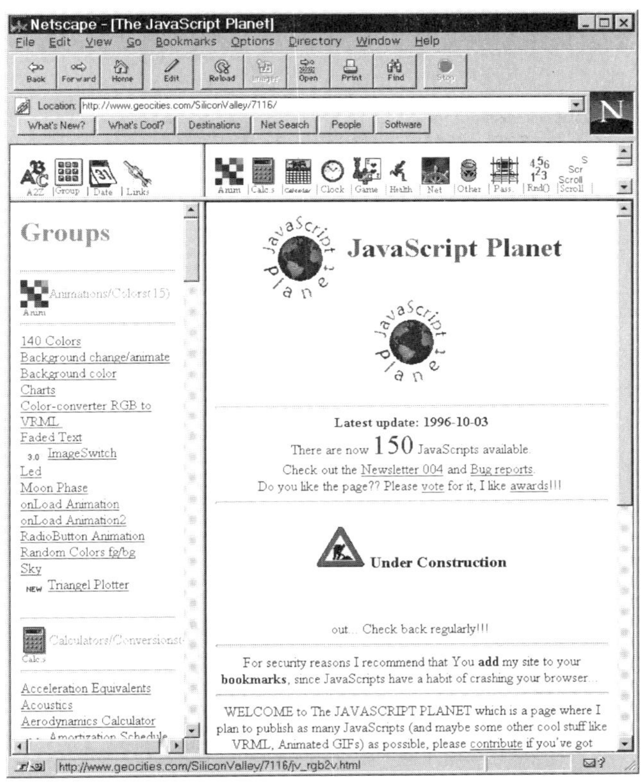

Figure 33.3 JavaScript Planet has lots of JavaScript you can borrow

From Here

- There's only one place to go from here, as far as Netscape Editor is concerned: Chapter 34, which shows you how to make your documents available to others on the Web.

Chapter 34

Publishing Your Page

Now that your page is finished, it's time to publish it! This means that you need to place your page on a computer that's running a Web server, a program that knows how to make your page available to others on the Web. You need to understand a few simple concepts, get some information, and configure Gold to do the job. After that, publishing is easy!

Introducing Web Servers

To make your Web page available so that others can access it, you must place your page on a computer that's running a web server. A *web server* is a program that intercepts incoming requests for Web documents and doles them out over the Internet.

For the Time-Challenged

- A *Web server* is a program that knows how to make your Web page available to the Internet. To run a Web server, a computer requires a permanent connection to the Internet, which is an expensive proposition. For this reason, you'll probably want to publish your page using Web space provided by your Internet service provider (ISP).
- To get your page to your ISP, you need to transfer it using the File Transfer Protocol (FTP). You could use an FTP program to do this, but Netscape Gold makes it much easier. Gold automatically transfers all of the images in your document. With an FTP program, you'd have to transfer these files manually.
- Once you've configured the Publish page of Editor's Preferences dialog box, publishing your pages is as easy as clicking the Publish button!

Can you set up your own Web server? Only if you have a permanent Internet connection and a permanent Internet address. Most people (including your author) connect to the Internet by means of a modem, telephone line, and a friendly local Internet service provider (ISP). In most cases, you don't get a permanent connection or address with this service. You could arrange for a permanent connection and address, but it would cost you some serious money: as much as $200 per month for a *leased line*, a specially conditioned telephone line that's connected 24 hours per day.

For most people, shelling out the money for a permanent Internet connection just isn't worth it. Besides, most Internet service providers give you some free space on their computers to place your Web page, and their Web server makes your page available to the rest of the world. Check with your ISP to find out whether Web publishing services are available and whether they're included with your basic subscription fee.

The only rub with publishing via your ISP is that you need to copy your Web page and images to your ISP's computer. That's where FTP, the File Transfer Protocol, comes in.

Introducing FTP

The File Transfer Protocol enables Internet users to copy files between dissimilar computers. If you've created your Web pages on a Windows 95 system, you can copy your pages—and all the images they contain—to a UNIX or Macintosh system, thanks to FTP.

Before Netscape Gold came along, the only way you could transfer your Web pages to your ISP's computer was to use an FTP program. There are several good Windows FTP programs that make transferring files to another computer on the Internet as easy as transferring files between folders on your computer. Still, it's a tedious job. You must manually make sure that you're copying all the images associated with each page. If you forget just one of them, your page will show a placeholder instead of a graphic, and the page will look unprofessional.

That's where Netscape Gold comes in. One of the coolest of Gold's many excellent features is one-button publishing. Once you've set this up, as explained in the next section, you can send your completed page to an FTP server just by clicking one button, the Publish button.

Setting Up One-Button Publishing

Most people publish their Web pages by sending their pages (and associated images) to an Internet service provider via FTP. If you can publish your pages this way, you can take advantage of Netscape Gold's one-button publishing. To do so, you must first obtain information from your Internet service provider, as explained in the following section. Then you type this information into the Publish page of Editor Preferences. The following sections detail these procedures.

Obtaining FTP Information

To get started with one-button publishing, obtain the following information from your Internet service provider:

- The exact address of the location where you are supposed to store your Web pages and graphic images. This address should be phrased as a URL, such as ftp://www.fictititious.com/~barney/. Be *sure* to tell your ISP that you need this address phrased as a URL.
- The exact Web address of pages in your directory—that is, the address that people will use to access your pages. This address should be a URL, such as http://www.fictitious.com/~barney/.
- The name you should give your home page, or any other page that you want to be displayed automatically when users access your directory (this will probably be *default.html* or *index.html*).

- Your *user name* or *login name* for FTP access. This might be the same as your login name for e-mail, but it might differ.
- Your *password* for FTP access. This might be the same as your e-mail password, but it might differ.
- Any file name restrictions that your ISP might have.

Make sure all your file names conform to these basic restrictions. In general, don't use more than eight characters (not including the extension .htm or .html) to name your files and don't include spaces. Also, use lowercase letters for all your file names. URLs are case-sensitive. If you include capital letters, users may have to remember to type capital letters to retrieve your files.

Using the Publish Page of Editor Preferences

Once you've gotten the information you need from your Internet service provider, you're ready to give this information to Netscape Gold. Choose Options/Editor Preferences, and click the Publish tab. You'll see the Publish page of the Editor Preferences dialog box, shown in Figure 34.1.

In the Links and Images area, you'll see a couple of options concerning how Gold deals with the links included in your document as well as the images you've included:

- **Maintain links** By default, Gold automatically adjusts the hyperlinks in your document so that they will work from the document's new location. You should keep this option selected.
- **Keep images with documents** By default, Gold automatically uploads the images you've added to your document. You should keep this option selected.

To finish filling out this dialog box, do the following:

1. In the Publish To box, type the exact URL you were given for uploading your pages via FTP.
2. In the Browse To box, type the exact URL you were given for people to access your page.
3. In the User Name box, type your user or login name.

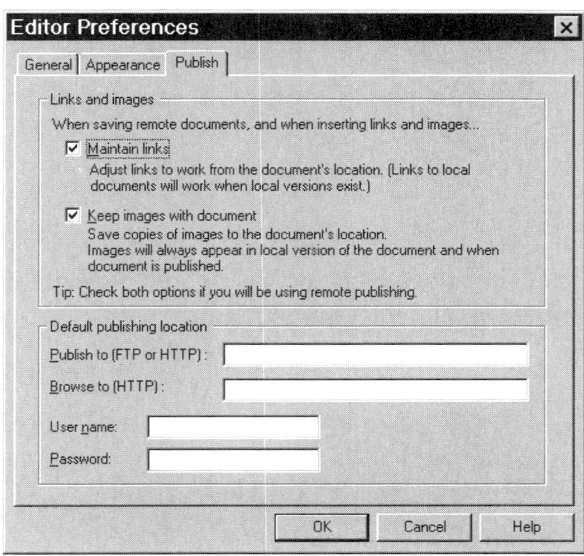

Figure 34.1 Provide your FTP information in this dialog box

4. In the Password box, type the password you were given for FTP access. Note that you can leave this box blank if you wish, and supply your password manually each time you publish. You should leave the box blank if your computer is used by other people.
5. Check what you've typed carefully! Remember that URLs are case-sensitive and you can't place any spaces within them.
6. When you're done, click OK.

Uploading Your Page to the Server

Once you've filled in the Publish page of the Editor Preferences dialog box, you can publish your Web documents!

To publish your page, do the following:

1. Click the Publish button, or choose File/Publish. You'll see the Publish Files dialog box, shown in Figure 34.2. This dialog box automatically shows the publishing location, user name, and password that you typed in the Editor Preferences dialog box (Publish page). In addition, it lists all the images you've included in your document.
2. In the Include Files area, choose whether you want to upload only the images in the document (the default option) or all the files in the current folder. The default option is fine for your first upload. For more information on the other option, see the next section.
3. In the Save Password box, uncheck this box if your computer is used by others. You'll have to supply your password manually every time you publish, but this will prevent someone from uploading something to your directory without your knowledge.
4. Just click OK to start uploading your files!

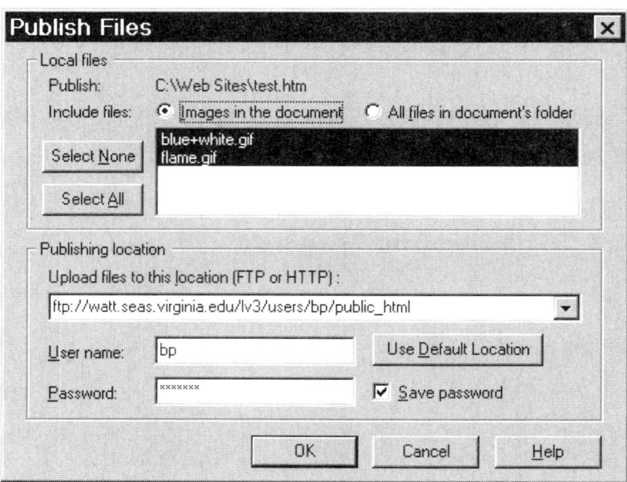

Figure 34.2 This dialog box enables you to publish your Web page

It didn't work! Problems, huh? Check the error message you're getting. Chances are you didn't type the FTP address, password, or user name correctly. Call your ISP and verify these.

I just uploaded my page, but then I found a mistake! Don't worry, you can correct it. Just make the correction with Gold and publish the page again. Your action will overwrite the old copy.

Publishing a Web Presentation

If you created a Web presentation that includes several linked HTML files, you can take advantage of special features of the Publish Files dialog box that enable you to upload the entire presentation easily.

To publish a Web presentation:

1. Click the Publish button, or choose File/Publish. You'll see the Publish Files dialog box, shown in Figure 34.2.
2. In the Include Files area, click "All files in document's folder." You'll see all the graphics and HTML files in this folder.
3. Click Select All if you want to upload all the files. Otherwise, click Select None and select only the files that are part of your presentation. (You don't have to hold down the Ctrl or Shift key to select more than one file—just click the ones you want.)
4. Click OK to publish your presentation.

From Here

- Thinking about setting up your own business on the Web, or just ordering something on-line? Understand the security issues, which are explained in Chapter 35.
- Check out the shopping opportunities on the Web in Chapter 36.

Part VII

The Netscape Marketplace

Chapter 35

Understanding Security Issues

Is a revolution under way? Will millions of people buy things through the Web, the way they do on the phone? It hasn't happened yet. Although a few businesses have been able to establish a business on the Web, on-line shopping is growing only at a slow pace. The reason that it's growing so slowly isn't so much that there's no solution to the problems of security on the Net, but rather that there isn't enough standardization to encourage both vendors and shoppers to leap into the fray.

This chapter provides an introduction to the security issues facing the would-be Web shopper.

For the Time-Challenged

- Security actually involves three different aspects: authentication (knowing who's sending you something), confidentiality (knowing that no third party can intercept and read the information you exchange with someone), and integrity (knowing that your message has not been tampered with or altered while en route).
- Public key cryptography, the technology that underlies Netscape's security features, enables any two people to exchange undecipherable messages without needing to exchange decoding keys via a secure channel.
- Netscape's security standard, called Secure Socket Layer (SSL), uses public key cryptography to enable you to establish a secure connection with a Web server.
- There is no single Web security standard yet; in fact, there are several competing standards. In the years to come it is likely that a single standard will emerge.
- Your credit card information cannot be intercepted en route, but you still need to use common sense when ordering via the Web. Order from trusted, well-established firms, and make sure you understand their policies.

What Is Security?

In the computer world, security has three distinct shades of meaning: authentication, confidentiality, and integrity, as the following sections discuss.

Authentication

In brief, *authentication* ensures that you are really who you say you are when you log on to a server. There's a flip side to this one: It also ensures that the site you're logging on to is actually the site that you think it is.

Authentication is very important. If criminals got hold of your credit card, they could log onto a commercial site that lacks authentication and order like crazy. By the same token, a criminal could set up a fake Web site, one that poses as a bona fide compact disc store, say, and get people's Visa numbers and expiration dates. They could then go on a phone shopping spree. Scary, huh?

Authentication is poorly developed. Most Web servers demand no authentication at all—they just let you in. However, virtually all Web servers support simple protection by password: You must type a login name (user name) and password to access the service. An example of a Web service that requires password authentication is HotWired, the on-line version of *Wired* magazine.

When you access HotWired for the first time, you're asked to create a login name and password and to supply your e-mail address. You then receive an automatically generated e-mail message that includes an authorization number. You must then supply this authorization number to access the system. What's gained from this? A modicum of assurance that you aren't accessing the site using someone else's name and e-mail address. But it's only a modicum. Computer criminals called crackers are notorious for getting past password-based authentication schemes.

And how do you know that the Web site you're accessing is really a bona fide site?

Confidentiality

Confidentiality refers to the protection of information while it is en route to its destination. It's not nice to think about, but none of the information you are transmitting via the Web is free from prying eyes. Hackers, criminals, or investigators can easily intercept, record, and print all the information you transmit.

Integrity

Integrity refers to the exact preservation of the transmitted data so that it reaches its destination without any alteration, accidental or deliberate. As with confidentiality, the Web provides absolutely no means of ensuring the integrity of transmitted data. It could be altered while en route, either by chance or deliberate interference, and the receiving computer would have no way of knowing.

A Solution: Encryption

The solution to the Web's security problems lies in the use of encryption. In essence, *encryption* is the process of converting a plain-text message (a message that could be read by anyone) into an unreadable ciphertext by means of a key (a method of transforming the message so that it appears to

be gibberish). The message can be read only by the intended recipient, who possesses the key and uses it (in a process called *decryption*) to make the text readable again.

Understanding Encryption

A simple encryption technique is ROT-13, which "rotates" all letters in the alphabet thirteen characters to the right. The ciphertext looks like gibberish, but it is easily decrypted by rotating the letters thirteen characters to the left. Encryption ensures integrity as well as confidentiality; if anyone or anything has altered the message en route, it won't decode 100% correctly, so you'll know that something has gone wrong.

ROT-13 is a poor encryption technique because its key is so simple. In fact, it's used on Usenet only to keep adult-oriented material away from the eyes of children or those who would rather not have such material thrown in their faces. More complicated keys are needed to ensure confidentiality and integrity. With more complicated keys, though, another problem arises: how to transmit the key to the recipient. Traditionally, this has been done by courier, but this is costly and time-consuming.

Public-Key Cryptography Explained

A new cryptographic method called *public-key cryptography* eliminates the need to deliver the key and raises the possibility that people who have never previously exchanged messages could send encrypted messages to each other that could not be intercepted by a third party. In public-key cryptography, there are two different keys, an encryption key and a decryption key:

- **Public Encryption Key** You make your encryption key public; people use it to send an encrypted message to you.
- **Decryption Key** This key is kept private. You use it to decode the messages sent to you. Nobody else can read the message without this key.

With public-key cryptography, there is no need to establish a secure channel to exchange the decryption key; the person who wishes to send an encrypted message to you merely obtains the public encryption key, encrypts the message, and sends it to you. Nobody along the way can decode the message, even if they have intercepted the encryption key; they would need the decryption key, and you keep that secret. Rightfully, public-key encryption has been described as a revolution in cryptography. It will make cryptography available to ordinary people.

Introducing the Secure Socket Layer Security Protocol

To provide secure transactions via the World Wide Web, Netscape Communications Corporation has proposed a standard called the Secure Socket Layer (SSL) protocol. This proposed Internet standard seeks to provide secure public key encryption capabilities so that people can exchange information securely via any established Internet protocol, including not only the Web but also Gopher, FTP, Telnet, and others. What's more, SSL seeks to do this without placing undue demands on users; much or all of the SSL processing goes on in the background, without requiring any intervention from the user.

An SSL session begins when an SSL-capable client (such as Netscape Navigator) contacts an SSL-capable server (such as Netscape's secure Web servers). A brief exchange of public keys occurs; from that point on, the client and server can exchange secure, encrypted messages, and no third party can intercept them. In addition, SSL includes integrity-checking features that assure both parties that the message has not been tampered with or altered during its transmission.

I read that somebody cracked the security scheme! Due to limitations stemming from Cold War–era export restrictions, Netscape's security can indeed be cracked—but only by running several expensive workstations for days on end. That's worth doing to make a point, perhaps, but not to decode your $29.95 order to Victoria's Secret.

How Netscape Addresses Security Problems

Netscape Navigator tackles the security problem in the following ways:

- **Secure Servers** Netscape's server programs incoporate a security scheme that enables secure, encrypted communication between you, the Web user, and an on-line vendor. That takes care of the

confidentiality and integrity problems pretty well. When you access a secure server, the broken key icon becomes whole, and you can proceed with the confidence that no individual could intercept your credit card information while it's en route.

- **Site Certificates for Vendors** These certificates establish that the vendor you're contacting is really a bona fide on-line vendor. To prevent people from forging certificates, they're issued and validated by independent certificate authorities, which do the job for a fee. When you first contact a vendor, Netscape examines the certificate to see whether it has been digitally signed by a recognized authority. Subsequently, Netscape stores the certificate (to see a list, open the Options menu, click Security Preferences, and click Site Certificates). This takes care of one half of the authentication problem.
- **Personal Certificates** These certificates establish that you're actually the person you say you are. You can create a default certificate, but many vendors will prefer that they send you their own. To obtain your personal certificate, see a list of your personal certificates, or set the default certificate, you use the Personal Certificates page of Network Preferences.

Does Netscape's solution make everyone happy? Nope. It's still not a complete solution. From the vendors' standpoint, there still isn't an agreed-upon mechanism for validating credit card purchases, the way clerks do at stores when they swipe your card through a validation reader.

Credit card companies aren't completely happy with this solution, either. The largest source of credit card fraud occurs on the vendor's end; peoples' credit card numbers and expiration dates are freely available to employees, and a lot of them get stolen and misused. Credit card companies want a system that simultaneously obtains validation and keeps the credit card number encrypted, so that the vendor never has access to it. Such a system would be very much in the consumer's interest.

What about Standards?

As of this book's writing, there is no official standard for the secure transmission of sensitive data on the World Wide Web. In an effort to gain acceptance for its SSL protocol as the standard security protocol for the Web, Netscape has published SSL's specifications and made the technology widely available. However, competing firms are attempting to do the same. The worst-case scenario is that two or more competing but incompatible security standards will exist. If this happens, the Web's budding commercial ventures could die on the vine; a user of Netscape would be able to access only Netscape-friendly secure sites, while users of competing browsers (such as Spyglass's Enhanced NCSA Mosaic) would be able to access only those sites conforming to Spyglass's protocol.

The most likely outcome of this struggle, in the short run, is that two or three competing security standards will exist and Web servers will have to recognize them all. This situation is very much to the disadvantage of the on-line business community, as well as to on-line consumers; it means that you may have to run Netscape to access one secure service, and Internet Explorer (or some other browser with a proprietary security scheme) to access another.

The SET Standard

Credit card companies themselves have taken the leadership to resolve the standardization issue. Visa International, working with MasterCard, Netscape, Microsoft, and other corporations, has recently proposed a single standard for dealing with all the issues of credit card security over the Internet. This standard, called Secure Electronic Transactions (SET), won't be finalized until 1997, but it offers the best hope yet that digital commerce will really take off.

SET directly addresses the remaining issues of Internet security by enabling merchants to obtain on-line validation, while at the same time protecting credit card numbers from the prying eyes of unscrupulous employees. With SET, nobody but the credit card company itself ever sees your credit card number, and validation is automatic and instantaneous.

The SET standard is good news for Web users because it resolves a major standardization issue. Previously, Visa had been working with Microsoft on one security standard, while MasterCard and Netscape had been working on a competing standard. Getting all four of these parties to agree and work together is in everyone's best interests; without cooperation at this time, Web commerce might not develop at all.

Accessing a Secure Server

Notwithstanding the security and validation problems that are still holding back many would-be Web vendors, a few pioneers have gotten into the act

(for some samples, see the next chapter). They're using Netscape's secure servers to implement Netscape's security scheme, sans SET.

You'll know when you access a secure server because you'll see the dialog box shown in Figure 35.1. This dialog box informs you that you are accessing a secure document. In addition, the broken key on the status bar is suddenly made whole.

If you don't want to see this warning again, deselect the check box next to Show This Alert Next Time.

Another way you can tell that you've accessed a secure server is to look at the Location box: A secure server's URL begins with https://.

To get more information about the document you have accessed, open the View menu and choose Document Info. This command displays the dialog box shown in Figure 35.2. When you access a secure document, you see the server's authentication certificate, which tells you that you really are accessing the service you think you're accessing (and not some clever hacker's "mock" service). This dialog box also indicates the level of security that has been established.

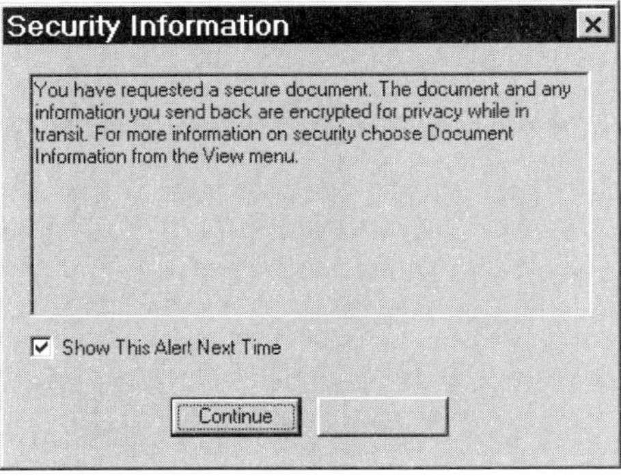

Figure 35.1 Secure server

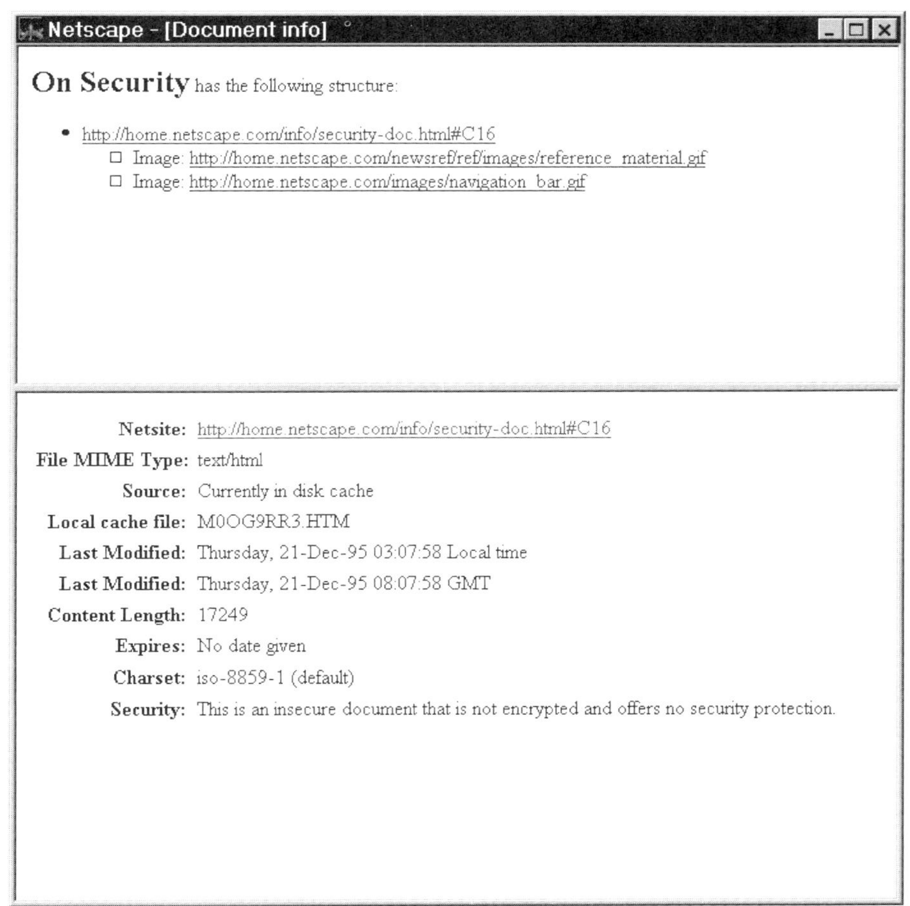

Figure 35.2 Document Info dialog box (insecure document)

It says the certificate can't be authenticated! A security certificate ensures that the service you're accessing is actually what it says it is, and not some fly-by-night imposter. In order to authenticate the site, Netscape examines the site certificate to see whether it has been signed by an independent certification authority (CA) that Netscape trusts. If not, you see a wizard

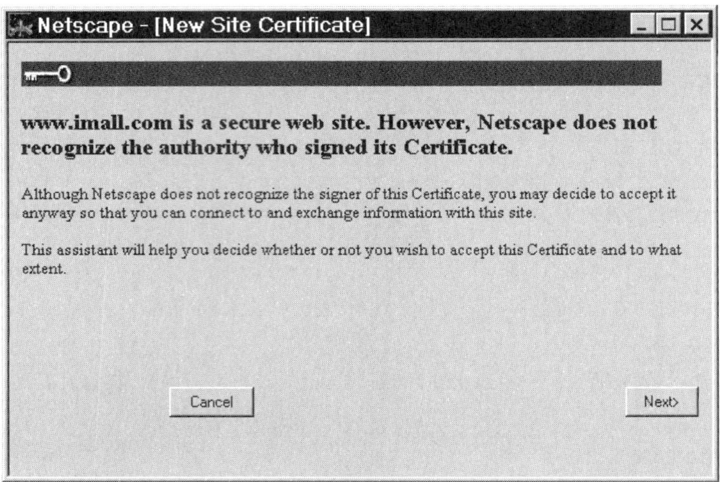

Figure 35.3 Certificate authentication warning

that warns you that the certificate isn't fully trustworthy (see Figure 35.3). You're given the option of accepting it anyway. Personally, I wouldn't.

Is My Credit Card Information Really Safe?

Once you've accessed a secure server, you can transmit your credit card number without fear of its being intercepted along the way. Does that mean your credit card information is safe? With Netscape's security features, you can be assured that nobody can obtain your credit card number by tapping your Internet connection. But sending your credit card number via a secure link is very much like giving it to somebody over the telephone: You're still dependent on the honesty and integrity of the person on the other end. In the end, ordering on the Web won't be any safer than any other form of mail or telephone order.

VeriFone/Netscape Deal Makes It Easier to Offer On-Line Ordering

When you charge something at a store, the clerk takes your card and swipes it through a little verifying machine. It's actually an on-line device; the card reads your information, contacts the verification service, and determines whether your card's valid and how much credit is available. Right now, there's no software available that does this automatically when you order on-line, unless vendors develop the software themselve—an expensive proposition. So somebody has to manually check all the orders before they can be processed. But that's about to change.

The maker of about 75% of those "swiping" devices, VeriFone, announced an agreement with Netscape to develop automatic verification for Netscape's Commerce Server. One of the Web-based vendors that welcomes this development is the Internet Shopping Network, of Palo Alto, CA, which currently processes some $1.4 million in credit card orders each month.

If you're thinking about ordering something by credit card on the Web, use all the common-sense rules that you would when ordering by telephone or mail. Order from well-established firms with good reputations. Make sure you fully understand the firm's policies regarding the delivery of ordered goods, returns and exchanges, and refunds.

What about "Cookies"?

While we're on the subject of security, there's one other aspect of Netscape that you ought to know about: cookies. No, we're not talking about Grandma's chocolate-chip delights, but something that some people think is a bit more sinister. In brief, a *cookie* is a small file that a Web server stores on your hard drive—that's right, your hard drive—that contains information about you.

According to Netscape, the information is quite harmless and benefits you. For example, a cookie could describe what portions of a site you've

already seen, so that the next time you log on you'll see portions that are new to you. Cookies also enable you to set up a custom home page on somebody else's server (for an example, see the custom home page accessible from http://www.msn.com). Netscape says that cookies cannot be used to steal your e-mail password, keep track of which sites you've visited, scan your hard drive for sensitive data, or compile sensitive private information about you. What they can do, though, is get your e-mail address—and now you know why you've been getting all that junk e-mail!

The problem with cookies isn't so much that they reveal information about you—they don't, for instance, upload a list of all the sites you've visited—but rather that people didn't know about them, as if something unseemly was being concealed. In response to this, Netscape 3 introduces a feature that lets you approve cookies before they're sent. Most of them have to do with pretty darned mundane stuff, as you'll see, such as how many times you've visited the site.

To give yourself the option of approving cookies before they're sent, choose Network Preferences from the Options menu, and click the Protocols tab. Select Accepting a Cookie to see an alert before any cookies are sent.

And While We're at It... JavaScript

JavaScript, as you learned in Chapter 13, is a Netscape version of Java that enables Web site developers to make things happen with Java applets without doing a lot of programming. The problem is that JavaScript isn't as secure as Java, and several teenage hackers have devised some very clever ways to make bad things happen to unsuspecting Web users. Unfortunately, all the bad things that people have been saying about cookies are actually true when it comes to JavaScript. Here's a sampler of some of the rogue JavaScript programs that have been developed:

- **History Tracker** This repugnant thing is able to keep track of where you've been browsing.
- **E-mail Robot** When you access this page, an e-mail message alert is sent to a snooper; it contains your e-mail address.

- **Read Your Files** This page can read and even retrieve files from your disk.
- **Write Something to Your Disk** This page can surreptitiously write a file, perhaps something containing obscene material, to your disk.

Netscape is trying to resolve these problems by performing fixes on JavaScript, and that's one very good reason to always use the latest version of Netscape.

To ensure your privacy while you're browsing the Web, you may wish to disable JavaScript until Netscape gets its act together. You can do so by opening the Options menu, choosing Network Preferences, clicking the Languages tab, and disabling the JavaScript option. You'll lose some of Netscape's functionality, but you'll be protected from malicious pages that exploit JavaScript's security holes.

From Here

- Want to take a look at some Web commerce pioneers? Check out Chapter 36.

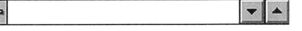

Chapter 36

Let's Go Shopping!

Secure Web Commercial Sites

To promote Web vendors who have adopted Netscape's secure server technology, Netscape Communications has developed a Customer Showcase page (Figure 36.1) featuring growing numbers of commercial Web servers. To access the Showcase, open the Directory menu and choose Customer Showcase. What you'll find, as this chapter attests, is that Web commerce is still in the experimental phase. What's going to sell on the Web? Are there some types of merchandise that aren't well suited to the Web commercial idiom? Do you offer just a few high-profile items or your whole catalog? Are Web commercial sites best deployed for one-of-a-kind, special-interest items or for huge shopping enterprises on a department store scale? As of yet, nobody knows, but there are plenty of experiments in all directions.

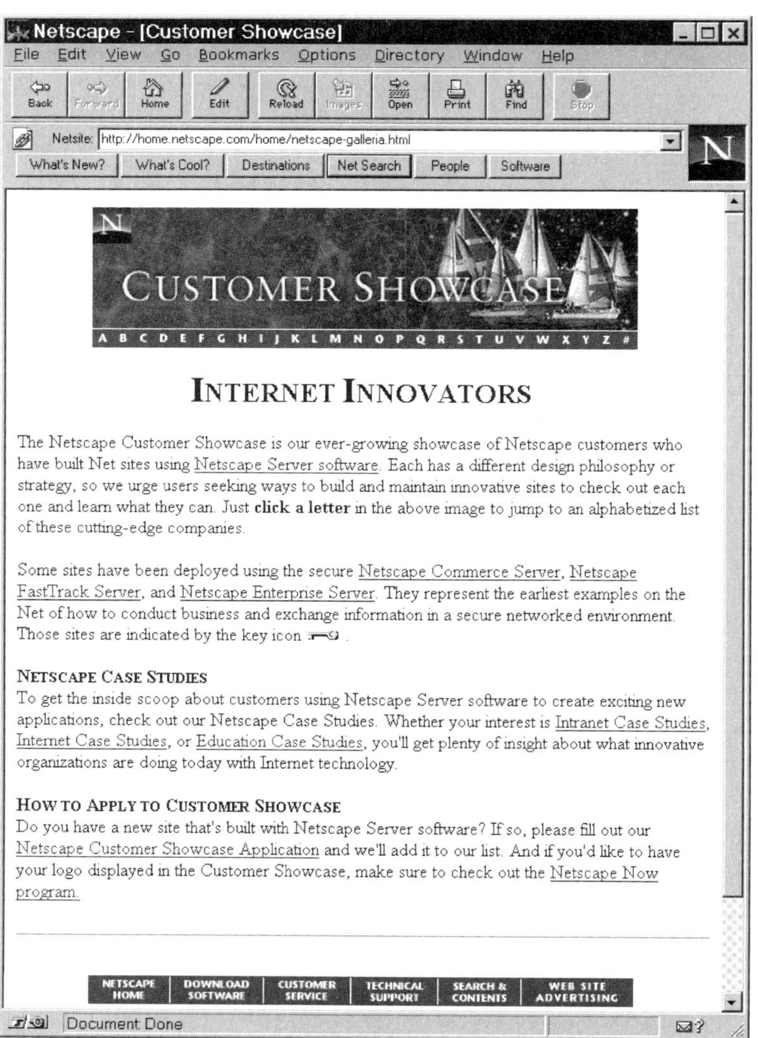

Figure 36.1 Netscape Customer Showcase page

This chapter provides an in-depth look at a few of the most interesting commercial Web sites that were on-line at the time of this book's writing; the Showcase page will certainly list additional vendors, so take a look.

For the Time-Challenged

- If you run into a secure Web commercial site, scope it out one step at a time. Be sure to display and read the fine print—when will your order be delivered, and how? What happens if you want to return it? Don't shut off your shopping smarts just because you're ordering on-line.
- You won't find full on-line catalogs—at least, not yet. The dominant philosophy seems to be "Let's offer a few good deals, and see who bites."
- Don't assume that the price is right—at least, not without checking around. Is it really worth the thrill to order something on-line if you could get the same article for less money at a local retail store?

Don't be shy about browsing these sites—there's no obligation. You can even fill out order forms, and then change your mind and cancel at the last moment.

The Grapevine

Here's a challenge. You own a winery. But most of your visitors and customers aren't young. How do you reach the younger generation and introduce them to the pleasures of fine wine?

The Grapevine (http://www.winery.com/) is one answer. It's a complete guide to wine, featuring the creations of more than 30 vineyards (Figure 36.2). To keep things fresh, the site features current news and events, such as the catalog from a recent Sonoma County wine auction. By means of an on-line toteboard, people browsing the site could relay their bids to the auctioneers!

The Grapevine relies on heavy-duty equipment: Several Sun workstations and Netscape's Commerce Server, which enables secure on-line ordering. Once within the site, you can navigate by means of well-designed icons (Wineries, Maps, Products, Events, What's New, Travel, Reviews, Judging, and On-Wine, an on-line wine newspaper).

What about the wineries? One of the things that's worrisome about Web commerce is that the vendors might not represent the best of the lot. But

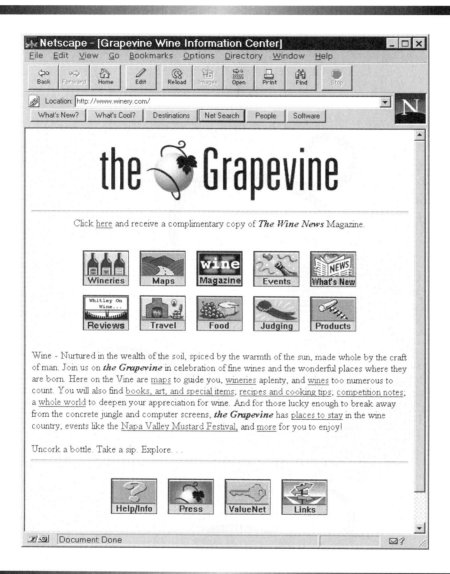

Figure 36.2 The Grapevine

you'll find some of California's best wineries on Grapevine, including the superb Matanzas Creek Winery, makers of what many wine aficionados believe is one of the finest Merlots in the entire world. And it's not just California that's represented. You'll find Oregon, Australian, and even Texas wineries in Grapevine—and doubtless more by the time you read this book.

SOFTWARE.NET

As an indication of what software retailing might be like in the future, software.net (Figure 36.3) goes the whole nine yards—not only can you take advantage of on-line ordering via secure Netscape transactions but you can also obtain some programs via electronic links. No packaging to fill up landfills, no old buggy versions to worry about, no truck making its way across the United States, no week-long delay—just instantaneous, environmentally responsible delivery. Don't think that the software distributed electronically is strictly no-name, low-quality stuff: For those taxing moments before April 15, for example, you can obtain H&R Block's TaxCut or Novell's TaxSaver.

software.net (http://www.software.net/index.htm) illustrates the First Rule of Web Marketing: Provide some freebies that make the site attractive to people. Not a site to mince words, software.net offers a Free Stuff page full of genuinely interesting stuff. At this writing, you could obtain the latest version of the Norton virus scanning software and a half-dozen sampler programs (full-featured but with built-in expiration dates). There's even a Usenet-like discussion system for software.net's products and services. To help you make the best selection, you can search a database of over 50,000 magazine articles from 16 major computer publications.

INTERNET SHOPPING NETWORK

It had to happen: Cable TV's Home Shopping Network was one of the first commercial ventures on the Internet, and it figures (Figure 36.4). After all, who else has more experience in high-tech marketing? Don't expect to find everything under the sun at ISN, though—the site specializes in the stuff its youthful browsers like to buy. Specifically, you'll find software, computer and electronics gear, photo and video stuff, equipment for home offices, and—naturally—flowers for those with romantic yearnings.

So how do you order? It's easy. When you find something you like you click the Buy button, and the server shifts into the secure mode. You'll see a page inviting you to become a member of ISN, if you're not already. If you

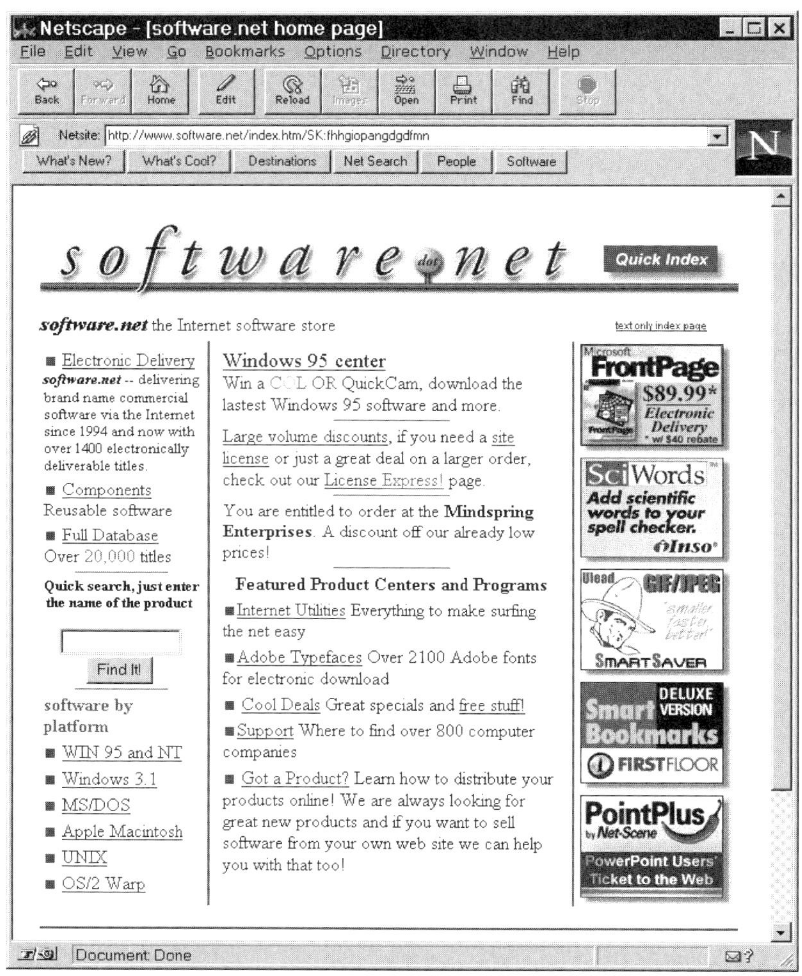

Figure 36.3 software.net

don't feel comfortable about giving your credit card information on-line, despite the security protection, or if you're accessing ISN from behind a firewall that disables security, you can call an 800 number, or fax the membership form. There's no charge for the membership.

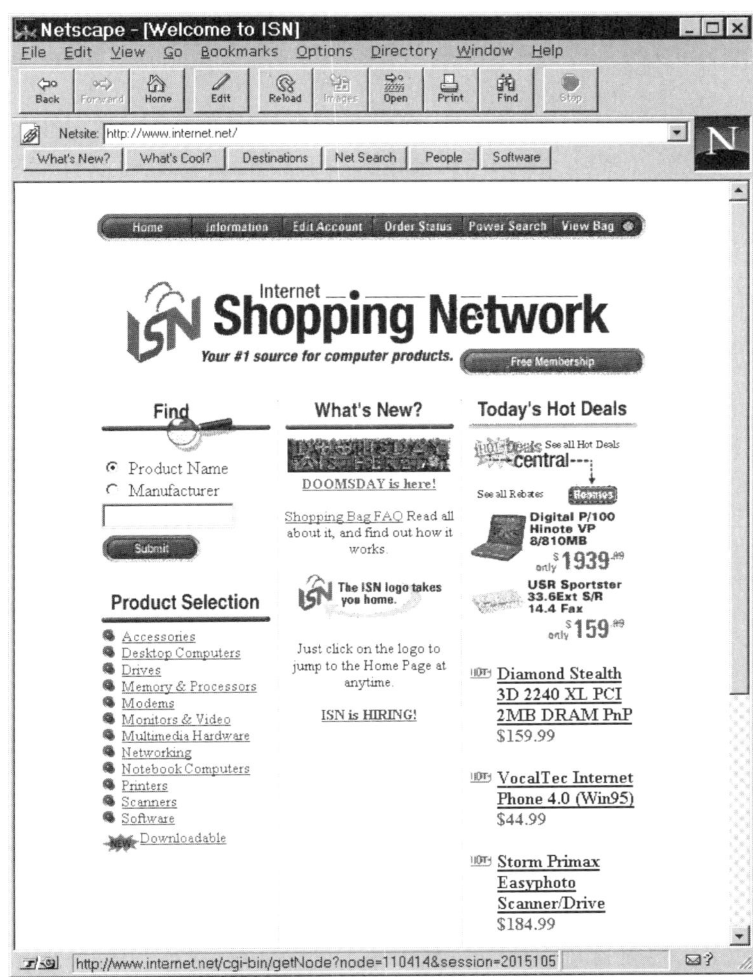

Figure 36.4 Internet Shopping Network

MARKETPLACEMCI

marketplaceMCI—the Web shopping arm of internetMCI, the long-distance company's foray into the Internet service provider sweepstakes—offers a

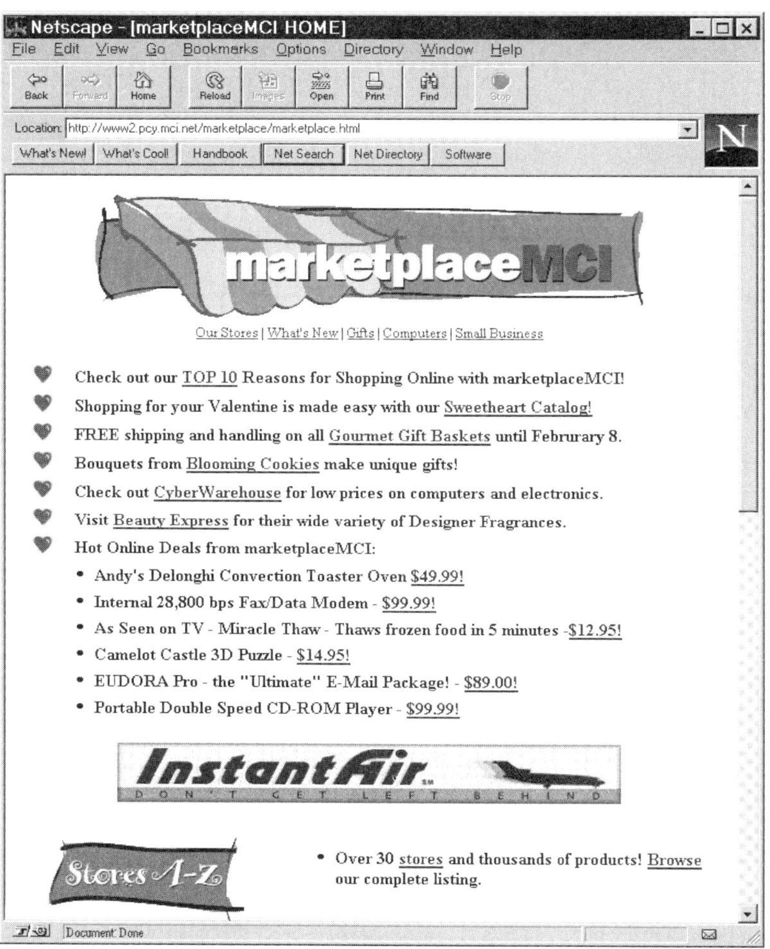

Figure 36.5 marketplaceMCI

number of storefronts (Figure 36.5). Each of them is accessible by means of Netscape's secure communications technologies. Here's what's available at this writing:

- **Andy's Garage Sale** Featuring all sorts of stuff dirt cheap! Andy's is an offshoot of Fingerhut Corporation, a direct mail marketing company
- **Blooming Cookies** Delivers "melt-in-your-mouth" custom cookie displays and individualized arrangements all over the world
- **Border's Books and Music** For your favorite books and CDs
- **CyberWarehouse** An online discount computer products superstore
- **Day-Timer** Personal planners, calendars, electronic organizers, and accessories
- **Express Lane** Universal Press Syndicate and Andrews & McMeel publishing company are home to the biggest names in comics and opinion, and Express Lane is home to their products on the Web
- **L'Eggs** Women's hosiery
- **The Mac Zone** and **The PC Zone** Low prices and overnight delivery of the hottest computer products
- **MCI Store** Communications products and services
- **Nordstrom** Shop via e-mail at one of the United States' leading fashion specialty stores
- **Travelers Personal Lines** and **Travelers Small Business** Fun facts, games, offers, tips, and online insurance quotes from the Travelers-Group

Access marketplaceMCI at http://www.internetmci.com/marketplace/.

From Here

- With this chapter, we've come to the end of this book. I hope you'll enjoy Netscape and the Web as much as I do!

Part VIII

Appendices

Appendix

Getting Connected

To determine which parts of this appendix you should read, please note the following:

- If you already have a copy of Netscape Navigator Gold 3.0 and you're already connected to the Internet, you don't need to read this appendix. It's for people who don't have the program.
- If you don't have Netscape, and you aren't yet connected to the Internet, read on.
- Do you already have a connection with an Internet service provider or live outside the United States? You can obtain a copy of Netscape Navigator Gold by using the Internet, as explained later in this appendix.

Connecting to the Internet

In order to browse the Web with Netscape Navigator, you need all of the following:

- **Internet software support for your computer** This is built in with Windows 95, but you'll have to add it if you're using Windows 3.1.
- **An Internet connection** You can obtain this from an independent Internet service provider (ISP) or an on-line service that enables you to use the browser of your choice.
- **A high-speed modem** You can use Netscape with a 14.4 Kbps (14,400 bits per second) modem, but you will get better results with a 28.8 Kbps modem.
- **A copy of Netscape** You can obtain a copy of Netscape by purchasing it from a software store or mail-order firm, or by downloading a copy from Netscape's site.

Don't drive yourself nuts trying to configure your Windows system for Internet use. It's a complicated job. Instead, find an Internet service provider who will give you preconfigured disks containing all the software you need (sometimes this includes Netscape). Installation should be as easy as clicking the SETUP icon on the disk and following a few on-screen instructions. For local Internet service providers, check in the Yellow Pages under Computers—Networks.

Obtaining a Copy of Netscape Gold

If you already have an Internet connection, this section shows you how to obtain a copy of Netscape Gold.

The Really Easy Way

Did your service provider give you a Web browser other than Netscape? You can use this browser to download Netscape Navigator Gold 3.0. To do so, simply type the following URL into your browser's Location box:

http://www.netscape.com

and follow the links to download the latest version of Netscape Gold.

According to Netscape's current licensing restrictions, individuals, businesses, and government organizations may evaluate Netscape Navigator free of charge for up to 90 days. After that time, you should purchase your copy of Netscape. Students, faculty, and staff members of educational institutions and employees of charitable nonprofit organizations may use Netscape free of charge.

The Easy Way

Purchase a copy of Netscape Navigator Gold. You can buy Netscape from just about any place that sells software, including office supply stores, software stores at shopping malls, and mail-order software suppliers.

The Slightly More Difficult Way

You can also obtain Netscape by using the Internet. To obtain Netscape Navigator Gold this way, you'll need an FTP program. FTP is short for File Transfer Protocol. With FTP, you can obtain files on computers that have set up *anonymous FTP* services. In anonymous FTP, the computer accepts requests from anyone who accesses the site, and lets you browse around the computer's file directories. When you find a file you want—here, Netscape Gold 3.0, of course—you can download it to your computer.

Where can you get an FTP program? If you're using Windows 3.1, ask your service provider. If you're using Windows 95, you're in luck—there's an FTP program included with Windows 95's Internet software. It's called FTP.EXE. To run the program, click the Start menu, click Run, type FTP.EXE in the dialog box, and click OK.

Once you've gotten your FTP program running, you'll need to configure the program to access a site from which you can download the Netscape software. For details on how to do this, consult the documentation of the FTP program you're using. In brief, you'll need to supply the FTP address of the computer that contains a copy of the Netscape software. Once you've contacted this computer, you'll need to navigate the computer's file directories so that you can locate and download Netscape.

This isn't quite as hard as it sounds. With most FTP programs, accessing an FTP server is as easy as typing the FTP address. To obtain Netscape, the address you'll need is one of Netscape's FTP servers. At this writing, the following servers at Netscape Communications contained copies of the Gold 3.0 software:

ftp2.netscape.com
ftp3.netscape.com

ftp4.netscape.com
ftp5.netscape.com
ftp6.netscape.com
ftp7.netscape.com
ftp8.netscape.com

It says "User anonymous access denied!" No, don't worry, Netscape still loves you. The problem is that so many people are trying to access Netscape's server that the server can't even send you a message informing you that it's too busy.

Once you've accessed one of these FTP sites, you may need to do some directory navigation to find the folder containing Netscape Gold. If you see a list of directories after you log on, look for the /pub directory—this is the one that usually contains files to download. You may need to hunt around a bit to find Netscape Gold. To learn how to navigate directories using your FTP client, see your program's documentation.

Appendix B

Using This Book's CD-ROM Disc

To access the programs and additional goodies on this book's CD-ROM disc, do the following:

1. Place the CD-ROM disc in your CD-ROM drive.
2. If necessary, start Netscape Navigator.
3. From the File menu, choose File Open.
4. In the Open dialog box, select the CD-ROM disc.
5. Select the file WELCOME.HTM.
6. Follow the instructions and links in WELCOME.HTM.

Appendix C

Configuring Plug-ins, Support, and Helper Applications

If you just want to browse the Web and view the text and graphics you'll find, you can use Netscape just as soon as you've established your network connection. However, you'll need to do some configuration and program installation if you would like to take full advantage of Netscape. The program needs help from the following:

- **Plug-ins** Netscape 3.0 comes with the LiveAudio, LiveVideo, and QuickTime plug-ins, which install automatically and require no configuration.
- **Support applications** To deal with Telnet and 3270 data, you need to install the appropriate applications and configure Netscape to use them.

- **Helper applications** Netscape 3.0 isn't as reliant on helper applications as previous versions of the program, thanks to the LiveAudio, LiveVideo, and QuickTime plug-ins. However, you still need to install and configure a few helper applications if you want to deal with the data types that these plug-ins don't cover.

Before proceeding, you will want to install the support and helper applications that are included on this book's CD-ROM disc. For more information, see Appendix B.

About Plug-ins

Thanks to the suite of plug-ins provided with Netscape 3, configuring Netscape to handle multimedia isn't the job it used to be. Plug-ins configure themselves automatically. You simply install the plug-in and it's ready to go to work for you.

Plug-ins live in the PLUGINS folder, which you'll find in Netscape's folder. If a plug-in is present there, Netscape loads it and uses it during that session. For this reason, you should be careful to safeguard the files in the PLUGINS folder. Don't erase or move them.

There's just one other thing you need to know about plug-ins. They override helper applications. To put this point another way, suppose you install a helper application for *.au (Sun/NeXT) sound files. Then you browse the Web and find a Sun/NeXT sound. When you click the link, LiveAudio starts, not your helper application.

If you really want to work with a helper application instead of LiveAudio or LiveVideo, your only option is to remove the plug-in from the PLUGINS folder, but I don't recommend this; you'll knock out the plug-in's functionality for the other file formats that the plug-in recognizes. What's really needed is a Helpers preference page that enables the user to configure plug-ins as well as helper application, but such a page hasn't yet been implemented in the Windows versions this book discusses. Look for this in more recent upgrades of the program.

To see the current file type (MIME type) assignments for the plug-ins your copy of Netscape has currently loaded, open the Help menu and choose Plug-ins.

Why Netscape (Still) Needs Helper Applications

By itself, Netscape can deal with GIF and JPEG graphics. In addition, the LiveAudio, LiveVideo, and QuickTime plug-ins can deal with many common multimedia formats. But there are many more types of multimedia files out there. Netscape needs the help of several helper applications to deal with some of the less frequently encountered sounds, as well as MPEG videos. In addition, if you want to be able to access Telnet resources (see Chapter 23), you need to configure Netscape to use support applications.

Configuring Support Applications

If you've installed Telnet and TN3270 helper applications, which enable you to access mainframe computer resources (see Chapter 23), you need to tell Netscape where these programs are located.

To configure your Telnet support applications:

1. From the Options menu, choose General Preferences. You'll see the Preferences dialog box.
2. Click the Apps tab. You'll see the Apps page.
3. In the Telnet Application box, click the Browse button, and locate your Telnet helper application.
4. In the TN3270 box, click the Browse button, and locate your 3270 helper application.
5. Click OK.

Configuring Helper Applications

When Netscape encounters a file that it can't directly read, the program tries to figure out what type of file it is. To do this, the program examines the file's *extension*. An *extension* is a three- or four-letter addition to a file's name. For example, "mov" is the extension of the file "sailboat.mov." Any

file with the extension "mov" is a QuickTime graphics file. The program then examines a table that associates QuickTime graphics files with a helper program. If a program is listed, Netscape starts the helper. If no program is listed, you see an on-screen error message informing you that Netscape can't display the data you've downloaded. You can save the data to disk, or you can browse for an application capable of displaying the data.

To prevent this error message, you should take a few minutes to link the various file types to applications. It's easy, and once you've done this, you can forget about it.

Remember, before proceeding, you need to install the helper apps as described in Appendix B.

Configuring Existing File Types

When you open the Helpers page of Netscape's General Preferences dialog box, you will see that many file types are already listed. The following instructions show you how to configure helper applications when the file type is listed in this way. If you're trying to configure a file type that's not listed, such as stereo MPEG audio (*.mp2), see the next section.

To link multimedia file types with helper applications:

1. From the Options menu, choose General Preferences.
2. Click the Helpers tab. You'll see the Helpers page. Take a moment to look at this dialog box. In the list box, you see the various file types. If an application is already associated with a file type, you see the application's name in the Action column; otherwise, you see Ask User.
3. Find and select a file type.
4. Click the Browse button, and use the Open dialog box to select and open the application.
5. In the Action area, make sure the Launch the Application button is selected.
6. Repeat steps 3 through 5 for the rest of the file types you're going to configure. See Table C.1 for a list of the file types and applications to install.

Creating a New File Type

Depending on which version of Netscape you're using, one or more of the file types in Table C.1 may not appear in the file type list. But don't worry—you can add new file types easily:

1. Click the Create New Type button.
2. In the Configure New MIME Type dialog box, type the part of the file type that comes before the slash mark (for "audio/x-mpeg," you type "audio").
3. In the MIME Sub Type box, type the part of the file type that comes *after* the slash mark (for "audio/x-mpeg," you type "x-mpeg." Do *not* type the slash mark—Netscape adds that automatically).
4. Click OK.
5. With the new type still selected, type the extension or extensions in the File Extensions box (separated by commas—no spaces, please).
6. Click Launch the Application.
7. Now, associate your new file type with an application, as you've done for the other file types.

Table C.1 File Types and Applications

File Type	Application	Extensions
application/pdf	Adobe Acrobat Reader	pdf
application/x-compress	WinZip	x
application/x-gzip	WinZip	Z
application/x-pan-realaudio	RealAudio Player	ra
audio/midi	MidiGate	mid
audio/x-mpeg	XingSound Audio Player	mp2
video/fli	Autodesk Animation Player	fli
video/mpeg	NET TOOB	mpg, mpeg

Appendix D

Netscape Navigator Quick Reference

This appendix lists the commands for Netscape Navigator and provides a quick summary of what these commands do. For Editor commands, see Appendix E.

FILE MENU

The File menu (Figure D.1) enables you to manage Web documents; specifically, you can open additional windows or open documents by typing the URL directly or loading them from disk. You can also open new Editor documents. You can save files, both in HTML and plain text; you can even mail documents to other Internet users. You can view hidden information about a document, including its security status. You can preview the printed

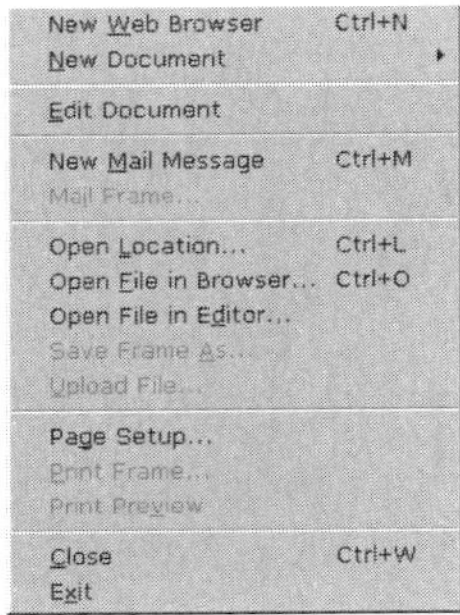

Figure D.1 File menu

appearance of a document on-screen and then print the document. A final option enables you to save all your preferences and exit Netscape.

New Web Browser

Opens a new Netscape window and displays the default home page. *Note*: By default, you can open a maximum of four Netscape windows. To increase this number, open the Options menu, choose Network Preferences, and click the Connections tab. Type the number of windows you want to open in the Number of Connections box.

Note that increasing the number of connections may slow down each of the connections. For optimum performance, set the number of connections at four.

New Document

Enables you to create a new document in Netscape Editor. You can start with a blank document, a template, or the Page Wizard.

New Mail Message

Displays the Message Composition window, which enables you to send an electronic mail message via the Internet.

Mail Document

Displays the Message Composition box, which enables you to send an electronic mail message via the Internet. Netscape automatically attaches the document you're currently viewing, and the program echoes the document's URL in the body of the message.

Open Location

Displays the Open Location dialog box, which enables you to type a URL directly.

It's easier to just type the URL in the Location box. To do so, click the current URL, and press Delete to erase it. Type your URL, and click OK.

Open File in Browser

Displays an Open dialog box that enables you to open a local file in the browser. Netscape can display HTML documents, JPEG and GIF graphics, and text files.

Open File in Editor

Displays an Open dialog box that enables you to open a local file in Netscape Editor. You can open HTML files only.

Save As

Saves the current document to a local disk drive. You can save the document with the HTML formatting (source) or as plain text (HTML codes are stripped from the document).

Upload File

Enables you to select a file to upload to an FTP server, as long as you have write permission on this server.

Page Setup

Choose margins, headers, footers, and other printing options with this menu command before you choose Print.

Print

Displays the Print dialog box, which prints the document you are currently viewing. You can select from a variety of print options, including number of copies, page range, and others (depending on your printer's capabilities).

Print Preview

Shows what your document will look like when printed. The Print Preview window draws on Microsoft Windows resources to display a one- or two-page graphic rendition of Netscape's print output. You can zoom in for a closer look, if you wish, and page through the print output. If it looks good, you can initiate printing from within this window without having to use the Print command.

Close

Closes the current window. If only one window is open, this command quits Netscape.

Exit

Saves the current configuration and quits Netscape.

Edit Menu

The Edit menu (Figure D.2) includes the standard Windows commands for editing text. There are great keyboard shortcuts for all of these commands (see Appendix F).

Undo

Reverses the last editing action, if possible. For example, suppose you type a new URL in the Location box. If you choose Undo, you see the previous

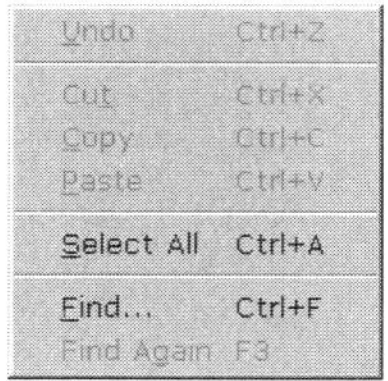

Figure D.2 Edit menu

URL. *Note:* This command is available only when it is able to reverse the last action.

Cut

Deletes the current selection and places a copy of the selection in the Clipboard. *Note:* This command is available only when it is possible to delete the selection (for example, you may use it within the Location box but not within a Web document).

Copy

Copies the current selection to the Clipboard.

Paste

Pastes the Clipboard's contents at the insertion point's location. *Note*: This command is available only when it is possible to paste text (for example, into the Location box).

Select All

Selects all the available text or items.

Find

Displays the Find dialog box, which enables you to search for a word or phrase within the currently displayed document.

Find Again

Repeats the search, using the settings you previously supplied in the Find dialog box.

View Menu

The View menu (Figure D.3) enables you to choose options for the display of Web documents; you won't use it much, though, because the most commonly accessed commands have more convenient equivalents on the Toolbar.

Reload

Retrieves a fresh copy of the current document from the cache or, if the original document has changed, from the Web server.

Reload Frame

Retrieves a fresh copy of the frame that's currently active (selected).

Load Images

If you have turned off the automatic display of in-line images (see Options), this command reloads all the in-line images in the current document. To

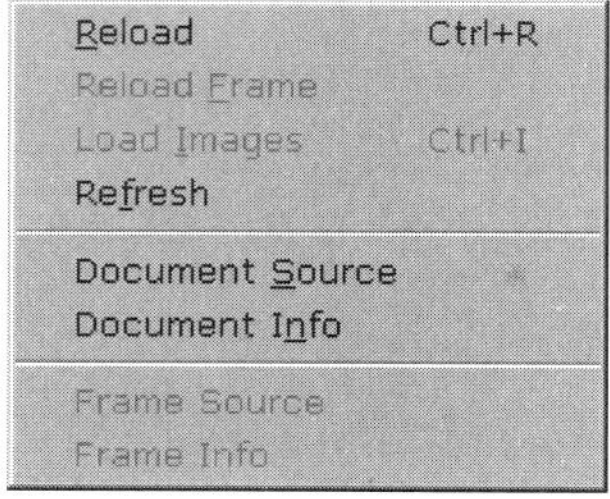

Figure D.3 View menu

load in-line images selectively, click the image you want to see with the right mouse button, and choose View This Image.

Refresh

Refreshes the screen from the cache, clearing distortion or errors in the display of fonts, colors, or backgrounds.

Document Source

Displays the HTML source code of the document you are currently viewing. In the Source window, you can scroll through the document. You can also copy text to the Clipboard (select the text and press Ctrl + C).

Document Info

Displays a View Source window that provides information about the Web page you're currently viewing, including security settings.

Frame Source

Displays the HTML source code of the frame you are currently viewing. In the Source window, you can scroll through the document. You can also copy text to the Clipboard (select the text and press Ctrl + C). This option is available only if you're viewing a document with frames.

Frame Info

Displays a View Source window that provides information about the frame you're currently viewing, including security settings. This option is available only if you're viewing a document with frames.

Go Menu

The Go menu (Figure D.4) provides navigation commands. You won't use the commands much, though, because the Toolbar offers a more convenient way of choosing these commands. The best thing about the Go menu is that it lists the last few Web pages you've visited, allowing you to go back to a

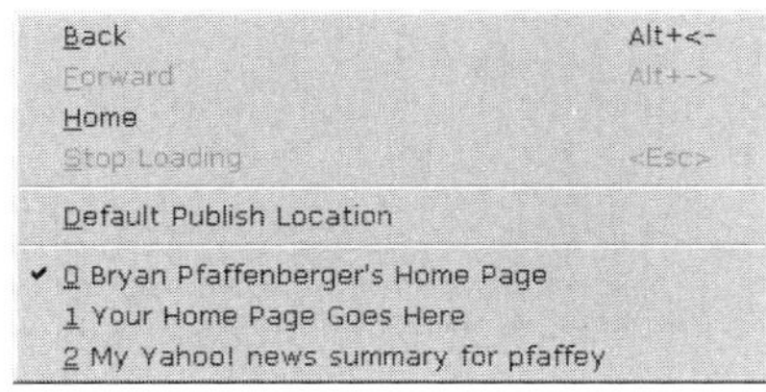

Figure D.4 Go menu

page you viewed several pages ago without clicking the Back button over and over.

Back

Displays the previous document (same as clicking the Back button). This option is dimmed if the current document is the first you've displayed in a new Netscape window.

Forward

Displays the document that was displayed prior to clicking the Back button or choosing Back from the Go menu (same as clicking the Forward button). This option is dimmed if you have not chosen Back or clicked Back.

Home

Displays the default start page (the document listed in the Home Page Location field of the Appearance page, General Preferences dialog box).

Stop Loading

Stops the retrieval of the current document (same as clicking Stop).

Default Publish Location

Displays the default location where you publish your Web documents. This is the location listed in the Default Publishing Location area of the Editor Preferences dialog box (Publish page).

History Items (0, 1, 2, 3, etc.)

Choose one of these options to redisplay previously viewed documents.

Bookmarks Menu

The Bookmarks menu (Figure D.5) enables you to add, view, edit, and organize bookmarks. Bookmarks that you've added appear on the lower portion of the menu.

Add Bookmark

Adds the current document to the bookmark folder that is currently selected in the Set to New Bookmarks Folder text box (Bookmarks window)

Go to Bookmarks

Opens the Bookmarks window, which enables you to organize your bookmarks.

Options Menu

The Options menu (Figure D.6) enables you to choose options for Netscape's operation, as well as to specify program configuration settings, the location of helper programs, and much more.

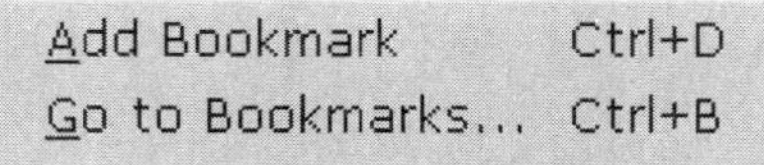

Figure D.5 Bookmarks menu

Figure D.6 Options menu

General Preferences

Displays the Preferences dialog box, which has the following seven pages. Note that essential configuration options are discussed in Appendix C.

Appearance	Choose Toolbar, startup, and link style options.
Fonts	Choose a different language encoding for foreign languages, if you're using Netscape in a non-English-speaking country. In addition, you can choose a font for the body text (proportional spacing) and the fixed font.
Colors	Choose colors for links, followed links, text, and background. You can also determine whether Netscape should override a document's colors.
Images	Choose options for displaying images, and determine when images are displayed (while loading or after loading).

Apps	Specify the location for supporting Telnet, TN3270, and text editor applications, and specify the default directory for storing files temporarily.
Helpers	Specify helper applications, as discussed in Appendix B.
Language	Specify which languages Netscape will accept when you download pages.

Editor Preferences

See Appendix E.

Mail And News Preferences

In this Preferences page, you choose options for electronic mail and Usenet newsgroups. You'll find the following tabbed pages:

Appearance	Choose the font to display e-mail messages and Usenet articles. You can also choose a character style for quoted text. In the Windows 95 version of Netscape Navigator, you can choose between Netscape and the Microsoft Exchange client to send and receive e-mail (I recommend Netscape).
Composition	Choose the encoding method for sending and receiving e-mail and articles (8-bit or MIME-compliant). You can also specify an e-mail address or a file to which to send copies of your e-mail and articles.
Servers	Here you specify the addresses of your mail and Usenet servers.
Identity	In this dialog box you type your name and e-mail address, as well as the location of your signature file.
Organization	Choose options for displaying e-mail addresses

Network Preferences

This option displays a dialog box that enables you to choose cache, connection, and proxy information. You don't need to worrry about the proxy

information unless you're using Netscape behind a firewall. There are three tabbed pages, as follows:

Cache	Choose the size of the memory and disk cache, specify the cache location, and choose how Netscape verifies documents.
Connections	Specify the number of network connections that Netscape can establish at any one time. Also, specify the size of the network buffer (the memory space set aside for network data transmission).
Proxies	If you are using Netscape behind a firewall, ask your network administrator how to fill out this dialog box.

Security Preferences

In this dialog box, you can choose how you want Netscape to handle communication with secure servers. You'll see two tabbed pages:

General	In this page, you can disable Java. You can also specify when Netscape displays those rather annoying security alert boxes.
Passwords	Enables you to set a password for your copy of Netscape, so that nobody else can use your security certificates.
Personal Certificates	Lists your current personal certificates.
Site Certificates	Here, you see a list of the site certificates that you have accepted. These certificates establish that the site you're contacting really is the site you think you're contacting.

Show Toolbar

Hides or displays the Toolbar.

Show Location

Hides or displays the Location box.

Show Directory Buttons

Hides or displays the Directory buttons.

Show Java Console

Hides or displays a window that monitors the execution of Java applets.

Auto Load Images

Disables or enables the automatic decoding of in-line graphics. If this option is switched off, you can view a single graphic by clicking it with the right mouse button and choosing View This Image from the pop-up menu; alternatively, you can choose Load Images from the View menu to view all the images in the current document.

Document Encoding

Specifies the current character set and language to be used to display documents.

Directory Menu

The Directory menu (Figure D.7) provides menu equivalents (and then some) for the Directory buttons.

Netscape's Home

Displays Netscape Communications Corporation's home page, which is the default home page for Netscape (unless you've changed the setting in the Appearance page of the Preferences dialog box).

What's New?

Displays Netscape Communications Corporation's What's New page, which lists new Web sites of unusual interest. Same as clicking the What's New? button.

Netscape's Home
What's New?
What's Cool?

Customer Showcase
Netscape Destinations
Internet Search
People
About the Internet

Figure D.7 Directory menu

What's Cool?

Displays a selection of unusual, interesting, or pioneering Web pages; well worth a look. Same as clicking the What's Cool? button.

Customer Showcase

Displays a list of Web servers that offer secure transactions using Netscape's Secure Socket Layer (SSL) technology.

Netscape Destinations

Displays a cool starting points page.

Internet Search

Displays a page that enables you to choose from several search engines and initiate searches.

People

Displays a page that enables you to search for people's e-mail addresses.

About the Internet

Displays a page that enables you to access information about the Internet.

Window Menu

This menu (Figure D.8) enables you to access Netscape Mail, Netscape News, the Address Book, the Bookmarks window, and the History window.

Netscape Mail

Opens a new Mail window.

Netscape News

Opens a new Usenet window.

Address Book

Opens the Address Book window, which enables you to add new e-mail addresses to your Address Book.

Bookmarks

Opens the Bookmarks window, which enables you to organize your bookmark items.

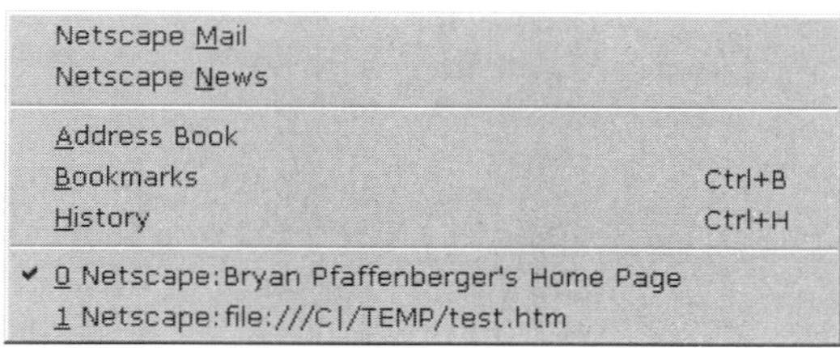

Figure D.8 Window menu

History

Displays the History dialog box.

Open Windows (0, 1, 2, 3, Etc.)

At the bottom of the Windows menu, you'll see a list of the Netscape browser windows that are currently open.

Help Menu

The Help menu (Figure D.9) accesses documents stored on Netscape Communications Corporation's server. It's loaded with interesting and helpful information, including an on-line Netscape handbook.

About Netscape

Displays a dialog box indicating which version of Netscape you're using.

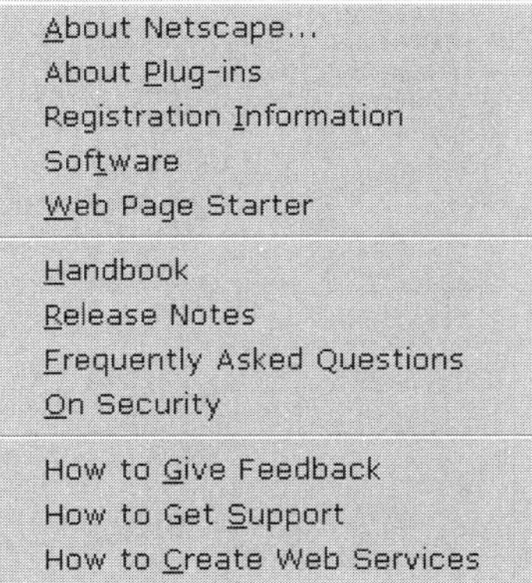

Figure D.9 Help menu

About Plug-ins

Displays a page of information concerning the version 3.0 plug-ins.

Registration Information

Displays information enabling you to register your copy of Netscape.

Software

Displays a page of information about Netscape Communication Corporation's software offerings.

Web Page Starter

Displays Netscape's Page Wizard, which enables you to create a home page quickly and easily.

Handbook

Accesses Netscape Communications Corporation's on-line help manual for Netscape.

Release Notes

Displays a page of notes about the version of Netscape you are using.

Frequently Asked Questions

Displays a page of frequently asked questions (and answers) about Netscape Navigator.

On Security

Displays information about Internet security and Netscape's Secure Sockets Layer (SSL) security technology.

How to Give Feedback

Displays a page providing instructions about submitting bug reports and providing feedback on Netscape Navigator.

How to Get Support

Displays a page providing instructions for obtaining technical support for registered users.

How to Create Web Services

Displays a page about creating World Wide Web sites. Tons of links to Internet-based information.

Appendix E

Netscape Editor Quick Reference

This appendix provides a quick guide to the commands on Netscape Editor's menus. For information on Netscape Navigator's commands, see Appendix D.

File Menu

Netscape Editor's File menu (Figure E.1) is almost the same as the one you see in Netscape Navigator. Only the commands unique to Editor are covered here; see Appendix D for information on the other commands.

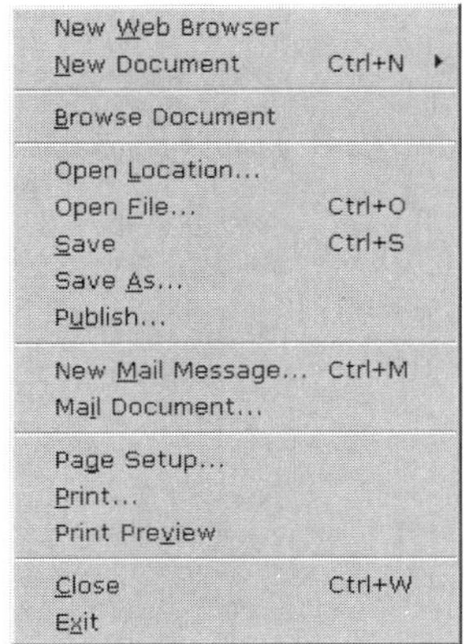

Figure E.1 Editor's File Menu

Browse Document

Displays the current Editor document in a browser window.

Open File

Opens a local HTML file for editing.

Publish

Opens the Publish Files dialog box, which enables you to upload your files to the Web server that you specified in the Publish page of the Editor Preferences dialog box.

Edit Menu

Netscape Editor's Edit menu (Figure E.2) provides an extended suite of Edit commands. These enable you to undo or redo your most recent editing change; cut, copy, or paste from the Clipboard; select and delete items, including selecting the entire document; select and delete table items; remove all the links from your document; or find text within your document.

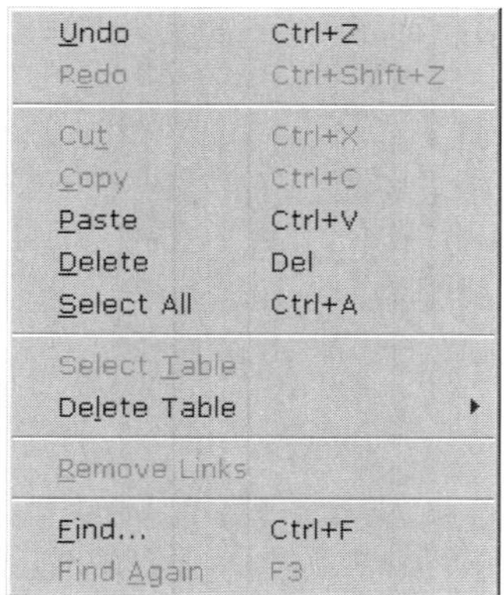

Figure E.2 Editor's Edit Menu

Undo

Reverses the last editing action, if possible. *Note:* This command is available only when it is able to reverse the last action.

Redo

Restores the editing change that was previously undone. If you reversed an editing change by choosing Undo, you can choose Redo to restore it.

Cut

Deletes the current selection and places a copy of the selection in the Clipboard.

Copy

Copies the current selection to the Clipboard.

Paste

Pastes the Clipboard's contents at the insertion point's location.

Delete

Deletes the current selection, but does not place a copy of the deletion in the Clipboard.

Select All

Selects all the available text and items.

Select Table

Selects the entire table. This command is very useful when you're trying to edit a table that has hidden borders (thus making the exact boundaries of the table invisible).

Delete Table

Deletes the selected table row, column, or cell, or the entire table.

Remove Links

Removes the hyperlinks from the selection.

Find

Displays the Find dialog box, which enables you to search for a word or phrase within the currently displayed document.

Find Again

Repeats the search, using the settings you previously supplied in the Find dialog box.

View Menu

Netscape Editor's View menu (Figure E.3) closely resembles the View menu you see in Navigator, except that it enables you to directly edit the underly-

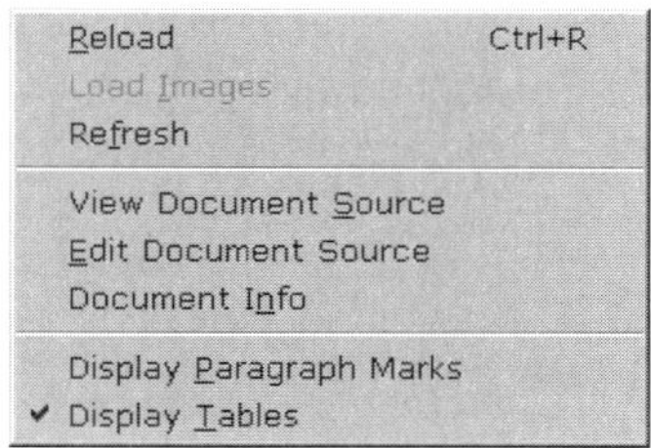

Figure E.3 Editor's View Menu

ing HTML (which may be necessary for advanced applications). In addition, you can display paragraph marks (the places where you pressed Enter or Shift + Enter) or hide tables.

Reload

Retrieves a fresh copy of the document from your disk. If you haven't saved your changes, you'll see a warning box.

Load Images

If you've turned off the automatic display of in-line images, this command reloads all the in-line images in the current document. To load in-line images selectively, click the image you want to see with the right mouse button and choose View This Image from the pop-up menu.

Refresh

Refreshes the screen from the cache, clearing distortion or error in the display of fonts, colors, or backgrounds.

View Document Source

Displays the HTML source code of the document you are currently viewing. In the Source window, you can scroll through the document. You can also copy text to the Clipboard (select the text and press Ctrl + C).

Edit Document Source

Starts the default HTML editor (as entered in Editor Preferences), enabling you to directly edit the underlying HTML. After you save the document in the default HTML editor and return to Netscape Editor, you'll see a dialog box informing you that the file you're working on has been saved by another application. Click Yes to reload the document and see the changes.

Document Info

Displays a View Source window that provides information about the Web page you're currently viewing, including security settings.

Display Paragraph Marks

Displays a large black box where you pressed Enter, and a small black box where you pressed Shift + Enter. Displaying these marks might prove helpful if you're trying to edit a document and can't figure out why a line break occurs, but they're visually distracting. Paragraph marks are turned off by default.

Display Tables

Displays tables so that they look like tables on-screen. You can still directly edit the text. If your system is slow, you may wish to switch this feature off. It's turned on by default.

Insert Menu

The Insert menu (Figure E.4) enables you to insert hyperlinks, targets, images, tables, horizontal lines, HTML code, line breaks, and nonbreaking spaces into your Editor document.

Link

Creates a hyperlink at the cursor's location.

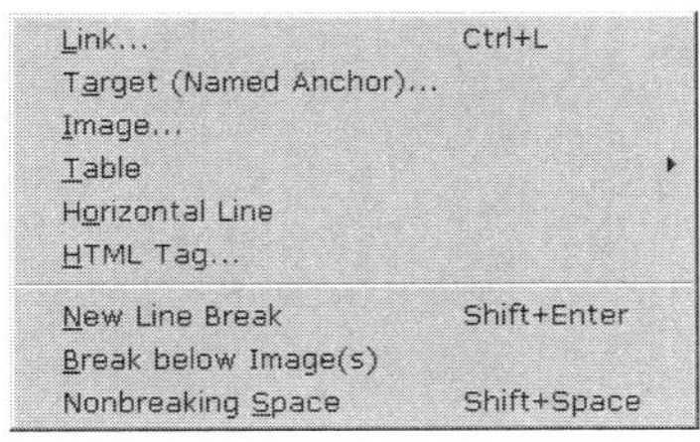

Figure E.4 Editor's Insert Menu

Target

Creates a named target for an internal hyperlink at the cursor's location.

Image

Inserts an in-line image at the cursor's location.

Table

Creates a table at the cursor's location. From the pop-up menu, you can choose options that insert a row, column, or cell at the cursor's location.

Horizontal Line

Inserts a horizontal line (rule) at the cursor's location.

HTML Tag

Displays the HTML Tag dialog box, enabling you to add an HTML tag to your document.

New Line Break

Inserts a line break without adding a blank line.

Break Below Image(s)

Inserts an invisible mark in your document. Text below this mark is wrapped to the left margin instead of floated around a graphic.

Nonbreaking Space

Inserts a nonbreaking space, which forces the browser to keep the two words linked by this space together on a line.

Properties Menu

The Properties menu (Figure E.5) lets you see and adjust the current properties settings for selected elements in your document, including text, hyperlinks, targets, images, tables, horizontal lines, HTML tags, and document features such as colors and backgrounds. In addition, you can enter character, font size, and paragraph formats from this menu.

Text

Displays the current properties for the selected text and enables you to change them. You can change font color, font size, or style (boldface, italic, superscript, subscript, and so forth).

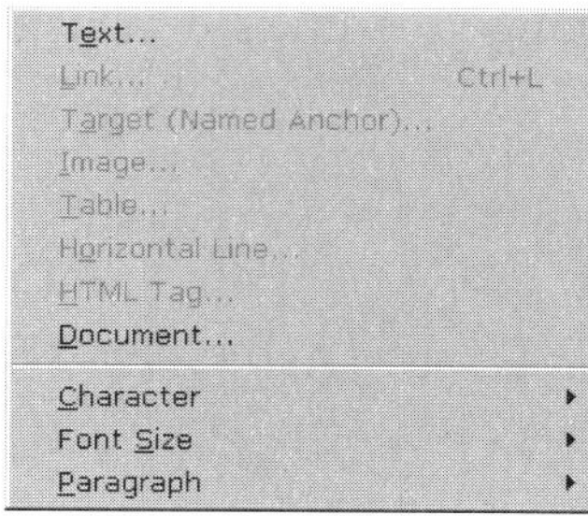

Figure E.5 Editor's Properties Menu

Link

Displays the current properties for the selected link and enables you to change them. You can change the URL or remove the link altogether.

Target (Named Anchor)

Displays the name of the selected target and enables you to change the name.

Image

Displays the properties of the selected in-line image and enables you to change them. You can change the image file, provide alternative text, adjust the alignment, specify the dimensions, add space around the image, or edit the image using the external image editor named in Editor Preferences.

Table

Displays the properties of the selected table, table row, or table cell, and enables you to change them. You can change settings for borders, cell spacing, cell padding, table width, table height, table color, table alignment, table caption, row alignment, row color, row and column spanning, text alignment within cells, text style within cells, cell width, cell height, and cell color.

Horizontal Line

Displays the properties of the selected horizontal line (rule), and enables you to change them. You can change the line's dimensions (height and width), alignment, and 3-D effect.

HTML Tag

Displays the selected HTML tag, enabling you to make changes to it.

Document

Displays the current document properties, including title, author, description, keywords, classification, color scheme, text color, link text color, active

link text color, followed link text color, background color, background image, and META tag system variables.

Character

Displays a pop-up menu from which you can choose font styles (bold, italic, underline, fixed width, superscript, subscript, strikethrough, or blink) colors (text color and default color), or JavaScript formatting. You can also clear all styles.

Font Size

Displays a pop-up menu from which you can choose relative font sizes (–2 to +4).

Paragraph

Displays a pop-up menu from which you can choose a variety of paragraph formats, including Normal, the six Heading styles, Address, Formatted, List Item, Description Title, Description Text, and indents.

Options Menu

Netscape Editor's Options menu (Figure E.6) enables you to display the Preferences menus discussed in Appendix D and adds several options that are valid only for Editor.

General Preferences

See Appendix D.

Editor Preferences

In this Preferences page, you choose options for Netscape Editor. You'll find the following tabbed pages:

General	Specify your name as the author of your documents, specify the location of external HTML and

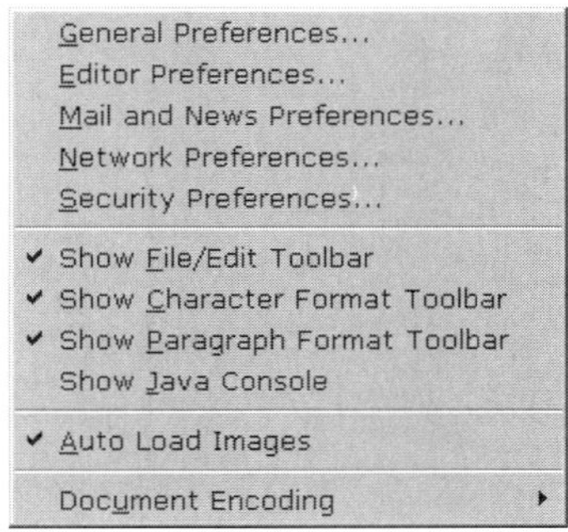

Figure E.6 Editor's Properties Menu

	image editors, specify the location of the default document template, and set up Autosave options.
Appearance	Choose between the browser's default color scheme or a named custom scheme; specify document-wide colors for normal text, link text, active link text, followed link text, and background; select a background graphic.
Publish	Specify options and locations for publishing your documents via FTP; specify your default document location for browsing via HTTP.

Mail and News Preferences

See Appendix D.

Network Preferences

See Appendix D.

Security Preferences

See Appendix D.

Show File/Edit Toolbar

Displays or hides the File/Edit toolbar (displayed by default).

Show Character Format Toolbar

Displays or hides the Character Format toolbar (displayed by default).

Show Paragraph Format Toolbar

Displays or hides the Paragraph Format toolbar (displayed by default).

Show Java Console

See Appendix D.

Auto Load Images

See Appendix D.

Document Encoding

See Appendix D.

Directory, Window, and Help Menus

These Editor menus are identical to the ones you see in Navigator; see Appendix D.

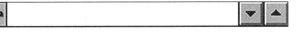

Appendix F

Netscape Gold's Keyboard Shortcuts

Navigator Shortcuts

To Do This	Press These Keys
Add bookmark	Ctrl + D
Close a window	Ctrl + W
Copy selection to the Clipboard	Ctrl + C
Create a new mail message	Ctrl + M
Cut selection to the Clipboard	Ctrl + X
Display Bookmarks dialog box	Ctrl + B
Find again	F3
Find text in current document	Ctrl + F
Go back	Alt + <
Open a local file	Ctrl + O (the letter)
Open a new browser window	Ctrl + N
Paste from the Clipboard	Ctrl + V
Print current document	Ctrl + P

To Do This	Press These Keys
Reload current document	Ctrl + R
Save a file to disk	Ctrl + S
Select all	Ctrl + A
Stop loading	Esc
Type a URL directly (Open Location)	Ctrl + L
Undo your last editing action	Ctrl + Z
View all in-line images	Ctrl + I
View the history list	Ctrl + H

Editor Shortcuts

To Do This	Press These Keys
Close a window	Ctrl + W
Copy selection to the Clipboard	Ctrl + C
Create a new document	Ctrl + N
Create a new mail message	Ctrl + M
Cut selection to the Clipboard	Ctrl + X
Delete without affecting the Clipboard	Del
Find text in current document	Ctrl + F
Find again	F3
Insert hyperlink	Ctrl + L
New line without blank line	Shift + Enter
Nonbreaking space	Shift + Space
Open a file	Ctrl + O
Paste from the Clipboard	Ctrl + V
Redo your last editing action	Ctrl + Shift + Z
Reload from disk	Ctrl + R
Save a file	Ctrl + S
Select all	Ctrl + A
Undo your last editing action	Ctrl + Z

Index

About AP Professional

AP Professional, an imprint of Academic Press, a division of Harcourt Brace & Company, was founded in 1993 to provide high-quality, innovative products for the computer community. For over 50 years, Academic Press has been a world leader in documenting scientific and technical research.

AP Professional continues this tradition by providing its readers with exemplary publications that bring new topics to light and offer fresh views on prominent topics. Often, today's computer books are underdeveloped clones, published in haste and promoted in series. Readers tend to be neglected by the lack of commitment from other publishers to produce quality products. It is our business to provide you with clearly written, educational publications that contain valuable information you will find truly useful. AP Professional has grown quickly and has established a reputation for fine products because of this commitment to excellence.

Through our strong reputation at Academic Press, and one of the most experienced editorial boards in computer publishing, AP Professional has also contracted many of the best writers in the computer community. Each book undergoes three stages of editing—technical, developmental, and copyediting—before going through the traditional book publishing production process. These extensive measures ensure clear, informative, and accurate publications.

It is our hope that you will be pleased with your decision to purchase this book, and that it will exceed your expectations. We are committed to making the AP Professional logo a sign of excellence for all computer users and hope that you will come to rely on the quality of our publications.

Enjoy!

Jeffrey M. Pepper
Vice President, Editorial Director

Related Titles from AP PROFESSIONAL

AHUJA, *Network and Internet Security*

AHUJA, *Secure Commerce on the Internet*

CAMPBELL/CAMPBELL, *World Wide WebPocket Directory*

CASEY, *The Hill on the Net*

CRANE, *Mutual Fund Investing on the Internet*

FEILER, *Cyberdog*

FOLEY, *The Microsoft Exchange Guide*

GRAHAM, *TCP/IP Addressing*

KEOGH, *Webmaster's Guide to VB Script*

LEVINE, *Live Java*

LEVITUS/EVANS, *Cheap and Easy Internet Access (Windows Version)*

LEVITUS/EVANS, *Cheap and Easy Internet Access (Macintosh Version)*

LEVITUS/EVANS, *WebMaster Macintosh*

LEVITUS/EVANS, *WebMaster Windows*

LOSHIN, *TCP/IP for Everyone*

MCKEEHAN, *Safe Surfing*

PAPPAS/MURRAY, *Java with Borland C++*

MURRAY/PAPPAS, *Visual J++ Handbook*

OZER, *Publishing Digital Video*

PFAFFENBERGER, *Netscape Navigator 3.0 (Macintosh Version)*

PFAFFENBERGER, *Netscape Navigator 3.0 (Windows Version)*

PFAFFENBERGER, *Publish it on the Web! (Macintosh Version)*

PFAFFENBERGER, *Publish it on the Web! (Windows Version)*

PFAFFENBERGER, *The Elements of Hypertext Style*

REINER/BLANTON, *Person to Person on the Internet*

REISS, *The Eudora User's Guide*

RIBAR, *The Internet with Windows 95*

SCHENGILI-ROBERTS, *The Advanced HTML Companion*

SINCLAIR/HALE, *Intranets vs. Lotus Notes*

SULLIVAN, *Using Internet Explorer to Browse the Internet*

TESTA, *Graphical Treasures on the Internet*

THOMPSON, *Internet Movies with Shockwave & Director*

TITTEL/ROBBINS, *E-mail Essentials*

TITTEL/ROBBINS, *Internet Access Essentials*

VACCA, *JavaScript*

VACCA, *VRML: Bringing Virtual Reality to the Internet*

VAUGHAN-NICHOLS, *Intranets*

WATKINS/MARENKA, *The Internet Edge in Business*

WAYNER, *Agents at Large*

WAYNER, *Digital Cash*

WAYNER, *Disappearing Cryptography*

WAYNER, *Java and Javascript*

Ordering Information

AP PROFESSIONAL
An Imprint of ACADEMIC PRESS
A Division of HARCOURT BRACE & COMPANY

ORDERS (USA and Canada): 1-800-3131-APP or APP@ACAD.COM
AP Professional Orders: 6277 Sea Harbor Dr., Orlando, FL 32821-9816

Europe/Middle East/Africa: 0-11-44 (0) 181-300-3322
Orders: AP Professional 24–28 Oval Rd., London NW1 7DX

Japan/Korea: 03-3234-3911-5
Orders: Harcourt Brace Japan, Inc., Ichibunan

Australia: 02-517-8999
Orders: Harcourt Brace & Co. Australia, Locked Bag 16, Marrickville, NSW 2204, Australia

Other International: (407) 345-3800
AP Professional Orders: 6277 Sea Harbor Dr., Orlando FL 32821-9816

Editorial: 1300 Boylston St., Chestnut Hill, MA 02167; (617) 232-0500

Web: http://www.apnet.com/

LIMITED WARRANTY AND DISCLAIMER OF LIABILITY

ACADEMIC PRESS, INC. ("AP") AND ANYONE ELSE WHO HAS BEEN INVOLVED IN THE CREATION OR PRODUCTION OF THE ACCOMPANYING CODE ("THE PRODUCT") CANNOT AND DO NOT WARRANT THE PERFORMANCE OR RESULTS THAT MAY BE OBTAINED BY USING THE PRODUCT. THE PRODUCT IS SOLD "AS IS" WITHOUT WARRANTY OF ANY KIND (EXCEPT AS HEREAFTER DESCRIBED), EITHER EXPRESSED OR IMPLIED, INCLUDING, BUT NOT LIMITED TO, ANY WARRANTY OF PERFORMANCE OR ANY IMPLIED WARRANTY OF MERCHANTABILITY OR FITNESS FOR ANY PARTICULAR PURPOSE. AP WARRANTS ONLY THAT THE MAGNETIC DISC(S) ON WHICH THE CODE IS RECORDED IS FREE FROM DEFECTS IN MATERIAL AND FAULTY WORKMANSHIP UNDER THE NORMAL USE AND SERVICE FOR A PERIOD OF NINETY (90) DAYS FROM THE DATE THE PRODUCT IS DELIVERED. THE PURCHASER'S SOLE AND EXCLUSIVE REMEDY IN THE EVENT OF A DEFECT IS EXPRESSLY LIMITED TO EITHER REPLACEMENT OF THE DISC(S) OR REFUND OF THE PURCHASE PRICE, AT AP'S SOLE DISCRETION.

IN NO EVENT, WHETHER AS A RESULT OF BREACH OF CONTRACT, WARRANTY OR TORT (INCLUDING NEGLIGENCE), WILL AP OR ANYONE WHO HAS BEEN INVOLVED IN THE CREATION OR PRODUCTION OF THE PRODUCT BE LIABLE TO PURCHASER FOR ANY DAMAGES, INCLUDING ANY LOST PROFITS, LOST SAVINGS OR OTHER INCIDENTAL OR CONSEQUENTIAL DAMAGES ARISING OUT OF THE USE OR INABILITY TO USE THE PRODUCT OR ANY MODIFICATIONS THEREOF, OR DUE TO THE CONTENTS OF THE CODE, EVEN IF AP HAS BEEN ADVISED OF THE POSSIBILITY OF SUCH DAMAGES, OR FOR ANY CLAIM BY ANY OTHER PARTY.

Any request for replacement of a defective CD-ROM disc must be postage prepaid and must be accompanied by the original defective disc, your mailing address and telephone number, and proof of date of purchase and purchase price. Send such requests, stating the nature of the problem, to Academic Press Customer Service, 6277 Sea Harbor Drive, Orlando, FL 32887, 1-800-321-5068. APP shall have no obligation to refund the purchase price or to replace a disc based on claims of defects in the nature or operation of the Product.

Some states do not allow limitation on how long an implied warranty lasts, nor exclusions or limitations of incidental or consequential damage, so the above limitations and exclusions may not apply to you. This Warranty gives you specific legal rights, and you may also have other rights which vary from jurisdiction to jurisdiction.

THE RE-EXPORT OF UNITED STATES ORIGIN SOFTWARE IS SUBJECT TO THE UNITED STATES LAWS UNDER THE EXPORT ADMINISTRATION ACT OF 1969 AS AMENDED. ANY FURTHER SALE OF THE PRODUCT SHALL BE IN COMPLIANCE WITH THE UNITED STATES DEPARTMENT OF COMMERCE ADMINISTRATION REGULATIONS. COMPLIANCE WITH SUCH REGULATIONS IS YOUR RESPONSIBILITY AND NOT THE RESPONSIBILITY OF AP.

About the CD-ROM

On this CD-ROM you will find a wide assortment of useful tools:

- **HOME.HTM** A new default start page that contains dozens of the Internet's hottest sites.
- **Helper applications** Included are freeware and shareware applications that can help you cope with just about any type of data that the Net can sling at you, including Adobe Acrobat, Autodesk Animation Player for Windows, MidiGate (for playing MIDI sounds), NCSA Telnet for Windows (for Telnet sessions), NET TOOB (for playing MPEG and AVI videos), QuickTime for Windows (for playing QuickTime videos), RealAudio (for playing 14.4 Kbps RealAudio sounds), Waveform Hold and Modify (for playing and modifying Sun and NeXT sounds), and XingSound Freely Redistributable Audio Player (for playing beautiful MPEG stereo recordings with near-CD quality).
- **Plug-ins** Explore the exciting new capabilities of Netscape's plug-ins with VR Scout, one of the highest-rated VRML plug-ins for the Windows 95 version of Netscape.
- **Pueblo** Chaco Communication's client program for accessing MUD games. It enables you to work with text-only MUDs. Pueblo also makes it possible to participate in growing numbers of graphics-based, three-dimensional MUDs. If you're talking to somebody who gives you a URL, you can click on it to view this URL with Netscape.
- **Graphics** Lots of public-domain backgrounds, arrows, lines, bullets, and icons for your Web publishing designs.

Running the Disc

To use this disc, place it in your CD-ROM drive and use Netscape's File Open command to open WELCOME.HTM. This file tells you how to install and configure all of the files on this disc.

System Requirements

If you choose to run Netscape Navigator Gold, you'll need a Microsoft Windows 3.1 or Windows 95 computer with a minimum of 8 MB RAM, and a 14.4 or 28.8 Kbps modem. Some applications require additional specific system requirements.